La Piscine

La Piscine

The French Secret Service
since 1944

Roger Faligot and Pascal Krop

Translated by W. D. Halls

Basil Blackwell

First published in France as *La Piscine: les services secrets français, 1944–1984* ©, 1985 Editions du Seuil, Paris
This translation © Basil Blackwell Ltd 1989.

First published 1989

Basil Blackwell Ltd
108 Cowley Road, Oxford, OX4 1JF, UK

Basil Blackwell Inc.
432 Park Avenue South, Suite 1503
New York, NY 10016, USA

British Library Cataloguing in Publication Data
Faligot, Roger
   La Piscine : the French secret service since 1944.
   1. France. Service de Documentation
Extérieure et de Contre-Espionnage, to 1987
   I. Title   II. Krop, Pascal
   327.1'2'0944

   ISBN 0–631–15656–9

Library of Congress Cataloging in Publication Data
Faligot, Roger.
   [Piscine, English]
   La piscine : the French secret service since 1944 / Roger Faligot and Pascal Krop ; translated by W.D. Halls
p.   cm.
Includes index.
ISBN 0–631–15656–9
   1. Intelligence service—France—History. 2. Secret service—France—History. 3. France. Service de documentation extérieure et de contre-espionnage—History. 4. France—Politics and government—1945-   I. Krop, Pascal.   II. Title.
JN2738.I58F3513 1989   88–6589
327.1'2'0944—dc19   CIP

Typeset in Ehrhardt 10 on 11½ pt
by Hope Services, Abingdon
Printed in Great Britain by
T.J. Press Ltd., Padstow, Cornwall

Through a kind of obscure foresight on the part of Nature, it so happened that in 1940 a section of the adult population was inclined in advance towards clandestine activities. In fact, between the wars young people had shown a great liking for stories about the Deuxième Bureau, the secret service or the police, and also for bold exploits and conspiracies. Books, newspapers, the theatre and the cinema were widely given over to the adventures of a more or less imaginary breed of heroes who, in the shadows, performed their feats in the service of their country.

Such a psychology was to facilitate recruitment for special missions. But it ran the danger also of introducing into them romanticism, a lack of seriousness, sometimes fraudulence, which would prove to be the worst snares.

Charles de Gaulle, *War Memoirs*

PISCINE   Basin for purificatory rites. Small bowl designed to receive the water that has been used at baptisms or for the purification of sacred vessels . . . Large swimming pool and the complex of installations surrounding it.

Petit Robert Dictionary

The headquarters of the French secret service are on the Boulevard Mortier in Paris, opposite the Tourelles swimming baths. Journalists have fallen into the habit of calling these services 'La Piscine'. But in the trade they prefer to call the headquarters something else: 'The Shack' ('La Boîte'), 'The Firm' ('La Maison'), 'The Dairy' ('La Crèmerie').

Contents

Acknowledgements   viii

Abbreviations   ix

Translator's Note   xiv

Prologue: Amid the Ruins of the Third Reich   1

Part I   The Birth of SDECE
1 *Ali Baba's Cave*   11
2 *Tracking down the Nazis*   27
3 *SDECE and the Socialist Party*   39

Part II   Operations on all Fronts
4 *The Cold War*   61
5 *Indo-China*   79
6 *The Secret War in the Maghreb*   105

Part III   The Gaullist Republic
7 *Grossin's 'Firm'*   135
8 *Signed: The 'Red Hand'*   157
9 *The Colonies are Finished*   173
10 *Secret Missions on the Dark Continent*   191
11 *The Hunt for Moles*   210
12 *In the Turbulence*   230

Part IV   From Pompidou to Mitterrand
13 *De Marenches at SDECE*   245
14 Coups d'état *in Africa*   262
15 *Mitterrand's 'Specials'*   276
16 *Mission 'Satanic': 'Sink the* Rainbow Warrior*'*   288

Notes   297

Index   322

Acknowledgements

Apart from publicly available sources (parliamentary and law reports, and newspapers and periodicals such as *Le Figaro, Le Monde, L'Humanité, Le Canard enchaîné, L'Express* and *Le Nouvel observateur*), the authors have systematically sought testimony from former officers of the French secret services. With rare exceptions both military and civilian personnel of SDECE agreed to recount some of their memories. From the founder of BCRA in London to the present directors of DGSE, as well as eminent specialists of the Gaullist period, they have all been kind enough to allow the authors to question them fully. Many of those who served SDECE in responsible positions regretted that no history of the service had been attempted before.

In all we conducted nearly a hundred interviews. Several agents asked us to preserve their anonymity, and we have respected their wishes. But for the first time officials of Action Branch and Counter-Espionage in charge of special operations have agreed to give the authors the benefit of their experience. We wish to thank them warmly.

Other former officers at SDECE have given us access to their personal files, and we wish to express our special gratitude.

Roger Faligot
Pascal Krop

* * *

The authors and publisher gratefully acknowledge permission given by the following copyright holders and agencies to print the illustrations in this book: © Agence France Presse (Plates 1, 4, 7, 9, 11); John Hillelson Agency Limited/Sygma (Plates 8, 10, 12); Popperfoto (Plate 13); and Frank Spooner/Gamma (Plate 6). The authors have granted permission for the use of Plates 2, 3 and 5.

Abbreviations

ACP   Agence Centrale de Presse
AFL   American Federation of Labor
AFP   Agence France Presse
ALN   Armée de Libération Nationale
AMT   Assistance Militaire Technique
AS   Armée Secrète
ASSDN   Association des Services Spéciaux de la Défense Nationale
ATP   Agence Transcontinentale de Presse

BAG   Bloc Africain de Guinée
BCRA   Bureau Central de Renseignement et d'Action
BDPA   Bureau de Développement de la Production Agricole
B-doc   Bureau de Documentation
BEL   Bureau d'Etudes et de Liaison
BfV   Bundesamt für Verfassungsschutz (West Germany)
BICE   Bureau Interallié de Contre-Espionnage
BND   Bundesnachrichtendienst (West Germany)
BOSS   Bureau of State Security (South Africa)
BR   Bureau de Renseignement
BSLE   Bureau de la Statistique de la Légion Etrangère
BSM   Bureau de Sécurité Militaire
BTLC   Bureau Technique de Liaison et de Coordination
BUPO   Bundespolizei (Switzerland)
BVD   Binnenlandse Veiligheidsdienst (Netherlands)

CCI   Centre de Coordination Interarmées
CDS   Christian Social Democrats (Portugal)
CE   Contre-Espionnage
CEA   Commissariat à l'Energie Atomique
CERM   Centre d'Exploitation du Renseignement Militaire
CFA   Communauté Française d'Afrique
CGC   Confédération Générale des Combattants
CGT   Confédération Générale du Travail

CIA	Central Intelligence Agency (USA)
CIC	Counter-Intelligence Corps (USA)
CID	Counter-Intelligence Department (USA)
CINC	Centre d'Instruction de Nageurs de Combat
CIR	Comité Interministériel du Renseignement
CIRVP	Centre d'Instruction des Réservistes Volontaires Parachutistes
CLD	Centre de Liaison et Documentation
CNEC	Centres Nationaux d'Entraînement Commando
CNR	Conseil National de la Résistance
CNRS	Centre National de la Recherche Scientifique
CNT	Confederación Nacional del Trabajo (Spain)
CRP	Chimie, Radio, Photographe
DCT	Direction du Contrôle Technique
DGD	Direction Générale de Documentation
DGER	Direction Générale des Etudes et Recherches
DGSE	Direction Générale de la Sécurité Extérieure
DGSS	Direction Générale des Services Spéciaux
DIRCEN	Direction du Centre des Experimentations Nucléaires
DIRDOC	Direction de la Documentation
DOM-TOM	Departements d'Outre-Mer/Territoires d'Outre-Mer
DOP	Détachement Opérationnel de Protection
DPU	Dispositif de Protection Urbaine
DRA	Direction de la Recherche en Allemagne
DST	Direction de la Surveillance du Territoire
ELP	Exercito de Libertação Português
EMIAT	Etat-Major Inter-Armées Terrestres
FAI	Federación Anarquista Ibérica
FBI	Federal Bureau of Investigation (USA)
FFI	Forces Françaises de l'Intérieur
FFL	Forces Françaises Libres
FHO	Fremde Heere Ost (Germany)
FI	[action team under] False Identity
FLB	Front de Libération de la Bretagne
FLEC	Front de Libération de l'Enclave de Cabinda
FLERD	Front de Libération et de Réhabilitation de Dahomey
FLN	Front de Libération Nationale (Algeria)
FLNC	Front de Libération Nationale Corse
FLNKS	Front de Libération Nationale Kanak at Socialiste
FLQ	Front de Libération du Québec
FNLA	Front National de la Libération de l'Angola
FTP	Franc-Tireurs et Partisans

GAM	Group Aérien Mixte
GCMA	Groupement de Commandos Mixtes Aéroportés
GCR	Groupement de Communications Radio-électriques
GEI	Groupe Etranger d'Intervention
GIC	Groupement Interministériel des Communications
GIGN	Groupement d'Intervention de la Gendarmerie Nationale
GLI	Groupement Léger d'Intervention
GMI	Groupement Mixte d'Intervention
GOC	General Officer Commanding
GPRA	Groupement Provisoire de la République Algérienne
GRE	Groupe de Renseignement et d'Exploitation
GRU	Glavnoye Razvedyvatelnoe Upravlenye (USSR)
IF	Identité Fausse
IHEDN	Institut des Hautes Etudes de la Défense Nationale
KARU	[Soviet Section of DST]
KGB	Komitet Gosudarstvennoi Bezopasnosti (State Security Committee: USSR)
MHBK	Magyar Harcosok Bajtarski Közössege (Association of Hungarian Freedom Fighters)
MI5	Military Intelligence, Secret Service Division (UK)
MINOS	Matériels d'Informations Normalisées pour les Opérations Spéciales
MLN	Mouvement de Libération Nationale
MNA	Mouvement Nationaliste Algérien
MNPGD	Mouvement National des Prisonniers de Guerre et Déportés
MPLA	Mouvement Populaire de Libération de l'Angola
MRA	Mission de Réforme Administrative
MRP	Mouvement Républicain Populaire
NASA	National Aeronautics and Space Administration (USA)
NATO	North Atlantic Treaty Organization
NKVD	Narodnyi Komissariat Vnutrennikh Del (People's Commissariat for Internal Affairs: USSR)
NTS	Natsiolno Trudoboy Soyuz (National Union for Labour: USSR)
OAS	Organisation de l'Armée Secrète
OCM	Organisation Civile et Militaire
OG	Organisation Gehlen (Germany)
ORAF	Organisation de la Résistance de l'Algérie Française
ORCG	Organisation de Recherche des Criminels de Guerre
ORTF	Office de la Radiodiffusion et Télévision Française
OSO	Office of Special Operations (USA)
OSS	Office of Strategic Services (USA)

PAIG	Parti Africain d'Indépendance Guinéenne
PAIGC	Parti do Africano da Indépendencia da Guiné e Cabo Verde
PCF	Parti Communiste Français
PCR	Police des Communications Radio-électriques
PDG	Parti Démocratique de Guinée
PFLP	Popular Front for the Liberation of Palestine
PIDE	Policia Internationale de Defesa de Estado (Portugal)
PLR	Poste de Liaison et de Renseignement
PPF	Parti Populaire Français
PSS	Parti de la Solidarité Sénégalaise
PTT	Postes, Télégraphes et Téléphones
RAP	Répression, Action, Protection
RCF	Rassemblement des Comoriens en France
RCMP	Royal Canadian Mounted Police
RDP	Régiment de Dragons Parachutistes
REP	Régiment Etranger Parachutiste
RIN	Rassemblement pour l'Indépendance Nationale
RPF	Rassemblement du Peuple Français
RPIMA	Régiment Parachutiste d'Infanterie de Marine
RLO	Regional Liaison Office (of MI5: UK)
ROVS	Russki Obshtche Voïenski Soyuz (USSR)
RTF	Radio Télévision Française
SA	Service Action
SAARF	Special Allied Airborne Reconnaissance Force
SAC	Service d'Action Civique
SAS	Special Air Services (UK)
SCE	Service de Contre-Espionnage
SDCI	[intelligence service of the Mouvement des Forces Armées]
SDECE	Service de Documentation Extérieure et de Contre-Espionnage
SDESC	Service de Documentation et d'Etudes de la Sécurité Camerounaise
SFIO	Section Française de l'Internationale Ouvrière
SGPDN	Sécretariat Général Permanent de la Défense Nationale
SID	Servizio Informazioni Difesa (Italy)
SIFAR	Servizio Informazioni Forze Armate Riuniti (Italy)
SIS	Secret Intelligence Service (UK)
SLNA	Service de Liaisons Nord-Africaines
SNEP	Sociéte Nationale des Entreprises de Presse
SOFRACOP	Société Franco-soviétique de Coopération Industrielle
SOFRES	Société Française d'Enquêtes et de Sondages
SR	Service de Renseignement
SRO	Service de Renseignement Opérationnel

SSD	Staatssicherheitsdienst (Germany)
SSM	Service de Sécurité Militaire
STB	Statni Tajna Bezpečnost (Czechoslovakia)
STO	Service du Travail Obligatoire
SURMAR	Surveillance Maritime
TR	Travaux Ruraux
UCR	Unité de Combat et de Renseignement
UDR	Union des Démocrates pour la République
UJP	Union des Jeunes pour le Progrès
UNR	Union pour la Nouvelle République
UPS	Union des Populations du Cameroun
UTA	Union Progressiste Sénégalaise

Translator's Note

In general the spelling of names is that normally used in French sources and in the original French version of this book.

The titles of ranks in the armed forces have been translated literally and no attempt has been made to replace them with British or American equivalents. It should be noted that 'Commandant' can be a generic title applied to all officers of 'superior' or 'field' rank in all three branches of the French armed forces. Its use in the secret services may have the advantageous effect of disguising the true rank of an officer and thus the importance of the mission on which he was engaged.

Prologue: Amid the Ruins of the Third Reich

Theirs was a perilous, almost impossible mission. Forty years on, without the testimony of the participants and the existence of archives, such adventures would seem to spring from the fertile imagination of some novelist. And yet . . . Jacques Foccart has not forgotten: 'We were to parachute in small teams into Germany in the winter at the end of 1944 and the beginning of 1945, in order to liberate the camps housing prisoners and deportees. It was planned that we should proceed by intimidation, telling their German commandants: 'If you stay quiet, and don't evacuate the camps or wipe out the prisoners, we'll give you credit for it at the end of the war.'[1]

For several months POWs had had their own intelligence agency, a kind of small secret service called the Liaison and Documentation Centre (Centre de Liaison et Documentation: CLD). 'I founded it in September 1944,' stated Jacques Benet, a former member of the Consultative Assembly, who was the representative for POWs.

Acting for the leadership of the National Movement for Prisoners of War and Deportees [Mouvement National des Prisonniers de Guerre et Déportés: MNPGD], to which I belonged, I prepared the text of the agreement between the minister for prisoners of war and refugee deportees, Henri Frenay, and Jacques Soustelle, then the head of the French secret services. From then onwards the CLD was placed under the dual protection of the ministry and the secret services, and increased resources were available to it.

The new task assigned to the CLD was to exploit the wealth of information gleaned from prisoners, and occasionally even from workers on forced labour [Service du Travail Obligatoire: STO] in Germany,[2] and to persuade the Allied armies to carry out operations to protect the prison camps and, above all, the political deportees. It was felt that they were marked for extermination, and that this would happen more quickly the nearer the German army came to final collapse. Our deepest motivation, even stronger than a certain conception of the duty of solidarity, was to save our comrades-in-arms, whom we knew well and respected, and who were daily threatened with extinction.[3]

Jacques Benet, about 30 years old and an archivist by profession, kept a careful eye on his charge. And the wheels of the CLD worked perfectly. A stream of information was coming out of Germany. Within the CLD itself there existed a body whose sole task was intelligence-gathering, under Colonel Jacques Pommès-Barrère, an officer in the pre-war intelligence service, who during the fighting had joined a network of the Free French Forces. The Colonel explained:

We centralized all intelligence relating to the 250,000 prisoners. We wanted to know where they were and what they were doing. At the beginning the Nazis used only German workers in their armament factories. But as and when they needed fresh military recruits, they moved in what they called 'free workers' [Tr. note: these were ex-POWs]. They put relative trust in them, and these prisoners were able to provide us with useful information. Thanks to them we were able to pinpoint the new factories that were building the V1 and V2 weapons.

Our information also allowed us to temper somewhat the enthusiasm of the Allies. The Germans fought to the very end. The very last intelligence report I received is actually dated 5 May 1945. It informed me that work gangs from Mauthausen were building new underground factories at Ebensee, in the Austrian valley of the Traunsee. Amid utter chaos they were busy tightening nuts and bolts and constructing towers – and this at a time when the German radio had already announced Hitler's death.[4]

The gathering of intelligence for the Allies was not the sole activity of the CLD – far from it. Contact with the French secret services was ensured by an air force colonel, Maurice Belleux, a former member of the Resistance.

Commandant Voltaire Ponchel, one of his aides, was an officer in the Central Bureau for Intelligence and Action (Bureau Central de Renseignement et d'Action: BCRA), the first Gaullist secret service, set up in London by 'Colonel Passy'. During the war Commandant Ponchel specialized in working inside Germany. In Berne he had got to know Allen Dulles, the future head of the CIA. Dulles worked under diplomatic cover in Switzerland, representing the US secret services. The two men were able to exchange and cross-check their intelligence. When he came to the CLD, Voltaire Ponchel, himself a former escaped prisoner, was given the task of screening the large number of them returning from Germany. He also selected officers suitable for participating in missions in the war now nearing its close.

Indeed, in London the countdown had already begun. Jacques Benet, François Mitterrand and their friends in the MNPGD had succeeded in convincing de Gaulle and General Juin, then commanding the French troops, that liberating the camps was a priority. In Paris several proposals to this effect had been made to the representatives of the Allied troops.

Who could have promoted the idea of such a mad expedition? Voltaire Ponchel stated: 'It was the MNPGD that suggested it. Its leader, François Mitterand, was thinking above all about the protection of the prisoners, now that the battle for Germany was beginning. In association with the French and Allied secret services based in London, some action was to be attempted.'[5]

Operation 'Vicarage': The Plan

It was August 1944 when Jacques Foccart arrived in the British capital, after a brief posting to the Fourth Military Region Command at Angers. His exploits in the Resistance had brought about his promotion to the rank of lieutenant-colonel in the BCRA. 'Two missions were proposed to us', he recalled. 'Either to parachute into Indo-China, landing on the Thai plateaux, or to attempt deep reconnaissance operations into Germany. I chose the latter.' Indeed Jacques Foccart was far from being a mere operative: he was the leader of the French volunteers. It was to him that at the end of 1944 Voltaire Ponchel dispatched some 40 escaped ex-prisoners, who were to take part in the venture because of their knowledge of the terrain.

These very special commando groups, placed in London under the command of the British General Nicholls, were called the Special Allied Airborne Reconnaissance Force (SAARF). For communication purposes, the plan for Operation 'Vicarage' involved parachute drops of small detachments supplied with radio transmitters. The training was very rigorous. It usually took place in the outer London area, at Virginia Water. All the men chosen to command the detachments were officers, either of lieutenant or captain rank. 'Our basic principle,' Voltaire Ponchel recalled, 'was to make up teams of three: a radio operator from the BCRA, a prisoner who knew the region, and an officer.' In practice, however, this principle was not always respected.

Reliable and experienced men were needed. Those coming from the Action group within the BCRA quickly outstripped the ex-prisoners. But were not the inter-Allied plans over-ambitious? Perhaps. The aims laid down were to liberate the concentration camps at Buchenwald, Bergen-Belsen, Mauthausen and Ravensbrück. The means envisaged were many and varied: 'Through intimidation or blackmail,' Jacques Foccart recalled, 'for instance, by sending in a commando group to parley with the Nazi camp commandant.' Sometimes the mission of these commandos was also to pave the way for the regular troops. 'Certain parachute drops, prepared directly by the CLD in conjunction with the Allies,' Jacques Benet explained, 'were to be effected not far from the camps housing political deportees, in order to trigger immediate intervention by lightly armed units.'

At the beginning of 1945 the go-ahead was given. But the operation was fraught with difficulty and the volunteers suffered a cruel disappointment. Dropped a few kilometres from Cologne, the team commanded by Captain Lacaze – who soon afterwards became President Coty's master tailor – succeeded in capturing the town prison. Alas, it was too late. In the underground cells of the sinister German gaols, the officer discovered to his horror the funeral urns of 150 Frenchmen. His mission had been in vain.

In March 1945 it was the turn of Lieutenant Pierre Cambon, of the family of diplomats, to try his luck. The objective was prison camp XIA at Altengrabow, where the singer Maurice Chevalier had been held in the 1914–18 war. Unfortunately the small commando unit was dropped too far from the camp. Poring over his staff map, Pierre Cambon could see only one solution. If he wanted to move quickly – in London the topographical detail had been carefully studied – he had to follow the route taken by the German soldiers and convoys. At the entrance to the first village a Wehrmacht officer roughly questioned the small clandestine group clad in the paratroop uniform of the Third Reich. Without hesitation Cambon, who spoke fluent German, hurled insults at the sentry in military slang. 'Ah, these paras,' sighed the officer and let them pass. Whilst the Allies were continuing their advance on Berlin, the French commandos presented themselves at the gate of Altengrabow prison. Pierre Cambon demanded that the camp commandant see him. The latter – an old Prussian soldier – was amazed at the audacity of this group of men. Knowing that Germany had lost, he was not one of those fanatical Nazis intent on fighting to the bitter end. He gave way to the intruders. Camp XIA was liberated and the mission accomplished.

Other detachments met with more serious difficulties. After being dropped in the wrong place, the commandos under Captain Paul Aussaresses were for a long time given up for lost. 'We left on board a Stirling aircraft in April 1945', said the BCRA officer. 'I was accompanied by Grangeaud, the radio officer, and Lieutenant Joseph Wagner of the BCRA. We were to liberate a camp manned by Wehrmacht troops in the Zerbst area, between Berlin and Magdeburg. We were dropped by mistake not far from the small town of Lubars, scores of kilometres from the place arranged.'[6] Aussaresses and his men found themselves in the thick of the fighting, but succeeded in carrying out their mission. Escaping from the terrifying Nazi 'sailors' of the Scharnhorst division, in Saxony, the commandos then fell into the hands of the Soviet Marshal Zhukov. Taken for spies, the Frenchmen were made prisoner and interrogated for several weeks. In London, they had long been given up for dead when in August 1945 they turned up again at the training camp in Virginia Water. General Nicholls came in person to congratulate Captain Aussaresses, and put him up for a few days.

What was the precise number of these astonishing missions? Opinions differ. 'Four,' said Jacques Benet. 'Six or seven teams left,' corrected Jacques Foccart, 'and many were killed.' 'Nine missions were carried out,' maintained Voltaire Ponchel, the CLD chief of staff. Colonel Pommès-Barrère was frank. 'I don't know,' he admitted, adding ironically, 'You know, we all risked being tortured, and this explains our extreme isolation from one another, and how little curiosity we felt.'

Suddenly the order was given to call a halt to the enterprise. In London Jacques Foccart was notified personally by General Nicholls. 'There may have been too many killed. It was really too dangerous,' said the former lieutenant-colonel of the BCRA with a sigh, still regretting this cancellation, given at the very moment when he and two of his comrades were at last going to be able to jump. General Pommès-Barrère, for his part, saw another explanation for it: 'The American advance was much faster than foreseen, and this made the SAARF plan redundant.'

'Many factors played a part in it,' concluded Jacques Benet of CLD:

The development of the military situation from the beginning of March 1945, the slow-moving and imperfect coordination between all the parties concerned, and also a few misunderstandings, kept the 20 other teams on the ground. They were split up among the forward echelons of the armies and, because of this, could not perform the tasks expected of them. The whole of the enterprise that I had headed and then sustained from the outside therefore led to limited results, and this was very detrimental to the survival of a large number of deportees. True, the experience gained by the CLD services involved was used to help in the general repatriation of the POWs, deportees and forced labour conscripts. But this became a task of a purely social kind. The CLD was disbanded in September 1945.[7]

The 'Calvary' Mission: The Freeing of Léon Blum

The French secret services did not operate only on the German front. Henceforth they participated fully in the many different military offensives waged by the Allies. From the autumn of 1944 onwards several teams were sent to the South Tyrol in Italy, in order to inform the Allied Command there about the German defences.

These missions behind the enemy lines, in especially hostile regions, were very dangerous. Eleven of them failed. But Passy, head of the French secret services, did not give up. In September 1944 he summoned to London two young officers. Passy did not hide the truth from these tried and tested men. 'It will be very tough,' he said, 'and I don't think you'll be coming back.' Hence the code-name 'Calvary' for this new Italian mission.

François Saar Demichel – code-name 'Coriolan' – who accepted responsibility for it, had already during the Resistance formed a 'fighting and intelligence unit' [Unité de Combat et de Renseignment: UCR] in the Corrèze. After the liberation of that area in August 1944 he got to know an officer recently parachuted in from London, Jacques Lebel de Penguilly, who suggested that he should take part in fresh operations in Austria. He accepted with enthusiasm. Lebel de Penguilly – 'Leb' or 'Lussac' – reports as follows: 'At that time the Allies thought that Hitler was going to concentrate his remaining forces in the notorious Tyrolean redoubt. We

were therefore to make contact with units of the Italian underground, inform
the Allies of German troop movements and, if possible, blow up whatever
lines of communication they might use.'[8]

Because of the anarchy then prevailing in the French services, the team
only left Paris at the beginning of February 1945, and reached Switzerland.
Besides Demichel and Penguilly it included a radio operator, André van
Laer, as well as two ex-officers of the Feldgendarmerie (the German field
security police), Leopold Auer and Olivier de Rességuier; these former
prisoners had agreed to work for the French. Direct access to Austria soon
proved impracticable: the Germans had reinforced their troops on the
frontier. Transit via Italy became imperative. Under false cover, generously
provided by a Swiss intelligence officer, the team finally crossed the frontier
on 19 March at La Drossa.

Immediately all hell broke loose. To escape Wehrmacht surveillance the
clandestine group was forced to take to the high mountain paths. In this way
Coriolan and Leb scaled the passes of the Etra (2,209 metres) and Foscagno
(2,291 metres), the Passo d'Eita (2,500 metres) and finally the Caretta Pass
(2,200 metres). Heavily laden, equipped with weapons and B2 radio sets, the
two men plunged up to the chest in the snow, which was just beginning to
melt. From 17 March to 28 April, in these conditions, the 'Calvary' mission
covered more than 400 kilometres behind the enemy lines, with Coriolan
and Leb, who had left the other team members behind in order to save time,
never forgetting to inform their Paris headquarters of the intelligence they
had gathered at every stage of their passage through the mountains.

Moreover, Jacques Lebel de Penguilly suffered from a grave disadvantage:
he did not speak a word of German. When the slightest check upon them
was made, François Saar Demichel, who fortunately spoke the language
perfectly, had to draw attention to himself by recounting any cock and bull
story. On 23 April they were stopped by three sentries at Mulbach. Whilst
Demichel was explaining to the Wehrmacht soldiers that his house had been
completely destroyed and that they had been forced to take to the roads,
Penguilly prudently kept his hand in his pocket, clutching the butt of his
revolver. Neither at this nor any other time did he ever need it. Demichel's
perfect accent convinced the occupying troops.

On 26 April the two men finally arrived at Pieve di Cadore, in the
Dolomites. François Saar Demichel explained: 'The Germans had begun
their fall-back upon the Bassano–Cortina axis towards Dobblach. The
collapse of the Reich was imminent, but any local capitulation could save
Allied lives. So I addressed an ultimatum to the German authorities in Pieve,
who still had a force several battalions strong, calling upon them to
surrender.'[9]

A written record of this improbable episode survives: Jacques Lebel de
Penguilly, once the mission was over, wrote a detailed report (hitherto
unpublished):

A neutral person delivered our ultimatum at 1600 hours. Half an hour later, we learnt that he was being held prisoner at the *Ortskommandantur*. We put on our uniforms and went to find the commander. His second in command, Captain Richter, pallid with amazement, received us and asked us what we wanted. Coriolan protested against the arrest of our emissary and repeated the ultimatum. Gradually the room filled up with almost all the officers of the garrison, drawn there by curiosity. Then the captain asked who we were and what we represented. Coriolan replied that we commanded a battalion of paratroops who were waiting in the mountains with 5,000 partisans,[10] under British and American officers. We had come, in the name of the Allied command, to demand their unconditional surrender, in order to avoid shedding blood to no purpose, since for them the war was lost. At this moment there appeared an enraged SS Panzer captain who was passing through Pieve and had just heard the rumour that two Allied officers were demanding the surrender of the town. He addressed Richter, asking him what it was all about. Coriolan answered in the same tone of voice. The other retorted that we could only be prisoners of war and permitted himself some insolent remarks about the Allies. Then Leb remarked to Coriolan that the captain should not speak to us with his hands in his pockets. Put out of countenance, the latter took his hands out of his pockets, and then burst forth in insults about the French.[11]

The two officers were arrested. Under strong escort, on the next day Demichel and Penguilly were taken a few kilometres from there, to Gestapo headquarters in Cortina, where they were again interrogated by a *Hauptsturmführer*, Dr von Lospichel. It was 28 April 1945. From then on the Frenchmen's bluffing knew no bounds. Having obtained the surrender of some hundred policemen in Cortina, François Saar Demichel established contact with the staff of General von Heer, commanding the German Tenth Army. After several interviews Colonel Beletz and Lieutenant Neumann, representing General von Heer, agreed on 1 May to surrender to the French officers. That very evening a huge Tricolor was hoisted over the main inn in Cortina. The following afternoon Wittinghof, the German general, signed the surrender of all German troops in Italy. This in no way detracts from the merit of the 'Calvary' mission, which by neutralizing numerous elements of the Tenth Army for several days, had prevented any last-ditch actions, which are often the most murderous.

Another surprise awaited the victors. The Germans indicated that they were holding a convoy of important political prisoners from the concentration camps. They had just been settled in at the Villa Bassa in Niederdorf. On 3 May Penguilly therefore went off to Niederdorf, travelling in a vehicle bedecked with a white cross of Lorraine, and driven by a German. The arrival of the first Allied officer in this camp produced a vivid impression. Leb, for his part, was stupefied. There he discovered Léon Blum and his wife, brought down from Buchenwald; Schuschnigg, the former Austrian Chancellor; the son of the Hungarian Miklos Horthy; Mgr Gabriel Piguet; the Greek General Staff in its entirety; Prince Xavier of Bourbon-Parma; Prince Frederick of Prussia; one of Churchill's cousins; and even a nephew of Molotov named Kokorin.[12] To these victims of Nazism must be added German VIPs such as Count von Stauffenberg and Dr Schacht, both involved in the assassination attempt against Hitler on 20 July 1944. Several weeks earlier these men had been snatched by the SS from the concentration camps. With such hostages the Nazis did not give up hope of negotiating favourable conditions for their own surrender.

On 3 May Jacques Lebel de Penguilly lunched with Léon Blum and his wife. 'The former prime minister and his spouse do not appear to have suffered unduly physically, but seem always to have been at the mercy of the camp commandant, who could have had them shot.' During the meal M. Blum declared that in his view the person of General de Gaulle was 'providential' for France, and that he foresaw a rapid revival of the nation. He questioned Leb about the different ministers, whom he generally did not seem to know, except for Tanguy-Prigent and Ramadier.

The election results and the successes of the Socialist Party seem especially to interest him. He thinks that Pétain was the instigator of the riots of 6 February [1934]; that he is a cunning, wily character; that Laval has never reached statesman class, and that it took tragic circumstances to make him one. At the end of the meal we drink champagne with Prince Xavier of Bourbon-Parma and Mgr Piguet, Bishop of Clermont-Ferrand. Leb has a quick conversation with Dr Schuschnigg who wishes Austria and Italy to be occupied by the Western powers.[13]

Political preoccupations, it seems, had already taken precedence over the war.

PART I

The Birth of SDECE

I

Ali Baba's Cave

The magnificent advantage of the General Directorate for Studies and Research (Direction Générale des Etudes et Recherches: DGER) just after the war was that in its basement it housed one of the most accessible restaurants in Paris, where, provided one had one's card (a secret agent card, and not a food ration card, like all other Parisians), one could eat one's fill, invite one's friends, and feast. This is the first image that most former members of the DGER summon up in describing the organization. But it is indissolubly linked with stories of a sorry muddle in which officers, under different pseudonyms, were receiving several salaries; Resistance networks were striving to 'assimilate' groups whose numbers were artificially swollen, despite the vigilance of the 'liquidation' commissions.

Who could have dreamt that, in spite of everything, a nucleus of resolute men from diverse backgrounds would be able, from this crude amalgam, to cast an alloy and forge a weapon, the cutting edge of the secret war in the post-Resistance era?

'Colonel Passy': André Dewavrin

On 6 November 1944, the General Directorate for Special Services (Direction Générale des Services Spéciaux: DGSS), headed by Jacques Soustelle since the unification of all the Free French networks, changed its name. For the remaining six months of the war, the new Directorate for Studies and Research (DGER) was to keep Soustelle as its leader. Then, on 19 April 1945, just before the capitulation of the Third Reich, Colonel Passy once again assumed control of the secret services, as he had done at the beginning of the world conflict.[1] The wheel of fortune had turned justly. At one time de Gaulle had asked him to set up the services of Free France; now he called upon him again to play midwife to what he himself called 'the intelligence service of the future'. From the very foundation of the Central Bureau for Intelligence and Action (Bureau Central de Renseignement et

d'Action: BCRA), de Gaulle's agency within the Resistance, the General
had weighed up his subordinate:

As soon as he was appointed, he was gripped by a kind of cold passion for this task,
which was to sustain him along a shadowy road where he found himself mixed up
with the best and the worst. . . . He was able to stifle his disgust and keep clear of the
boasting that are familiar devils in this kind of activity. This is the reason why,
whatever changes the BCRA had had to undergo in the light of experience, through
thick and thin I kept Passy in his post.[2]

In reality there was nothing that especially singled out Colonel Passy to
become the founder of our modern special services. André Dewavrin was
born in Paris in 1911 into a rich northern industrial family. In 1932 he
entered the Ecole Polytechnique, after having been a brilliant pupil at the
Lycée Louis-le-Grand. Two years later he passed into the Military
Engineering College (Ecole Militaire et d'Application du Génie). Here we
see the budding technician and planner: he was appointed an assistant
professor at the Special Military College (Ecole Militaire Spéciale). It was at
this time that sympathies for the Cagoule group were attributed to him.[3] The
allegation lacked any foundation and arose from a combination of
circumstances: in fact, his 'brains trust' in London was to be led by several
former Cagoulards, among them Colonel Fourcaud and Maurice Duclos
('Saint-Jacques'). A captain in 1939, Dewavrin volunteered for Norway and
took part in the Narvik operations. De Gaulle, whom he joined on 1 July
1940, appointed him head of his Deuxième Bureau, in Duke Street,
London, and two years later, head of the BCRA.

With Pierre Brossolette – whose portrait continues to grace the wall of his
Paris drawing-room beside a signed photograph of the General and among
works by Matisse, Maillole and Magritte – Colonel Passy parachuted into
France in 1943. What other head of a secret service, anywhere in the world,
has taken such risks? The British chided him roundly for it – not forgiving
him for an expedition that had as its outcome the independence of Free
France, through the setting up of the National Resistance Council (Conseil
National de la Résistance), and the staff of the Secret Army (Armée Secrète:
AS). In November 1943, as already noted, the secret services of de Gaulle
and Giraud were amalgamated in Algiers, under the direction of Jacques
Soustelle: Passy became technical director of the DGSS. Shortly after the
Normandy landings, after having been parachuted into Brittany, he became
head of intelligence and counter-espionage in the DGER, and soon after, in
May 1945, its director-general. By the end of the year he had mapped out
the outlines of an organizational structure for SDECE, but, with the
departure of de Gaulle, was to leave the special services and official politics
for good. He states: 'With the exception of people like Fourcaud, in the main
the BCRA was organized by men of the Left, such as Jacques Bingen, Tony
Mella, Jean-Pierre Bloch and Stéphane Hessel . . . I have always been on the

Left, despite my origins (and in spite of the lying assertions concerning the Cagoule). But I have never joined a political party.'⁴

The General Directorate for Studies and Research
(Direction Générale des Etudes et Recherches)

As for the Left, the communists and their Francs-Tireurs et Partisans had no part in the birth of the DGER. Nor were they invited to do so. But all the former networks 'who carried out intelligence work' in the Resistance seem to have been absorbed 'naturally' by the new DGER. It soon numbered over 10,000 officers and agents – four times more than its successor in 1989, the DGSE.

At the time there was no security office really capable of vetting those who wished to become 'secret agents'. Their motives and technical ability were in fact often questionable. The patriot who had rallied from the very first had nothing in common with the schemer of any and every camp who rallied to the Resistance at the 25th hour. And even a Resister, a genuine one, who had counted the number of Wehrmacht trains passing in 1943, did not change automatically into an officer capable of managing a network of agents behind the Iron Curtain in 1946.

Yet, in spite of everything, the framework of the special services was a solid one. Those who were to be its officers for 20 years principally belonged to two schools that the War had fused together in the crucible of action. There were some snags: sometimes two generations confronted each other. It is helpful to distinguish between them: on the one hand, the 'traditional' secret services, created in the last century and amply provided for in the 1930s; on the other, the services contingent upon the presence in London of de Gaulle, whose work certainly needed a secular arm.

The first group was immortalized by the writers of the period between the wars: Robert-Charles Dumas, Pierre Nord, Pierre Benoît and many others. The cinema also exploited this vein. So much so that all over the world the Deuxième Bureau became synonymous with spying *à la française*. The image it conjured up was of haughty officers, immaculately turned out, with neat moustaches and white gloves, and just a suspicion of roguery, yet chivalrous in spirit, even on the darkest missions. Contrary to legend, the Deuxième Bureau was merely a body devoted to intelligence studies that was attached to the Army general staff. The daring exploits, the thefts of documents, the recruitment of double agents – in short, all the secret operations that inspire the novelists – emanated from another headquarters; this was 2 bis, Avenue de Tourville in Paris – '2 bis', as it was familiarly called – which housed the intelligence service (Service de Renseignement: SR) and its inseparable complement, the counter-espionage service (Contre-Espionnage: CE). In the simplest terms, the SR carries out the search for intelligence and

manages agents abroad, and the CE ensures that the foreigner does not do
the same thing in France. They are the sword and buckler. It was these two
entities that, month after month before 1939, rang the alarm bells, warning
irresponsible French governments against the Nazi peril.

After the collapse in 1940, these services chose to remain attached to the
Armistice Army, and to carry on their activities against the Germans, using
various forms of cover. Thus there was 'Monsieur Perrier', who ran a
business called 'Rural Works' ('Travaux Ruraux'): this enigmatic character
was none other than Commandant Paul Paillole, one of those responsible for
counter-espionage. After the Nazis invaded the Unoccupied Zone, he joined
up in Algiers in 1943 with his former colleagues: his pre-war chief, General
Louis Rivet, his friend Henri Navarre and many others. Close to the British
and American secret services, they did not trust de Gaulle, and preferred
General Giraud to him. After a few skirmishes, the secret services of the two
generals merged in time into the DGSS, then the DGER, and later the
SDECE (see figure 1.1).

Commandant Paillole played a decisive role in their coming together.[5]
Without a shadow of doubt he summons up the perfect picture of the 'boss'
of the secret services, whether the intelligence service or the Deuxième
Bureau, as depicted in novels and films. His tall stature, his Grecian nose,
his gaze, penetrating and amused by turns, his cold-blooded approach to
problems and paternal stance towards his men made him a redoubtable
technical expert in German counter-espionage. But this type of traditional
officer, whose professionalism and integrity are equalled only by the strength
of his temperament, was opposed to de Gaulle's decision of 17 November
1944 to split counter-espionage into two groups. Military security was to be
attached to the Ministry of War, whilst Paillole's team was to form the
counter-espionage section proper in the new DGER. Logically the DGER
should have been headed by Paul Paillole, but he, outraged at the breakup of
his old service, handed in his resignation, whilst suggesting to his colleagues
that they should carry on their activities within the new services.[6]
Occasionally their integration proved to be a delicate matter. Certain voices
reproached them with not having been involved in the clandestine
Resistance before 1943. They proved that, even within the Vichy special
service, they fought the Nazi occupier. Their merits were to be recognized:
right up to the 1960s they were at the very heart first of the DGER, and then
of the SDECE.[7]

For the time being, in the spring of 1945, it was the other wartime secret
service, General de Gaulle's BCRA, headed in London by Colonel Passy,
that constituted the other wing of the DGER and, for the most part, took
over its leadership. In contrast to the old intelligence service, the BCRA was
a structure dictated by circumstances, the child of chance and necessity,
born from the will of the Resisters who, under the influence of General de
Gaulle, had been emboldened to build up intelligence and operational

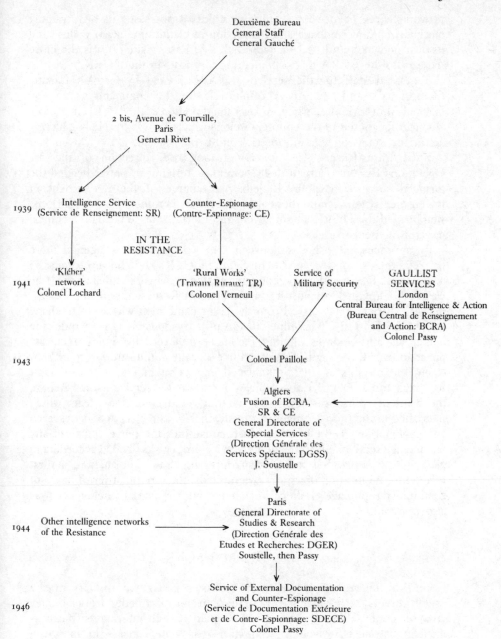

Figure 1.1 Development of the secret services established under Generals de Gaulle and Giraud

networks. Free France meant nothing unless it possessed its own training mechanisms for espionage and instruction in clandestine activity, directing its own networks and its own radio links. At Passy's side, it was therefore those from the BCRA that occupied the top posts in the DGER.

A general staff for the services was coordinated by Captain Lahana ('Landrieux'), and the officer responsible for the command group was Colonel André Manuel, who took over the direction of the DGER in Passy's absence. Promoted to the counter-espionage service was François Thierry-Mieg, the scion of a family of rich industrialists, and a POW who had escaped from Russia; Captain Dutet took over direction of the Air Operations Bureau (Bureau des Opérations Aériennes); Saffar headed the financial services; Captain Belleux had charge of the department of intelligence synopses; and there also were the two brothers Fourcaud: Boris, who headed the DGER air squadron, and Pierre, soon to become technical director of special services.

By a process of osmosis between the two 'families' of agents, there emerged the organizational structure of the DGER. To it, however, must be added those responsible for secondary resistance networks, such as the 'free corps' of Captain Hounau, the future head of Research, and the socialist network 'Libération-Nord'. From the latter came men who were to shape the SDECE: Guy Marienne ('Morvan'), responsible for clandestine operations, and Georges Lionnet, the linchpin of Security. The Directorate presided over three main divisions. First was the administration, very busy when one considered that it managed 10,123 members, a total of 123 buildings and a fleet of 1,400 vehicles. Next was the service named Action, the band of specialists in shock operations and commando feats which flourished in the Indo-China war. Finally, there was the service for research and exploitation of intelligence, which constitutes the nerve centre of any intelligence service. The intelligence service proper was divided according to geographical sectors. It fed headquarters with 'raw' information, at first relating to the hunting down of war criminals, then to the order of battle of communist espionage. Political, economic and industrial intelligence was also gathered.

The SR and the CE

Faithful to the pre-war tradition, in embassies an assistant military attaché usually directs the intelligence arm. He gleans his information from a motley crew of 'honourable correspondents', unpaid French informants: business men, industrialists, travelling academics – or 'static' ones – in any given country. But he gains it even more from 'agents', natives of the country in which his post is located: these are officials, politicians, journalists, clerics etc.[8] Moreover, in the same embassy, 'vice-consuls' or 'attachés' watch over, collate and protect intelligence activities. They replicate the research, to make it more reliable.

They belong to the other main section, that of Counter-Espionage (CE), which is also divided into geographical sectors. Their role consists in protecting the activities of their intelligence colleagues and in blocking any infiltration from opposing services. They tend to resort to what is termed 'offensive' counter-espionage. In order to ward off any attack from their adversaries, they proceed to infiltrate them first, to recruit an agent from within their services, and even to win over an agent of the opposing camp who has been sent to penetrate the French service, and who immediately becomes a 'double' agent. Finally, it is even conceivable that they can 'turn' once more an agent of their own whom they wished to infiltrate into the opposing camp but who in the meantime has been recruited by it. Here matters become endlessly complicated, and one enters the realm of literature.

It should be noted that up to the 1950s, in the colonies, and above all in Africa, only the counter-espionage section was really represented in the French possessions, side by side with various services of the colonial police.

From the mass of information arriving from the various departments of the DGER a 'third section', the service devoted to 'Studies', produces a synthesis. Editors, analysts – specialists in various countries and in many subjects – finally draw up the Intelligence Reports (Bulletins de Renseignement: BR) which, after approval by the directorate, finish up on the desks of the various ministries and, most importantly, on that of the prime minister.

The DGER 'Listens in' to France

In January 1945 the heads of mission of the DGER received a circular entitled 'Instructions to agents concerning the nature of the intelligence to be sought, the manner of classifying it and of passing it on'. This document bears witness to the fact that even before World War II was over, a transition was occurring to peacetime espionage, in which politics was to occupy an important place. The circular merits citing at length: it may be summarized as follows:

Section I: The internal situation and public opinion. Ascertaining and foreseeing reactions to government decisions, and those of the regional Commissioners of the Republic and the prefects. The state of mind of prisoners and deportees returning from Germany. The situation in ecclesiastical circles. The open or covert survival of the Vichy mentality. Possible manifestations of anti-Semitism. Evaluation of opinion regarding the Consultative Assembly, parliamentary and municipal institutions etc.

Section II: The political parties. Status, programmes and development of the parties. Their leaders and their standing. Main trends in ideas and in slogans. Demonstrations. The financial resources of parties. Number of members and real standing of the parties. Election forecasts.

Section III: The Resistance movements. The Council of the Resistance. The Liberation committees, their composition and activities. The Resistance movements that have developed from clandestine activities: *Combat, Libération, OCM, MLN, Front National* and branches. Their present role, status, developments and changes.

When it was made public this memorandum raised a general uproar in the Assembly.[9] However, in the event the DGER proceeded to carry on its enquiries on the classical lines, and these later became the task of Renseignements Généraux (the French equivalent of Special Branch). Several years were to elapse before Jules Moch asked the DST (Direction de la Surveillance du Territoire) to open files on each and every member of the Francs-Tireurs et Partisans (the FTP, of whom only a handful had been able to inveigle themselves into the French secret services).[10] The reaction that the activities of the DGER aroused in certain quarters arose from its omnipresent nature. Its reports were passed on to Gaston Palewski, the head of General de Gaulle's Private Office, which also acted as a centre for intelligence emanating from the Sûreté Nationale, which was run by other long-standing former members of the BCRA in North Africa, Charles Luizet and André Pelabon.

Finally, with its considerable budget,[11] and its 10,000 agents, it also covered surveillance of the mail and telephone tapping, via the PTT (Postes, Télégraphes et Téléphones). Under the title of Directorate of Technical Control (Direction du Contrôle Technique: DCT), the DGER intercepted suspect letters and telephone communications. In Paris its technicians operated from the Anjou, Elysées, Etoile, Jasmin, Littré, Marcadet and Montrouge telephone exchanges. In Lyons a similar body was attached to the DGER centre at 68, Rue des Belges. The scenario was the same in Clermont-Ferrand, Bordeaux, Nancy and Strasbourg. At Marseilles the matter was more delicate, and the French had to take back control of the listening services from the Americans. Lieutenant Stasia O'Neill, an Irish woman attached to American counter-espionage based in Marseilles from 1944 to 1946, recalled:

Our service had as its cover name Signal Communication Installation of Delta Base Section. I worked under Colonel Ira P. Doctor, of the Signal Corps, and Captain Fitzpatrick of the CIC [Counter-Intelligence Corps]. Our entire set-up in the Rue de la Bourse at Marseilles was linked to the telephone exchange. Sixty-two persons were then working day and night at the exchange. We listened in to people suspected of collaboration during the war, and also to Resistance groups or French political groupings. The section for civilian enquiries [CID] was concerned above all with the 'purge' of collaborators and the Information Service with the provision of intelligence to the secret services in Washington.[12]

By the end of 1944 the postal censorship employed 3,000 people and was costing the DGER 15 million francs.[13] In August 1945 the DCT budget was transferred from the Ministry of War to the Ministry of the Interior. In February 1946, with the creation of the SDECE, these services were abolished.

The DGER: A Shambles

There were 10,123 members of the DGER, of whom 9,971 were on the permanent staff. They were – naturally – members of the Resistance, people to whom the war had imparted a taste for the secret, the shadowy and the clandestine. It was a sort of virus. But there were also crooks, former 'big shots' in the black market, or – even worse – sometime 'collaborators' who had undergone a timely conversion.

'Taking advantage of the general disorder,' wrote the clear-sighted Colonel Passy, head of the DGER, 'a flood of shysters, *agents-provocateurs* or more than dubious agents had poured into the DGER.'[14] He also wrote: 'Numerous professional brigands had no difficulty in obtaining documents of assignment, on DGER notepaper, which allowed them, in the name of counter-espionage, to swindle a few gullible unfortunates.'[15] Indeed a survey of the press of the time reveals the extent of the phenomenon. Let us look at it more closely.

The first time, Lieutenant H. pushed Mme Gardel over a dam 18 m high. By good fortune she escaped from danger, so he then fired at her point-blank, emptying the magazine of his pistol. But the lady had nine lives. The third time H. ordered one of his assistants to assassinate her. It came to nothing. In March 1946 she was the principal witness at the military court at Lyons before which H. appeared. What was the motive behind these attempts at murder? The reader of the daily press was never to find out. On the other hand, it was emphasized that the officer belonged to the DGER.[16] 'Yet again,' journalists were tempted to say, hinting that the DGER smelled rotten. The long catalogue of small news items that filled the newspaper columns would make a book.

Let us consider a few typical cases. Jean D., a native of Lille, a senior officer in the DGER, was arrested at a wedding in September 1945 on a charge of swindling and for the illegal wearing of decorations.[17] Two days later, gendarmes questioned Georges M., a second lieutenant in the DGER, who was carrying in his vehicle 1,600 gold coins belonging to 'Mme Huss, interned in the camp at Tourelles, who had entrusted them to her sister, who lived in Cours (Rhône)'.[18] Yet another example: Paul B., an industrialist from Corpeau (Côte d'Or), was receiving payments from the DGER until the day in September 1945 when he was arrested. He had belonged to the collaborationist Parti Populaire Français (PPF) during the War, had been in constant touch with the Propagandastaffel, and had even denounced his brother-in-law to the Gestapo for concealment of weapons, only shortly before he had joined the Resistance in 1944.[19] Another example is hardly more edifying: Captain G., a former high official in the youth movement Chantiers de Jeunesse, was arrested in 1944 for his collaborationist activities. Temporarily set free, he succeeded in joining the DGER.[20] That same September Captain L. ('Brival') was arrested at the Swiss frontier with 4 million francs in gold coins in his possession.

An even more serious case was that of four DGER officers who were transporting prisoners who had been members of the collaborationist police force Milice. Near Nice they murdered them, making off with 10 million francs they had stolen from them. The newspaper *Franc-Tireur* waxed indignant: 'After all, what on earth is this all about? Under the sign of those four mysterious letters DGER, not a day goes by without an offence being reported, or a scurrilous action, or even a crime, committed by the members of this special, secret and private police, which is exempt from any form of control.'[21]

Colonel Passy reacted immediately. On 22 September 1945, the prime minister's Office drew up a statement that set out the tasks assigned to the DGER. It said:

Various news items that are basically untrue, if not tendentious, have recently appeared in certain organs of the press concerning the General Directorate of Studies and Research [DGER]. About these matters it is necessary to make clear the following:

1 The BCRA, set up in London in June 1940 by the Free French, had as its essential task the installation and organization of an operational and intelligence-gathering network in French enemy-occupied territory. It fulfilled that mission at the price of heavy losses, but we owe invaluable results to it.

2 Its successor, the DGER, after the liberation of the national territory, was entrusted with the mission of organizing, on the lines of a model already existing among our principal allies, a counter-espionage service devoted solely to activities beyond our frontiers, whilst playing in Indo-China the role previously assumed by the BCRA. On the one hand it was a question of replacing the former French services, whose activities had been almost entirely suppressed by the Vichy government, and, on the other, of giving these new services a structure that corresponded to future needs. . .

3 The DGER plays a part in safeguarding our national interests beyond our frontiers; it fulfils no role within them. Bound by its duties of discipline, it can answer neither attacks nor hostile insinuations except by performing conscientiously the task with which it is entrusted.

In more than one respect such observations were wholly justified, since the abuses and offences committed by DGER members were hardly out of proportion to the total number of its agents. But it was probably high time to undertake a thorough purge, for scandals concerning the DGER continued to break. In October 1945, an ex-lieutenant in the DGER, Jacques F., by trade a butcher's boy, was arrested in Neuilly for the theft in Verona of jewels worth 12 million francs.[22] For his part, Lieutenant Robert H. had installed himself in the home of the actor Victorien Sardou, in order to devote himself to trafficking in old bank notes and to dealing in wine and spirits on the black market. Yet another former member of the DGER, Paul de L., was interrogated for 'dealings with the enemy and economic collaboration'. Simone C., a woman lieutenant in the special services, was wont to steal several cars every week, doubtless for want of anything better to do. Etc., etc.

Let us leave the list there, except for two outrageous cases: that of D., the Paris administrator of the DGER, who turned out to have been the administrator of Jewish property during the Occupation; and worst of all, that of Henri Soutif, an officer of superintendent rank in the Renseignements Généraux. Soutif was notorious for his brutality, and was reported to have murdered many Resistance members in Quimper. Arrested by the Bureau of Military Security, he was taken over by the DGER, and, to the bewilderment of former Breton Resistance members, succeeded in getting himself enrolled in that organization. The official version was that Soutif had already been enrolled in the BCRA under reference number C.XC 6/5–30.410. In fact, he had enthusiastically carried out torture in order to strengthen his cover as a secret agent of the Free French. Fearing reprisals by the Resistance, he had disappeared for a while, and then surfaced again in 1947. So many scandalous cases demonstrate that the Organization for the Investigation of War Crimes (Organisation de Recherche des Criminels de Guerre: ORCG), then attached to the DGER, in the end encountered greater difficulties in Paris than beyond the frontier.

Commandant Gilbert Mantout, who directed the ORCG from the former headquarters of the Gestapo in the Avenue Victor Hugo, wrestled with immense problems. To build up a sound intelligence service and to carry out the 'purge' of collaborationists were two very different matters. Colonel Passy realized this, and he was to reorganize his services from top to bottom – not before time. 'The DGER had become a veritable Ali Baba's cave. A clean break was needed,' Passy recalled 40 years later.

What mattered was to retain what would be indispensable later on, for the intelligence services of the future. In July or August I took a radical decision: I showed 10,000 people the door. I gave up 101 out of 105 buildings. I kept 50 vehicles. In view of the spectrum of political opinion represented among those who were dismissed, I was attacked by the extreme Right and the extreme Left. Then I told de Gaulle that I had to leave in other hands 'the secret services of the future'. He replied, 'One does not abandon a ship when it is taking in water.' So I founded the SDECE [Service of External Documentation and Counter-Espionage]. But a little later the socialists and communists mounted a harebrained plot against me involving BCRA funds that had remained in London.[23]

There is no doubt that Colonel Passy had made many enemies. He became aware of this somewhat later, when the affair that bears his name 'broke'. For the time being, the French Communist Party (Parti Communiste Français: PCF) went all out to destroy the fledgeling secret services.

The French Communist Party Confronts the Secret Services

In the campaign orchestrated first against the DGER and then the SDECE, the communists were especially virulent. They probably realized that, with a few exceptions, it would be impossible to integrate their members into the secret services on an equal footing with other former Resistance fighters. The DGER was crucified by the communist press for being the heir of the BCRA, namely of a mechanism for 'coercion and a Gaullist seizure of power', a 'super-police',[24] or, to adopt the slogan of André Wurmser, the vitriolic polemicist of *L'Humanité*, 'DGER = Direction Générale des Ennemis de la République [General Directorate of the Enemies of the Republic].'[25] Clearly the muddle that reigned at the DGER left people aghast, and the communists had an easy time in denouncing the daily petty scandals that marked its brief history, from the liberation of Paris to the winter of 1945. But the Gaullists and former BCRA members alone were incriminated in this way, whereas they were far from constituting a majority in the DGER. It was really from the autumn of 1944 onwards that the PCF violently attacked the intelligence agency, then headed by Jacques Soustelle and still called, as it had been at Algiers since 1943, the Directorate General of Special Services. At that time it certainly bore the mark of Gaullism.

And the Party specialists threw themselves into the attack. On 27 October 1944, at a meeting held at the Mutualité, Jacques Duclos denounced the DGSS, the 'super-police' that had emerged from the Gaullist BCRA: 'This BCRA organized parachute drops of arms, but so contrived it that the FTP received none. Several of its members are known to be Cagoulards or notorious anti-communists, and the body provided arms for anti-communist groups, whilst denying them to patriots fighting the Boches.' Nor did the second secretary of the PCF draw any fine distinctions: the service, now styled the DGSS, was tending 'to become a police organ built on the model of the Gestapo.'[26]

Georges Beyer, the underrated coordinator of the special services of the FTP during the War, the mysterious 'Service B', posed the question in *France d'abord*:

Where did the billions of francs of the BCRA go to? The Resistance must ask for the accounts. It has the right, and it is the duty of all in the Resistance to do so, both those who remained in France and those who left for London. The FTP never received a penny from the subscription opened in Algiers on their behalf. Resisters and patriots have the right and the duty to join with [the FTP] in demanding that Passy's accounts, and those of Soustelle, Frenay and others, be published.[27]

In 1946 the Gaullists, and Passy in particular, were the favourite target of the PCF. The members of the BCRA were depicted as sometime troublemakers and conspirators. The proof? Maurice Duclos ('Saint-Jacques'), Pierre Fourcaud ('Barbès'), and even, it was falsely claimed, Dewavrin ('Passy'), the head of them all, had a troubled conscience. 'Let us not say that the BCRA was full of Cagoulards – that would be absurd,' asserted André Wurmser. 'Let us say more simply: the enemies of the Republic had the BCRA in their hands. But, after all, you will say, what kind of person is Passy, the head of this BCRA? Passy is a swindler.'[28]

Another manifestation of this vituperation: on 20 April 1951 Marcel Servin, head of the leadership cadres promotion section, the security services of the PCF, sent to section secretaries a document that was plain and unambiguous, emanating from Raymond Guyot, a member of the Party executive 'Be on your guard against militants who, during the period of clandestine activities, had active connections with the networks called DGER, BCRA, etc.'[29]

Later the former leader of the PCF, André Marty, expelled from his party, was to pose this pertinent question:

Why, at the beginning of our participation in government, when the secretary-general of the Party was deputy premier, when moreover Maurice Thorez was one of the government delegates on the commission of control for that ultra-secret police body called the DGER, and then the SDECE (which the PCF said had been penetrated by Cagoulards and fascists), why did not the Communist ministers demand to know the names of the principal 'moles' and *agents-provocateurs* planted in the PCF and the CGT [Confédération Générale du Travail]?[30]

All the evidence collected by the present authors adds up. There were no more than a handful of self-confessed communist members or sympathizers in the SDECE and the DST, and these were generally former FTP members and were involved only at the very beginning; Clément, the head of the scientific section, was one, and another was an officer attached to Colonel Verneuil's counter-espionage group. The best agents for Soviet penetration of the SDECE were not men of the Left, but the adepts of anti-communism. The typical recruit was the officer who had collaborated with the Nazis or betrayed a Resistance network, whose existence the Russians had learnt of by searching through Gestapo or Abwehr files. It only remained to blackmail him.

Between the communists and the special services, in any case, there was total war. The 'Passy affair' provides a good illustration of this.

The Passy Affair

In February 1946 Colonel Passy – and we shall return to this – handed over to his successor. Two months later, in April 1946, Colonel Fourcaud, Passy's former assistant at the BCRA, undertook an inspection of the London base of SDECE. 'Ugly rumours' were then circulating concerning Captain Lahana ('Landrieux'), the former station head in Britain. On his return to Paris Fourcaud reported to the new director of SDECE, Henri Ribière, Passy's successor. The colonel was later to say, 'An unfortunate mischance put me at cross-purposes with one of my comrades whom I still esteem highly, Colonel Passy. Although painful for me, I did not shirk my duty.'[31] Pierre Sudreau, in charge of the administrative and financial affairs of SDECE, led an enquiry into deposits of money that had remained in London and had not been accounted for. Worse still, Captain Lahana admitted to 'having trafficked in gold, underwear and furs', and to having opened two secret accounts at Barclays Bank in Liverpool and the National Provincial in London.[32] Another SDECE officer, Captain Nocq, disclosed that he was still in possession of 25 million francs, which had been handed over by the British but had proved impossible to parachute into France.[33]

The detailed enquiry quickly led back to Passy. 'It was on his orders,' asserted Colonel André Manuel, then secretary-general of SDECE, 'that I established three clandestine deposit accounts. They had been set up on the orders of Colonel Dewavrin in order to constitute a "war chest", and reasons of state were invoked.'[34] Fearing an armed coup by the communists, had Passy amassed this nest-egg in order to allow the BCRA, which became the SDECE, to set up a 'new Resistance' movement? Passy, when interrogated, explained:

In November 1945 it had been agreed, in the event of international complications, to set up a war chest. I took this decision on my own, because of the atmosphere then prevailing. I wish to make it plain that I alerted General de Gaulle to the existence of this deposit at the beginning of April 1945. He sent me a reply a few days later through Captain Guy to the effect that I was immediately to return this sum to the government to which it belonged.[35]

On May 20 Henri Ribière submitted to the government a detailed report prepared by Louis Fauvert, the new officer responsible for the finances of SDECE. It attacked Colonel Passy on the following grounds:

1 Having established two secret deposits in England amounting in all to £16,664, $45,615 and 20,000 Swiss francs:
2 Having used part of these deposits with a view to setting up an import and export company:
3 Having established a deposit in Paris amounting in total to £8,275 and $36,000:

4 Having used a sum of 15 million francs originating from the British services, handed over to him by Captain Nocq:

5 Having exceeded the expiry date on [old] banknotes worth 6 million French francs, Treasury bonds to the value of 11.7 million francs and 5 millions' worth of cheques found at the home of M. Anglard, in the London area:

6 Having agreed to a loan of 10 million francs to the newspaper *France-soir*, in order to further his personal ends in matters of internal politics, which was outside the terms of reference of the service he directed:

7 Having disposed of a sum of 4.5 million francs, in non-accountable funds but belonging to SDECE, on 3 March 1946, when he was no longer director-general:

8 Having falsified the account books, a set of which was handed over to him, in order to cover up the irregularity of his actions.

9 Having been involved in trafficking in gold and currencies, in particular through the intermediary of M. Roberty, concerning whom unfavourable information had been given him by the deputy director of his Office, M. Vaudreuil.[36]

10 Having committed an outright swindle at the expense of his colleagues by inciting them to act irregularly, claiming that he was following the orders of General de Gaulle, whereas the latter, having been informed late in the day of the existence of these various deposits, had given orders that they should be handed back without delay to the government to which they belonged. The use for his personal ends of these sums, the total of which it has not been possible to determine, is apparent from the various testimonies given by his oldest colleagues, who all make it plain that they had been shocked at the life style of Colonel Passy.[37]

Before the report was made public, Félix Gouin informed General de Gaulle of its contents. Whilst expressing the wish that the 'Passy affair' should not become public knowledge, the General suggested that his 'Compagnon' should be placed under close arrest. On 5 May 1946, the former head of the secret services was incarcerated in the fortress of Metz, where he remained for four months. Was he let down by his own people? And, above all, was he indeed responsible for what he had been accused of?

For the communists, seething with indignation, there was no room for doubt. Their acknowledged polemicist, André Wurmser, wrote:

What is serious – very serious – about this affair is that the DGER, packed with enemies of the Republic, led by Passy and covered by General de Gaulle, set up a state within a state, and even went so far as to refuse to submit accounts, or to deem valid the votes of Parliament, changes in the ministries and the orders of the Republic. . . . It is possible that Passy abused the trust of General de Gaulle. It is certain that the General's trust in Passy was ill-founded.[38]

During a press conference held shortly after his release Colonel Passy made this laconic comment: 'It was frequently the case that certain funds, particularly from extra-budgetary sources, were not automatically passed on to a direct successor, but occasionally to "other responsible persons", provided that they remained available for the objectives of the SR.'[39] Retaining his rank, Passy resigned from the Army at his own request in January 1948. Forty years later he harbours bitter memories of this episode.

When we pointed out to him that the archives of the Office of Strategic Services (OSS), which can now be consulted, suggest that he frequently met the American special services at that time, in order to work out a joint defence in case of a communist armed coup, the first head of our modern secret services replied unhesitatingly:

No. A communist *coup d'état* was to be feared in 1944, but not afterwards. When I left the SDECE in 1946, if there was a Russian danger, it could only come from a war. De Gaulle thought that such a conflict would occur. At the beginning of 1947 I paid him a visit. 'Truman should bang the table,' de Gaulle shouted. When I telephoned my friend David Bruce, a former OSS man, to inform him of these views, he merely replied: 'That's crazy.' In March came the birth of the RPF.[40] But I would not join. I had turned away from politics. Now the affair of May 1946 had been political. The socialists and communists had dreamt up a crazy Gaullist plot. They had allegedly found 10 billion francs. I didn't understand the matter at all. This represented the remaining funds of the BCRA, but the banknotes were invalid, because there had been the currency revision. This clearly proves there was no ulterior motive on our part, since they were unusable.[41]

To write about the 'services', as the reader will easily discover in the pages that follow, is to plunge into a troubled world where the rock of utter certainties and the whole truth often disappears in the mists of what remains unsaid. Reference points are blurred, and the investigator's compass swings wildly. But before rancour, bitterness and time separated the comrades of former days forever, a common struggle brought them together for a brief space of time after the War. It united the long-serving officers and the more recent recruits, the London agents and the veterans of intelligence. For some months, hunting down the Nazis was the central preoccupation of the services.

2

Tracking down the Nazis

'What kind of face would the Americans have pulled if we had abducted Barbie, as we could have done, when he was one of their agents?' asked Colonel Paul Paillole 40 years later. One of the chief architects of French counter-espionage during the War, he knew what he was talking about. 'It was my service, the team based at the time in Wiesbaden, with Colonel Gérar-Dubot, Captain Dumont, Superintendent Bibes, and then Lieutenant Whiteway, who, through their American contacts, found Barbie. And it was under these conditions that we were able to interrogate him and that he made the remarks that are at the root of the Jean Moulin affair.'[1]

Klaus Barbie, acting with unsurpassed ferocity, orchestrated the Gestapo's operations against the Resistance in Lyons. In 1983 he was extradited from Bolivia to France. An action squad of the French special services went out from Guyana to pick him up and bring him back to French territory. They were too young to have known the Occupation, but they carried out a mission that their elders would have dearly liked to accomplish. In the 1940s the French came up against the Americans, our allies, so the matter was a delicate one, and Klaus Barbie neatly eluded them the first time, like many others the Americans rescued. Immediately after the Liberation, knowledge of the battlefield in Eastern Europe, which the Germans alone possessed, was a trump card in the Cold War that was opening up. However, on the part of the French, there was no thought of giving up the chase. Above all else they sought to apprehend the war criminals who had exercised such a tyranny in France. The Anglo-Americans did not always understand this stubbornness – doubtless because they had not known the German yoke. In October 1944 Commandant Paillole created an organization to operate in the French occupation zone across the Rhine, the Inter-Allied Bureau for Counter-Espionage (Bureau Interallié de Contre-Espionnage: BICE).[2]

Its head was certainly one of the most astonishing figures in French intelligence during the twentieth century. Born in 1888, Paul Gérar-Dubot (GD, as his friends called him) had made his career in journalism. From 1911 onwards he became an 'honourable correspondent' for Counter-Espionage. Although he fought in the war of 1914–18 and had waged an unceasing struggle against German militarism, he had ended up, monocle and all, by resembling a Prussian officer of the kind played by Eric von Stroheim in *La Grande illusion*. As chief editor of *Le Journal*, the Paris daily, through correspondents such as Georges Blun in Berlin, he provided valuable information on Nazi Germany. In 1940, as a colonel in the reserve, he devoted himself to counter-espionage. Under his leadership *Le Journal* furnished an effective cover during the Occupation. His regional Service of Military Security (Service de Sécurité Militaire: SSM) disguised its meetings under the anodyne name of 'Sporting Club of the Marne' (Société Sportive de la Marne), which, swapping its straw boaters for other accessories, was to take part in the liberation of the capital. As regards his own fate, he was arrested and deported to Cologne, but returned at the right moment to start the special unit that was to dismantle the last remnants of the Nazi secret services in Germany.[3]

On 11 August 1944 General de Gaulle's BCRA in London had sent out the following message: 'Lists persons to be arrested prepared by Section CE [Counter-Espionage] of BCRA. Stop. Forwarded to Military Security for implementation. Stop. Will be handed immediately after Liberation to police services. Stop. Message ends.'

To promote effective tracking down of war criminals, the former counter-espionage section in Algiers contributed a powerful weapon: an up-to-date reference book of war criminals, a veritable bible for the Nazi-hunters. Commandant Paillole brought copies over by plane, and his assistant, Captain Germain, by ship. It was distributed to the various bodies entrusted with the task of winkling out the guilty. A painstaking undertaking started in 1943 and requiring the compilation on cards of descriptions of tens of thousands of people, it was entitled *Synthesis of the Organization of the German Special Services and their Activities in France, 1940–1944*. This document (J.32519–44), endorsed 'Top Secret', was to facilitate the identification of German spies, double agents, collaborators and war criminals. The *Synthesis*, 500 pages in length, contained a total of 3,800 names of agents in the Nazi services, as well as a supplementary list of 5,000 suspects, divided into geographical zones.[4] It bristled with accounts of German agents and collaborators. Breaking the seal of secrecy, let us extract three examples:

BEUGRAS (Albert), alias BERGER. French nationality. Aged 40–50. Born Altkirch, 1.8 m, light chestnut hair, green, deep-set eyes, wears glasses for working. Ex-captain in Syria. Officially, corporate national secretary of the PPF. Unofficially, head of the PPF intelligence section, liaising with the Alst [Abwehr] and then the SD [Sicherheitsdienst] . . . Posted to Tunisia in April 1943; left before its liberation.

Still under the letter 'B', there follows:

BICKLER (Hermann), Dr. SS *Standartenführer*. Of Alsatian origin, before the war lawyer at the Strasbourg bar, aged about 40, 1.68 m, dark hair receding at forehead, full-faced. Arrested during the war of 1939–40, was freed by the Germans. In 1941 negotiated with Breton autonomist movement. In March 1943 was a mere *Untersturmführer* [Lieutenant in Waffen SS], in charge of propaganda.

Or, for example, this very French profile:

MERODE (Rudy von). Really MARTIN (Frédéric Hubert), alias MALTNER, alias MONTAIGU (de). Born 28 December 1905, Silly-sur-Neid (Moselle). French nationality. Engineer in ministry of Public Works. About 1.70 m; light chestnut hair, slightly wavy; grey-blue eyes; fairly stout; slightly bald. Sentenced 10 October 1936 by military tribunal, Strasbourg, to ten years' imprisonment and 20 years' residence exclusion, for espionage. Freed by the Germans, appeared in Paris end 1940 working for their services. . . . Cover function seems to have been within the OTTO organization. In reality, in 1943–4 appears as head of agent network tracking down Resistance elements and committing large-scale theft at their expense, in liaison with Section III of Alst or with Gestapo.

These three represent admirable prototypes of the selected prey the DGER intended to flush out.[5] As the special services had foreseen during the War, with the defeat of the Reich numerous ex-'collabos' (collaborators) of yesteryear had turned their coats. It seems that Jacques Doriot himself, from Sigmaringen, may have attempted to contact the Military Security Bureau (Bureau de Sécurité Militaire: BSM) at Strasbourg before he met his end in circumstances that remain obscure.

Sometimes extreme means were resorted to. In January 1945 four DGER men, one of them an immediate assistant of Colonel Passy, executed 'Monsieur Michel' in Spain. The Civil Guard discovered that the body was that of Michel Szkolnikoff, and were informed of his lurid past through the press: a dealer in cheapjack goods before the War, particularly in clothes, he had made his fortune by re-selling to the German Army. This was done under the egregious protection of the Gestapo, to whom he passed information concerning Resistance 'terrorists'. Szkolnikoff had been betrayed by his Gestapo friend Rudy von Merode, also exiled in Spain.

Others went on the run, but the French services closed in on them. This was due to the vast networks established during the War, particularly in Latin America, where Jacques Soustelle, then Director of the DGER, first won his spurs as a secret agent – in Mexico – at the same time becoming an undisputed expert on Aztec civilization. Using a car firm as cover, Commandant Victor Sapin-Lignères established his counter-espionage organization in Brazil. Its aim was simple: to locate the collaborators and Nazi agents on the Latin American sub-continent. In Argentina also, where numerous escape routes from Europe ended, two former members of the DGER, officially retired, kept a look-out. Maurice Duclos ('Saint-Jacques'), one of the first BCRA agents to be parachuted into France, kept bees and angora rabbits there. Jean Rousseau-Portalis ('Parent') also chose Argentina to live in, directing an agricultural undertaking there. Naturally both were numbered among the host of 'honourable correspondents' of the DGER (and subsequently of the SDECE).

The destinies of the former 'collabos' turned out to be very diverse. Auguste Ricord, a member of the French Gestapo in the Rue Lauriston, the moving spirit behind SS escape routes, was to perform some tasks for the SDECE before plunging into more lucrative activities, such as trafficking in heroin for the French Connection and undertaking missions funded by the CIA. Jean Vaugelas, Milice chief, on the other hand, was not so lucky. He had been responsible for many atrocities in the Limousin, and had then become a captain in the SS, protecting the last perimeter around Sigmaringen and Pétain. After his arrest he managed to escape while being extradited to France, but he was to die in Argentina, in a terrible car accident that was attributed to the SDECE.

The Hunt for 'Brainpower'

In destroyed Vienna, the capital of European espionage, the tide of Displaced Persons – Hungarian, Czech and Croatian refugees – flooded in. The mind boggles at the spectacle of all those clandestine networks of the victorious Powers, former Nazi connections, bounty hunters, professional informers and black market bosses, not to mention infiltrating agents of every description.

The French established their set-up at Seefeld, above Innsbruck. Vienna was its outpost. It had as its leader a technician famous for his skill: after the Liberation, Colonel Lucien Lochard headed the Research branch in Austria. He had been trained in the pre-war intelligence service, and was then promoted to head the clandestine SR – the 'Kléber' network. Backed by a force of some 60 active agents, 'Jojo' Lochard pursued two passions: the *Kriegsspiel* against the Soviet services, and pike-fishing. The same attention to detail, the same patience, were needed both to hook 'the shark of the rivers' and to build up a network in the Russian zone.

Supported by Colonels Jean Mercier ('Big Mercier') and Henry de Buttet – colleagues from the former SR – Colonel Lochard directed his research towards the Eastern bloc countries. As always, he was accompanied by 'Edward', whose real name was Yevgeny Delimarsky, and who was born in 1893 at Ekaterinoslav. A White Russian officer, at the end of the civil war he had fled to Constantinople, the key post for the French SR, and became its 'eye' on the Bolshevik revolution. Recruited in 1920, Delimarsky was able to 'manage' numerous Russian émigrés.[6] In Austria he was both interpreter and guide, together with another agent, Soldos, a Hungarian. The DGER – later SDECE – station under Colonel Lochard, before he left to control the Russian section in Paris, did not hesitate to use former Nazi networks against the Soviets. But at the same time it was involved in the hunt for an animal of a particular species, a hunt that set all the special services against one another.

It fell to Lochard, and then to his successor in Austria, Henri Gorce-Franklin, to round up as many scientists and scientific researchers as possible – the 'brains' of the Third Reich.[7] In this task they were pitted against the Russian, US and British secret services. It was a closely fought struggle, and one gloomy day in 1947 the Viennese police fished the corpse of a Frenchman out of the Danube with a bullet in his head. The SDECE got the message: the Russians had killed this young engineer from the National Centre for Scientific Research (Centre National de Recherche Scientifique: CNRS) as a warning. The 'honourable correspondent', probably over-zealous, belonged to a contingent of French scientists engaged on a temporary basis to evaluate the calibre of Nazi scientists it might be deemed appropriate to ship back to France.

The SDECE also cooperated with civilian ministries. Léon Kastenbaum – an astonishing character whom we shall meet again – supervised the activities of the service within the 'Reparations and Restitution' department of the Ministry of Industrial Production, which for a time was in the hands of Marcel Paul, the Communist deputy. Engineers and architects combed Germany and Austria, indicating their 'prey' to the special services. In 1951 the French, helped by the Allies, located the Messerschmitt works, where the 220 and 250 jet planes and the improved V2s (styled V3s) had been designed. These works were in underground factories near Wiener Neustadt, not far from Vienna, and were in the Soviet zone.

A little earlier the French had tracked down a former research director of the Junkers aeronautics firm. He had taken refuge at the home in Vienna of Magda Schneider, the actress. Little Romy Schneider, her daughter, then ten years old, could not believe her eyes when the men from the SDECE seized the scientist. He later became a naturalized Frenchman, and was to follow a discreet career in the French aerospace industry, where, with Dassault, he became one of the creators of the Mirage aircraft. The same was true of his colleague Helmut von Zborowski, the inventor of the curious vertical take-off plane, the 'Coléoptère', that was to astonish visitors to the Le Bourget Air Show in 1956.

Porsche to Renault, and Joliot-Curie at Tübingen

In mid-December 1945 the SDECE snatched the engineer Ferdinand Porsche on German territory. Raymond Hamel, a young officer in the service, brought him back to France. The Austrian engineer, son of a small artisan tinsmith of Bohemia, was a very valuable technician. Before the war he had worked at Austro-Daimler and at Mercedes-Benz in Stuttgart, and had invented the prestigious SSK series. Then he built the first Volkswagen cars. Throughout the war, from 1939 to 1945, he was attached personally to Adolf Hitler. Ferdinand Porsche carried out the most secret German projects, among them the monstrous Mouse tank, which weighed 188 tonnes.

With the fall of the Reich the Allies quite naturally took an interest in the engineer. In July 1945 the Americans interned him, and he spent three months being interrogated in a castle in Hesse. When he was released he was restricted to residence on his estate at Zell-am-See. In Baden-Baden, Meffre, the French colonel responsible for the surveillance of industry in the Occupation zone, watched his prey. Removed to France with his son-in-law, Dr Piech, Ferdinand Porsche was imprisoned at Dijon.

In Paris, Marcel Paul, the Communist who had then just succeeded Robert Lacoste at the head of the Ministry of Industrial Production, decided to exploit this prisoner to the full. The 'Reparations and Restitutions' department in his ministry, which was in constant touch with the SDECE, advised that he be assigned to the state-owned Renault company, to make suggestions for the '4CV', which was soon to be manufactured. But by July 1946 only a few weeks remained before the official launching of this 'people's car'. The French engineers who had designed it jibbed at having their work judged by a foreigner, however competent he might be. Thus Ferdinand Porsche, who was met with frank hostility by Pierre Lefaucheux, the head of Renault, and his staff, confined himself to a few remarks purely on detail. 'The advanced state of the tooling-up for factory-line production', he asserted, 'now made unfeasible any possible modifications of any importance.'[8]

Ferdinand Porsche made other contributions at Renault apart from the 4CV. He gave useful advice to the Trucks Division, and worked out plans for the first factory at Flins. But at the end of 1947 Marcel Paul left the government. The Renault management got rid of Ferdinand Porsche, who was sent back to prison in Dijon, before being freed a few months later.[9]

Another body, a military one this time, the Operational Intelligence Service (Service de Renseignement Opérationnel: SRO), attached to the French First Army, followed the same line of action. Its head, Colonel Léon Simoneau, recalled that in 1945, with the advance of the army of de Lattre de Tassigny, he had appointed as head of the scientific section Saint-Guilly, a corvette captain. The latter recruited French scientists who were to accompany the SRO commando groups on their man-hunts, unbeknown to the Americans.

Colonel Simoneau reported:

For this scientific section we had assembled some top people: Professor Spiteri of the Tunis Academy of Sciences, Professor Jean-Jacques Trillat, a physicist at the Sorbonne, and also a 'Jack of all trades', the excellent Professor Marcheboeuf of the Institut Pasteur. Trillat and Marcheboeuf had helped our services to hide heavy water in France during the War. I set up my headquarters at Gernsbach, and we started on the hunt. It was a real race to capture 'brains', people who would help us to make the atomic bomb. We succeeded in bringing back two or three scientists whom we had snatched from the Russians. The help of 'Captain Durand' was invaluable to me. The person to whom we had given this name was there in order to assess the quality of the scientific intelligence from the standpoint of nuclear physics. One day in the mess, one of my assistants studied this tall officer at length. He was visibly ill at ease in a uniform that made him look somewhat awkward. My assistant told me confidentially: 'It's astonishing, don't you think, how much Captain Durand resembles Joliot-Curie.' And indeed it was Joliot-Curie, the father of the French atomic bomb. He had agreed to disguise himself for a few weeks as an intelligence officer, in order to study incognito the documents relating to Nazi nuclear research we had uncovered at Tübingen.[10]

This episode caused more than one top member of French counter-espionage to shake in his shoes, because of Joliot-Curie's political leanings and his links with the Communist Party.[11]

The Research Directorate in Germany

At the end of the 1940s, various intelligence structures were flourishing in Germany and Austria side by side with one another. The Organization for the Search after War Criminals [Organisation de Recherche des Criminels de Guerre: ORCG], headed by Commandant Gilbert Mantout, had been formed under the aegis of the DGER. It was sited on the Avenue Victor Hugo in a private mansion that had once been a Gestapo headquarters. Charles Mittel, one of Mantout's former assistants, recalled:

I was the garage man at the office for war criminals. In my family there had been a fair number of deportees, and I was out for revenge on the Germans. I worked with Captain Lécole, Marcel Guetz and Germain Lybine, a former bodyguard of General de Gaulle. We arrested, for instance. 'The Tigress', a German woman in the Gestapo. We came from the Second Armoured Division. But I left the organization very quickly. In my view it was not efficient enough.[12]

Indeed, as Charles Mittel implied, the nature of the hunt for the Nazis was changing.

Colonel Passy, as head of the SDECE from April 1945 onwards, considered that these police operations no longer fell within the province of the secret service, but were a matter for the DST and Renseignements Généraux. To the 'services' fell a much more exhilarating task: the mission of special agents in Germany was visibly changing. It was no longer merely a matter of dismantling the Nazi services, but actually of 'hooking up' these German networks for the new struggle looming ahead: the fight against communism. Here the French were not the only ones in the field. The British and Americans also joined in, working on their own behalf.

In spite of everything, a certain degree of cooperation was inevitable. One of the assistants of Colonel T. A. Robertson, of MI5, the British counter-espionage agency, one day had several tons of archives delivered to Colonel

Gérar-Dubot: they consisted of the complete order of battle of the German secret service from October 1939 to February 1945, supplemented by thousands of biographical records. The head of 'B-Doc' was over the moon. The Englishman who had discovered this mine of information in Frankfurt had been unable to arouse any interest among his own countrymen, and had therefore decided to address himself elsewhere.

Doubtless other archives that the French perused were more interesting: those of Section III.F – Abwehr counter-espionage; of the *Sonderkommando* Pannwitz on the 'Red Orchestra'; and of the wireless intercept section (Funk Abwehr) concerning the 'Drei Roten' – the 'Three Reds', the Soviet network in Switzerland.[13] Cross-checked against interrogations of Abwehr specialists and of specialists from the Sixth Bureau of Reich Security (Amt VI/RSHA), this intelligence allowed us to reconstruct the organizational structure of the special Soviet services right up to the collapse of Nazism: the remnants of the 'Apparat', the secret organism of the Komintern which had been officially dissolved in 1943 and consisted of special units entrusted with the job of 'Smersh' executions (*Smiert Shpionam*: 'death to spies'), became Section oo, then the NKVD, and finally the MVD.

In 1946 the whole of the post-war services were unified in a Research Directorate for Germany (Direction de la Recherche en Allemagne: DRA), with its headquarters in Baden-Baden. The DRA was a branch of the SDECE. Its purpose was political, economic and military information in the Federal Republic, but also, and above all, in the German Democratic Republic, the USSR and the various communist countries. Colonel, later General, Paul Lombard was to direct Research in the DRA up to 1951. A native of Draguignan, during the War he had commanded the clandestine SR in Lyons. In 1943 he had been arrested and then deported by the Nazis. His *alter ego* in the counter-espionage section was another veteran of 2 bis, Avenue de Tourville, in the pre-war services: Jean Fontès had been fighting the Nazi services in Belgium and Holland since 1937, from his station in Lille. Based during the war in Tunis, more than anyone else he had paved the way for the American landing there in 1943 by 'turning round' German networks and feeding misleading information to the enemy.[14]

There was a third man at the Berlin station, Commandant Léon Müller, an Alsatian. Like his friend Lombard a former deportee, he was to replace him as the head of Research in Germany, a post that he held from 1951 to 1958. The path followed by all three – Lombard, Fontès and Müller – demonstrates the upheaval that the French services had undergone immediately after the Liberation. They were men who did not need to prove their courage, since they had often risked their lives in the struggle against the Third Reich. But at the end of the 1940s they threw all their experience of underground warfare into secret operations against the communist bloc. The Cold War was raging in all its fury, utterly transforming a generation of secret agents.

Nazi Leaders as Candidates for SDECE

In the climate that set in from 1945 onwards, the future US CIA and the British Secret Intelligence Service (SIS) recruited Nazi elements to fight the Russians earlier than did the French. It was a matter of employing the top people in German intelligence, who brought with them trunks full of archives and any of their networks behind the Iron Curtain that had remained intact. At the time they were no more than valuable auxiliaries. Later, in the new Germany, they were to occupy commanding posts in the special services. General Reinhard Gehlen, the best-known and soon to become the most powerful of them, had been the chief of Fremde Heere Ost (FHO), German military intelligence in the East, during the War. He offered his services to the Americans, who were to assist him and a number of other former members in rebuilding a clandestine organization – the OG (Organisation Gehlen). In 1955 this was to become the official central intelligence body – the Bundesnachrichtendienst (BND) – of Konrad Adenauer.

In the East they were equally busy, and the Soviets likewise recruited former officers. Thus General Rudolf Bamler, the former head of Abwehr III, the counter-espionage section under his friend Admiral Canaris,[15] became adviser to the Staatssicherheitsdienst (SSD), the East German service, which took into its ranks former SS leaders such as Ludwig Hagemeister, Johann Sanitzer, Reinhold Tapper and many others.

Each side advanced its pawns. Each one groomed its favourite. The British SIS and the French SDECE put forward, as head of the new German services, two allegedly anti-Nazi candidates, both formerly wanted for their involvement in the attempt on Hitler's life in July 1944. The British proposed that Otto John, their former agent, should head the anti-espionage branch. For their part, the French wanted Friedrich Heinz to take control of military intelligence. This was a real slicing-up of the cake, since, on their side, the United States supported Gehlen as the head of external intelligence, the future BND. In this game of chess Gehlen, who detested the other two candidates as traitors to the Third Reich, succeeded in discrediting them.

Yet Friedrich Wilhelm Heinz, the SDECE candidate, had only opposed Hitler at the very end. Beforehand his career as a Nazi officer had been 'beyond reproach'. His career is worth dwelling upon. Heinz was an intellectual, a chronicler of the Freikorps of the 1920s, the author of enthusiastic books favouring the 'national revolution', a member of the SA and also a friend of Admiral Canaris, who in 1935 put him in charge of a section (III.C1) in his military intelligence organization, the department concerned with counter-espionage within the Hitler state. As early as 1938 he had taken part in a first plot against Hitler, which leaked out, but had successfully avoided being purged. Seeking a change of atmosphere, he took command of the First Brandenburg Regiment, which was the 'Action' arm of the Abwehr. In 1941 he was the first to penetrate into the USSR with his commando shock troopers. The Ukrainians in his 'Redbreast' battalion distinguished themselves by the massacre of civilians during their advance. Then, in the following year, in Serbia, Heinz joined with General Mihajlović's partisans in putting down Tito's partisans. Such a knowledge of the Ukraine and Yugoslavia was to prove valuable to the SDECE in the future. In July 1944 Heinz joined the conspiracy against Hitler. Arrested by the Gestapo, he was tortured but not executed. Contacted by the French, he agreed to pass on information about the Red Army in East Germany.[16] This first-rate agent thus began his momentous upward rise.

In December 1950 Count Gerhard von Schwerin, Chancellor Adenauer's military adviser, appointed Lieutenant-Colonel Heinz as adviser for intelligence questions. Then, in the following year, he became the head of the Abwehr in the Amt Blank, the office founded by Theodor Blank, which was the embryo of a new military intelligence entity. Thus the head of the secret services of the German Army was a French agent. In the SDECE his cover-name was 'Tulip', and he was controlled in tandem by Captain Elsaneaux of Coblenz and by 'Courby', the code-name of an officer of the SDECE attached to the Napoleon Camp in Berlin. 'Tulip's' reports were brilliant and were of the utmost importance concerning the Russian zone, so the Berlin station assured headquarters in Paris.

But the situation deteriorated. Otto John, the man whom the British had placed in the security services, the BfV,[17] complained about not being able to de-Nazify the special services, especially that bastion of former Nazi officers, the Gehlen Organization. Was he merely naive, or an agent of the East? 'Dr John' became much talked about. In 1954 he crossed the zonal border and held a resounding press conference in the Eastern zone, in the course of which he denounced the neo-Nazi networks that proliferated in the West. A decidedly unusual turncoat, John resurfaced in the Federal Republic in the following year, asserting that he had been kidnapped and had been made to speak under constraint. This scarcely credible version of his disappearance was not to save him from prison. Gehlen had won the first round: one of his own men replaced John at the head of the BfV.

On the military side there remained Heinz, the French nominee. Here again a skilfully manipulated campaign put it about that he was working for the Russians. On 31 March 1954 Gehlen finally brought about his resignation and replacement by another of his wartime assistants, Gerhardt Wessel. This was a setback for the SDECE, which, however, was able to 'hook in' the network of informers that Heinz had implanted in the Russian sector of Berlin. In future the French would have to deal with Gehlen.

The Heinz affair is not the only instance where former Nazi intelligence specialists were scooped up by the French. Let us return to Austria. At Friedrichshafen (West Germany) and Bregenz, on Lake Constance, in 1946 the SDECE opened two camps to house prisoners from the Abwehr and the SD (the secret service of the SS), in order to sort out the 'war criminals' from professional agents 'worthy of interest'. At Friedrichshafen, Raoul Kaiser, an Alsatian, picked out those that were 'viable'. In Bregenz, the local head of the SDECE, Captain Maurice Blondel, uncovered a 'jewel': Wilhelm Hoettl, SS *Sturmbannführer* No. 309510. Hoettl, an Austrian, had directed the SS special services in the Balkans, and had forged exclusive links with secret agents of the Vatican. Would he agree to work for the French? The former head of the section for south-east Europe in Amt VI, Schellenberg's external services, gave his assent. He would even be prepared to search for the celebrated treasure hoard of the SS, supposedly dumped in a lake.

However, as soon as he was freed, Major Hoettl had talks with the CIC, the American counter-espionage service, which was only too pleased to put him in contact with the Gehlen Organization. He was to become the head of the Austrian service.[18]

A Slight Change for Skorzeny

'Very stout, 1.92 m, full-faced, dark hair, grey eyes, eyebrows meet, large mouth, thin lips, strong, determined chin, cauliflower ears, deaf in one ear, broad hands . . .' This is the description in SDECE archives of one of the most astonishing agents of the Third Reich. A man of action without equal, whose biographical record, established by the French, is a particularly full one:

Entered the SS as early as 1934. Took an active part in the *Anschluss*. In 1940 served in the Waffen-SS with the rank of *Obersturmführer* (Lieutenant). With the Reich Division took part in the campaigns of France, the Balkans and Russia. In it acquired a reputation for great bravery. Transferred in 1943 to the SD, with the rank of *Hauptsturmführer*, where he recruited and trained agents for a special mission. In September 1943 this turned out to be the freeing of Mussolini, which constituted a great success for him . . . He inspired sabotage missions on every front and was equally trusted to ensure the security of Hitler's HQ, set up pursuit commandos, strong-arm units, and mount impossible operations.

The Americans dubbed him their 'most dangerous man', and posted his picture and description throughout Germany. Finally he was captured by their services. Otto Skorzeny, the leader of the Brandenburg Division, the SS component of the Action Branch of the Abwehr, did not, however, remain a prisoner for long. On 27 July 1948 SS Captain Karl Radl, Skorzeny's assistant and lifelong friend, contrived his escape from the American camp at Darmstadt – in a vehicle, and through the main gate. In his memoirs Skorzeny naturally gives himself the credit for this miraculous operation. However, almost 40 years on, the French colonel, Michel Garder, for the first time gives another version: 'I organized Skorzeny's escape. We snatched him from the Americans in order to get information. He seemed to be an outstanding informer. The operation, it is true, was only partly authorized by Paris HQ. But he knew a lot about the Russians. I gave him a Saarland passport.'

Colonel Garder was in fact one of the leading lights in SDECE counter-espionage in Germany at that time, working from stations in Baden, the Rhineland and the Saar. Alas, he knew Germany well. In 1943, as a clandestine counter-espionage officer, he had been arrested and deported. Skorzeny was the archetype of the Nazi machine that Garder had fought ferociously. And now there he was, having fled to Italy, Ireland and then Spain, free to participate right up to the 1970s in all the neo-Nazi plots of Europe. What are we to make of that? His rescuer explained: 'You must realize that the tracking down of Nazis very quickly became transformed into the anti-communist struggle.'[19]

By a quirk of history this anti-communist struggle was to devolve upon services that were taken over by the socialists.

3

SDECE and the Socialist Party

In the summer of 1945 Colonel Passy, as yet untouched by the financial scandal that was to be uncovered in the following year, assumed command of the French secret services. The former head of BCRA wished to transform DGER, the new name for the 'Firm' since November 1944, into a real headquarters, modern and efficient. The first task – immense – was to weed out the overgrown wartime staff. By the end of the year the reorganization was complete. But under whose authority was the new body to function?

The Service of External Documentation and Counter-Espionage (Service de Documentation Extérieure et de Contre-Espionnage)

'I suggest the British solution, where MI6 comes under the Permanent Under-Secretary of the Foreign Office,' announced Passy. 'Let us link SDECE to the Quai d'Orsay.' This solution presented one theoretical advantage: special agents could be deployed using diplomatic cover, which meant that they would be easily integrated into the embassy organization, and were consequently more difficult to detect. In practice the French tradition in Foreign Affairs went against it. Inclined to be condescending, the diplomats, from ambassadors downwards, had nothing but contempt for the agents of the secret services, fearing that their covert activities undermined the prestige of diplomatic missions and tarnished the French image abroad. In the cruel world of the Cold War such a viewpoint was laughable. The consequences were clear: apart from the posts of military attaché or assistant military attaché, a title that automatically identifies the function of the person who holds it, the Quai d'Orsay conceded to SDECE agents only titles hardly less blatant: 'vice-consul', 'assistant consul', 'counsellor', as well as 'attachés' of every description.

Moreover, de Gaulle could not permit SDECE to function under Georges Bidault, a minister of Foreign Affairs whom he greatly feared. In the end, it was attached to the prime minister's Office, and – a fact that is always forgotten – placed under the supervision of the inter-ministerial

Council for Documentation. 'The funds for the new service,' its founder noted, 'were approved by the Chamber of Deputies at the end of 1945 by over 500 votes (including a considerable proportion of Communist members), after a motion was put forward by President Vincent Auriol.'[1]

On 28 December 1945 the Cabinet adopted the decree announcing the setting-up of the Service of External Documentation and Counter-Espionage (Service de Documentation Extérieure et de Contre-Espionnage: SDECE). This decree, promulgated on 4 January 1946, was not to be published in the *Journal Officiel*. SDECE's mission was defined as follows:

1 To gather any intelligence and documentation abroad that might provide information for the government.
2 To detect agents of foreign powers whose activities might be detrimental to national defence or State security, and to inform the departments concerned.

Finally the Organic Decree made it plain that 'the mission of SDECE precludes any investigations in overseas territories under French sovereignty. These continue to be a matter for the ministries for French Overseas Territories and of Foreign Affairs. It follows therefore that in regard to the gathering of intelligence and countering foreign infiltration into territories not under French sovereignty, SDECE alone is empowered to undertake these tasks.'

Thus the foundations of the modern secret service were laid. As the target of numerous personal attacks, Colonel Passy was not free to watch over his brainchild. This was even more the case when, a few days later, on 21 January 1946, de Gaulle quit the government. On 26 February Félix Gouin, the new prime minister, designated Henri Ribière to replace Colonel Passy as overall head of SDECE. But André Dewavrin had not entirely severed his links with the service. He still had to deal with the affair of the 'subverted' funds, which we have already described.[2]

Henri Ribière, a Socialist Director

According to Louis Mouchon, one of the socialist activists in the 'Firm':

After Passy's removal – he had been denounced to the French government by members of the British Intelligence Service – it was Henri Ribière, a good member of the Resistance and a good socialist, who became the head of the service, assisted by Fourcaud and Sudreau. At that time, in 1946, the service was still in a state of disorder. In spite of Passy's initial reforms, a rather cosy atmosphere still prevailed in the various headquarters, which were located in the Bois de Boulogne, on the Avenue de Maréchal Maunoury and the Avenue Georges Mandel. In fact, security was slapdash. For example, the door of each section bore a notice such as 'Monsieur X, head of the Latin America department'. In short, when Ribière arrived he had to clear up the mess. In particular, he attached the Political Service to the General Directorate, the central body. He got rid of still more agents, in addition to those already dismissed by Passy. This was a shame, because he was thereby to deprive himself of a network of Resistance personnel who by the end of the War had become really outstanding.[3]

But Ribière stood for the Resistance within France, in contrast to those heads of department who had come from the traditional intelligence services in Algiers, or from the BCRA in London. He was also the forerunner of the socialist substratum within SDECE, whilst the Gaullists, still well represented in the secret service, lost control after Passy's departure.

Aged 49 – he was born on 27 December 1897 at Montluçon – Henri-Alexis Ribière ploughed stubbornly through the files. Always a militant socialist, in the early 1930s he had been dismissed from the merchant bank where he was employed, because of his trade union activities. Initiated into the mysteries of the Third Republic, he joined the Popular Front and in 1936 became the deputy head of the prime minister's Office, and then worked in the office of Marx Dormoy, the Minister of the Interior, who was assassinated during the Occupation by the Cagoule. He was appointed Secretary-General of the Ardèche department, and then in 1941 counsellor at a prefecture. He plunged into covert activities, becoming a moving spirit in the Resistance in the Allier department. Finally, he participated in the clandestine reconstitution of the Socialist Party and, shortly afterwards, the Libération-Nord. A member of the National Council of the Resistance, at the Liberation he was elected first to the provisional Consultative Assembly, and then, until 1946, became a member of the two Constituent Assemblies.

Thus in February 1946 he was faced with one of the highest responsibilities in a stormy and – in the eyes of the Resistance and the governing Socialist Party – impeccable career. The responsibility laid upon him was that of Director-General of SDECE. A trade unionist master spy caused titters among the specialists beforehand. They were wrong. Henri Ribière was not an expert in intelligence work, but he was a man determined to ensure that the scandals surrounding the DGER at the time should not recur, and that from then on the Socialist Party should exercise control over the secret service. The new director had nevertheless to reckon with a particularly turbulent assistant, Colonel Pierre Fourcaud.

Pierre Fourcaud, 'the Slav'

A scintillating personality, a maestro in intelligence work, the Saint-Just of espionage – or a shadowy individual, enigmatic, Machiavellian, unstable and insane? Descriptions abound – and contradict one another. The man with the mischievous look who received us in the Invalides office of the Association of ex-members of Action Branch, whose president he was, may have been all these in one.

Colonel Pierre Fourcaud, nicknamed 'the Slav', was born at St Petersburg in 1898. Enlisting as a volunteer, he fought on the French front and was wounded in 1918. 'I have been in intelligence since 1919,' he would explain with a note of pride in his voice.[4] But the young subaltern left the army the following year. In 1939 he rejoined it, in the 6th Battalion of the Chasseurs Alpins, commanding a band of irregulars. In the meanwhile, had Pierre Fourcaud really taken part in the Cagoulard plot against the Popular Front? He was usually careful not to deny the legend, since it added greatly to the air of mystery about his character.

On the other hand, he was certainly among the first volunteers for the Free French Forces in July 1940. He recalled with emotion the half a dozen men who had founded the secret service of General de Gaulle. He undertook numerous missions to France for the BCRA, establishing certain contacts with former Cagoulards such as Colonel Georges Groussard, then head of one of Marshal Pétain's security services. Colonel Groussard remembered him:

A nice chap, Fourcaud. In 1914–18 he had had a splendid war, and his conduct in 1939–40 had been equally outstanding. Fairly tall and thin, with a dark moustache and small eyes with a piercing gaze, he was devilishly lively and inclined to be longwinded, but all the same he was never muddled or indiscreet. Quite the contrary: he had a wonderful gift for holding his tongue. I can still see him in those dark days continually exuding enthusiasm and good humour, and with a serene and utter confidence in victory. Every time I saw the big fellow appear – he was as strong physically as he was morally – I felt really heartened.[5]

By contrast, Colonel Passy had a completely different memory of 'Barbès', Fourcaud's *nom de guerre* in the BCRA:

Into his forties, clean-shaven with dark hair, thin, but of average height, a sallow complexion, he reminded one of a *condottiere*, but from his Russian mother he had inherited the slightly mysterious air of the Slav. With his direct but hesitant gaze, he used always to speak fairly loudly, occasionally verging upon the pretentious, and retailing his exploits with immodest frequency. He cut a magnificent figure as an adventurer; he was one who wanted to play the great lord, but who, now and then betrayed his origins by minor slips.[6]

A controversial figure, then. The animosity that Colonel Passy and his assistant, Roger Wybot, bore him went back to 1941, when Barbès was the BCRA representative in Marseilles. Its origin lay in a garbled story about an arrest attributed to his 'imprudence', and an incredible escape. As ever with Fourcaud, nothing was simple. But it is notable that he returned to London in September 1942 at the side of Emmanuel d'Astier de la Vigerie, one of the leaders of Libération-Sud. Above all, he was on friendly terms with Louba, d'Astier's wife and the daughter of the former Bolshevik ambassador in Paris, Leonid Krassin.

Colonel Fourcaud's strength lay in the fact that from 1945 onwards he knew how to manipulate a range of relationships, which covered the whole political chess-board, from extreme Right to extreme Left. All in all, despite his title of 'technical director' in SDECE, Fourcaud played a predominantly political role. This was frequently to be held against him, and partly accounts for the violent altercations he had with Ribière.

Above all, Fourcaud did not shrink from any and every kind of cooperation, no matter whence it came. Claude Bourdet, then editor-in-chief of *Combat*, recalled that Fourcaud had been thunderstruck upon reading some small news items published by Daniel Nat, one of his journalists, who had Trotskyist leanings.

'How do you go about getting such information, particularly on Asia?' asked Fourcaud with astonishment, at a meal organized expressly for this purpose – Fourcaud paid his informants well.

'It's very simple, you need only to subscribe to press agency reports and throw in a ha'porth of Marxist analysis.'

Straight away Fourcaud ordered syntheses of these reports from the journalist, for his own guidance.[7]

What power did Colonel Fourcaud really have at his disposal within SDECE? He was accustomed to say: 'I am deputy director-general of a service that has a triple objective: intelligence, counter-espionage and action.' But Jean-Marie L'Allinec, his assistant and a specialist in the world of diplomacy, made matters plain: 'Colonel Fourcaud has no financial resources available at SDECE. All financial operations, or any flights by the air squadron etc. fall within the exclusive province of M. Ribière.'[8] The 'technical director' had therefore only limited powers of operational decision. This was to be modified, however, for in 1946 it was, in fact, Fourcaud who resurrected Action Branch, so that it could operate in Indo-China. 'Yes,' he said, 'I created Action Branch (Service Action: SA), but only the Americans gave me credit for it, for the branch is the ancestor of the Green Berets.'

But Fourcaud's reign was brief. In 1950 Pierre Fourcaud, who had been a thorn in the side of many, was discreetly eased out of SDECE. But – and this is unique in the annals of the French secret service – the government then offered the colonel a mini-intelligence service attached directly to the prime minister's Office.[9]

Colonel Verneuil, Nicknamed 'Little Father'

Counter-Espionage, by contrast, was ruled by a much less controversial figure, Colonel Verneuil. In 1947, when Pierre Nord, the author of many spy novels, published his documentary work *Mes camarades sont morts*, which traced the history of French counter-espionage in its fight against the Nazis, an icy silence was preserved at SDECE. Even though he had changed the names of the principal characters, Pierre Nord was reproached with having handed over a wealth of information regarding the French organization to the secret services of the Eastern bloc. In fact, the leading cadres of 'Rural Works' (Travaux Ruraux: TR), the cover organization for these secret agents during the War, were for the most part to be found in 'Service 23' – Counter-Espionage – at SDECE.

In the novel, Nord calls the main character, the head of 'Rural Works' in Occupied France, Vauthier Laforêt (thus the pseudonym in the book began with the 'V', like the name of his real life prototype; while the 'real' name in the book began with the letters 'LAFO', with a 'T' at the end as did Verneuil's real name, Lafont). Pierre Nord wrote of Vauthier: 'His calm, firm voice was that of a leader whose authority had never been questioned. His wandering gaze, through his myopic glasses, took on a fixed, vacant look, and a leaden opaqueness. . . . The gaze was thoughtful and worried, profound and hard. The colourless, Courteline-like character of the guest at table had changed into the man of action, one who commanded.'[10] The description is faithful to its model. In 1971, in a fresh work on espionage, *L'Intoxication*, Pierre Nord disclosed: 'There is no longer any bar to my stating that Colonel Verneuil was the Vauthier Laforêt of my book *Mes camarades sont morts*. Verneuil survived the War, but died prematurely in harness as head of Counter-Espionage, a post that fell to him by right.'[11]

But the man whom those in SDECE Counter-Espionage affectionately called 'Little Father' was not called Verneuil either. As it was also known as 'Service 23', its head, 'Verneuil', was designated by the number '2301'; his deputy, 'Colonel Germain', by '2302', and so on. These were the same old mirror-image games, those sets of Russian dolls fitting inside one another, with the purpose of protecting SDECE against infiltration – and also of penetrating the set-up of the other side, 'turning' enemy agents, and controlling double agents.

In civilian records, Verneuil was really called Roger Lafont. In 1917, at the age of 20, he had been wounded under fire. He later became head of the intelligence station located on the outskirts of Frankfurt – his first experience of the invisible world of intelligence. 'He had a rare aptitude,' recalled General Louis Rivet, head of Intelligence from 1936 onwards, 'an exceptional intuition for his age of the future of France and Germany, and this instinctively led him to those who worked in the vanguard of our security'.[12]

In 1920 he was posted to Constantinople, where he remained for two years. The city was then the listening post for French intelligence on the Soviet Union. Agents were trained there, together with specialists, both Frenchmen and White Russians who followed passionately the development of Russian policy. Beside the Bosphorus, during this stay in Turkey, Commandant Lafont took his first steps into the labyrinth of international politics. Who could predict that one day he would become the undisputed master in Europe of anti-Soviet counter-espionage? But the Nazi danger was looming. Upon his return to France he coordinated many operations against the Abwehr, working from the stations scattered along the Franco-German frontier.

In the occupied zone during the war, Colonel Verneuil became a legendary figure. As the head of 'Rural Works' he escaped from every trap that was set for him, and succeeded not only in protecting the 'Kléber' intelligence networks directed by his friend Colonel Joseph Lochard, but in penetrating the German services. When SDECE was reorganized in 1947 everyone agreed that Verneuil would be the ideal person to head Counter-Espionage. Authoritarian, but with a smile on his face, occasionally giving the impression of a clergyman in mufti, prudent and wily, he slotted exactly into a post that required skill, precision and a certain good-heartedness, but also real rigour. Whereas those in Research Branch could allow themselves a certain margin of inaccuracy in their reports and an artistic vagueness about their information, Counter-Espionage acted as the buckler of SDECE. The lives of agents in the field sometimes depended on the analyses it produced.

Colonel Verneuil reorganized the Counter-Espionage branch that his predecessors had bequeathed him from top to bottom, beginning with the removal of General Chrétien. On the Boulevard Suchet, a sifting process was carried out: cross-checks, assessments and verifications were made of those taken on by SDECE. No more letting slip through the net those former collaborators who had become members of the Resistance at the last minute, nor Soviet 'moles'. Counter-Espionage was divided up into geographical departments: Europe, America, the Middle East and Africa. In embassies abroad its representatives, masquerading as 'vice-consuls' or 'attachés', supervised the entire SDECE set-up, as well as seeking to recruit agents on the ground. This applied in particular for the Eastern bloc and the Arab countries, not forgetting Latin America, where SDECE was never so active as during these years.

Colonel Verneuil was not above putting a shoulder to the wheel himself. The average Frenchman, 'Mr Everyman', he went about unnoticed and crossed the Atlantic several times in order to give a helping hand to counter-espionage stations in Argentina or Brazil. '"Little Father" was very cautious regarding the Russians,' asserted Colonel Germain, his deputy and also his friend at the time. 'But it is an exaggeration to say that he changed his lodgings every night for fear of being followed by the NKVD.' The daily round in Counter-Espionage might have seemed humdrum. In fact the staff worked hard, analysing files, collating reports from officers in stations abroad, and carefully verifying the tiniest piece of information. The 50 officers and 200 others in Service 23 formed a closely knit team, working in a very discreet, quiet and almost family atmosphere. A modest and yet a legendary figure, Colonel Verneuil died without fuss on 1 December 1952. He was, it has been said, the buckler. His *alter ego*, who brandished the sword, was Henri Trautmann.

Henri Trautmann, 'the Admiral'

In contrast to the British tradition, until the appointment of Admiral Lacoste in 1982 to head French intelligence, naval men had hardly played a prominent role in the French secret services. There was one notable exception: Captain Trautmann, nicknamed 'the Admiral', was in charge of Research Branch from the end of the War until 1958, and then, for a further ten years, trained secret agents.

That choice was a judicious one: as a full naval captain, Henri Trautmann, 'the Admiral', possessed the soundest kind of experience, acquired throughout the world. In fact, from 1924 onwards, as a junior lieutenant, and using the cover of a Swiss commercial firm, he had strengthened links with the French networks in Asia, China and particularly with the strategically placed station at Singapore. The Middle Kingdom was at the time shaken by a gigantic struggle between the Guomindang and the Chinese Communist Party.[13]

Of Alsatian origin, and possessing a perfect command of German, Henri Trautmann was clearly equipped to man the front line against the Nazi machine before 1939. He directed the stations at Düsseldorf, Mainz, Metz, Strasbourg and Dunkirk. Then, fleeing from the Vichy regime, 'the Admiral' arrived in Algiers in 1943, from where he directed the naval branch of intelligence until the Liberation. He himself has related the final stage:

I returned to France, and afterwards I installed myself in the DGSS, as head of the naval division of special services. It was Colonel Dewavrin who, seeking to restore order in the huge muddle that prevailed on the Boulevard Suchet, invited me to work out a plan for civilian and military intelligence in peacetime. Finding my plan to be a reasonable one, he put me in charge of the Intelligence directorate. Passy was perfectly aware that, in order to restore a great secret service in France, it was necessary to amalgamate all the branches and put at their head people with a certain degree of experience.[14]

Those who served with him were unanimous in their opinion of Captain Trautmann as director of Research, despite the various quarrels that shook SDECE in the 1950s and 1960s. For everybody he remained 'a great figure in intelligence'. Until shortly after their wedding his wife, whom he had met in China, did not know that Trautmann was an intelligence officer. Until the birth of their first child she assisted him on his secret missions. 'Not all my former colleagues had my good luck,' Henri Trautmann stressed, adding:

Secret services usually jib at using the wives of their intelligence officers. It's already a great concession if they occasionally do not mind certain wives knowing what their husbands do. Although it breaks the rules, it is justifiable. It is impossible to share the life of another person and conceal this particular occupation. One of our colleagues received an order forbidding him from revealing his activities to his wife. There was a terrible row at home, and a succession of scenes occurring sporadically one after another. Our colleague appeared always to be in the wrong, as if he were leading a dissolute life. Finally he gave up the job.[15]

Strengthened by collaborators of the calibre of Verneuil and Trautmann, Henri Ribière, as head of the secret services, was able to speed up the establishment of SDECE.

Those of the 22nd, the 27th and the 29th

First of all, there was the move. Ribière installed his services in the barracks of the Tourelles, in Paris, on the Boulevard Mortier, in three blocks of buildings surrounding a courtyard shut in by high walls – a French barracks of the most traditional kind.[16] Later the whole complex bristled with aerials, and new wings were built on. The secret services gradually assumed the shape that was to remain theirs until de Gaulle came to power in 1958: 1,480 persons were confirmed permanently in their posts as SDECE officers or NCOs in France and in the stations abroad. To be precise, there were 880 civilians, 600 military personnel and 750 others hired under contract. The proportion of civilian to military favoured the former, in accordance with socialist inclinations at the time.

Almost every day the Director-General would call a meeting at noon of his directors and heads of services. Each director had carved out his own domain. Before 1949, as we have seen, Fourcaud had controlled Action Branch, known as 'Service 29', which was now directed by Henri Fille-Lambie, nicknamed Jacques Morlanne from the name of a castle near his native village. With the war in Indo-China, Service 29 was to grow out of all proportion. It grouped together commando 'shock troops', who carried out raids and paramilitary infiltrations. To cite one example typical of the times: Action Branch had drawn up a list of all the key points in Germany that it would be necessary to sabotage in order to halt an invasion by the Red Army. At Montlouis Captain Paul Aussaresses was about to set up the 11th Regiment of 'shock' paratroops, from which Action Branch was to draw its reserves in the future.[17] Pierre Fourcaud's half-brother, Commandant Boris Delocque-Fourcaud, commanded the SDECE airborne section based at Persan-Beaumont: Squadron 1/56 – 'Vaucluse' – was equipped with Fieseler Storch aircraft, Junkers JU52s and Dakota DC3s. This squadron had originally been set up in 1943 by Henri Boris, who was responsible for BCRA air communications. An ex-pilot, he was nicknamed 'SVP', and was so shortsighted that people said he was as blind as a bat. 'It doesn't matter', he used to say, 'since I only fly at night'.[18]

To complete the account of Fourcaud's domain in SDECE, it is fitting to add that he 'naturally' retained for himself Service 27, the department dealing with migrants from the East, which was under Commandant Jacques Pommes-Barrère and Captain René Bertrand ('Beaumont').

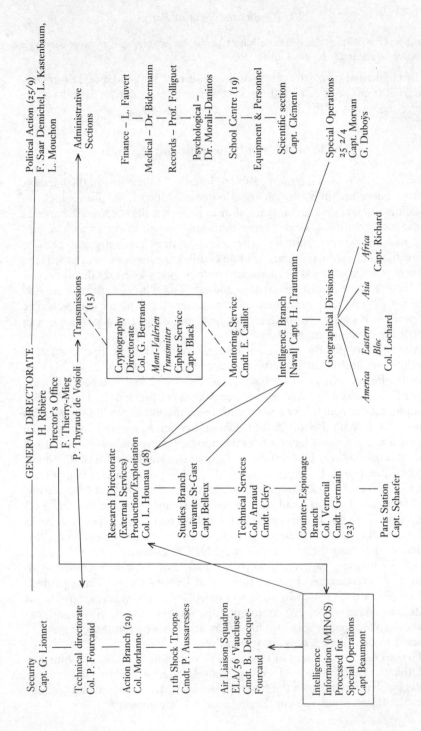

Figure 3.1 The SDECE under H. Ribière (1,480 established staff; 880 civilians, 600 military; and 750 on contract)

Another deputy to the Director-General was Colonel Gustave Bertrand.[19] He did not get on well with Fourcaud, although the two men had both begun their career in intelligence in the same year, 1919. In 1949 Colonel Bertrand was the top European expert in cryptography, the decoding of ciphered messages. He had a way of breaking an enemy code with consummate art. Nor was he lacking in humour. He recounts: 'One day, having occasion to stand in for my boss – when I was deputy to the Director-General of SDECE in 1949 – I had the key of the safe; this contained, among other things, the personnel files, which were strictly confidential. I then conceived the unhealthy idea – oh, the demoniacal spirit of intelligence – of raiding my own file, from which I noted only the following excerpt: "Was the most notable technician in the war intelligence provided by Intelligence Branch during hostilities."'[20] Nothing could have been more true.

Indeed, during the War Colonel Bertrand had succeeded in getting hold of the Wehrmacht's Enigma machine, used for encoding the Germans' most secret messages. At SDECE he directed the transmitting and interception centre at Mont-Valérien, which was linked to the decoding and cipher service. His assistant, Colonel Black, did not linger long in the 'Firm'. Shortly after having taken over as head of the unit for forging passports and false papers, he was thrown out because his secretary was found to have been recruited by the Russians.

The third director was a truculent sort of person: Lieutenant-Colonel Léonard Hounau, who directed the branch for the exploitation and production of intelligence. He was a man who liked to live well, and possessed a keen sense of humour. 'I am a Polytechnique graduate just like Passy and Bertrand,' said General Hounau, who gave a warm welcome to the authors at the computing firm where he works as a consultant.

I took part in the war in Syria, and then in the Resistance I joined the 'Martial' network that organized the second liberation of Tulle, after confrontations between our independent group and the Francs-Tireurs et Partisans. We retook the town from the communists. At the Liberation Passy, my fellow student at the Polytechnique (class of 1933), asked me to come and help him. This time I was to remain in SDECE until 1952.[21] According to orders from de Gaulle, we were to organize a service that would resemble the British Intelligence Service. I directed the branch concerned with the production and exploitation of intelligence, which included the sections for Studies, technical services, and counter-espionage and monitoring.[22]

Thus Lieutenant-Colonel Hounau supervised the whole apparatus for intelligence gathering. Eugène Caillot organized the monitoring service so efficiently that in the 1970s he became the leading light in telephone interception in France. The section for Studies, controlled by two former members of the BCRA, Paul Guivante Saint-Gast and Maurice Belleux, later replaced by one Maigret, centralized documentation and records, liaising with Professor Folliguet, the head of 'Service 22' – the central registry. This drew up the daily intelligence reports that buttressed the decisions of the prime minister's staff. It was a matter of analysing, classifying, ordering and summarizing intelligence, so as to clarify the main political, economic and military developments that might cause the world to tremble. The whole art lay in assessing them, explaining their importance, and stressing the possible consequences. Without this, an item of intelligence classified A1 might pass unnoticed.

'Morvan' and the Safe-Breakers

'My main job was to break into and intercept the diplomatic bags. It all began because one day a foreign diplomat allowed his bag to be stolen. "Morvan" saw the advantage that might accrue from this, and from this the unit grew,' Jules declared, watchful behind his tinted glasses, as doubtless he had been all his life, for fear of being caught in the act of opening the safe in some embassy or other. 'The "plumbing" work, the placing of microphones and the opening up of safes were exhausting tasks. Michel Bommelaer, our medico, first prescribed me Maxiton, to stimulate me, and then a tranquillizer, since I had so nervous a disposition.'[23]

By the end of 1947 Jules had quite naturally found his niche in a new unit, that of special operations. In fact, section 25 2/4 was set up inside the Intelligence Branch. Its head, Guy Marienne, known as 'Morvan', had fashioned a tool suitable for obtaining 'raw' documents, the reports of foreign military attachés, personal correspondence, and confidential economic and financial files – in short, all the information that normally eludes the classic type of SDECE officer.

Morvan left behind the memory of a lively, bespectacled fellow, with a long face. He had been divorced, but had remarried a brilliant analyst of the Russian section of Intelligence Branch. He was a freemason in the socialist manner. But Morvan, the onetime head of the 'Darius' network in the Resistance, also retained a sound peasant-like common sense, which his rough accent highlighted. His feet were planted firmly on the ground. This former naval officer made an impression because of his good humour; if one of his subordinates was in trouble, he would move mountains to get him out of it. He was the exemplar of the kind of man that enabled a service such as 25 2/4 to recruit hundreds of 'honourable correspondents'.

His deputy, Guy Duboÿs, was the complete secret agent, as he had amply demonstrated in the BCRA during the War. Dealing with the records from October 1941, at the request of Colonel Passy he had organized the general archive section in London. Yet he was none the less a man of action: having transferred to the intelligence section in 1943, he was to set up 'Prometheus', the headquarters in France of the BCRA. 'Duboÿs,' declared Passy, 'quickly succeeded in establishing his own skeleton headquarters which was linked to "Coligny" headquarters by a communications system. This was to prove its effectiveness, because when Duboÿs was arrested by the Gestapo some weeks later, no harm came to either of the two headquarters, thanks to the courage he displayed.'[24] Lieutenant Duboÿs was to experience the horrors of the concentration camps. Upon his return from deportation he participated enthusiastically in the building up of the new services. But a certain detachment peculiar to former deportees led him to view philosophically, and from a distance, the host of intrigues within the secret services, from which he was to suffer somewhat during his long career in SDECE.

It was this team, of Morvan and Duboÿs, and the Arsène Lupins of espionage such as Jules, that made SDECE one of the best Western services for the gathering of covert intelligence.

There remain the technical services, under Colonel Arnaud. Since 1937, in the old intelligence service, he had been a specialist in the CRP (chemistry–radio–photography) section, as it was then styled. Up to 1964 he was to direct the technical services of SDECE, together with his assistant, another former member of the old service, Commandant Bernard Cléry, *the* expert in radio transmissions. Transmissions was 'Service 15'. It occupied a key position in the training of agents and technicians, which was planned by 'Service 19' – the SDECE school. To complete the 'organizational chart', we might also mention the registry, directed by Professor Folliguet, which was the heart and memory of the 'Firm'. Finally, to look after the recruits, and also to follow up and care for the officers and men, and their families, there were the medical services of Dr Bidermann and Dr Bommelaer.

Security Branch

Tall – 1.76 m – weighing 80 kilos, with close-cropped hair, light-coloured eyes behind thick-framed glasses, a round face and prominent nose, Georges Lionnet had belonged to Libération-Nord, the socialist covert Resistance network. In August 1944 Paris rose up. Lionnet, with his wife, who was a nurse, at his side, seized the German *Kommandantur* on the Place de l'Opéra. A few yards away Henri Ribière, his friend and leader, was also fighting. So it is understandable that he should have agreed to enter the secret services. He remained in them for a quarter of a century, and was undoubtedly the longest-surviving section head, since, he said, he had known 'seven director-generals of SDECE'. In the beginning he was responsible for the legal section of the DGER, given the job of vetting the employment of Resisters, although at the time, as he declared, 'Things were in a right old mess.' In SDECE from 1948 onwards Security Branch, directly linked to the general directorate, was to play a central role. The external stations of both Intelligence Branch and Counter-Espionage had to be supervised, to guard against the risk of agents being 'turned' (from time to time Lionnet accused Verneuil and Trautmann of 'slackness'), and to organize the physical security of the Tourelles barracks and other SDECE bases in Berlin and inside France.

Lionnet was responsible for hiring the guards, secretaries and charwomen. It is too often forgotten that the Soviet KGB is in the habit of recruiting the female employee who empties the waste paper baskets rather than the minister himself. This was equally true for SDECE. Colonel Lionnet therefore planned in the utmost secrecy the move of the formerly dispersed departments to headquarters on the Boulevard Mortier.

But his knottiest problem was clearly the protection of stations outside France:

You must realize – everybody aspires to a posting to a foreign station. Madame can wear her glad rags and go to cocktail parties. Monsieur benefits from diplomatic status. A mere sergeant-major from Paris headquarters gets the fictitious rank of colonel. It's a wonderful life. If one considers the case of the Eastern bloc countries, the difficulty is that the French never believe they will fall victim to attempts to recruit them. The Frenchman goes off to Eastern Europe, priding himself on being the more wily one. But the fellows from the Eastern bloc – and all the communist services that are dependent upon them – resort to methods very much below the belt – of a kind that our secret services are not in the habit of employing.[25]

When General Jacquier took over as head of SDECE in 1962 he assembled all the heads of departments in order to make himself familiar with their work. Each one in turn explained his work. Then he turned to Lionnet and said, 'And you, what's your line?'.'Me, general?' he replied, 'I'm the watchdog, the cop, the fireman, the chucker-out – all rolled into one.'

Léon Kastenbaum, Jules Guesde's Secretary

Strongly stamped with his socialist commitment, and working outside the traditional structures of SDECE, Henri Ribière assembled a special group for 'reserved matters'. This was a body that worked outside the directorates for Research and Counter-Espionage, fulfilling a straight political function: a service for relations with 'allied' parties.

A derisive borrowing from Soviet jargon, the appellation merely designated a liaison group between the SDECE directorate and foreign social-democrat organizations. But an ambiguity prevailed: was it merely a question of helping the 'fraternal parties' of the Socialist (Second) International, or of recruiting from within them 'honourable correspondents', or, in the end, of gathering intelligence about such parties? The extraordinary life-story of the head of this 'ghost' service adds to this confusion further. Léon Kastenbaum was a strange man, a figure both picturesque and enigmatic within SDECE, who seemed to vanish round the corner of a corridor whenever one thought one had pinned him down.

Tall, lean, fleshless, stooping, his ebony-coloured hair plastered back, somewhat distant in manner (though he did not hide his friendship with Ribière) – and, moreover, a doctor of science – Léon Kastenbaum was, or anyway claimed to have been, one of the private secretaries of the Socialist deputy Jules Guesde, in the 1920s. During the next decade he had figured among the directors of the Tour de France. Being the friend of Gilbert Novinat, the pre-war president of the Association of Socialist Party Ex-Servicemen, he it was who regularly brought to the *Populaire* the obituaries of comrades who had recently died. This bird of ill omen is still remembered by editors. The youngest among them used to make jokes about him.

A descendant of Polish Jews, in 1945 Kastenbaum embraced with a will the task of tracking down war criminals. From this, and a desire to be effective, he was led to join SDECE. He directed the Reparations and Restitution section that was jointly controlled by Marcel Paul's ministry and the secret services.[26] We have already seen the hunters of Nazis in action in Austria. Here links with the Austrian socialists had proved very useful. Gaston Goldschild, the socialist in SDECE's Vienna station, maintained contact with them. Toussaint Raffini did the same with the Italian socialist party,[27] and Bloch, Ribière's son-in-law, looked after the Spanish. Henri Damon had some involvement in all this, but had no special territorial responsibility.

The person coordinating this 'political' sector was a former member of the BCRA, Louis Mouchon. Kastenbaum's assistant had shone successively as head of BCRA's missions department, and then on the staff of General Koenig.[28] For him, the role of the group that dealt with foreign parties of the same political complexion was not restricted to analyses or assessments of the future. SDECE officers belonging to other branches criticized Kastenbaum's group for excessively favouring civilians, and consequently introducing a political element. They resented it for trying, at Kastenbaum's instigation, to win civilian status, modelled on that of civil servants, giving security of tenure to staff. They also voiced another criticism: that Ribière and his little coterie of socialist agents carried out 'operations' using the SDECE infrastructure, but outside the usual channels, so that no one really knew whether they were serving their country or their party.

François Saar Demichel: A Gaullist 'Condottiere'

Thus within SDECE the socialists met with opposition, including that of François Saar Demichel. A kind of haughty 'condottiere', he did not conceal his admiration for de Gaulle. The little unit dealing with 'allied' parties abroad was in competition with an equally mysterious unit, 'Political Action'.

Jacques Loquin was quickly replaced at its head by François Saar Demichel, a well-bred Austrian brought up in the splendour of pre-war Vienna. It was in Paris, where he had come to continue his studies, that he learnt of the *Anschluss*, and then of the occupation of Czechoslovakia. In 1939 he requested naturalization, and this was granted. A courageous member of the Resistance, he belonged to the Gallia network, and had specialized in intelligence. At the end of the War he was sent by Colonel Passy into northern Italy to blow up the last German strongholds.[29]

He then went to Vienna, where he found Charles Albert Mouriot, a former member of the Dunkirk Intelligence group. It was also in the Austrian capital that he joined up with Lieutenant Pierre Cambon. François Saar Demichel was to be particularly affected when this young officer committed suicide in Innsbruck in 1947.[30] Recalled to Paris by Henri Ribière to lead the 'Political Action' unit, this convinced Gaullist, soon to become the semi-official treasurer of the Gaullist Rassemblement du Peuple Français (RPF), had frequent brushes with Kastenbaum and Mouchon. He accused them of favouring their socialist comrades instead of serving the State. Nevertheless the Political Action unit functioned well. 'We couldn't do everything at once,' François Saar Demichel reports, 'so we concentrated our efforts on Germany and the Eastern bloc. In peacetime intelligence resembles crosswords. With time, and by working at it, one must try to fill in the blank squares.'[31] In spite of some fine, successful operations,[32] François Saar Demichel met with difficulties. At the National Assembly one deputy spoke of his astonishment that such responsibilities could be entrusted to one only so recently naturalized. And suddenly he made a mistake – an enormous blunder. On a trip to Vienna in 1948 he quarrelled with the station head, Colonel Jean Mercier, who had succeeded Mouriot, 'I challenged him to a duel, as was frequently done in Austria during my youth. For a moment I had forgotten that I was resident in France. I handed in my resignation.'[33]

Helping Salvador Allende

The departure of François Saar Demichel strengthened the position of the socialist group within SDECE. Henceforth it could carry on its operations with the personal blessing of Henri Ribière.

Robert Lemoine – No. 90 in the Libération-Nord Resistance movement and concentration camp prisoner No. 77,708 at Buchenwald – took part in several missions with this team. One of the least publicized, carried on over several years, concerned South America. The SDECE line was to support strong characters hostile to the US presence: Juan Perón in the Argentine, and Salvador Allende (Allende already!) in Chile. SDECE arranged the covert sale of bauxite stocks to the USSR – at double the price – in violation of the Neutrality Act, using ships flying flags of convenience.

Thus the 'Lemoine' mission, under cover of a 'front' company in Buenos Aires, realized substantial profits. Helped by a network of 'honourable correspondents' revolving round the Association France-Amérique Latine and the Lycée Français in Buenos Aires, SDECE then bought up copper in small quantities, thus circumventing the US monopoly, and this was then conveyed to France. These fresh profits swelled the coffers of Salvador Allende's Socialist Party, which was preparing for important elections in 1952, and again in 1954.

Throwing General Franco Off Balance

For Spanish refugees in France – above all, those from the civil war – who had helped the French Resistance, the war did not finish on 8 May 1945. In all logic, after the fall of the Duce and the Führer, the fate of the Caudillo, Francisco Franco, remained to be settled. French opinion in general shared this view, beginning with de Gaulle, who strongly disliked the dictator beyond the Pyrenees. The situation at the frontier was tense. From 1944 to 1952 7,359 guerrilla operations were counted. These were launched by the combined forces of the members of the Spanish Communist Party, the anarchists of the FAI (Iberian Anarchist Federation) and the CNT, and other socialist groups – an average of 1,500 raids, ambushes in the countryside and attacks right in the heart of Madrid, during each of the two hottest years, 1946 and 1947.[34]

The most celebrated figure behind the anti-Franco guerrilla operations, Cristino Garcia, was arrested by the Civil Guard in September 1945. In France he had been one of the leaders of the 3rd Division in the Free French Forces of the Interior (FFI). He had risked his own neck for the liberation of the country that had given him asylum. Thus when Franco had him shot in 1946 the National Assembly unanimously demanded the breaking off of diplomatic relations with Madrid. For a year the Franco-Spanish frontier remained closed.

In this atmosphere the role of SDECE was not an easy one. During the War Franco had played the neutral card, and BCRA had exchanged information with SIM, its Spanish counterpart. Thus when French collaborators went to ground in Spain, a gentleman's agreement was arrived at: if Franco's men left the Republican refugees that had fled to France in peace, ORCG and SDECE counter-espionage would not 'liquidate' the collaborators. Apart from a few exceptions, such as Szkolnikoff,[35] the majority, in particular Darquier de Pellepoix,[36] would be merely kept under surveillance.

In Toulouse Colonel Verneuil set up a strong counter-espionage organization directed against Spain. During the war its head, François Bistos ('Colonel Franck'), had directed one of the most important operational, escape and intelligence networks in the south-west, named 'Andalusia'. He had been aided by Déodat du Puy-Montbrun, and had controlled Alain Roy, one of the best French agents to penetrate Franco's Spain.

On the other hand, certain agents were run directly from Paris. Thus Louis Febvre, a former policeman and an 'honourable correspondent' of the Deuxième Bureau before the War, revealed to the authors that Colonel Verneuil allocated him 1,200 francs a month to work against Spain, 'because the government wanted to eliminate Franco'.[37] However, according to Colonel Passy, under his direction SDECE had aimed above all at a certain balance: 'In Spain we were in touch with three leaders: Maora, who was a man of the Centre; Franco; and a notorious communist who had taken refuge in France, Cristino Garcia. But since Ribière, my successor, didn't understand anything about intelligence work, he committed many blunders in Spain. He placed too much confidence in his socialist comrades as "honourable correspondents". The result was that his networks were liquidated.'[38]

Colonel Passy was well qualified to know how politics can impede the smooth running of the secret services. But Spain also aroused strong emotions. Very many Resisters drew their inspiration from the memory of the Stukas that had strafed Guernica. Shortly before his death Commandant Trautmann, head of Research at SDECE, recalled with feeling the meeting just after the War in Marseilles between the French, Americans and the British. On the agenda: should Franco be 'destabilized'? The British used their veto. At the same time, in September 1945, the press retailed an account of a special mission of the DGER, organized by Captain Mansard, who smuggled in FAI pamphlets.[39] But the episode that reveals most about the state of mind at the time has remained unknown until the present day: SDECE seems not to have opposed the assassination of Franco!

Paul-Louis Aussaresses was a privileged witness to this. During the War BCRA had sent him as instructor to the Spanish Republican maquis of the FAI in Ariège. He recalled: 'At the Liberation the FAI, led by the Royo brothers, decided to carry out operations in Spain. At the time it was said that the movement even wanted to assassinate Franco, and that SDECE knew of this, that Passy was personally in favour, and allegedly even wished the Spaniards good luck. Indeed de Gaulle detested Franco, and considered him a fearful military dictator. This is the reason why one could believe that the French were behind the Spanish underground.'

It was to no avail: anti-Francoism did not last. Soon SDECE was keeping up friendly contacts with the Spanish authorities. Three years later René Pleven, the prime minister, gave the go-ahead to Plan Bolero-Paprika. On 8 September 1949, in the most extensive police operation since the War, the DST, the Renseignements Généraux and others launched a vast dawn raid that led to more than 200 arrests all over France. Three-quarters of these were Spanish activists, among them the principal communist leaders, the very ones who were organizing resistance to the Franco regime. At the height of the Cold War, and at the Kremlin's instigation, some of them also indulged in activities that were less commendable, and against French interests.[40] It was the end of a chapter for guerrilla warfare in Spain.

The Rescue of Ripka

In 1948 SDECE was not caught off its guard by the communist coup in Prague. The warning signs had been discerned by the French for several months beforehand. 'We drew our information from the best sources, thanks to our "honourable correspondents" among socialists or the clergy,' stated General Hounau, then head of Research at SDECE, and later military attaché in Prague. 'We were even in the confidence of top communist officials.'

As economics minister in a government deeply penetrated by the pro-Russian communists of Klement Gottwald, Hubert Ripka doubtless hoped for the nation to react. In 1939, before the War, he had voluntarily gone into exile with President Benes, first in Paris and then London, fleeing from Nazi oppression. For the French he was the genuine representative of a free Czechoslovakia, in 1948 as much as in 1939. Then came the February coup. The government of national unity was reduced to nothing. The social-democrat head of state, Jan Masaryk, the son of the founder of the Czechoslovakian republic, died suddenly. SDECE was the first secret service to obtain a copy of the confidential report of Dr Jaroslav Teply, which concluded that the death was not a natural one. Dr Teply was assassinated in his turn.

Meanwhile SDECE had not remained idle. On the orders of Henri Ribière, the director-general, the special Squadron ELA 56 ('Vaucluse') ordered one of its planes to take off from Austria. Two former members of the BCRA, Marcel Chaumien, alias Monsieur Armand, a wartime specialist in 'pick-ups', the air-lifting of Resisters, and Ferdinand Mischke, a Czech, were given the task of rescuing Ripka and bringing him back to France.

In Prague, the station head of SDECE, François Saar Demichel, had organized everything. He had known Hubert Ripka for a long while, through his brother-in-law, Maximilian Schlokow, who, under the name of 'Captain Max', had belonged to the 'Gallia' network during the War.

Captain Vincent, the military attaché at the French Embassy, was instructed to drive Hubert Ripka to the rendezvous in a car that could not be traced. At the pre-arranged time the SDECE plane touched down in a field alongside the Kunice road, only a few kilometres from Prague. Ripka flew off to Paris, where he was soon to become president of the Free Czech Movement.[41]

Not all opposition leaders had such good fortune. An attempt by the French secret services to arrange the escape of General Pika, the former head of the Czech military mission in Moscow, failed, and shortly afterwards General Pika was sentenced to death and hanged. With the powerful backing of the Soviet secret services, the new regime was henceforth on its guard. The Cold War had well and truly begun.

PART II

Operations on all Fronts

4
The Cold War

At the beginning of 1947 the Cold War really began to rage. Immediately the attention of the French secret services was concentrated on the Communist Party and on the directives that Moscow might give it. The political climate was tense. The embryonic CIA – it officially saw the light of day on 25 April 1947 – was pouring oil on the fire. Moreover, SDECE noted with consternation how greatly the French political scene was obsessed with American reports, which were couched in gloomy terms. Apart from the exaggerated stories of arms being stockpiled by the former Francs-Tireurs et Partisans, an American-fabricated document, for example, detailed a meeting of the Communist Party at which Fried, the 'Red Eminence' of the Comintern in Paris, was present. But the latter had been assassinated in Brussels in 1943! On the Boulevard Mortier the door remained almost closed to the CIA liaison man, Philip Clark Horton, who, all smiles and speaking in a slight Marseilles accent, regularly delivered batches of reports that were progressively more alarmist.

'There is no question of our involving ourselves in French internal affairs,' said Colonel Verneuil, 'It is not within SDECE's province: it can only act outside the country.' However, 'Little Father' knew full well that his Counter-Espionage Branch was at the centre of the apparatus set up to 'catch the Communist Party and the Russians with their hands in the till'. Surveillance of Alexander Bogomolov, the Soviet ambassador, constituted a kind of 'right of hot pursuit'. Within SDECE the monitoring services of Captain Eugène Caillot worked hard day and night, and achieved some results: the communists were ordered to raise the temperature, to harden their social and economic positions, and stir up a succession of strikes.

In fact a dispute at the Renault factories served as a pretext for the breakup of the alliance within the government. The five Communist ministers were forced to leave the Ramadier administration.

The Blue Plan

'At that time I was living in Sète, at the home of Commandant Benet, a DGER officer formerly stationed in India. Numerous meetings took place at his house. One day, after a visit by Lieutenant Jellicoe of the British SAS, the commandant told me: "We are setting up an armed organization, especially in Brittany." '[1]

Thus began the operation baptized 'Blue Plan'. Victor Vergnes, who describes it here, was one of its authors. The idea was to set up armed networks over France, to combat a possible armed coup by the communists. From 1946 on, the Anglo-American secret services redoubled their activities on French territory. Earl Jellicoe, the British lieutenant who had already distinguished himself in 1944 during the crushing of the Greek resistance, arrived in south-west France.[2] At the same time two members of the American OSS, formerly in the 'Jedburgh' commandos,[3] Tom Braden, the future assistant to Allen Dulles at the CIA, and Phil Chadbourne, were encouraging a split in the Confédération Générale du Travail (CGT), the communist-led trade union organization in Marseilles. After being parachuted into Finistère, Chadbourne had later become the US consul in Marseilles.[4] With Irving Brown, the European representative of the American unions, he contributed to the birth of the breakaway Force Ouvrière. Not only did the British and Americans put up the money for most of the so-called 'independent' unions, but they also took an interest in the political parties. The SFIO (Socialist) and especially the RPF (Gaullist) parties benefited from their largesse.

James Burnham, the special adviser to President Truman, did not rule out alliances from time to time with the Gaullists. 'In the world struggle against the communists,' he wrote, 'the United States needs firm friendships. The Gaullist movement is the most significant force in France. The movement has attracted to it a certain scum element, like all movements of its kind. But the RPF also includes a greater number of Frenchmen upon whom we may count to resist communism to the very end.'[5] Thus the Americans helped the Gaullists to prepare in material ways to respond to a possible offensive by the Communist Party. At the beginning of 1947 the wave of social unrest in the country seemed to confirm their fears. In Paris Colonel Simédéï (alias 'Servais'), who had just left the DGER to take over the political organization bureau of the RPF, received numerous emissaries from the small anti-communist groupings that were proliferating all over the country. One of the most active was the General Confederation of Ex-Servicemen (Confédération Générale des Combattants: CGC), led by Count de Vulpian. And it so happened that the CGC shared an address on the Avenue de l'Opéra in Paris with the Committee for Economic and Social Studies (Comité d'Etudes Economiques et Sociales), controlled by Irving

Brown, the representative of the American Federation of Labor (AFL).

Occasionally the clergy were also drawn in. Thus Fr Dominique Bulley, of Dombes Abbey, near Lyons, started the 'Balkan' network, whose task it was to collect money from the religious communities. In eastern France it was the industrialists who tended to be approached. 'I saw the Peugeot brothers at their offices,' stated Victor Vergnes. 'We discussed what should be done if there was a strike and their factories were occupied. For two months we worked to draw up a plan of action. We were divided up into sections, and had vehicles, garages and hotels at our disposal.'

All this organization was aimed at preventing an armed coup by the Communist Party. But this did not mean that the American and British secret services favoured an armed pre-emptive strike, so they were stunned to learn of a real 'plot' against the French government. On 30 June 1947, the socialist minister of the Interior, Edouard Depreux, disclosed the affair at a melodramatic press conference. 'At the end of 1946,' he revealed, 'we knew there existed a "black" maquis, made up of extreme right-wing Resisters, Vichyites and monarchists. They had a plan of attack, known as the "Blue Plan", which was to be launched either at the end of July, or on 6 August.' Count Edme de Vulpian was arrested. In his château of Bois, near Lamballe, in the Côtes-du-Nord, where the preparations for the conspiracy had been finalized, Superintendent Ange Antonini uncovered 'heavy weapons, battle orders, and fire plans'. The plotters had a taste for the theatrical. To spark off an uprising in the country, they conceived the idea of creating a scare about an imminent communist threat. Maps marked with the hammer and sickle were sent to prominent Bretons. The assassination of de Gaulle was even envisaged, in order to heighten popular indignation.

For the socialists the affair was timely. They wished to blow it up out of all proportion, because it would moderate the growing unrest in military circles close to the RPF. A government report cited Generals Koenig, de Larminat and Béthouard. There were rumblings in the army. Paul Ramadier, the prime minister, back-pedalled and gave an assurance that these prestigious leaders would not be prosecuted. On the other hand three other soldiers, General Maurice Guillaudot, the head of the Breton gendarmerie and a courageous member of the Resistance,[6] General Jean Merson, a former director of the intelligence service in the 1920s, as well as the former Cagoulard Colonel Loustanau-Lacau, were arrested. The files of the investigation were patently rigged. After a farcical trial, the accused were acquitted.

However, the enquiry, carried out simultaneously by Pierre Boursicot, the director of the Sûreté, and Henri Ribière. 'Number One' at SDECE, uncovered some curious foreign ramifications. The weapons found all over France had been paid for in part by London and Washington. But they had been given to resist the communists and not to provoke a *coup d'état*. Was de Gaulle aware of these preparations? In any case he did not believe any movement inciting to insurrection would be successful. He later confided to his collaborator Louis Terrenoire, 'Koenig, who headed the occupying forces in West Germany, would not have gone along with it. And then, I saw clearly that revolutionary Paris would not move.'[7] In 1947 André Malraux, for his part, regretted this passive stance.

General Aussaresses, then the commander of the 11th Shock Troops at Montlouis, said with a sigh: 'You should remember the atmosphere at the time. Everybody felt pretty low. At the end of 1947 I saw General Roger Oliva-Roget, who told me: "The RPF leaders have been to see me and informed me of communist preparations for a *coup d'état*. They offered me command of an armed militia." I replied quite tersely: "Can you imagine André Tournet, the Communist senator and a Compagnon de la Libération, organizing an armed coup? No, it's impossible!"'[8] In fact, the French secret services, with a few exceptions, took no action.

The Whitsun Conspiracy

No, the 'Gorilla' wouldn't play. Dominique Ponchardier, the author of the famous adventure stories about the *barbouzes* (as French secret police agents were called), and head of the Gaullist bodyguard and crowd control contingent after the War, had had enough of all these comic-opera plots.[9] 'The Old Man', as his friends called him, who with his brother Pierre had founded the Resistance network named 'Sosies', detested the communists, but mistrusted even more the swarm of adventurers who, in the depths of the Cold War, gravitated around the RPF and the secret services.

Lieutenant-Colonel Roger Decore, whom he had summarily turned out of his office, belonged in that category. During the war he had directed the 'Darius' network, and then worked for the DGER. In 1948, under the false name 'Jean Devis', he travelled to the United States, and there raised funds to mount an anti-communist operation. With these he sought to recruit from Gaullist circles. Not all the RPF leaders displayed the same stern disapproval as Dominique Ponchardier. Several dozen militants, among them Jacques Rateau, an RPF Paris town councillor, allowed themselves to become involved in a tenuous 'Whitsun Plan', so called because the date envisaged for the insurrection coincided with Whitsun weekend.

During the spring of 1949 Decore visited several French towns looking for weapons and financial support from former Resisters who had been connected with the American secret services during the War. After the failure of the 'Blue Plan', those approached showed prudence, and in general did not respond to these visits. Finding himself isolated, Roger Decore threw caution to the winds, with the result that certain of the officers he approached immediately alerted their superiors.

Captain Girard, commanding the First Squadron of the Garde Républicaine, reported these contacts to Commandant Delpal, the Garde's military security officer. He was ordered to wire his apartment for sound and invite the conspirators to his home. Captain Blondeau, another military security officer, likewise attended meetings at Le Vieil restaurant on the Boulevard de la Madeleine in Paris. Going one better, Roger Decore got in touch with a Resistance friend, Superintendent Ange Antonini, who had already taken charge of the investigation into the 'Blue Plan'. This senior official in the political section of Renseignements Généraux was thereafter invited to the meetings at Le Vieil restaurant. What Antonini did there was to gather information, whilst 'running' his friend Decore. It was customary throughout the Fourth Republic not to unmask conspiracies except at the ideal moment when it was in the political interest to make such a revelation. In the present case, the main accused was the RPF.

On 2 March 1949, Superintendent Romain, of Renseignements Généraux, in charge of the enquiry, arrested most of the plotters at La Passerelle restaurant in St Cloud, without a blow having been struck. The plot turned into a tragi-comedy. For instance, at Périgueux Bernard Marty, a dental surgeon by profession, had promised Roger Decore that he would assemble fifty men and march on Paris. At the appointed time, only Maurice Chatelain, an employee of the Périgueux Chamber of Commerce, and Albert Pradel, the managing secretary of a local newspaper, turned up. Moreover, in order to recruit them Bernard Marty had led them to believe they would be going by coach to a protest meeting, which would be followed by a banquet. This silly escapade ended at Longjumeau with the arrival of the police.

On 17 June 1949 Roger Decore was found hanging in his cell. Officially the conclusion was suicide. During the investigation of his case the colonel had several times declared that he was still working for the French secret services.

Operation 'Rainbow'

'Our chief in Lyons, Gilbert Union, who had carried out several missions for the BCRA during the War, was a silk manufacturer who was mad on cars – and he killed himself in one. As his replacement, SDECE recruited François de Grossouvre in 1950. His sugar firm, A. Berger & Co., provided opportunities for all sorts of different covers. He was a man who really did have a lot of contacts.'[10]

Louis Mouchon, one of SDECE's 'political experts', who had known François Mitterrand in London in 1944, recalled Operation 'Rainbow' perfectly. It was imperative in this affair that François de Grossouvre should become 'Monsieur Leduc'. Henceforth he was in regular contact with Morvan, the head of special operations in Research Branch. He was what was called an 'honourable correspondent'. The industrialist could scarcely imagine that, 30 years later, his task would be to oversee the intelligence world from the Elysée Palace.

It was Henri Ribière who conceived the idea of Operation 'Rainbow', also christened 'Compass Rose' or Mission '48', since it began in that year. In socialist circles, very influential within SDECE, there was a growing fear of the Soviet threat. The end of 1947 was particularly disturbing. Since the formation of the Comintern at the meeting of European communist parties held in Slarska-Poreba, the communists had adopted a strategy of confrontation. Obsessive fears were growing within the political parties.

During the same period Jacques Chaban-Delmas, the Gaullist who had lately been elected mayor of Bordeaux, made straight for the American consulate there to announce that the Communist Party was doubtless going to attempt to play its trump card. Riots broke out in Marseilles. In November the CGT brought the mines of the Nord and Pas-de-Calais departments to a standstill. Dockers blocked the ports of Bordeaux, Le Havre, Marseilles and Nantes. There was general disarray. In this intensely over-heated atmosphere the head of SDECE worked out a plan to hit back in case of a Soviet invasion. But unlike Passy, his purpose was not to secure the return of de Gaulle to power. Plans were merely made, in the event of a Russian occupation, to evacuate the government to North Africa. To this end buildings were requisitioned in Morocco. From then onwards, acting providently, SDECE sent some of its archives off to Dakar, having microfilmed them first.

Henri Ribière envisaged the creation of a network of several thousand persons throughout France. It was more or less a matter of constructing a new BCRA. In order to recruit agents SDECE officers would not hesitate to allude to the heroic actions of General de Gaulle during the last War. If a crisis arose SDECE, whose general staff would have been transferred to Morocco, would rouse these networks of 'sleepers' and spark off a new Resistance movement throughout the country.

It fell to Morvan, who headed Service 25 2/4 and was in fact the person who ran the SDECE's 'honourable correspondents', to carry through this ambitious programme. Henri Trautmann, director of Research, supervised the affair, but at arm's length. France was divided into geographical zones, each sector being entrusted to one of the staff of '25 2/4'. Raymond Hamel, Louis Mouchon and Marcel Le Roy ('Finville') dealt with recruitment. Guy Duboÿs, Morvan's assistant, was to train the troops of Mission 48. Practice exercises were rudimentary. They consisted of initiating the fledgeling spies into the methods of transmitting and encoding; they learnt how to operate radio transmitters and photographic apparatus. Above all, they were pledged to observe the utmost discretion.

At the height of the Cold War, Operation 'Rainbow' could not proceed without running certain risks. If the communists learnt about it they would make a great furore, both in Parliament and in the country. Thus the matter of recruitment was particularly delicate. There was no question of turning for support to members of small political groupings, even if they were anti-communist. Their supporters were far too talkative. On the contrary, it would be necessary to enrol as agents those who had never belonged to a political party, but whose connections would allow solid networks to be built up.

For the Lyons region François de Grossouvre, the peaceable managing director, presented the ideal model. He had no political label, but many friends. Nor did SDECE wish to call upon former Resistance members, because their networks were too well known and too vulnerable in case of foreign occupation. The principle adopted was to mobilize 'Mr Everyman', those whose files were almost blank. This was so in the case of François de Grossouvre.

The structures built up for Operation 'Rainbow' were to remain in place for a decade. But once the Cold War was over, SDECE scarcely concerned itself any longer with its secret organization. 'Service 25 2/4' became 'Service 7' and kept less and less closely in touch with its agents. And in 1958 Mission 48 disappeared from the records. There remained the friendships that had developed over these years. When François de Grossouvre arrived at the Elysée in 1981 he called upon a number of former members of these 'phantom' networks to assist him.

The Death of the 'Little Fathers'

On 4 March 1953, at 8.30 a.m., a toneless voice proclaimed on Radio Moscow: 'The Central Committee of the Communist Party of the Soviet Union and the Council of Ministers of the USSR announce the misfortune that has befallen our Party and people: the grave illness of Comrade Stalin. In the night of 1–2 March Comrade Stalin, whilst in his Moscow apartment, suffered a cerebral haemorrhage that attacked the vital areas of the brain. The use of speech has been lost. Grave cardiac and respiratory difficulties have arisen.'

The Russians were bewildered, but, under the fitful sunshine, went about their business. In Bolchevaïa-Jakimanka Street, at the French embassy, Louis Joxe, the Quai d'Orsay's representative, exploded, as did Commandant Perret, SDECE's head of station. Radio communication had broken down, and it was impossible for them to dispatch to their respective headquarters the ciphered telegrams declaring that it was all over for the Georgian dictator. It was no matter: two days later a laconic communiqué was published: 'On 5 March, at 9.50 p.m., cardio-vascular and respiratory insufficiencies worsened, and Joseph Vissarionovich Stalin died.'

On 6 March in Paris, a Cabinet meeting presided over by René Mayer endorsed a decision that everybody at SDECE had been expecting for three months: Lieutenant-Colonel Maurice Dumont would take over direction of the Counter-Espionage Branch.

That very evening, at the government's request, Dumont paid a visit to his technical aide, 'Domino', temporarily in hospital as a result of his war wounds:

'Tell me, while you are lying idle here, could you draft me a short paper intended for the President and the prime minister – two pages at most – on the succession to Stalin, seen from the intelligence viewpoint? Have you any ideas?'

'Yes, I can already see its beginnings . . . "The leopard may change its spots but not its nature." '[11]

Dominique Loisel was in fact one of the shrewdest officers covering the Soviet Union, a man of tremendous drive, which sometimes had to be curbed, but very gifted. A senior official of Action Branch recalled:

I knew him very well, because he was next to me on the same floor at the Pension Verdin, one of SDECE's 'hotels' at 102, Avenue Victor Hugo. His story is one of the most outstanding I know. Before the War he was a student in the Faculty of Letters at Strasbourg, and had won a travelling scholarship to study Greek temples. But he was contacted by a captain in the Deuxième Bureau and handed a questionnaire about the Balkans. Dominique Loisel came back with answers to almost all the questions. 'Monsieur Loisel, we shall remember this,' said the captain. And sure enough the following year Loisel won another scholarship. But this time he was to go and scout out the Siegfried Line, moving from one youth hostel to another. He was caught and received a monumental beating-up before being conducted *manu militari* back to the frontier. The final humiliation was a hefty kick in the backside. Loisel used to say, 'It was to avenge that assault that I chose later to go into intelligence.'

Both Dumont and Loisel were trained in Colonel Paillole's school, and were in Madrid during the War, and then in Germany, in order to dismantle the German secret services and embark upon the struggle against the Russians and their allies. In 1948, after their return to SDECE headquarters, they assisted Colonel Verneuil. But he died in December 1952, and from then on everyone at SDECE waited impatiently to learn who would replace the 'Little Father'. Dumont, the replacement, was appointed upon the death of the 'Little Father of the People'. It was true that the changes there, on the other side of the Iron Curtain, would be much more considerable than those on the Boulevard Mortier.

Three years later SDECE delivered to the prime minister's Office a document marked 'Secret' and entitled *Documentary Memorandum for Political Counter-Infiltration: The Twentieth Congress of the Soviet Communist Party – 14–25 February 1956*. Whereas, in his secret report, Nikita Khrushchev denounced the crimes of Stalin, and above all those of the chief of his secret service, Lavrenti Beria, for its part SDECE's report announced the changes going on in the Soviet intelligence community.

The Polish Drama

Shortly after the Prague coup a number of French networks were undermined. In January 1951 Colonel Gastaldo, a military attaché, was virtually kidnapped. The Czech secret service attempted to compromise him in an affair with a woman. As a last resort he took refuge in the French Embassy.[12] In 1950 Léon Lamy was expelled from Romania for espionage. This former seaman and radio expert had worked in Bucharest in the heyday of pre-war intelligence. A fluent Romanian speaker, he was one of SDECE's finest 'pianists'.[13] The same was true of Captain Georges Barazer de Lannurien, military attaché in Bucharest since 1947, where, for budgetary reasons, he functioned as head of both the SDECE station and the Deuxième Bureau. It would be understating the case to say that he knew the Eastern bloc countries. During the War, with another Breton, Captain Michel Bourel de la Roncière, he had led a detachment of Frenchmen, alongside Slovakian and Russian partisans, right up to 1944. La Roncière was also to make his career in SDECE, becoming the head of the Yugoslavian station in 1954.

Meanwhile, in 1948 Lannurien had undertaken a raid into Czech territory to rescue some senior Catholic dignitaries who had been threatened: 'When I arrived in Prague they were under lock and key, and I finished my mission with my wife in a spa resort.'[14]

The Hungarian secret services under General Gabriel Peter watched Lannurien very closely. On 5 June 1950 he was expelled from Hungary, in a blaze of publicity. The Hungarian 'specialists' were ruthless: Hungarian citizens, undoubtedly considered to be SDECE agents, were hanged, beginning with the Director of Customs and the Chief of the General Staff.[15]

But the most serious event occurred in Poland. Through contacts established before the War, as well as the non-communist resistance of General Anders and the traditional Franco-Polish friendship, SDECE had built up a vast network. On 21 November 1949, the Polish government announced the arrest of André Robineau, the consular agent at Szczecin. Abducted a few days previously, he had implicated two members of the embassy staff: 'The Polish government requires MM. Aymar de Brossin de Meré and Fernand Renaux, unmasked as having committed acts of espionage, to leave the territory of the Polish Republic immediately.'

Then the situation grew worse. In its turn, the consulate at Wroclaw came under fire. Scores of agents were arrested. At SDECE Colonel Verneuil paced up and down: the intelligence coming in to the 'Firm' was disturbing. Had Robineau betrayed them? Shipped back to Paris, Brossin de Meré and Renaux were interrogated unremittingly at SDECE Security. They had been so diligent in gathering intelligence concerning the Red Army stationed in

Poland that they had neglected to exercise prudence. But treason was ruled out. Franco-Polish relations deteriorated. In a series of trials at the beginning of 1950 André Robineau, and then Yvonne Bassaler, a secretary in the Wroclaw station, as well as a radio operator, Gaston Druet, who had helped Robineau to recruit agents, confessed to their spying activities. SDECE's Polish agents, once in the dock, had reason to fear the outcome of the trial: so they split on their leaders. The French nationals were sentenced to twelve years' imprisonment, their official diplomatic status being disregarded.

By way of retaliation, and above all to get back its men, SDECE collaborated with the DST to mount a number of operations. In fact one of these had been under way since 1947: the infiltration of SEPIC, a Franco-Romanian company directed by a Cominform agent, David Chaim Jallez, alias Albert Igouin. He was associated with Aronowicz, a Polish national, and with the director of the Crédit Franco-Roumain, Chunowsky. Now Igouin had selected as his technical director a former Resistance comrade and member of Libération-Nord, Robert Lemoine. In reality the latter, after his return from deportation, had joined the DGER, and then SDECE. He told his story as follows:

For that first infiltration into a Soviet network, Henri Ribière, my former chief in the Resistance, and now head of SDECE, told me: 'You'll have to resign.' I was furious but it was necessary, for he asked me to penetrate that network, in order initially not to destroy it, but to watch it and learn whether it was engaged in trading in war materials. In short, we were receiving from an allegedly technical association, called 'Importers of Polish Coal', the supposed profits from the sale of this coal, which were paid into a special account. At Warsaw's request, we bought machine-tools for heavy and light industry. In theory at least, their destination was Portugal. In reality, we sent surveying equipment, together with maps, to Poland, Russia, Yugoslavia and China. Everything passed through our office. So long as it concerned civilian materials there was no problem. But soon military orders arrived: I was sent an order for Type 550 torpedoes. We were therefore obliged at SDECE to contemplate liquidating the network, especially with the Wroclaw trial going on in Poland.

One day Colonel Fourcaud summoned me, together with my control officer, Colonel Fournet, and said to us both: 'For once we have reached agreement with the DST. Starting at 7 a.m. tomorrow morning we shall pick up the network members. Some 250 people will be arrested.' And in fact many Poles were expelled. However, with SDECE's agreement a certain number were allowed to escape to Canada, where the authorities were able to monitor the rebuilding of new networks.[16]

In Paris, Myjzkiwski, the assistant military attaché, was arrested. In Lille Szczerbinski, the Vice-Consul, was convicted in 1951. After an exchange of prisoners, carried out with due formality, SDECE learnt the inside story of the Wroclaw affair. As frequently in spy stories, its mechanism was very simple. Yvonne Bassaler and Robineau were interrogated and cleared. The latter was to continue his career at headquarters until 1960. The consulate secretary, recruited by General Teyssier, the military attaché, to deal with shorthand-typing and the preparation of intelligence reports, had probably been having an affair with the general. The latter died. Shortly afterwards, when the trials were getting under way, his widow refused to return to France. SDECE was quick to realize that it was she who had denounced the French organization to the Urzad Bezpieczenstwa – Polish military security – quite simply out of jealousy.

Ten Years in a Gulag for the 'Little Cleric' of SDECE

Lieutenant Lucien Gouazé had a religious vocation. If the War had not turned his life upside down, he would have become a priest. Taken prisoner in Hungary, he gave his Nazi jailers the slip and succeeded in escaping from the fortress of Königsberg. Understandably, at the Liberation the secret services sought to recruit him, all the more so because his fortunes had changed when he decided to marry a ravishing Hungarian lady.

Since he knew the Eastern bloc countries, SDECE decided to post him to the Vienna station, under Commandant Mouriot. As we have seen, Vienna was strategically located. But it was an ill-fated station, exposed as it was to all the tricks of the Soviet services. Some fifty French agents were working there, including some of Austrian nationality. How could security be maintained when the attempts of the other side to breach it were on the increase? An SDECE case officer committed suicide rather than withstand the pressure; people disappeared. In the 1950s the station, in which counter-espionage was run by Captain Humm and Maurice Clément, was to be infiltrated by the KGB. 'Vienna' was so 'contaminated' that Trautmann, the head of Intelligence Branch at SDECE, advised his officers based on the other side of the Iron Curtain to cut off all contact with it.

An extremely agreeable man, a dynamic person who saw his involvement with SDECE as a kind of priesthood, Lucien Gouazé was sent on many different missions to communist countries. In September 1948 he arrived in Budapest. The Belgian Embassy served as a dropping-off point. There he deposited his bag, which contained his uniform and pistol. Then he paid a visit to SDECE's head of station, Captain Lannurien. Somewhat disconcerted, the latter explained that he was delighted to see him, but that he was risking a great deal, because the Hungarian security services were tightening their grip. The next day Gouazé retrieved his case but as he emerged from the Belgian diplomatic mission he found himself face to face with some men in plastic raincoats. No more was heard of him. But a rumour circulated that a 'French spy' had been sentenced to 15 years in prison – the Gulag.

In Tokyo in 1954, at an embassy cocktail party, the head of SDECE in Japan was clinking glasses with his counterparts of various nationalities.

'I would love to visit France, such a fine country,' a naval officer in the

Japanese equivalent of the Deuxième Bureau, Captain Medea, confided to him.

The SDECE man stared at him. His companion had been discussing poetry – Villon, Rimbaud, Aragon.

'But come now, Captain, how is it that you speak such good French, when you have never been to our country?'

'Ah, unfortunately it's only too simple: I was a prisoner of the Russians for several years.'

'The Russians?'

'Yes, and in the prison where I was there was a Frenchman who taught us his language. He was a great chap.'

You will have realized that the Japanese officer had met up with Lucien Gouazé. But years had still to pass before the French officer could be got out of the Gulag. In 1957 General Grossin, then head of SDECE, intervened to secure the release of his subordinate, who had disappeared ten years previously. 'It was one of the first files I found on my desk upon my arrival,' the General said. 'On his return to Paris in May 1959, Gouazé told me: "I promised the Russian services never to do any more intelligence work. Please help me to keep my word."'[17]

The Surveillance of French Territory

He had been a colleague of Dzerzhinsky, the founder of the Cheka, Lenin's secret police, and assistant to Beria. But in August 1959 Lieutenant-Colonel Siegfried Dombrowski opted to seek refuge in the West, arriving with his cases stuffed full of records. His documents were gone through with a fine toothcomb by the analysts of the French secret services. They revealed that 'Eleven' – Section 11 of the First Division of the KGB – comprised 800 agents with the job of cross-checking intelligence originating in France and neighbouring countries. 'Subsection R' ran 200 'settled' and 'travelling' agents in France, Russians with diplomatic cover or there illegally, or indeed Frenchmen, most of whom were not in the Communist Party. The counter-espionage men were on their guard – not only those in SDECE, but also their colleagues in the Directorate for Surveillance of the National Territory (Direction de la Surveillance du Territoire: DST).

Abolished by Marshal Pétain in 1942, the DST arose again from the ashes on 16 November 1944. It was included by statute among the directorates run by the Ministry of the Interior, and in theory it came under the Director-General of the Sûreté Nationale, André Pelabon, the former BCRA representative in North Africa. In practice, however, 'Roger Wybot' – his real name was Warin – a former head of counter-espionage in the BCRA, who later became its director, dealt directly with his minister.

Covered by the seal of secrecy attached to national defence, the DST claimed to work under a different system.

Breaking with a pre-war tradition whereby offensive counter-espionage and the running of agents were attached to the military intelligence service, Wybot set up an extensive apparatus for research, analysis and agent management. It was inevitable that occasionally SDECE and the DST would hunt over the same territory. Following the example of the American FBI, or the British MI5, Roger Wybot was even to request that some of his officers should be posted to embassies abroad. The idea came to nothing. As well as its central Research service, the DST equipped itself with a Management Directorate and a monitoring service, the Agency for Radioelectronic Communications (Police des Communications Radio-électroniques: PCR). Twenty brigades covered the national territory, and North Africa. From his Paris office on the Rue des Saussaies Roger Wybot, aided by Stanislas Mangin and Alain Montarras, headed the section for the control of agents (E:2 – hence the pseudonym of its head, 'Monsieur Aideux'), documentation, operational services, and the radio direction-finding and monitoring centre. At regional level the service was divided into nine brigades, each with the same sections.

From 1944 to 1958, under the Fourth Republic, during the period when it was headed by Roger Wybot, the DST provided the best 'copy' for journalists, so deeply was it involved in all the explosive affairs of the time. However, the communist bloc remained its chief preoccupation. With SDECE and Section 7 of Renseignements Généraux, DST then decided to begin penetrating the groups of migrants coming from the Eastern bloc countries.

Immigrants from the East in the Service of SDECE

The satellites of the Soviet Union sheltered behind the Iron Curtain. The Cold War was at its height. Anti-communist émigrés were flooding in, forming a pool of potential recruits for the French secret services. Yet let us be candid here. We are dealing with an assortment of people of different generations, united in their hatred of the Reds, but divided by their political affinities, ethnic origins and personal quarrels. Systematically the DST, Section 7 of Renseignements Généraux, and a special section of SDECE worked their way through these immigrants with a fine toothcomb. This was necessary not only to protect the dissidents, but also to detect false émigrés, who were in fact Eastern bloc agents. Certain groups claimed to have maintained strong networks behind the Iron Curtain, and could provide up to date information to the French.

This was so in the case of the National Union for Labour (Natsiolno Trudoboy Soyuz: NTS), founded in 1930. The 'Solidarists', as they are still called, had sworn to overthrow Russian communism. In the 1950s the Gehlen Organization in the Federal Republic and the CIA acted as 'godfathers' to them, but SDECE remained wary. The French section of the NTS, in exchange for down payments in cash, provided only stale information, often gleaned from Soviet press cuttings. 'The NTS people are joking,' was the view commonly expressed in SDECE's Russian section directed by Colonel Lochard and even in the minor 'K (for 'Kominform') Service' controlled by a man called Poujat, a fiery young intellectual, clearly planted in SDECE by the Socialist Party.

This, however, was not a view shared by Pierre Faillant de Villemarest, a member of SDECE until 1950, who 'personally followed the work of the Cominform and the NKVD on the international plane', and who maintained privileged connections with the NTS leaders in France, Michel Slavinsky and Vladimir Stolypine.[18]

Nevertheless, SDECE opted to recruit only a handful of people coming from the NTS. One such was Yevgeny Ivanovich Sinitzin, alias 'Garanin', an officer first in the Red Army and then in the Vlassov Army, which was a Nazi puppet. After the War he fled to Morocco, and there was taken on by SDECE. Another agent from the NTS was Nikolay Ruchenko, who was to cause a dispute between SDECE and the CIA, by attempting to enlist an American agent in the French organization.

Situated in the Rue Mérimée in Paris, another staging-point was the General Federation of Associations of Russian Ex-Servicemen in France (ROVS), comprising 500 members and run by Alexis de Lampe and Vladimir Popoff. But these White Russians were completely out of touch with reality. Nostalgia for a past that had gone for ever, which caused them to meet in certain cafés in the evenings, turned them into gentle dreamers, but not top-quality agents. They also liked to associate with officers from various secret services, and their lack of exclusiveness devalued the quality of their intelligence. Thus in Paris Konstantin Yeveyevich Istomin, who had a good entrée into political circles, sold his information to SDECE, the British SIS and the German BND in turn.[19]

Recent immigrants from Soviet satellite countries provided the best raw intelligence: their information was fresh. A Central Committee of Ukrainian Organizations in France grouped together 17 associations under the presidency of Simeon Sorontiev. The Association of Hungarian Fighters (Magyar Harcosok Bajtarski Közössege: MHBK) of Joseph Szen, in Paris on the Rue de Vézelay, numbered 7,000 members, 400 of whom were in the Paris area, thanks to the influx of immigrants in 1956. Yugloslav immigration was divided between Serbs and Croats: for the Croats there was the United Croats of France (Ujedinjeni Hrvatski Francuska), led by Istvan Tsukor;[20] for the Serbs, the main organization was the Cetniks, a nationalist and royalist movement, made up of former soldiers in the Royal Yugoslav Army and former Yugoslav Resistance members under General Mihajlović, which was led in France by Lazar Dabetić and Miloslav Popović. Finally, among those most eager to cooperate with SDECE were the former members of the Romanian Iron Guard. A complete list of these organizations would be very long.[21] Certainly not all of them were 'managed' by SDECE or the other French secret services. Yet they provided the best recruits for one of SDECE's most mysterious post-war operations, when it parachuted agents behind the communist lines.

MINOS: A Secret Cell

With all lights extinguished the Douglas DC3 Dakota flew at low altitude over the Slovak forests. As yet the Eastern bloc countries possessed no radar detection apparatus, and anyway the Czechs might mistake the plane for one of their own Dakotas, built under Czech licence and renamed Lisunof LI-2.

The fighters in the secret war who plunged into the darkness were all clad from head to foot in leather. Their equipment was similar to that of the 'Smoke Jumpers', the American football rig that had been in fashion in the USA since 1942. The 'flying firemen' liked to wear it. For a jump from about 500 feet, an automatic opening belt, rather than a lap-pack, was used. So who were these ghostly spies? They were émigrés, trained by SDECE and equipped with radios, survival rations and light weapons. Their objective was to carry out intruder intelligence missions in depth, and even to start guerrilla resistance groups – and this was only three years after the Prague coup.

This is the first time that these French operations behind the Iron Curtain have been revealed. From 1949 to 1954, almost a hundred covert parachutists were dropped into the unknown in this way, in Czechoslovakia, Yugoslavia and Romania, and even into Byelorussia and Lithuania. This was the doing of one of the most secret SDECE units, which was directly attached to the General Directorate. Under the banner of 'intelligence materials standardized for special operations' (Matériels d'Informations Normalisées pour les Opérations Spéciales: MINOS), France embarked upon this venture, sometimes with the logistic support of the CIA, which was very active in this field.

The American services, in cooperation with the Gehlen Organization in Germany and the British SIS, in fact mounted the same type of operations in Eastern Europe. Thus Mission 'Valuable' aimed at stimulating guerrilla warfare in Albania and the Ukraine.[22] Up to 1952 impressive formations of 'White' guerrillas, the heirs of the war-time non-communist popular resistance, were implanted in Croatia, the Ukraine and Poland. And the Russians had to commit several divisions in order to wipe them out. However, the secret CIA missions were a lamentable failure. When the parachutists landed they ran straight into local security forces. It came out too late that the whole plan had been betrayed in Washington by one of its British organizers, Kim Philby, who was in Stalin's service.

It so happened that SDECE frequently kept out of this kind of joint venture. Operation MINOS remained so secret that even today often those who took part in it – and whom the authors have been able to question – only knew bits of it. To a large extent the operation remained outside the purview of Henri Ribière and the General Directorate, and was principally run by its technical directors, Colonels Hounau and Fourcaud.

As Colonel Germain, the deputy director of Counter-Intelligence Branch recalls, 'Counter-espionage was given the task of studying the files of several dozen émigrés from the East. In this way we got to know that Intelligence Branch was organizing drops, but did not know the details. We must not forget that everything was very compartmentalized.' One can, however, put together the plan of the operation like a jigsaw puzzle. As a first step, a special section recruited immigrants from the Eastern bloc, from among the anti-communist groups, or even outside them. The section was handed over to Colonel Jacques Pommès-Barrère and his assistant, Colonel Beaumont. The latter, like Lieutenant-Colonel Ferdinand Mischke,[23] had been a member of the Czech Army and attached to the BCRA during the War, and afterwards to the Air Ministry.

'Monsieur Armand', in real life Marcel Chaumien, a former member of the Frce French 'Météo' network, and an air force commandant, trained the commandos. They followed an accelerated technical and paramilitary training course, given at Neuilly and Longjumeau. Close combat, sabotage techniques and parachuting were taught at the Action Branch centre directed by Colonel Morlanne, near Luzarches in the Val-d'Oise.

So far as possible, subordinate officers of the commando groups were drawn from escapees from behind the Iron Curtain. One such was Dragan Sotirović, a former commander in the Cetniks, the anti-communist fighters of General Mihajlović's army, opposed to Tito during the War. Acting for both CIA and SDECE, he ran the school for agents that were to be parachuted into Yugoslavia.[24] The same was done for Romania. At the beginning of 1953 émigrés parachuted in by SDECE were captured by the authorities. Among them were Alexander Tanase and Mircea Papovici. Their trial opened in August before a Bucharest military tribunal. Tanase declared, 'For our training in Paris we were entrusted to a former Iron Guard, Mircea Musatescu.' This same Musatescu, during the spring and summer of 1952, served as liaison officer between the Romanian volunteers and the SDECE instructors and later with the CIA.

The secret of Operation MINOS was all the more closely guarded because it demanded the cooperation of the special SDECE squadron based at Persan-Beaumont. The successor of Squadron 1/56 ('Vaucluse'), set up by the BCRA in 1943, it bore the same emblem – an eagle and the three keys of Avignon. It was led by Commandants Boris Delocque-Fourcaud and

Charles Christienne.[25] At that time it was called the Air Liaison Squadron ELA 56 'Vaucluse', and was made up of Junkers JU52s as well as Dakotas. It was the latter, which had a range of 3,000 kilometres, which took off from airfields at Innsbruck in Austria and Lahr in Germany to drop these night commandos. During the War the pilots of the Franco-Russian Normandie-Niemen squadron flew over this terrain hundreds of times. Those who after the War agreed to continue to fly for SDECE were very valuable in such circumstances. During one night flight a Fairey-Barracuda, a two-seater monoplane, crashed on a training exercise in the Rhine Valley, near Freiburg. Its pilot, Lieutenant Gabriel Mertzisen, had been an ace of the Normandie-Niemen squadron, with eight victories to his credit and had been awarded the Legion of Honour, the Military Medal, the Ordre de la Guerre pour la Patrie, and the Victory Medal. After the War he opted to work for SDECE. Officially Mertzisen 'died on active air service for France on 30 September 1951'.

By an irony of fate those who earlier had fought side by side with the Russians against Nazism were, five years later, dropping 'ghost fighters' by parachute into the Soviet camp to organize guerrilla units. This was what the Cold War demanded.[26]

How many of them were there? The evidence is conflicting.[27] What is certain is that few émigrés were to return to France after their mission, and several radio operators were 'turned' by the local counter-espionage service in order to 'contaminate' SDECE. One day, however, there was a strange episode. Action Branch parachuted into his native land a Pole who was to carry out a liaison mission. Then no more was heard of him. Silence: failure was assumed. He was believed lost. This was a mistake. Some weeks later the Pole presented himself at 141, Boulevard Mortier and, to general amazement, demanded to see Colonel Morlanne, the head of 'Service 29' – Action Branch. How was it that a covert agent, infiltrated with an extraordinary wealth of precautions behind the Iron Curtain, could calmly walk into headquarters in this way to report on his mission, when he was plainly under surveillance by the secret services of the other side? Colonel Morlanne was astonished.

'As soon as I landed,' recounted the MINOS escapee, 'I was arrested by the Poles. So, to get out of the mess, I told everything.'

'What, precisely?' anxiously enquired the head of Action Branch.

'Everything, really. I told about the house in the suburbs, the training, the Boulevard Mortier, Action Branch, commanded by a man named Morlanne.'

'And they let you go?'

'Undoubtedly, since I'm here now.'

Colonel Morlanne might have reflected that the story was straight out of Alfred Jarry's *Ubu Roi*, particularly since he knew that the Polish services were called 'UB', and their head Jarry!

This far-fetched event could not conceal the fact that essentially

Operation MINOS was a failure. Pierre Nikitine, secretary of ROVS, appears to have been a fatalist: 'I must confess that every time émigrés had been sent into the East European countries, on foot before the war, and after 1945 by parachute, they returned only rarely. The Soviets seemed aware of their movements. Who gave them away? I can't make up my mind about it.'[28]

Numerous senior members of SDECE shared the same opinion. In general they thought the operation had been compromised, because it had been betrayed by one or more of those who had dreamed it up. Twenty years later the affair was to surface again, discrediting one particular person. On the other hand, a former member of Counter-Espionage affirmed, 'It was too much like a game. You have to know the émigrés. They were incapable of keeping a secret. And above all, in police states such as the communist countries, the chances of success were very slim.'

5

Indo-China

At the beginning of 1945 the first Frenchmen who had been parachuted into Indo-China, which was still in Japanese hands, succeeded in sending Colonel Passy the following note: 'All went off very well. We fell into a bog. When we had got out of it about a hundred Japanese were waiting for us. So we are prisoners.'[1]

Black humour. But in Paris Passy had scarcely had a choice. He had to reorganize the DGER in the Far East and catch up with all the Powers that coveted Indo-China: the Japanese, who were starting a tactical withdrawal, but had not yet capitulated; the Chinese and the British, who, in accordance with the Potsdam Agreement, wanted to share out Indo-China along a North–South dividing line; and finally, the Americans of OSS, who were backing the nationalist troops of Ho Chi Minh.

That fatal spot, Dien Bien Phu, was where Colonel Passy and François de Langlade jumped in their turn on 10 March 1945. This was shortly after the capture of Hanoi by the Japanese, who had decided to liquidate the French power base, despite the fact that it had previously rallied to the Pétain regime. The Vietminh Politbureau then decided: 'Faced by Japanese fascism, the single enemy of the Vietnamese revolution, we must ally ourselves to the French and Americans.'

De Langlade, who accompanied the deputy director of the DGER, was a specialist on Asia. A rubber planter in Malaya, in 1943 he had set up a BCRA network, with the help of the writer, Pierre Boulle. The latter was captured and horribly ill-treated by the Japanese. De Langlade appointed another former member of his Malayan network, Colonel Léonard, as the DGER's general representative in the Far East. His mission, which was continued by Joseph Roos, his successor, was to set up intelligence networks working with the DGER stations in Calcutta and Kandy, which up to then had functioned under the British action unit Force 136. In Laos an action unit was already operating. Soon over 3,000 men, stood down from the European front, were to form a vast reserve in Calcutta for Action Branch in Indo-China.

The situation was complicated. As Colonel Passy was folding away his

parachute on 10 March, the Japanese, scenting the wind of change, decided
to confer power in the territories they had conquered upon local rulers loyal
to them. Thus on the next day, 11 March, at the invitation of the Japanese
occupying forces, Bao Dai, the young emperor of Annam, proclaimed the
independence of Vietnam and, with the same eagerness, gave his assent to a
general manifesto in favour of a greater East Asia under Japanese protection.

Colonel Passy, before returning to France to assume the directorship of
DGER, studied the situation closely. Much though he admired the
Americans, their ambiguous attitude amazed him:

At Dien Bien Phu, in order to combat malaria, which was endemic, planes of OSS,
the American secret services, brought in medical supplies. We went to meet them in
order to take over the consignment. We told them that we were the representatives of
Free France, and that the supplies should be handed over to us to distribute to the
population. They refused. There was no question of their recognizing French
authority: they would deliver the supplies to the natives themselves. We protested.
They replied, 'Orders are orders.'[2]

Ho Chi Minh's Briefcase

On 1 June 1946 the plane carrying Ho Chi Minh, Pham Van Dong and their
four secretaries landed in France. Georges Bidault, the prime minister, and
Marius Moutet welcomed them as they got off the plane. Moutet, a Socialist
minister in liberated France, had been an acquaintance of the Indo-Chinese
leader since the 1930s. A man to trust? During the War he had been one of
the agents in Switzerland of the Soviet espionage network led by Sandor
Rado . . .

On 6 July the Fontainebleau conference began. Four months earlier, on
2 March, Ho Chi Minh had become the president of the Democratic
Republic of Vietnam. Thus on 6 March he had signed an agreement with
Jean Sainteny, Commissioner of the Republic for Tonkin, which recognized
Vietnam as an autonomous republic within the French Union. For three
months, although President Ho Chi Minh had been welcomed in France
with all due honour, the Vietnamese had been convinced that the French
government was playing for time by inviting Ho and his entourage on a visit
that took them from Biarritz to Lourdes and then to Deauville, closely
followed by a Mercedes of SDECE (which had belonged to the German
military governor of Paris). The *modus vivendi* finally agreed on
15 September 1946 concerning the status of Vietnam was a mere expedient,
for want of anything better. It proved all the more so because, even during
the negotiations at Fontainebleau, disquieting events were taking place in
Indo-China. Whilst the conference was talking about Franco-Vietnamese
cooperation, on 21 June Admiral Thierry d'Argenlieu let loose his French
troops on the plateaux of Vietnam. It was not surprising that at Fontainebleau

Ho Chi Minh and his delegation became increasingly convinced that the Bidault government could not be relied on to find a peaceful solution to the Indo-China question.

On 19 October 1946, Ho Chi Minh and his companions embarked on the patrol boat *Dumont d'Urville* in order to return to Indo-China. The stage was set for an incident that has become a legend within SDECE, but which is revealed here for the first time. Colonel Morlanne, head of Action Branch, succeeded in fact in placing on board two of his best agents. The two men, 'Pioche' ('Pick'[3]) and 'the Austrian', almost succeeded in getting into the Vietnamese leader's cabin and photographing the documents in Ho's briefcase. It was a failure, but they let the Vietnamese think they had managed to read their documents prior to the Conference. For history this failure became a magnificent feat – and a subject for jokes in the SDECE training courses for years to come!

Some weeks later, SDECE's Studies Branch, under Paul Guivante ('Saint-Gast') and Colonel Maurice Belleux, soon to be SDECE's representative in Saigon, submitted a report to Prime Minister Bidault. Action Branch became a part of folklore. Nevertheless, for 40 years this first unbelievable mission has remained unknown to the public. The substance of the report was: 'Ho Chi Minh has no faith in the decisions arrived at in Fontainebleau. On the slightest pretext he will launch open guerrilla warfare against France.'

People in SDECE were amazed when their finest operation was not followed up. However, in Indo-China events moved rapidly. From 2 November 1946 onwards, Admiral Thierry d'Argenlieu ordered the bombardment and then the recapture of the city of Haiphong, where Vietnamese troops had barricaded themselves in. On 20 December, taking advantage of the uncertain situation in France, where Georges Bidault had handed in his resignation but Léon Blum was not yet prime minister, Uncle Ho issued his call to rebellion: 'Let all Vietnamese, men and women, young and old, regardless of religion, party or nationality, rise up to fight the French colonialists and save our country.'

Bagheera the Panther

The mouth of a ferocious black panther, Bagheera, as in *The Jungle Book*, was the emblem of the 11th Shock Troops. It evoked the involvement of the commandos in Indo-China. Lieutenant Jacques Dupas, a frogman of long experience, formerly with the Sahara units, and then a marine commando who had taken part in the landings in June 1944, ever the humorist, had chosen this symbol after a row with his wife, a Niçoise.

Whilst the war in Indo-China was spreading, tens of thousands of kilometres away a group of ex-soldiers of the assault troops of the Free French forces were building up a regiment specializing in secret warfare, and from whom SDECE was to draw its Action Branch troops. The 11th Shock Troops Battalion was started on 1 September 1946. From the former SAS troops, the 'Jedburgh' teams, and the Action unit in BCRA, a small nucleus of the best were chosen, those who had won their spurs in the most daring missions, the most audacious raids against the Nazis. After a period with an interim commander, the battalion's real architect was selected from the Jedburgh contingent. He was discreet and reserved, quite the opposite of a loud-mouthed go-getter: for Captain Paul Aussaresses, to accomplish physical feats depended first of all upon one's state of mind, psychology and convictions. He had given proof of this, as we have seen, by parachuting into Germany in order to protect the concentration camps. Aussaresses was an intellectual; but this was to prove a drawback. In 1948 Yves Godard, after many intrigues, ousted and then replaced the commander of the 11th Shock Troops.

The fact remains that Paul Aussaresses, who had the makings of a possible leader of Action Branch, succeeded in assembling 35 men, training them in the snowbound fort of Montlouis, and preparing them to assume command of 800 operational troops. They got together sports equipment and tons of arms and explosives. The fundamentals of their training were based on guerrilla warfare, infiltration behind enemy lines, and the setting-up of a counter-insurgency force. The 11th Shock Troops were a politico-military unit, and one cannot forget that they were formed at the height of the Cold War. Mountaineering, dangerous route marches, survival exercises, frogman combat training, handling explosives and special weapons, unarmed combat, low-altitude parachute drops and night drops – at the time all this initial training for the special units was conceived of with an eye to the enemy of the moment, communism.

Were the 'Red hordes' of the Soviet Army about to fan out all over France? If so, the 11th Shock Troops, working in conjunction with SDECE, were to organize 'white' counter-insurgency units. Was the Communist Party preparing for insurrection? In 1947, during the widespread miners' strikes in Northern France, commandos of the 11th Shock were dispatched, clad in the uniform of Jules Moch's Gardes Mobiles, to familiarize themselves with social 'counter-subversion'. In reality, it was in Indo-China that they were to encounter communism.

From 1948 onwards Captain Aussaresses followed the usual career pattern of the time. For three years, with the 'Paras', he trained the shock units who were to organize the counter-insurgents against the Vietminh. In 1952 we then find him at the head of the celebrated B3 Section of Action Branch at Cercottes, which dealt with troop numbers, the provision of officers and instruction, and was assisted by a small 'brains trust' made up of Philippe Salmson, Robert Caillaud and Commandant ('Papa') Perrin. The

Section was to train hundreds of special agents, reserve cadres and operational officers.

There was no talk as yet of 'dealing with' (that is, executing) people or of 'the killer gang under FI' (Action team under a false identity: Equipe action sous Identité Fausse – IF). The Resistance was still represented. One could imagine that one was present at meetings of the association of former members of the BCRA Action group. Jacques Foccart was pleased to pay them a visit, and there came across another 'honourable correspondent', Roger Bellon, the head of the pharmaceutical trust of the same name. As and when necessary Father Guétct, a Benedictine who in the BCRA had been called 'Debrand', officiated at services for reservists. At the request of Morlanne, their leader, a young lawyer named Maître Jean Viollet attended some short practical courses. Didier Faure-Beaulieu, who was to replace Aussaresses in the training of Action Branch, worked with Louis L'Helgouach, Morlanne's assistant, and Nicole Follot, his secretary. L'Helgouach, a Breton, was later to distinguish himself brilliantly as station head of SDECE in the Eastern bloc countries. As for Nicole Follot, she was not the only woman in Action Branch. On the ski slopes at Toussus-le-Noble Elizabeth Lion, who richly lived up to her name, trained nurses to jump, as well as Morlanne's radio operators, among them Edith Fournier. And another incurable 'honourable correspondent' was Countess Vassilissa Salomé Evain Pavée de Vendeuvre.

Members of the strange small world of the secret war liked to take a drink at Luigi's Bar, in the Rue du Colisée, owned by Maurice Boymond. Who would have suspected that gathered there were the architects of all the clandestine operations in Indo-China and Algeria?

The 'Little Liars' of Colonel Belleux

Colonel Maurice Belleux, a flyer, had distinguished himself in the Resistance within the BCRA network 'Phratrie' ('Brotherhood') It was only natural that he should organize 'Hunter', an air intelligence group. He was the kind of officer who, unlike some of his colleagues, had his gaze resolutely fixed upon the future, a desirable trait, given the astounding progress made in his arm of the forces. A man of his calibre was needed to direct intelligence work in Indo-China. Clear-sighted and without political prejudices, until December 1947 Colonel Belleux familiarized himself with the work of SDECE. In the nerve centre on the Avenue Maunoury he took over the supervision of the central registry and the job of documentation and studies, compiling the intelligence syntheses derived from the work of two of the principal directorates: Research and Counter-Espionage. His team wrote up the analyses and the intelligence bulletins (Bulletins de Renseignement: BR), the 'little liars', as he humorously termed them, that were to land up on the desks, and often in the waste paper baskets, of ministers and the prime minister's Office.

When he was sent to Saigon at the end of 1947 his mission was clear-cut: to coordinate SDECE operations in the Far East, but not to intervene in any way in Indo-China, which came under the Sûreté Nationale, since SDECE was forbidden to work on 'French territory'.

The task was immense. China, his main target, was also immense. During the War the French secret services had established a link at Kunming with the head of the Guomindang's secret service, Tai Li. After Mao's victory in 1949 the forces of Chiang Kai-shek fell back on Taiwan: SDECE was to maintain a link with them, but realized that espionage in Nationalist China was henceforth a branch of the CIA, and therefore a less trustworthy source. From Hong Kong, even today still considered to be one of the best surveillance posts together with Tokyo, SDECE agents studied carefully the links between Red China and Ho Chi Minh. From within China itself clerics such as Father Maillot acted as SDECE informants. In Thailand SDECE agents competed with the small network set up in 1952 by Colonel Jacques Guillermaz, which worked directly with the Deuxième Bureau in Paris. He had arrived from Peking, where he was military attaché, and in the 1960s was to become, after a further stay in China, one of the best Sinologists and historians of the People's Republic.

Colonel Somer, head of Dutch Intelligence, could hardly have found a better ally than Maurice Belleux. In Jakarta, in accordance with the TOTEM agreements,[4] they exchanged intelligence information. Both were fighting communist guerrillas, and were mistrustful of their Anglo-American friends, always prepared to double-cross them. The Intelligence Service and the CIA were playing the decolonization card, hoping to supplant their two European allies. But in Malaya, a British colony, the Malay Races Liberation Army, led by a Chinese, Chin Peng, was hitting the British lion hard. The upshot was that Singapore became a market-place for TOTEM intelligence. And in Indo-China the CIA man, Bob Jantzen, and the SIS man, Trevor-Wilson, strengthened their links with SDECE.

There were a few flies in the ointment. General de Lattre de Tassigny violently criticized Trevor-Wilson and Graham Greene, his friend: 'These Intelligence Service agents are stabbing the French in the back.' The reality was more complex: Greene, who was guided round Indo-China by a former member of the Francs-Tireurs et Partisans, was preparing an explosive novel directed against the CIA. And Trevor-Wilson, 'the friend of France' – he had been a liaison officer with the French secret services in Algiers in 1943 – especially criticized the political orientation given to the French war.[5]

On the American side, there were contradictions. On a study mission for the CIA Colonel Mervin Hall recalled his admiration for France. A keen student of the French Middle Ages, he published article after article on Vézelay Cathedral and the pilgrimages to Santiago de Compostela. He even presented two superb Dakota planes, of South African origin, to Colonel Belleux, who – alas – was ordered to send them back to France for use by Action Branch.

Yet at the same time the behaviour of the CIA agents, who had maintained contact with the Vietminh, became disturbing. All at once their vehicles and apartments were mysteriously blown up – as a warning. Albert Meyer, the man who organized this firework display, knew the Americans well. Having been responsible during the war for the Swiss outpost of Intelligence Branch, he had come into contact with Allen Dulles, later the head of the CIA. Meyer, a future general, did not belong to SDECE but to the operational intelligence service (Service de Renseignement Opérationnel: SRO). Colonel Belleux was to learn the details of this story only later, in France, when Meyer became his assistant on the air force staff. He did not approve of this kind of operation, for, after all, the TOTEM exchanges with the Anglo-American allies were occasionally very useful. Belleux willingly assented to this: 'One example was when SDECE had infiltrated some excellent agents into China. They were providing good information about the Chinese Army and the Communist Party, etc. One day, within the framework of the TOTEM agreements, I spoke about this to our Anglo-American allies. What a surprise: these same agents were inventing information and selling it to everybody – information that paid big money but wasn't worth a piastre.'[6]

The Colonial Intelligence Service

In 1950, when the war in Indo-China was at its height, Colonel Belleux saw his responsibilities increased. Henceforth SDECE was to head all the intelligence organizations. It was about time: up to then a host of services flitted around here and there. André Bass, adviser to Léon Pignon, the High Commissioner, ran a miniature network of political and 'high society' intelligence. Also under the High Commission was a small service called the Technical Bureau for Liaison and Coordination (Bureau Technique de Liaison et de Coordination), which was found to be deeply involved in two scandals that were to shake the Fourth Republic: the affair of the generals, and the traffic in piastres. An officer in the colonial infantry, Commandant Maxime Maleplate, was the director of the Bureau in Paris, with Colonel Guy de Saint-Hilaire as deputy. He wrote:

At the beginning of 1948 M. Coste-Floret, who had been minister for France Overseas for only two or three months, had me attached to his office and told me: 'Having learnt from my experience at the Ministry of National Defence, I would be glad if you would study the organization of the secret services in the overseas territories.' I set up the Technical Bureau for Liaison and Coordination, but at ministerial level, that is at the level of the man responsible, who needed the documents, and was able to exploit the intelligence we received from the overseas territories. So I established no new posts: on the contrary I reduced staff to such an extent that this Bureau, half civilian, half military, at present comprises only three persons: an administrator, an officer who acts as my military assistant and is in charge of coding services, and myself.[7]

Thus it was a mini-service, but one that liked to tread on SDECE's 'patch'. Its head in Indo-China was another Marine, Colonel Maurice Labadie. He explained the limits of his duties:

I arrived in Indo-China in May 1950 to take over a newly instituted service entitled the General Directorate of Documentation for the High Commission of Indochina (Direction Générale de la Documentation du Haut-Commissariat de l'Indochine). Before this body was set up there had been a service known as the Technical Bureau for Liaison and Coordination (BTLC). In fact, because of its own statutes the Bureau was not in a position to obtain from the various services all the intelligence they gathered. Consequently at the request of M. Pignon, the High Commissioner, the authorities sought to establish a special structure, so as to ensure a bare minimum of centralization and coordination between the services. The object of my work remained roughly the same as that of the BTLC, but with a greater potential. Moreover – and this remained within the purview of the BTLC after its integration into the Directorate under my control – the BTLC had as its task to follow the activities of certain persons or associations who appeared intent on wiping out or reducing the Franco-Vietnamese war effort, and even favouring that of the Vietminh.[8]

Whilst giving this testimony, which had been provoked by the scandal of the trafficking in piastres, Colonel Labadie emphasized what was self-evident: 'There were – and still are – a very large number of services devoted to intelligence.'

The Traffic in Piastres

La Moqueuse did not defy the police for long. Arrested in 1948, the French ship was relegated to a corner of the port of Saigon. Pierre Périer, director of Security services in Indo-China, surveyed with satisfaction the 19 metal cases lined up on the quayside. They contained 15 million 'Ho Chi Minh' piastres, recognizable by their red colour. These coins, issued by the Vietminh, were worth less than the French piastres and were used in the areas conquered by the 'rebels'. In Hong Kong the Chinese half-breeds from Cochin China had specialized in trafficking in the red currency.

It was a windfall for the police. Unhesitatingly Pierre Périer busied himself with the transfer to Hong Kong of his precious cargo. As an additional security measure he used the diplomatic pouch of the High Commissioner at the time, Eugène Bollaert. But the plane was searched and everything discovered. For a long time afterwards the police chief could not see anything culpable in his actions. He scarcely even felt the need to justify himself: 'The secret funds I had available were clearly insufficient to deal with the situation. Certain police stations received absolutely nothing, others received only a few hundred piastres a month. In the atmosphere of insecurity that prevailed at the time it was impossible to carry on with so little money.'[9]

At the height of the Indo-China war the police services had absolutely no control over Mathieu Franchini and his gang of crooks who spent their afternoons swaggering along the terraces of the Hôtel des Nations or the Continental. Under the shaded lights of the Ferme des Jeux du Grand Monde or the Casino de Cholon false secret agents rubbed shoulders with genuine Vietminhs, and traffickers and politicians of every hue mixed freely. In Saigon the war was a billion-piastre bonanza. Industrialists rushed to make their fortunes. The famous restaurant owner Jacques Borel, then the IBM representative, made his first large business deals here. At the head of the airline Aigle Azur Extrême-Orient Sylvain Floirat, its manager – and the future head of Europe I, the radio network – set about building up his empire. The port of Saigon was booming, at the pinnacle of its splendour. But it was a veritable crossroads of corruption. On the Boulevard Charner, the main artery of the town, where, incidentally, SDECE had set up shop, every kind of trafficking flourished. The most considerable was in piastres. The piastre was worth 8 francs in Indo-China, but was exchanged in France at 17 francs. The cycle of fraud was simple. A dollar bought in Paris for 350 francs was worth 50 piastres in Saigon. The trick was to obtain a currency authorization transfer, and then to sell these piastres in France at the official rate of 17 francs. For an initial outlay of 350 francs, you picked up 850 francs. And then the whole merry-go-round could begin again.

In Haiphong, Phnom Penh and Saigon it was the Office Indochinois des Changes that granted the necessary authorizations. In fact, this office had little control over anything. Its scanty personnel – fewer than 15 – did not allow it to make any serious investigation. All in all, permits granted as 'favours' were plentiful. The matter was all the graver because the traffic extended to the sale of arms to the Vietminh. 'Our soldiers are falling to bullets sold by the traffickers,' according to a report to his superiors from Inspector de Nouillan, the youthful head of colonial intelligence (the BTLC) in Saigon. He submitted hundreds of reports to Colonel Maurice Labadie, the head of the General Directorate of Documentation (Direction Générale de Documentation: DGD), who, as we have seen, supervised all the secret services in Indo-China on behalf of the High Commissioner. All the documents were microfilmed and sent to Paris. But this, despite the protests of Marshal de Lattre de Tassigny, was not followed up by any concrete measures.

In Paris the Office Indochinois des Changes came directly under the Finance Ministry, and on the Rue de Rivoli they scarcely showed any sense of urgency in arriving at decisions. The traffickers benefited from the presence of accomplices even in the Office of Antoine Pinay himself. In spite of the advice tendered by the Indo-Chinese branches of the Office, Paris granted authorizations for some very curious transfers. Thus several million piastres came to replenish the coffers of the daily newspaper *L'Aurore* and those of the publishers Editions Richelieu. In France the latter's head office bought up thousands of crime novels at a bargain price, which were then sold in Saigon at the price indicated by the publisher. The branch naturally paid for them in piastres. Once the transfer had been authorized and the money banked, the volumes were simply pulped.

One day Jacques Despuech, a humble clerk in the Office des Changes, went of his own volition to the office of Inspector de Nouillan. He came to denounce trafficking by the Torre brothers, a pair of notable businessmen, who were re-selling material to the Vietminh. Some months later military supply officers at the port of Haiphong indeed noted a cargo of 100,000 wire-cutters that had been mislaid on a quay. They were destined for Vietminh troops in order to cut the barbed wire that surrounded the French garrisons. At the same time another inspector of the BTLC, Fernand Amédée Thierry, discovered that the director of the Franco-Chinese Bank was none other than the French treasurer for the Vietminh. But the reports served little purpose. Still the government did not act.

Disheartened, in autumn 1952 Jacques Despuech left Indo-China for France. He had lost his job in Saigon and had been the target of many threats of one kind and another. Back in Paris the former correspondent of the BTLC got his revenge by publishing a very well-documented book.[10] It caused a scandal. Parliament appointed a commission of enquiry under Frank Arnal, a Socialist. During their investigations the deputies themselves encountered some difficulties. In the Rue de Rivoli finance officials were forbidden to give evidence to the commission. In spite of this handicap, the members of Parliament made some startling discoveries. For example, over 17 million piastres had been transferred illegally to the account of the RPF. But Louis Terrenoire, the general secretary of the Gaullist party, refused to answer the investigators' questions. Finally it was the devaluation of the piastre from 17 to 10 francs, decided upon on 11 May 1953 by René Mayer, the Radical-Socialist, that put an end to this traffic. But the war in Indo-China had not finished producing its crop of scandals.

The Monks of Dalat

When, in December 1947, Colonel Belleux took charge of SDECE in Asia, one fact was very clear to him: the intelligence from human sources, coming from agents scattered from New Delhi to Tokyo, was very mediocre in quality. Moreover, the analysts, the station heads or case officers, were very often content to draw up their reports using the local press, the official government gazette, radio news flashes or rumours hawked around in the bars of Cholon and elsewhere. Finally, the protection of secrets was very poor. Each week the commanders of French army units in Indo-China received their 'little liar', the SDECE report, which was then passed from hand to hand.

Maurice Belleux intended to restore good order. Above all, with the technical assistance of Service 15 (transmissions) and Service 28 (transmissions, cipher, radio intercepts, decrypting), he thought up the most effective of all intelligence systems in the Indo-China war, with the exception of commando operations. It consisted of a vast organization for radio interception, reinforced by direction-finding cross-checks from Hong Kong and Taiwan. In Belleux's words:

As soon as I arrived I tackled these problems. At Dalat, dozens of men, grouped into an interception unit, devoted themselves to the task. For every code I set up two-man teams. They lived like monks: they were separated off, working feverishly, shut away until they had succeeded in breaking 'their' code. Then, and only then, did I send them off on leave to relax and rest. And through this system we obtained a 60–80 per cent success rate: the messages of the Vietminh general staff were decoded. Then we passed on the reports, so that they could be acted on. Unfortunately at GHQ there were many recipients who did not believe the reports. It was absolutely incredible. General Salan was one of those who gave us due credit for our work.

Thus, at the time of the Cao Bang disaster in 1950,[11] SDECE was able to reveal that eight Vietminh battalions were being trained in the People's Republic of China. The warning was not heeded in high places, where the enemy was underrated. Informed of this by his agents, General Giap was put on his guard. Six years later, shortly before Dien Bien Phu, the Vietminh changed their operational codes. But SDECE could still follow their movements because their supply and equipment codes had not changed. And by assessesing the volume of an army's material needs one can understand its movements.

The GCMA

Let us go back a little. At the beginning of 1950, when passing through Hanoi, Colonel Fourcaud, the technical director of SDECE, in conjunction with Léon Pignon, the High Commissioner, studied the possibility of setting up an Action Branch unit to enable an original form of offensive to be launched – guerrilla war against the Vietminh. In other words, certain sections of the population would be mobilized so as to catch them at their own game. The idea was not new: it arose from the commando operations of the Second World War, and French officers, just like the Vietminh political commissars, had devoured the works of Mao Tse-tung, who had just assumed power in China, concerning 'the people's war'.

Today Colonel Pierre Fourcaud admits it: 'I committed an enormous blunder. When de Gaulle withdrew from public life in 1946, Action Branch no longer existed. I had let it run itself down. Shortly afterwards I suggested to Morlanne that an Action Branch should be organized once more. On the SDECE establishment there were six posts to be filled. These constituted the first nucleus of an Action Branch.'[12] In reality the idea was inherited from the BCRA during the War.

For his part, the American 'big wheel' in the struggle against insurrection, Colonel Edward Landsdale, put up a similar suggestion to that of the French: to set up an Action Branch of their own. As the head of the CIA in Asia – Graham Greene has immortalized him in *The Quiet American* – he had just suppressed the revolt of the Huks, the communist guerrillas in the Philippines. But plainly his plan had an ulterior motive. From that time on the Americans set their sights on taking over from the French in Indo-China. Landsdale's suggestion was turned down, but the French authorities received logistic help from Washington all the same.

Installed in Saigon, first on the Boulevard Charner and then at the military camp, and using the cover of 'Fifth Section' of the EMIAT (Etat-Major Inter-Armées Terrestres: General Staff of Joint Land Armies), in theory SDECE subsumed the various intelligence services, military security, the operational intelligence service (Service de Renseignement Opérationnel: SRO) etc. Colonel Belleux was in charge of operations. As an expert on the races and national minorities in Indo-China Colonel Gracieux took over as the head of the General Directorate for Documentation (Direction Générale de la Documentation: DGD).

Having returned to headquarters, Colonel Fourcaud, with Colonel Morlanne head of Action Branch, appointed the first instructors for Ty Wan, the Action training school at Cape Saint-Jacques. General Belleux told us:

Shortly after the defeat at Cao Bang, I sent an urgent telegram to Henri Ribière, the SDECE director. Its terms were clear: 'This is the greatest defeat in our colonial history. We have six months left in which to review our policy from top to bottom; otherwise we shall have lost in Indo-China.' After Cao Bang, Colonel Fourcaud laid the basis for Action Branch. The idea was to train and equip, at Cape Saint-Jacques, commandos drawn from the Meo and Thai populations. We would have 120 parachute officers leading 40,000 to 50,000 guerrillas. But in my opinion, that structure was too military.[13]

In May 1951 Action Branch assumed the name of Mixed Airborne Commando Group (Groupement de Commandos Mixtes Aéroportés: GCMA). The GCMA was under the DGD and SDECE, but its troops were placed at the disposal of the High Commissioner, who delegated his powers to the GOC. In other words the GCMA operated under a dual command, the regular General Staff and SDECE. Its commander, Lieutenant-Colonel Edmond Grall, laid down a huge programme for these 'shock-troop commandos': guerrilla and counter-guerrilla warfare, the mobilizing of ethnic groups hostile to the Vietminh, raids to infiltrate and penetrate the enemy positions, intelligence in depth, the penetration of Quan Bao, the Vietnamese intelligence service,[14] sabotage and destruction of lines of communication, and abduction and assassination of enemy cadres. These GCMA commandos were quickly to become the *bête noire* of the Vietminh troops, so much so that Ho Chi Minh decided to throw his best divisions against the French Action Branch units.

The first large-scale operation, led by Captain Prévôt of the 11th Shock Troops, consisted in building an air base in September 1951 on the island of Cu Lao Rê, south of Da Nang, and a bridgehead for his small fleet of pinnaces. Like pirates from another age, his commandos intercepted junks crammed full of weapons and carried out raids up the coast.

From that time on Captain Paul-Alain Léger, who distinguished himself particularly in Algeria, and who assumed command of these operations in 1953, said:

I commanded a base on an island of Cape Guang Ngao which is called Cu Lao Rê, where I had 300 auxiliary Vietnamese paratroops. Using sea transport, we began the work of landing and infiltrating agents. We acted on information received, and occasionally our men were disguised as Bo Doî. Apart from my deputy and a few officers, the commandos were Vietnamese. At the same time the GCMA had changed its name to 'Mixed Intervention Group' (Groupement Mixte d'Intervention) and from December 1953 was under the orders of Colonel Trinquier. In it were to be found all the big names in Action Branch: Puy-Montbrun, Hentic and others. The GMCA ran all the counter-insurgency units in North Tonkin and Laos, as well as the groups on the high plateaux. In fact, I took part in two kinds of operations: landings in combination with naval commandos, for large-scale operations; and for the smaller ones, with the means at my own disposal – raids in pinnaces and junks.[15]

Meanwhile the GCMA had extended its connections to cover the whole of Indo-China, beginning with Thailand, the banks of the Delta and Annam. The links built up in Thailand were to be severed during the Vietminh offensive of October 1952. Along the Delta and the Chinese frontier, particularly at Tien Yen, for which Lieutenant Pierre Dabezies was responsible, they were temporarily put into cold storage. The links in Annam proved more effective; from the island of Honh Mê Captain René Bichelot, a veteran of the nucleus of men that had preceded Action Branch, organized raids along the coasts of Thanh Hoa. As we have seen, on the island of Cu Lao Rê, first Captain Prévôt and then Captain Léger launched their commandos on the Lien Khu V region. Finally, in the Kontum area Captain Pierre Hentic, and then Lieutenant Thébault, two Action Branch experts in counter-guerrilla warfare who were to prove their worth against the FLN in

Algeria, were working with the Hre tribes, and, with these indigenous peoples, breaking the main lines of Vietminh communications.

This was indeed the GCMA speciality: to recruit and provide cadres for those elements in the ethnic groups that hated the Annamites of the Delta, on whom the Vietminh forces relied. The task was easy on the Moi plateaux of South Annam, but more delicate with the Meo and Man mountain peoples, who, from 1,500 metres up, contemplated without interest the struggle between the Vietminh and the French expeditionary force.

Yet in 1952 General Giap's troops crossed the Red River. The result was that henceforth the Vietminh controlled whole regions that contained restless national minorities: the black, red and white Thais, the Yaos, the Lolos and above all the Meos. From the very beginning the Meos had jealously guarded their independence and set up their own clandestine groups to fight the communists. One objective was to to cause disruption behind the Vietminh lines.

Operation 'X': The SDECE Opium

The war was changing in nature. A new era, that of subversive warfare, was replacing conventional fighting. This explained the expansion in clandestine operations, particularly of GCMA missions. At the beginning of the 1950s some tough, innovative young officers were undermining the military arts of the old school. For them the Indo-China war proved to be a huge game of chess, in which politico-military action reigned supreme. One has only to read the writings on strategy of their main opponent, Vo Nguyen Giap, or those of Mao Tse-tung: power grows out of the barrel of a gun, but politics are at the command post. Whether French or Vietnamese, victory would fall to the one who could rally to his side the religious and ethnic groups that in Indo-China constitute a vast mosaic.

Among the foremost theorists of counter-subversive warfare and practitioners of covert operations, two men stand out. The first, Commandant Roger Trinquier, born in 1908, a graduate of the infantry school at Saint-Maixent, had learnt his lessons before the War on the Tonkin frontier. At Shanghai, as deputy to the commander of the French troops, in the eye of the hurricane, he had observed the struggle between the Reds and the Whites, between Mao Tse-tung and Chiang Kai-shek. Action Branch was not new to him: in 1946 he had led one of the 'Ponchardier commandos' in Indo-China. He returned to it after having been in charge of the Instruction Centre for colonial troops at Fréjus, his head full of sound theories regarding revolutionary warfare. An ascetic personality, a soldier-monk, a 'gut-reaction' anti-communist, and a leader of men, Trinquier was to make his name in Algeria as a strategist of counter-guerrilla warfare, according to the methods he set out in his book *La Guerre Moderne*.[16] Appointed deputy to

Colonel Grall in the GCMA in May 1953, Trinquier was to command all its special missions.

The second man, Captain Antoine Savani, was undoubtedly more pragmatic. An officer in the Deuxième Bureau, he undertook a detailed analysis of Indo-Chinese society. In 1945, in his *Notes sur les Binh Xuyen*, he made a study of the river pirates who were protecting Saigon, certain that such 'social banditry' could be won over to the French cause.[17] Independently of SDECE, the military intelligence section of the Deuxième Bureau constituted clandestine bands that rallied to the French side, including former Vietminh fighters. In Cochin China its head, Captain Savani, thus ensured the loyalty of the Binh Xuyen pirates. Such men had mastered the art of changing sides. During the Second World War they had served as auxiliaries to the Kempeitai, the Japanese Gestapo. Then they flirted with the Vietminh. Finally the Binh Xuyen offered their services to the French. The flag was of no importance – only the rewards counted.

Savani held Cochin China. Trinquier rallied the hill tribes and dug himself in on the high plateaux as far as the Chinese frontier. In 1954, with his GCMA, he was to lead over 40,000 irregulars. But these operations cost dear, and the funds voted in France were paltry.

Was it the need to obtain special funds or to win the support of the Meos that swung the decision to give the green light for Operation 'X'? Doubtless both at the same time. Colonel Trinquier recalled:

In particular, the plan envisaged the implantation of resistance groups capable of acting against the Vietminh rear. Touby Lyfoung, the Meos' customary chieftain, brought the support of his people, with their warrior traditions. But he imposed an economic condition: we were to provide the means of selling his country's opium crop. Certainly we could have virtuously refused to help the Meos solve their economic problem, and so thrown them straight into the enemy camp. But the communist authorities, for their part, had no scruples in buying up the opium crop and using this 'strong currency' in external markets.[18]

As we have seen, the GCMA was also attached to the expeditionary force, and therefore to General Raoul Salan, as well as to SDECE under Colonel Belleux. From 1951 to 1954 Operation 'X' was protected at the highest level. The process was as follows: GCMA officers attached to the Meo irregulars bought up at a competitive price the spring crop of poppy seed. A DC3 crammed full of this unusual cargo took off from Tan Son Nhut for the plain of Jars. In reality it unloaded its cargo at a secret air strip near Cape Saint-Jacques, where SDECE's Action Branch trained GCMA commandos. Trucks covered the 90 kilometres from the landing strip to Binh Xuyen headquarters in Saigon. Bandits and drug traffickers operated there without fear, for the good reason that they were the Saigon militia. Their military leader, Lai Van Sang, was the chief of police. And their supreme commander, Le Van Vien, was to become prime minister of

Vietnam in 1954. On paper SDECE had merely transferred the cargo to its
opposite number, the Deuxième Bureau, and that was all.

Alfred McCoy's testimony shows what really happened:

The Binh Xuyen ran two large factories for the preparation of opium in Saigon (one
was situated near their GHQ at the Y bridge in the Cholon quarter and the other
near the National Assembly). There they transformed the raw juice of the poppy into
a smokable product. Bandits distributed the treated opium to all the opium houses
and shops of Saigon and Cholon, several of which belonged to Binh Xuyen (the
others paid over a substantial share of their profit to gangsters in exchange for
protection). The Binh Xuyen shared the takings with Trinquier's GCMA and
Savani's Deuxième Bureau.[19]

If the Binh Xuyen did not succeed in selling all their opium, they disposed
of it through Chinese merchants who had connections in Hong Kong, and
through the representatives of the Union Corse, the local Mafia. The latter
dispatched it to their correspondents in Marseilles, four large families who
for 20 years made the drugs traffic headline news. The names of their
leaders are notorious: Joseph Orsini, a former Gestapo agent, linked to the
American Mafia; the brothers Jean and Dominique Venturi, whose partner
in Tangiers, Jo Renucci, also worked for SDECE; Antoine Guérini, an
occasional 'honourable correspondent' of SDECE; and finally, Marcel
Francisci.[20]

Undoubtedly Operation 'X' paid dividends in Indo-China. In the province
of Xieng Khouang, in Laos, the GCMA successfully ran the Meo resistance
against the Vietminh. Touby Lyfoung, the 'king of the Meos', and his deputy
Vang Pao (later leader of the anti-communist irregulars under the auspices
of the CIA) were entirely happy with the alliance with SDECE. But the drug
shipments to Marseilles reached American shores, and now Colonel
Landsdale, the CIA strategist, turns up again: in 1952 he carried out an
investigation on the spot and assembled a devastating file against the French.

It was at the time that an enquiry was ordered in Indo-China, without the
knowledge of the French public. Colonel Belleux, the SDECE head in
Saigon, decreed the seizure of the opium stocks stored on GCMA premises.
Worried at the possible repercussions of the operation that Grall and
Trinquier were running, he sent to Pierre Boursicot, the new SDECE
director at the Mortier HQ, a report that led to his being treated as a
'troublemaker'. Thirty years later he explained his position as follows:

The GCMA/GMI was under Colonel Grall, who knew Indo-China well. He was
aided by Commanders Trinquier and Rozenne (who was killed in North Africa).
During his enquiry Colonel Bertin, of military security, uncovered hundreds of kilos
of opium in the GCMA buildings. General Salan blamed us for it: in theory we
should have passed on the opium. But this opium, from Touby Lyfoung, had to be
bought by someone. If it had not been for SDECE, the Viets would have gained the
allegiance of the Meos. The opium was to have been sent in part to the 'Golden
Triangle' in Burma, with the help of the Chinese connection. If a slip-up occurred,

the CIA, and not SDECE, would have been involved. The Americans were being hoodwinked. Moreover, another part of the cargo was to have been dispatched by Bai Vien to the Roger Bellon pharmaceutical laboratories, on board Jacquier's planes. It was envisaged that Trinquier's operation would be covered by Salan. Yet in the end Colonel Grall was sentenced to 45 days' close arrest, which enabled his deputy, Trinquier, to replace him.[21]

And Roger Trinquier continued the operation, but doubtless with greater discretion. When the battle of Dien Bien Phu set in, Trinquier tried, within the framework of the Condor operation, to infiltrate five GCMA units from Laos to relieve the besieged garrison, but he failed.

On 8 May 1954 the Geneva Conference marked the beginning of the end. SDECE did not consider itself beaten. It decided that, 'if the Geneva talks should lead to a cease-fire the resistance should, if not continue their action, at least go underground, in order to constitute a possible force that could be used when circumstances required.'[22]

The Demise of the GCMA

The end of the GCMA was a sordid affair. The resistance bands built up by the French were abandoned, and the Vietminh troops went all out to destroy them. Some people still recall the desperate appeals over the air to the French, and then to the Americans, by these fighters, asking for arms and ammunition drops in order to face up to the communists. Acting on his own initiative, Commandant Trinquier, who had set up a Liberation Committee for the upper Red River, hoped that he could continue to harass the Vietminh after the Geneva agreements, and thus save the necks of thousands of maquis who had been armed by the GCMA.[23] In bad odour with SDECE in Paris because of various incidents, Trinquier was sentenced to ten days' close arrest, because 'he has taken initiatives of a political nature that were in no way urgent, without the authorization of higher authority.'

The final collapse of the GCMA justifies our dwelling upon another matter that former members of the secret services are loath to recall: the desertion of GCMA officers to the Vietminh, which affected the whole of the French Army, in which a clandestine organization existed of soldiers belonging to the French Communist Party. Roger Trinquier mentioned the case of Captain Banhiot, of the GCMA Deuxième Bureau, who ran the Tien Yen station, which then passed to Lieutenant Pierre Dabezies. A former lieutenant-colonel in the Lyons section of the Francs-Tireurs et Partisans, one day in 1952 Banhiot was summoned before the general staff to answer accusations levelled against him concerning his precise role in the Resistance. He went over to the Vietminh at the little town of Luc Nam.[24] The historian Yves Roucaute states that a semi-official decision had been taken to execute certain communist officers. He gives names, and adds: 'At other times it was to their own coolness that soldiers owed their lives. Thus Captain Richon, a former lieutenant-colonel in the Francs-Tireurs et Partisans, as if in a "B movie" fired more quickly than the sergeant-major who had orders to liquidate him, and wounded him.'[25] After numerous enquiries the present authors are convinced that this man was in fact Captain Richonnet, who had led the first Laotian commando in 1946, formed from elements of the DGER, and who then entered the GCMA and was officially posted missing on 12 September 1952. Likewise it would be interesting to learn in what conditions Captain David, of the GCMA, disappeared on 26 June 1954.

Finally, a former head of the Deuxième Bureau, General Henri Jacquin, drew our attention to a strange story. As he told it:

On 15 January 1954 a GCMA captain deserted.[26] As an officer responsible for counter-espionage within the GCMA, he had knowledge of reports derived from radio intercepts. He was living with a Vietnamese woman, by whom he had several children. His desertion did not seem greatly to have surprised Trinquier, to whom I spoke about it. He remained in Indo-China after the Geneva agreements, in the North, where an American journalist met him. He confirmed to the journalist that he had joined the Vietminh out of idealism, and had alerted them that the French forces at Dien Bien Phu had been warned of an imminent attack. He was taken to the scene of operations and showed Giap the French preparations to go over to the offensive. Giap put off his own offensive.[27]

The match had merely been postponed.

The Treason of the Generals

It occurred in Paris near the Gare de Lyon, on 17 September 1949. On the platform of the 91 bus a fight broke out. Thomas Perrez, a soldier back from Indo-China, violently attacked Do Dai, a Vietnamese.[28] The police intervened and took the two protagonists to the police station. In the briefcase of the Vietnamese, who turned out to be the president of the Vietnamese Association in Paris, they discovered a copy of a document marked 'Top Secret: Defence'. It was a report signed by Revers, the chief of staff of the French Army.

In May 1949 Henri Queuille, the Radical prime minister, had sent General Revers to carry out an investigation in Indo-China. There, on the ground, the situation was none too bright. The expeditionary corps, torn between conflicting orders, had not succeeded in putting a stop to Vietminh agitation. Accompanied by Colonel Fourcaud, SDECE's 'Number Two', General Revers undertook a lengthy tour of Indo-China.

As soon as he returned to France the chief of staff drew up a very severe report concerning both the lack of coherence in French policy and the corruption of Emperor Bao Dai's regime in Vietnam. The general recommended a single command for Indo-China, wielding both civil and military powers. On Fourcaud's advice he also suggested dispatching special units of SDECE, comprising members both of Intelligence and Counter-Espionage branches, as well as Action troops. This was to constitute the future Mixed Airborne Commando Group (GCMA).

Revers's document was put into its final form on 29 June. Fifty copies carrying the 'Top Secret' classification were printed at the Ecole Militaire. Fifteen soldiers of the Garde Mobile were specially assigned to mount guard over the operation, directed by Captain Georges Rohmer, head of the army printing service. As printing proceeded the printing-blocks were burnt. Finally, 35 copies were distributed against a receipt. However, very quickly rumours circulated that the contents had been disclosed. Commandant Maleplate, the head of Colonial Intelligence, informed the government that he was in possession of the notorious document, with its three annexes. A telegram from Saigon informed Paul Coste-Floret, Minister for the Colonies, that the 'Voice of Vietnam' radio station was broadcasting the political conclusions of the report in Tonkinese.

Then catastrophe struck. The brawl in the bus and the arrest of Do Dai clearly showed that the Vietnamese colony in Paris had knowledge of the document. Roger Wybot, head of the DST, was officially commissioned to conduct an enquiry. In Do Dai's address book DST inspectors found a large number of Vietnamese names. They included Trang Ngoc Banh, the representative of Ho Chi Minh in Paris, who had taken the wise precaution of fleeing to Prague. Copies were also seized at the house of Vin Xa, a Vietnamese favourably disposed towards Ho Chi Minh, although he claimed to be a cousin of Emperor Bao Dai.

On the morning of September 20 the DST searched the premises of the Vietnamese delegation in Paris. The Revers report, in typed form, was spread out on a table, together with 38 other roneoed copies. The police haul was not yet complete. The delegation head, Huang Van Co, possessed two other copies at his personal residence. Moreover, at the house of this adviser to Emperor Bao Dai the police unearthed a very curious account book, in which against certain sums of money were entered against the names of several French politicians.

When interrogated at the DST offices Van Co asserted that he had been handed the document by a certain Roger Peyré. The latter, brought in his turn to the Rue des Saussaies, confessed immediately. He had obtained the report from General Mast, Director of the Institute for Higher Studies in National Defence (Institut des Hautes Etudes de la Défense Nationale: IHEDN).[29] In exchange the general had allegedly received a million francs to promote his candidacy for the post of High Commissioner in Indo-China. It was a spicy affair, all the more so because Roger Peyré declared that he had handed over the sum of money to General Revers so that he might support the candidacy of his friend Mast. Nobody at the DST was ready to believe all this, although Roger Peyré's address book looked like a copy of the social register. But so many glittering connections contrasted with the modest appearance of this little, bald-headed man. However, the evidence was there, and could not be ignored. At Peyré's home in the Rue de Prony Wybot's inspectors seized numerous letters signed by General Revers. The two men belonged to the same masonic lodge.

Roger Wybot was now convinced of the importance of the affair. For a connoisseur in such matters, there was the unsavoury odour of a political scandal. He immediately notified Jules Moch, the Minister of the Interior. The government was greatly embarrassed. At a time when the North Atlantic Treaty had just been signed, it would be inappropriate for the scandal to become publicly known, because it would risk upsetting France's powerful American ally. In contrast to Moch, the Socialist, who advocated an exemplary punishment, the Radical Henri Queuille, the prime minister, plumped for moderation. Paul Ramadier, the Socialist Minister of Defence, for his part came round to the view of the head of government. Some days later he affirmed that the report was not subject to military secrecy, and therefore leaking it could not constitute grounds for a charge of endangering the external security of the State.

On 23 November an ordinance was promulgated stating that there was no case to answer. Roger Peyré and his accomplices left the Cherche-Midi prison. Even better, the principal witness in the 'affair of the Generals' was authorized to retrieve most of the documents seized at his home. On 6 October, the Queuille cabinet fell. Georges Bidault, the MRP leader, formed a new government. Do Dai fled to Prague to join Ngoc Banh. On 30 November Roger Peyré was allowed to sail for Brazil without hindrance.[30] Generals Mast and Revers were placed discreetly on the retired list.

The Conjuring Colonel

Roger Peyré had been an SDECE agent, recruited at the end of the War and given the number AP 475. The affair of the generals flared up again. Two days before Christmas 1949 the weekly magazine *Time*, acting on a report from its Paris correspondent Jacques Laguerre, a fiercely militant Gaullist, published a violent attack on General Revers. Not only was the chief of staff responsible for important military leaks but, according to the American periodical, these had been passed on to Russia. A scandal broke out. On 17 January the new prime minister, Georges Bidault, was obliged to reveal the story to the National Assembly. The deputies immediately decided to set up a committee of enquiry.

Pierre Fourcaud recounted the following story to the astounded deputies: 'Peyré's contacts with our Paris station go back to 1 September 1944, at the time when Commandant Paillole was in charge of military security.

We uncovered the "Amado" affair (a conspiracy mounted by former collaborators) as a result of information provided by Peyré, himself a former collaborator, and we proceeded to make some 40 arrests.'[31] Recruited by Lieutenant Rollet, the new agent had as successive controllers Captains Sapin-Lignières and Schaeffer. From then on he worked regularly for the Paris base of the secret services under Colonel Jonglez and then Lieutenant-Colonel Leroux. With the active assistance of the secret services Roger Peyré attempted to open a gaming club in the basement of the Gramont Theatre. Colonel Morand, who shortly afterwards was dismissed from SDECE because of 'financial misappropriations', spared no effort to realize this project. French counter-espionage used these playgrounds to trap foreign diplomats. A few weeks before the affair of the generals broke, Roger Peyré had in fact been given the task of contacting several members of the Yugoslav embassy in Paris. His mission was only interrupted when the scandal unexpectedly broke.

As the parliamentary commission probed the underworld depths of the secret services, it was stunned to discover the poor coordination and muted rivalries that afflicted the various intelligence bodies. Although not officially dealing with the affair, SDECE was implicated up to the neck, because Roger Peyré was among its personnel. It was Henri Trautmann, head of Research Branch, who gave this dismaying piece of news to Henri Ribière. The SDECE director then asked 'Verneuil', head of Counter-Espionage, to contact Peyré and learn more about the leaks to the Vietminh.[32] In ordering this fresh enquiry Henri Ribière did not yet know that he had launched the French services on a fateful course.

On Verneuil's orders Captain Girardot, a specialist in the struggle against the Eastern bloc countries, who had already acted as controller to Peyré on his Yugoslav mission, got in touch with him again. On the night of 13 or 14 October, the officer even proceeded to carry out a fresh interrogation. A report was drawn up and on 20 October it was handed to Henri Ribière, who passed it on to Roger Wybot, the head of the DST. It appears that this new interview revealed nothing that was not known already: it agreed with the first statement that Peyré had made in the DST offices.

What Ribière and Wybot did not know was that Captain Girardot had submitted two very distinct reports. One went via Counter-Espionage and the usual channels up to the head of SDECE. The other was handed over to Colonel Fourcaud who delivered it in person to the government. Ribière and Wybot were never to see this second document. But it contained a totally different version of Peyré's interrogation. It completely exonerated General Revers. According to this document Roger Peyré denied ever having passed money to the general.

In fact, it was on Fourcaud's orders that Captain Girardot had altered his second version. Later he was to confess that it was because of a mission. Before the deputies he admitted that he had been manipulated by the deputy director: 'Colonel Fourcaud told me that at all events his [Revers's] name must not be dragged in the mud, defamed, or put at risk of being compromised.'[33] Having been present at the interview in Counter-Espionage offices on the Boulevard Mortier, Captain Vaudreuil bore out this viewpoint: 'Colonel Fourcaud placed the general above all suspicion. He stressed the general's importance internationally.'[34]

What were the reasons for all this manoeuvring? What were the motives that impelled Colonel Fourcaud? First, he had purely personal reasons. This hot-headed Slav had not forgiven the socialists for having appointed one of their number, Henri Ribière, to head SDECE. He was conceited enough to feel that the top job was his by right. Through this tortuous affair he was attempting to get rid of his chief by discrediting him with the political authorities. At the same time he was very much attached to General Revers, whose views on Indo-China he shared. With the complicity of Jacques Locquin,[35] the head of the European Press Agency (which had just launched a weekly entitled *Synopsis*), he spread the wildest rumours about Ribière.

In reality, there was no second affair of the generals. From the very first interrogation Roger Wybot, the head of DST, had unravelled all the threads in a matter of hours, tracing things back to Generals Mast and Revers.[36] But Queuille, the prime minister, had not wished to punish them publicly. It was this wish to hush up the scandal that caused the affair to explode. When the deputy director had handed over the second 'Peyré' version to the new prime minister, the MRP leader Georges Bidault, the latter had not been displeased at being able to place the Socialists, Moch and Ramadier, in a difficult position. On the commission of enquiry the various political parties were to show themselves more anxious to pay off personal scores than to seek out the truth. The *Delahoutre Report* was presented to the Chamber of Deputies on 22 November. After a particularly stormy session the Socialist Jules Moch escaped by a hair's breadth from having to appear before the High Court. Parliament utterly lost its head and contemplated punishing the only minister who had displayed any firmness since the beginning of the affair. As for Colonel Fourcaud, he was discreetly removed from SDECE. So too was Henri Ribière, a sick and terribly disappointed man, who said: 'I did everything I could. I defended the interests of my services against everybody.'[37]

The Republic that 'Leaked'

Encircled in the Dien Bien Phu basin, bombarded by day, and harassed every night by thousands of determined Vietminh troops, the 15,000 men of the French garrison went through hell. Dien Bien Phu fell on 7 May 1954. It was at this exact moment that General Raoul Salan chose to give the press some new military information. He could not bear having been replaced as head of the French forces in Indo-China by General Henri Navarre in May 1953. It was with an especially critical eye that he had just participated in a government fact-finding mission to Vietnam, accompanied by Generals Ely, Pelletier and Navarre.

'One day,' said Henri Noguères, the lawyer who then headed the Central Press Agency (Agence Centrale de Presse: ACP), 'Raoul Salan asked me to come and see him at his private address. He handed a file to me, saying, "Read this carefully," and left me alone in the room. The file contained a very confidential military report. When Raoul Salan returned I said to him, "Well, general, you were right to show me this file, but, aware of the military interests at stake, I shan't pass it on." Plainly,' concluded Henri Noguères with a laugh, 'that was not at all what Salan was hoping for. Less than a week later, *L'Express* used the documents I had read.'[38] On 27 May 1954 Jean-Jacques Servan-Schreiber's weekly in fact published, with a great splash, an unsigned article by General Salan that divulged the gist of the report submitted to the government by General Ely on his return from Indo-China. In the event the leak came from an identifiable source, which cannot be said of the leaks that came later.

On 2 July 1954, Christian Fouchet, the Minister for Moroccan and Tunisian Affairs, urgently requested an interview with the prime minister. This convinced Gaullist informed Pierre Mendès-France that the Communist Party possessed a complete report of the most recent meeting of the Higher Defence Committee. This committee, whose headquarters were at 51, Avenue de Latour-Maubourg, was ultra-secret. It discussed both the developments in the war in Indo-China and the first steps being taken towards a French nuclear weapon. All its decisions were in the 'classified' category, 'Top Secret: Defence'. The ministers involved in the questions discussed, as well as the military 'top brass', were normally present at the meetings, which were organized by the Permanent General Secretariat of National Defence (Secrétariat Général Permanent de la Défense Nationale: SGPDN). All the personnel involved underwent military security vetting. The head of the SGPDN at the time was Jean Mons, formerly Resident-General in Tunisia. It was this reserved and rather austere man who, after each meeting, drew up the minutes of the Committee's decisions.

Ostensibly the Republic's secrets were well guarded. Leaks seemed to be unthinkable. Pierre Mendès-France was aghast – particularly because he learnt that this was not the first time it had happened. Leaks had already occurred in February and May. But Joseph Laniel had not breathed a word about it when he had handed over the reins to him. It was as if he did not trust his successor. The last meeting of the Defence Committee had taken place on 28 June. On 2 July Pierre Mendès-France received an exact report on it from Christian Fouchet. The documents had clearly been passed on with incredible speed. This point struck Mendès-France, who instructed André Pelabon, the head of his Private Office, to mount an enquiry that was to be as discreet as possible. Pierre Mendès-France even refused to allow François Mitterrand, the Minister of the Interior, to be informed. It was only at the end of the summer that the head of the government finally told him what was brewing. Another meeting of the Defence Committee was to be held on 10 September. A subject of prime importance figured on the agenda: the initial stage in making the French atomic weapon.

As soon as he learnt about these leaks, François Mitterrand assembled his closest colleagues, among them André Dubois, the prefect of police, and Roger Wybot, the head of the all-powerful DST. Their task was twofold: to find out who had informed Christian Fouchet and to discover the origin of the leaks. Roger Wybot had no difficulty in solving the first conundrum. It was Superintendent Jean Dides who had handed over the file. He was in charge of Section 7 at the Préfecture de Police, which was especially concerned with communist affairs. He was a militant of the extreme Right, who had salvaged part of the archives of Doriot's PPF and of Vichy itself. Moreover, he had taken on to his staff a former criminal, Alfred Delarue, a onetime inspector in the Renseignements Généraux, a member of the infamous 'special brigades' who from 1942 onwards had been engaged in hunting down communists. He had succeeded in piecing together the anti-communist records of the Préfecture de Police during the Occupation.

The DST also tracked down Dides's informant. He was André Baranès, a parliamentary journalist on the newspaper *Libération*, the progressive daily directed by Emmanuel d'Astier de la Vigerie. For four years he had been the Prefecture's favoured source on the Communist Party. This affable, smooth-talking little man from Constantine had managed to win over leading officials in the Ministry of the Interior: the two Jeans – Baylot and Dides – swore by him. He was a valuable agent. Had he not stolen a personal telegram from Stalin off Jacques Duclos's own desk? Better still, it was he who, under the Laniel government, had been appointed to head the enquiry into the first leaks concerning national defence. Was he not best placed to know who had brought the precious documents to the Communist Party? To set up another enquiry might compromise this talented informant, to whom the Prefecture was paying impressive sums. One might say that at the time Baranès reigned supreme over the Paris police.

For Roger Wybot, an intelligence fanatic and a true professional, the story did not hang together. He asked his inspectors to follow both Dides and Baranès. But on 9 September his men came up against a police patrol from the Prefecture outside Baranès's home. The two groups came to blows. That very day Jean Mairey, director of the Sûreté Nationale, requested Roger Wybot to stop following Baranès: the Prefecture would take this over. The detail was not unimportant. The shadow of the Baylot–Dides duo loomed over this initial manoeuvre.

The next day another meeting of the Committee took place. On 18 September Superintendent Dides contacted Christian Fouchet again. A meeting was arranged at the ministry. There Roger Wybot, following Mitterrand's instructions to the letter, arrested the superintendent, who had in his possession a summarized version of the latest Defence Committee meeting. André Baranès was arrested in turn. In his house were found several reports of the Committee meetings. The manuscripts were in rough, without any annotations by the communist leaders. Henceforth it was clear that the documents had never passed through Communist Party HQ in the Rue Châteaudun. There was another surprise: the Baranès papers were an exact reproduction of the notes taken by Jean Mons, the man in charge of the Permanent General Secretariat of National Defence. Roger Wybot had both the originals in his hands.

There was no doubt that the Baranès trail led back to Jean Mons. This distinguished senior civil servant, a personal friend of Pierre Mendès-France, was summoned in his turn to the Rue des Saussaies. The head of the DST interrogated him remorselessly, bringing to light numerous contradictions. Two other officials of the SGPDN, René Turpin and Roger Labrusse, were likewise brought to the DST buildings. The first was Mons' private secretary. As for sub-prefect Labrusse, he had never concealed his opinions. He proudly asserted that he belonged to the management committee of the Union Progressiste and contributed regularly to *Libération*. A determined and militant pacifist, he was ready to sacrifice himself for his ideals. He confessed to having provided Baranès – and also d'Astier de la Vigerie, who thus acquired a leading role in the affair of the leaks – with information concerning the Defence Committee meetings. René Turpin had been copying the notes taken by Mons at the Committee. On the other hand both men asserted that the secretary-general himself was in ignorance of this. Roger Wybot, head of the DST, was never to accept this version as true. But after a lively trial Mons, the high official, was whitewashed and effectively allowed to resume his career.

A Secret Note to Mendès-France

While the war in Indo-China was tailing off, SDECE continued its work. A 'Confidential Note for Prime Minister Mendès-France', dated 13 November 1954 and classified 'Top Secret', which was written by a high official in the Ministry for Associated States, threw a penetrating light on what was to happen to Indo-China in the next 30 years. It ran:

From an interview I had today with a SDECE senior officer it would appear: (1) that the prime movers in US policy in Vietnam may be the secret service (Mr Allen Dulles's CIA), and in particular Colonel Landsdale (who arrived in Vietnam two months before the appointment of Ngo Dinh Diem, and who 'installed' President Magsaysay in the Philippines . . . (2) that these persons, determinedly hostile to French influence, may have persuaded Washington that it would be sufficient for the nationalists to take over power and for the French to withdraw, for the population in the South to bestir themselves and make common cause against the communists in the North.

Moreover, in Bangkok a certain Colonel Thomson, also a member of the US secret service and a great adventurer, may be supporting Prince Petsarah against the present king of Laos and Prince Savang, in spite of the denials made to us. It would not be too far-fetched to think that he was the real instigator of the recent assassination of the Laotian Minister of War. His attachment to Petsarah may be linked to interests relating to the opium traffic originating in the northern plateaux of Thailand.

From the same source, intelligence considered to be reliable establishes that Ho Chi Minh always takes his lead from Moscow, but never from Peking. My informant considers that the leaders of the Democratic Republic of Vietnam are indeed communists, but that their regime, particularly after being reunited with the South, might well become stabilized, and its institutions settle midway between those of the free world and the communist world.'[39]

Thus, even as it was folding up its networks during the French retreat, SDECE foresaw with uncanny perceptiveness the second war in Indo-China, the real role of the United States, and then the conflicts between Vietnam and China.

6

The Secret War in the Maghreb

On 22 October 1956, at the height of the war in Algeria, the French secret services seized the aeroplane of Ben Bella, the head of the Front de Libération Nationale (the FLN). In school children are taught that: 'The initiative of an irresponsible officer immediately soured our relations with Morocco.'[1] Thus history has been written for 30 years. An impulse, a warning, a strong-arm action. 'Ben Bella should not have been kidnapped,' the socialists declared in October 1956. 'It was the initiative of an irresponsible officer.'

'Ben Bella should not have been kidnapped,' a former high official of SDECE confirmed for the first time. 'And for the very good reason that we had received orders to assassinate him, a year and a half previously. After several failed attempts, we seized the first opportunity to get hold of him. Hence the first hijack in the history of aviation.' Colonel Germain's statement was categorical. This astonishing episode began in the spring of 1955.

Mission 'Out'

Edgar Faure, who was preparing for independence for Tunisia and Morocco, decided to announce a state of emergency in Algeria in order once and for all to crush the 'rebellion'. Cabinet meetings and interministerial meetings followed one another. On 11 May 1955, an 'inter-ministerial decision' was agreed that aimed at the 'neutralization' of the principal leaders of the FLN. SDECE was charged with executing it. The General Directorate entrusted the task to Colonel Morlanne's Action Branch and to a special delegation set up in Algiers whose sphere of action was defined as 'the African arena'. 'Neutralization' of the FLN leaders, for any secret service in the world, meant 'physical liquidation'. The operation lived up to its name: Mission 'Out'.

The head of this operation, Germain, a history professor, belonged to that astonishing breed of intelligence officers who would doubtless have remained in civilian life, but whom the world conflict had propelled towards a world of shadows. In 1942 he had been the deputy in Algiers to the head of Counter-Espionage, Colonel Paillole. He collaborated with the US Office of Strategic Services and with the SIS Head of Station in Algiers, Trevor-Wilson, as well as Kim Philby, who often visited North Africa, sent by SIS Headquarters! There he took part in vast inter-Allied disinformation operations, at the same time assembling the famous records that were to make possible the hunting down of Nazis after the Liberation. Having joined the DGER and then SDECE, Germain remained as assistant to Colonel Verneuil, the director of Counter-Espionage Branch. Then he left headquarters in 1951 to become director of the counter-espionage station in Tunis, where he was backed by a permanent resident, Commandant Paul Conty.

At Christmas 1954, I tried to imagine what the following year would be like. In 1954 Mendès-France, the prime minister, had come to Tunis, accompanied by Marshal Juin, and on 31 July, in his 'Carthage speech', he had promised internal autonomy. A little later, on 1 November, the Algerian 'rebellion' broke out: 1955 could not therefore fail to be a difficult year. As for myself, I was hoping to be promoted to the next rank. My friend the minister, Jacques Chevallier, had promised to get me put on the promotion list. As long ago as 1941 he had put me up when I was running the counter-espionage station in Algiers, and after 8 November 1942 he had served under my command, in the same town, at the Directorate of Military Security. How was the Algerian question, which risked assuming international dimensions, going to develop? Closer to home, the Tunisian problem was likely to go beyond internal autonomy and end in independence. Under these conditions, it was appropriate for me to consider what new form should be given to counter-espionage in the region.[2]

The questions raised by Colonel Germain, at any rate those concerning his immediate future, received a reply: Louis Lalanne, the director of the office of SDECE's head, arrived in Tunis. With effect from 1 June 1955, Germain was posted to Algiers. Before then he went to Paris headquarters on the Boulevard Mortier, in order to study in outline the instructions for Mission 'Out', which was to last almost three years.

Germain put forward suggestions. His *modus operandi* was to be independent of the SDECE organization in Africa; his ultra-secret mission would be solely under the General Directorate – in fact, under Lalanne. Nevertheless, Germain's branch was to be represented a little later in the new intelligence structure that had been adapted to Algeria, the Inter-Army Coordination Centre (Centre de Coordination Interarmées: CCI), directed by his friend Colonel Léon Simoneau. Working at the point where Counter-Espionage and Action Branches intersected, he would have access to 'technical means', from telephone-tapping services to the use of commandos of the 11th Shock Troops. As for the rest, the man who was already called 'the Peaceful Father' was to be left to use his connections and social skills to forge links with various networks and create his own, as well as to secure his communications with the general staff and the governor-general.

SDECE had drawn up a list of six men to be 'neutralized'.[3] For four of them the task fell to Commandant Germain; the other two remained as targets for Action Branch at Headquarters. In memorandum No. 546 of 13 July 1955, Pierre Boursicot gave the green light to Mission 'Out'. In Algiers Germain had already set to work. He installed himself in a modest office in the Charron barracks, aided by the station head of Counter-Espionage Branch, Lieutenant-Colonel Nougaret. He gathered round him a small team: a deputy; an NCO from Tournai as cipher clerk; sergeant-major 'Désiré'; one of the five sons of Jacques Chevallier to act as secretary; and a sailor as his driver. To 'close in on his objectives' Lieutenant-Colonel Germain (after Tunis he had been promoted to this rank) thus had at his disposal all the counter-espionage posts in North Africa,[4] and could call upon the 11th Shock Troops, based in Kabylia, liaising with Action Branch under Captain Erouard.

Germain had a cover that fitted in well with his former occupation as a professor: 'The School and University Liaison Service' (And in fact he worked with his former schoolmate Lucien Paye, a member of Robert Lacoste's staff, on the creation of new Algerian departments, and recruited 'honourable correspondents' among university graduates introduced to him by his sister, the headmistress of the girls' secondary school in Oran.) His first 'action' network, Network A, was to assist him in mounting operations, including attacks on the targets of Mission 'Out', the first name on the list being that of Ahmed Ben Bella. Its leader was André Achiary, who was paid monthly by SDECE to locate Ben Bella and his men.

André Achiary, Called 'Baudin'

This white Algerian of Basque origin had the secret action virus in his blood. Before the war he had headed the DST in Algiers. Though a Gaullist from the very beginning, he worked with Counter-Espionage, under Colonel Paillole, and with his deputy in Algiers, Germain. On 7 November 1942 he became the ruler of the city by seizing the main police station on the Boulevard Baudin – hence his nickname in SDECE. He took part in the plot that allowed de Gaulle to gain control of North Africa, just as in 1958 he was to take part in the plot that hastened the General's return to power. He then joined up with the head of Special Services, Jacques Soustelle, as well as with the mayor of Algiers, the liberal politician Jacques Chevallier.[5] It was the time of the so-called 'D Measures', the execution of traitors and collaborators, and Axis agents: corpses floated on the waters of the Bay of Algiers.

For Achiary the secret war did not stop on 8 May 1945. Nor did it stop for the Algerians. The Sétif riots of 1945 caused the deaths of 20,000 Arabs – the official figure – as reprisals for the murder of 104 Europeans. As Sub-Prefect of Guelma, André Achiary had led the repression. He was to be imprisoned, then freed through the intervention of his friend Chevallier. His life of adventure started again and proceeded at a headlong pace, amid the acrid fumes of opium and the crack of revolver shots. Then came All Saints' Day 1954 and an outbreak of attacks by the newly founded FLN. He placed himself at the disposal of his former leader at the DGSS, Jacques Soustelle, the governor-general. Achiary was needed by anybody who wished to control the situation. From his house in the Rue Saint-Saëns he pulled the strings of a thousand networks. He could equally well organize a triumphal departure for Soustelle as, in February 1956, he could mount a resounding conspiracy, when Guy Mollet wanted to install Catroux as the new governor-general. This was 'the tomato demonstration'. Through his informants in criminal circles he fought the FLN unremittingly.

Then he was also a close acquaintance of Dr René Kovacs, the leader of the Organization for Resistance in French Algeria (Organisation de la Résistance de l'Algérie Française: ORAF), a group of activists. Sporadic operations began: on 10 August 1956 there was the bombing in the Rue de Thèbes.[6] The commando group that carried out the attack was not unknown to SDECE. Thus Philippe Castille, who placed the bombs, was a former member of the training section in Action Branch, and was still a reserve officer in SDECE. The man who had founded the counter-terrorist groups, Jo Rizza – called 'The Hedgehog' – was contacted as early as November 1954 by an SDECE network led by Lieutenant Gaby Allenan from the Villa Madeleine, situated on the heights above Algiers. Allenan was to be stripped of his position after the attack in the Rue de Thèbes, and went on to join the Secret Army Organization (Organisation de l'Armée Secrète: OAS). It was not an operation commissioned by SDECE, but one mounted independently by former agents. It had terrible immediate consequences: on 30 September bombs were planted by the FLN in the centre of the town.

The same team of Achiary, Castille and Kovacs, with several other future leaders of the OAS, organized the failed bazooka attack on General Salan of 16 January 1957.[7] Yet, besides these semi-official operations, André Achiary assisted his friend Colonel Germain, the Algiers head of SDECE. The latter did not hold himself bound by the freelance activities of his agent. 'Baudin' set up his Network A, consisting of informants. In accordance with his assignment Germain pursued the lengthy task of tracking down the leaders of the 'rebellion'. Within the framework of Mission 'Out', he also called upon members of Action Branch and the telephone-tapping service directed from the Rue Michelet by Captain Tesseyre.

Target Ben Bella

On several occasions the teams of Mission 'Out' came close to assassinating Ben Bella. Did he know that he was being hunted? In any case, since moving to Cairo he had been acting openly under his real name. At the beginning of the summer of 1956 Achiary personally mounted an operation in Tripoli, where the head of the FLN was due to go. But the killer given the task of shooting him down failed to keep the appointment.

In October 1956, whilst in Paris feverish preparations were being made for the Suez operation, Lieutenant-Colonel Germain finally hoped to achieve his aim. Within a few days he was to orchestrate the first air hijack in history, and secure the person of 'Target A', as designated by SDECE. On 16 October 1956 Ben Bella was in Nador, in the Spanish Sahara. He was expecting to take delivery of the considerable cargo of arms being transported in the hold of the British-built minesweeper *Athos*, then flying the Sudanese flag, which was officially carrying material destined for the Moroccan Liberation Army. Major Fathi Ed Dib, the head of the Maghreb section of the Egyptian secret services, was personally supervising the transportation of 70 tonnes of weapons, enough to equip 3,000 men. The SDECE station in Beirut announced the departure of the ship. Cairo signalled that it called at Alexandria. The head of the Intelligence station in the Egyptian capital, Colonel Georges de Lannurien, was following the trail of the ship's owner, Ibrahim ben Mohamed ben Mayel. Back in July his counterpart in Berne, the 'commercial attaché', Marcel Mercier, had informed headquarters that a considerable lump sum had been paid into the account of the Sudanese owner at a Zurich bank.

'Contrary to what certain people have stated, Israel's MOSSAD had no hand in the affair,' Colonel de Lannurien explained recently. 'SDECE infiltrated the crew, an operation that I mounted from Cairo, and through the Beirut station, which was still very active.'

In fact, the Greek radio operator was being paid by SDECE, as was the Italian chief officer, a combat frogman in the special forces of the 'Black Prince', Valerio Borghese. (General Grossin, when he took over as head of SDECE at the end of 1957, was to notice that they had forgotten to pay the latter.) Moreover, the Italian secret service, SIFAR,[8] informed SDECE in mid-September that a Milan firm had supplied 2,000 Lee-Enfield rifles, officially destined for Pakistan. They would be found in the *Athos*'s cargo. Then on 4 October, in the military harbour at Alexandria, SDECE agents were observing Major Fathi Ed Dib and his men as they were loading the cargo. The alarm was given: '*Athos* is to sail during the night'. SDECE followed its movements day by day. On 15 October, a reconnaissance plane of the maritime surveillance branch (SURMAR), spotted the *Athos* off Algiers. The patrol-boat *Commandant-de-Pimodan* arrested it. This was a severe blow to the Algerian revolution.[9] And, for the French, it was indisputable proof of collusion between Egypt and the FLN.

It was precisely in Egypt, far from the gaze of the indiscreet, that a strange game was being played out. One day in October, Air Lieutenant Henri Geniès left the French Embassy near the Nile on foot. After many detours to throw off anyone that might be following him, he arrived at his meeting-place. The background was magnificent: in the shadow of a pyramid he met a 'university graduate', known to us as Lieutenant-Colonel Germain.[10]

The discussion centred on Ben Bella. Geniès provided the information required: the Algerian leader – still in Morocco – stayed at the Minerva Hotel when he came to Cairo. Almost every day he went on foot to the offices of the North African Liberation Committee at 32, Rue Abdelkhalek-Sarouat. He liked to lunch at the Bamboo Restaurant. Germain was to reconnoitre all these places. He even got into the room where Ben Bella normally stayed. If they failed to intercept him within a few days they would need an alternative plan. A year and a half after Mission 'Out' had been launched, it was time to get it over with, one way or another.

'The Sorcerer' of Cairo

For a target as important as Ben Bella SDECE pulled out all the stops. From Algiers, Germain was pursuing him relentlessly. In mid-December 1955, a killer of the 'Achiary' network even succeeded in getting into the room in the Hotel Mehari in Cairo where the Algerian leader was resting. He fired at him but missed. Afterwards it was alleged that Ben Bella was on the verge of a nervous breakdown.

In the summer of 1956, preparations were being made for a meeting on the island of Brioni in Yugoslavia of the spokesmen for the non-aligned states, Tito, Nehru and Nasser. It was the moment chosen by Action Branch to strike once more, directly from Paris. In July three men from the branch, staggering under the weight of their cases, turned up at the Cairo embassy. The cases were packed with explosives. Colonel de Lannurien, the station head, welcomed them, but wondered whether the execution of Ben Bella would be opportune. A previous attempt, on the railway station square in Cairo, had killed some 30 civilians when a booby-trapped vehicle blew up. Above all, the political climate did not favour it. In September, in the greatest secrecy, Guy Mollet was sending two emissaries, Pierre Commin and Pierre Hermault, to have talks with Ahmed Francis and M'hamed Yazid. What was more, on Brioni, as the French knew, Tito and Nehru were seeking to persuade Nasser to tone down his attitude over the Algerian question, and even to urge the 'Provisional Government of the Algerian Republic' (Gouvernement Provisoire de la République Algérienne: GPRA) to negotiate. In the circumstances would it not be bad timing to attack Ben

Bella? The Cairo head of SDECE hesitated. At the very least he demanded a written order from headquarters that Commandant François Blouin's mission should be carried out.[11] It was not given. De Lannurien cancelled the operation – and has been criticized for having done so.

In November 1956 came the Suez operation. SDECE packed its bags – but the explosives remained in the embassy. And the astonishing part was that they remained there up to 1963, when diplomatic relations between France and Egypt were re-established. They were now a threat to the diplomatic mission under Henri Froment-Meurice, and General Jacquier, then head of SDECE, secretly dispatched a bomb-disposal team to the embassy. Two men known for their coolness, one from Service 7 and the other from Action Branch, both explosives experts, were to defuse the bombs intended to kill Ben Bella. The second one, whose nickname was 'The Sorcerer', was Jeannou Lacaze, who in the 1980s was to become chief of staff of the French Army. Luckily for Ben Bella, in spite of all these attempts at assassination, it was the most spectacular but least final solution that prevailed.

Mission Accomplished

It was Monday, 22 October 1956. For several days SDECE had known that Ben Bella and his friends were to leave Rabat on board the Super-Constellation belonging to King Mohammed V, in order to take part in the Arab summit in Tunis. Thus they would overfly Algeria. As if by chance, on 19 October, Pierre Chaussade, the Secretary-General, had dispatched to General Frandon, commanding the 5th Air Region, Directive No. 4273/CM (Cabinet Militaire), which set out the procedures to be followed for arresting aeroplanes that might violate Algerian airspace.

Was the intelligence coming from Rabat reliable? Colonel Ducournau, head of the military staff of Robert Lacoste, regularly received confidential information by telephone from a journalist of the Central Press Agency. The Deuxième Bureau, run in Rabat by Colonel Jean Gardes, a future OAS leader, was in direct contact with Algiers. At about half-past eight that morning Colonel Ducourneau announced to Pierre Chaussade: 'Ben Bella is about to cross Algerian skies.' The heaven-sent opportunity. All the staff headquarters of the Algerian Army were in the picture and would not understand if nothing was done.

The countdown began according to the timetable that Colonel Germain had been carefully planning for months. As he described it:

In the beginning, it must be acknowledged, there were a few difficulties with the military office (of the governor-general), and the discussion was getting bogged down over the problem of time zones. Once these difficulties had been overcome, we went down to regional staff headquarters, where Colonel de Massignac, head of the

Deuxième Bureau, who had been won over, set up an impromptu meeting for 10 a.m. This had been made easier because, confirming the intelligence I had received from Counter-Espionage in Morocco, the Algerian press were talking openly of a trip eastwards by Ben Bella and his staff, leaving from Rabat. But that was not enough. Wheels had to be set in motion and the operation had to be carried out. I found valuable assistance in the person of the head of Air Security, Lieutenant-Colonel Andrès, as well as total understanding on the part of Frandon, the General commanding the 5th Air Region, and his chief of staff, Colonel de la Source, who opened their doors wide to me, and implemented the directive from the Secretary-General for Algeria.

Clearly Mission 'Out' was henceforth no longer a task for one individual with a certain amount of help, but one for the whole of military Algiers. It only remained to obtain the consent of the political authorities in Paris for an operation that no longer concerned SDECE alone (although the change of government, with the replacement of Edgar Faure by Guy Mollet at the beginning of 1956 had in no way modified the SDECE assignment concerning Mission 'Out'). But the green light from Paris was necessary, all the more so because there was a risk that the Sultan of Morocco might be on the plane. Now Robert Lacoste, the resident minister, was resting at his home in Périgord; Guy Mollet, the prime minister, was in the Pas-de-Calais; and Bourgès-Maunoury was taking part in one of those ultra-secret meetings with the Israelis and the British to study plans for the Suez invasion. On the other hand, Max Lejeune, the Secretary of State for Defence, did not beat about the bush when General Lorillot, commanding the 10th Military Region, put it to him: 'Ben Bella will be going through our air space. May we arrest the plane?' 'I'll cover you,' replied Max Lejeune.

The pace of events speeded up:

1130 hrs Rabat radios the flight plan of the Sultan of Morocco's Super-Constellation, but at the same time the Central Press Agency – a decidedly inexhaustible source of information – warns that Ben Bella will fly in another plane. Doubtless Mohammed V wanted to avoid any provocative gesture towards France. The main difficulty is thus eliminated.

1300 hrs The military control tower of the Maison-Blanche airfield at Algiers receives the flight plan of a DC3 of the Air-Atlas airline. SDECE, for its part, learns that Ben Bella, Mohammed Khider, Mohammed Boudiaf, Aït Ahmed Hocine and Moustapha Lacheraf are on board this aircraft, which will follow a course Casablanca – Salé – Oujda – Tunis. At the last moment the French pilot of the DC3 modifies the flight plan, at the request of Aït Ahmed, who is worried at overflying Algeria, and plans to make a stopover in the Balearic Islands.

1600 hrs The control tower at Oran contacts Commandant Grellier, the pilot; the ensuing exchange has gone down in history:

Oran: Say you've got engine trouble. Come in and land at Oran.
DC3: What's all this about?
Oran: You have five 'villains' on board, and we want them. (*The identity of Ben Bella and his colleagues is then revealed to the crew.*)
DC3: Who is giving this order?
Oran: The Ministry of National Defence.[12]

The crew plainly hesitates. The operation seems to have got off to a bad start. After the stop in Majorca, the control tower at Maison-Blanche takes over the task of convincing the pilot. On board the DC3 they are worried: the plane is not French. What will happen to the journalists accompanying the Algerians? And the crew's families, left behind in Morocco:[13]

1900 hrs The DC3 asks permission to return to Morocco.

2000 hrs Algiers replies: 'Negative for Morocco. Come down here. We are covering you.' Soon Mistral fighters and a B26 take off from Oran. 'Orders to fire at the starboard engine if the plane tries to escape,' the captain hears, for the message is deliberately translated in plain language in order to intimidate him. He makes up his mind: he will land.

The passengers themselves have noticed nothing. The air hostess, Claudine Lambert, has managed to distract the attention of the Algerian travellers, who are chatting and playing cards. They are armed and she must keep a cool head. This is all the more necessary because, in relation to the expected time of arrival in Tunis, the DC3 is naturally very early. So it is going to circle for a time. Will Ben Bella and his colleagues notice that the setting sun is constantly changing direction? The hostess draws the curtains, *in extremis*. . .

2027 hrs The DC3 sets down on the landing strip at Maison-Blanche. Jeeps surround it, machine guns at the ready. Armed with submachine guns, Colonel Andrès's men burst into the plane.

'Don't harm us,' shouts Ben Bella, asking his friends to surrender, as he does. Then he regains his self-control: 'I would never have thought the French were capable of this.'

They were taken to El-Biar, where superintendent Rauzy of the DST was awaiting them. Then operation 'Skorzeny' took over: an SDECE plane was to take them to France, where they were to finish the war in prison.

The news brought an instant burst of reactions. The European community in Algeria was jubilant. The army drank champagne: 'It's the end of hostilities.' Guy Mollet, when he learnt the news, judged it to be 'very grave'. Two of the kidnapped FLN leaders, Mohammed Khider and Aït Ahmed, had met emissaries of the French prime minister on two occasions, in Rome and Belgrade. SDECE knew of this, and had been watching Lieutenant-Colonel Tharwat Okacha, the military attaché and representative of the Egyptian secret services in Paris. It was he who had arranged the interviews. However, although the Socialists would admittedly have liked to achieve a cease-fire, they did not interfere with the hunt for the FLN leaders in any way. Few officials were disturbed by the idea that men who had been chosen as emissaries had been deliberately kidnapped. But the Secretary of State for Moroccan and Tunisian affairs, Alain Savary, the head of his Private Office, Claude Cheysson, and the French ambassador in Tunis, Count Pierre de Leusse, handed in their resignations.

Lieutenant-Colonel Germain himself had undoubtedly pulled off his finest operation. As soon as the landing of the DC3 and the intervention of the 'reception committee' had been confirmed, he had rushed to the telephone to contact Paris headquarters. The only director available, the head of Counter-Espionage, Colonel Dumont, his old friend, merely heard him pronounce triumphantly the agreed message: 'Targets A and C: mission accomplished.'[14]

On a more modest scale, Mission 'Out' was to continue up to 1958, under the command of Captain Thébault, 'Pat' of Action Branch.[15] The main target at the time, Ahmed Ben Bella, was already 'out'. Paradoxically, Lieutenant-Colonel Germain would soon be out as well. What the professionals judged to be 'a fine feat', the politicians perceived as 'yet another dirty trick by the secret services'. This was particularly true after the return of de Gaulle. On 3 October 1958, the Director-General of SDECE offered Germain a grandiose posting, stretching 'from the Indus to Fujiyama'; the Far East station. Since he was entitled to expect a post in headquarters, on the Boulevard Mortier, it was clearly a blind alley job. He resigned from the Army and returned to history teaching.

Operation 'Musketeer': Target Nasser

Some members of Guy Mollet's government clearly had a liking for the secretive, a taste they had inherited from the Resistance. They were in their element when preparing for the intervention against Egypt. Christian Pineau, the Minister of Foreign Affairs, had been the head of the intelligence network 'Cohors', belonging to Libération-Nord, the socialist underground Resistance movement. Bourgès-Maunoury, the Minister of Defence, had belonged to the BCRA, as had Louis Mangin, who had coordinated its paramilitary operations. In 1956 he was officially 'detached for service with the ministry of National Defence' and staged a furtive entrance into the SDECE Directorate. Finally, Boursicot, the head of

SDECE and a former socialist Resister, supervised the various meetings which worked out the plan for the Suez expedition, which took the code-name Operation 'Musketeer'.

His was the decisive role: for this occasion he brought together the Israeli and British secret services, which only a few years earlier had been waging a pitiless war against each other.

Nevertheless relations between the French and the Israelis had not always been easy. In September 1948, an Irgun commando team assassinated the emissaries of the United Nations in Israel, Count Folke Bernadotte and Colonel André Sérot. Colonel Sérot, a universally esteemed former member of Intelligence, had been a pioneer in Air Intelligence, and an observer for the French secret services in Palestine. The group that killed him was led by the future prime minister of Israel, Itzhak Shamir.[16] The fact remained that in 1956 the three – Israel, France and Great Britain – joined together to face Nasser, whom Anthony Eden, the British prime minister, had dubbed 'the Hitler of the Nile'.

In June Pierre Boursicot launched operation 'Diaspora II'. Its assignment was the reception of an important Israeli delegation, after an exploratory meeting between the French government and Shimon Peres and General Moshe Dayan. On the night of 17 June 1956, a Nord 2000 plane from Tel Aviv landed at the SDECE air base at Persan-Beaumont. The first meeting took place at the house of a friend of Bourgès-Maunoury, in the neighbourhood of Chantilly. Attending on the Israeli side were Moshe Dayan, Shimon Peres, Colonel Nishri, the military attaché in Paris, Colonel Habaki, the head of military intelligence, and Joseph Nahmias. On the French side were Lieutenant-General Lavaud, General Challe, Louis Mangin, Pierre Boursicot and his deputy in SDECE, the prefect Louis Lalanne, and finally Colonel Branet, from the private staff of the Minister for Algeria. The purpose was to discuss direct intervention against Nasser with the agreement of the British.

On 26 July the crisis intensified: the Raïs nationalized the Suez Canal. In October, after the affair of the *Athos*, the French became convinced that they must strike hard. SDECE then organized a fresh conference in a house at Sèvres. The Israeli Minister of Defence, Shimon Peres, General Dayan, and Golda Meir, the Minister of Foreign Affairs, met Bourgès-Maunoury, Abel Thomas and Louis Mangin. A military agreement was concluded, according to whose terms, in particular, France was to deliver Mystère IV planes to Israel. Shortly afterwards there was a final summit meeting: Guy Mollet found himself face to face not only with Ben Gurion and Dayan, but also with Selwyn Lloyd, the British Foreign Secretary, once again at the SDECE house. The green light was given for Operation 'Musketeer'.

At Aubagne SDECE had set up a special body to direct the operations of Action Branch in Egypt. Its code name was RAP 700, and it was supervised by Captain Paul Léger. He was to head the activities of two 'hundreds' of the

11th Shock Troops which had arrived in Cyprus. Only the group under Lieutenant Moutin, a specialist in subversive operations, were to be dropped with the men of the 10th Paratroop Division. In Cyprus itself, on the spot, one of the key missions of the 11th Shock Troops was clearly defined: to put an end to the war of the airwaves. In Cairo, the 'Voice of the Arabs' was preaching the nationalist revolution and its listening public was very numerous. Against it, in Cyprus the French launched Radio 'Somera', financed by the Quai d'Orsay. For their part, the British launched their station, 'Sharq al-Adna', rechristened the 'Near East Arab Broadcasting Corporation', based at Zyghi in southern Cyprus, which was funded directly by the British Intelligence Service. Both beamed their broadcasts towards Egypt, but without much success. Moreover, as soon as Operation 'Musketeer' started the Arab staff of the English station went on strike, whilst the BBC criticized the military adventure. To have selected Cyprus as its departure base was particularly perilous for the British, since EOKA, the Cypriot clandestine army led by General Grivas, was fighting a guerrilla war there.

SDECE had made up its mind, whatever the outcome of the Suez intervention, to destroy Radio Cairo. Captain Paul Léger recalled this in these terms:

Radio Cairo being at the time the main channel for broadcasting the propaganda of the Algerian rebels, I was designated to study the best way of causing maximum damage to it. I therefore contacted the service concerned in order to obtain all the intelligence needed to mount such an operation. In spite of my repeated demands, the agents on the spot provided me with only some very fragmentary information and details, although this was indispensable in order to work out the sequence of operations and the means required. Having exhausted all arguments, and against all logic, I prepared to go myself to see on the spot what was required. In the end, given the hostility of the representatives of Intelligence Branch, who did not appreciate anyone disturbing the fine structure of their networks, the mission was cancelled.[17]

What was the sense of an isolated operation aimed merely at the destruction of Nasser's radio station, if the French, Israeli and British general staffs were jointly preparing as well to defeat the Egyptian army and to overthrow the Raïs? The whole ambiguity of the mad venture of Suez is encapsulated in this enigma. Well informed, SDECE was not convinced that the vast military operation would attain its objectives. On the other hand, it could facilitate isolated raids. That would always be something gained, in case of failure. Action Branch also hoped to capture all the FLN files held in the Rue Abdelkhalek-Sarouat.

What is more, they dreamt, not for the first time, of assassinating Nasser. In 1954 a 'hit man', a paid killer, a reservist of Action Branch, had been sent to organize an attack on the spot. Jean-Marie Pellay, called 'Steamboat' in the BCRA, just missed the Raïs. It was only a postponement.[18]

In November 1956, there was a fresh attempt. General Henri Jacquin, head of the mysterious Bureau for Studies and Liaison (Bureau d'Etudes et de Liaison: BEL), confirmed this to the authors:

Regarding the assassination of Nasser, the order was passed on to Action Branch of the French force in Cyprus in November 1956. The order could only come from the prime minister of the time, who alone possessed authority to designate the 'Homo' targets of Action Branch. Why was this order not carried out? It was because, from July 1956, Nasser had 'decapitated' the French and British networks – and even the Israeli ones – through information that had allegedly been provided by arrested Egyptian communists.[19]

On 5 November 1956, at dawn, British and French paratroops from the 10th Parachute Division and the 11th Shock Troops jumped – over Port Fuad and Port Said. At the waterworks two of the men from the 'hundred' of the 11th Shock Troops led by Lieutenant Moutin got their parachutes entangled in the undergrowth and were finished off with a bayonet. But the commandos, in accordance with the plan, seized the works. On the whole, Operation 'Musketeer' successfully carried out its programme. Supported by the Israeli Army on the eastern front, the Franco-British troops were preparing to win the battle. But on the international plane the war was being lost. Acting in concert, the USSR and the USA insisted upon the withdrawal of the expeditionary force from Egypt.

In so doing, the United States indulged in a few diversionary manoeuvres. Thus on 6 November NATO sent out a false communiqué: 'From SACEM, very reliable source, report message received from Ankara. Turkey overflown by jets. Stop. Turkish air force alerted. Message ends.' This implied Soviet intervention. Misled, the SDECE station in Ankara confirmed the news. For the special services the contradictory nature of the operation was obvious. One picture demonstrated this to them: it was of the commandos of the 11th Shock Troops, whom General Beauffre had decided to link to the advance of the British Centurion tanks; in other words, the mobile infantry of the secret war were to be pinned down behind these sluggish steel juggernauts.

The troops were withdrawn. Lieutenant Moutin returned to Tipaza, the rear base of the 11th Shock Troops in Algeria. Whilst the battle for Algiers was about to begin, they continued to hunt down the Fellagha (the Algerian nationalists) in the desert. He found some difficulty in explaining to his comrades that while the Egyptian 'Fedyahin' were running in all directions from the advance of the French paratroops, the French advance had suddenly been called off.

In Algeria, after the arrest of the *Athos* and the kidnapping of Ben Bella, the general staff were hoping that these blows would hamper the pursuit of the war. But it was to continue, even more cruel than before. Yet, since a scapegoat is always needed when mistakes are made, certain errors in the Suez operations were laid at the door of SDECE. However, up to the end of

1957, when General Grossin became its head, SDECE continued its operations against Nasser. One of the leaders recalls of Action Branch:

Yes, there were several assassination attempts against the Raïs, in cooperation with other countries, and in particular with the complicity of the Muslim Brotherhood. In 1957 one such attempt was made exclusively by the French. Two agents, equipped with a bomb, were landed by boat. But the leader of the mission realized they were being followed. Needless to say, they had to abandon the attempt. And, having been closely tailed, they did not know how to get rid of their explosive charge.

The DST in Algeria

'My love, in thinking of you and of us, I know that on Sunday I shall take communion in a state of mortal sin . . .'

One letter among many. Intimate correspondence laid bare to unhealthy curiosity in order to satisfy the needs of an investigation. Ardent words, too many words. The letters were addressed to one of the leaders of the FLN's Federation of France by his mistress, a member of a Catholic group supporting the Algerians. The woman was married, the mother of a family, and known for her strong, almost mystic religious fervour. In her eyes to help the FLN was not to betray one's country but to apply the principles of Christ. But taking a lover was certainly a betrayal. Her letters were filed in the records of the DST under Section E2, 'Manipulations'. By tailing her day and night the DST was able to infiltrate certain networks helping the FLN.

'The most interesting part of this affair is the way in which a flaw in the personality or psychology of a "targeted person" is exploited,' stated a superintendent in the DST who had known about this case during the Algerian war. 'For us every individual has a flaw, a weak point that one can work upon. And in this particular case it can be seen that people motivated by a rigorous morality or ardent religious principles are more vulnerable. If this woman had made a habit of sleeping with other men, she would have felt less sinful, and immediately less manipulable from our viewpoint. The same would have applied if she had a much freer relationship in her marriage.'

Such techniques were of course not peculiar to the DST in its battle with the FLN. But during these years both Roger Wybot and his successor, the prefect Gabriel Eriau, who was well versed in Maghreb affairs,[20] somewhat neglected the agents of the KGB. In mainland France, faced with the Federation of France and the various European networks providing covert assistance, the DST took the lion's share of the work.

Nevertheless, in Algeria it progressively lost its predominant position to military counter-espionage. Naturally the DST in Algeria worked in close cooperation with Paris. It was divided into four geographical areas, in each of which were branches matching those in the capital: operational services, documentation and 'manipulations'. Algiers was an area like the rest, but in addition was responsible for the coordination of the DST in Algeria. Superintendent Rauzy had been appointed to head it and had the privilege of being the first to interrogate Ben Bella. 'Manipulations' Branch was in the hands of Maurice Lassabe, who, it must be freely admitted, did not always enjoy success in the sometimes very complex operations he had to carry out. Moreover, his assistant, an unstable person, had been 'turned', and passed on a lot of intelligence to the FLN, who finally executed him in 1962. In the Documentation Section, Inspector Héblé ran the registry, which had benefited from the work carried out during the War, when André Achiary identified the dangerous connections that had been built up between the Nazi secret services and certain Arab nationalists.

The Constantine area was headed by Chief Superintendent Elbling, the former head of the DST in Tunis. In Oran Louis Schneider displaced his colleague Honoré Gevaudan, who, all in all, was to lose nothing by quitting the DST for the criminal investigation department, where he enjoyed a glittering career. Finally, the Sahara area, by far the most peaceful, came under Marcel Chalet who, after his irresistible rise, was to occupy the top position of all in 1975.

Although it embarked upon the infiltrations and manipulations necessary to combat an insurrectionary movement, the DST lacked the experience of SDECE or the shock units which had operated in Indo-China. The consequence was that, setting aside the successful interceptions made by the Radioelectronic Communications Police (PCR), who were attached to the DST, the DST rapidly wore itself out. As we have seen in the case of the deputy to Superintendent Lassabe, 'manipulation' activities left much to be desired. This was also the case with Souchen, an Arab agent recruited by the DST but 'turned' by the FLN, and finally executed by Ourkla's Operational Protection Detachment (Détachement Opérationnel de Protection: DOP) in 1960.

The Inter-Army Coordination Centre

Apart from the DST and the Army security services, at the beginning of the insurrection there existed in Algeria only a small colonial intelligence service, comparable to the BTLC in Indo-China, Colonel Paul Schoen's Liaison Service for North Africa (Service de Liaisons Nord-Africaines: SLNA).[21] In Algiers, as in numerous French African colonies, there was also an SDECE counter-espionage station, whose task was essentially to uncover foreign interference, particularly by the British and the Russians. From 1950 onwards it was under Commandant Nougaret, who benefited from records that went back to the War, when Algiers was the French capital for intelligence matters. This station also operated in close liaison with the

Statistical Bureau of the Foreign Legion (Bureau de la Statistique de la Légion Etrangère: BSLE), the Legion's secret service directed by Colonel Henri Jacquin.

In 1955, with the arrival of Colonel Germain, SDECE expanded. He could only elude the administration by asking it to intervene in Algeria: in the so-called 'French departments' this was done by a stroke of the pen, exempting SDECE from the stipulation that it should only intervene abroad. But in Algeria there prevailed a subtle mixture of types of intelligence. Counter-subversion activities required the army to carry out tasks normally falling to the police, and through a process of osmosis the police, in particular the DST, employed methods that ran counter to their original brief.

The field of activities of the secret services grew larger. Colonel Trinquier, the principal strategist of 'modern warfare', applied his experience in Indo-China to urban counter-guerrilla warfare. 'To carry the revolutionary war into the enemy's camp', was Roger Trinquier's theme. It was a matter of destroying the politico-military machinery of the FLN, in order to 'liberate the population from the grip of terrorism'. Counter-guerrilla warfare and 'the reconquest of the population' went hand in hand. Firstly, this was done through psychological action, a speciality of the Fifth Bureau under Colonels Goussault, Lacheroy and Gardes, then by close control of the population, through the technique of 'block control' (*îlotage*) thought up by Trinquier and installed in March 1957 under the title 'Arrangements for Urban Protection' (Dispositif de Protection Urbaine: DPU).

These various stages naturally meshed in with the search for intelligence:

Information is nothing in itself, particularly in a period of crisis, if it is not rapidly exploited. The forces for maintaining order will set up an 'Action Branch' of their own capable of exploiting intelligence as quickly as possible. Certain members of the local intelligence service, having demonstrated their exceptional qualities, will enter Action Branch of the secret services . . . The best agents will be recruited from the enemy itself. The interrogation teams will always have in mind the fact that most of those arrested, if flexibly manipulated, may change sides . . . The Action Branch of intelligence will have to be constantly renewed. In close contact with those entrusted with the exploitation of intelligence participating in police operations, it will be kept informed of all arrests, in order to exploit to the utmost every possibility for recruiting of agents.[22]

It was in response to these preoccupations that, with the arrival of General Raoul Salan in Algeria, a vast intelligence service was formed, grouping together all the special military services and called the Inter-Army Coordination Centre (CCI). Colonel Léon Simoneau, head of the CCI, had spent his whole career in intelligence. After working in the Resistance in a covert intelligence network, he had directed the operational intelligence service in Germany, and participated in the Research Branch of SDECE, in particular in the famous 'hunt for Nazi brainpower'. Head of the Russian section in the Deuxième Bureau, and then of the Deuxième Bureau attached to the General Staff, it was therefore he who was invited in 1957 to create the CCI, from scratch. As he described it,

The first name found for this body was RAP – 'Repression, Action, Protection'. But psychologically this was inappropriate. I therefore selected the anodyne title of 'Inter-Army Coordination Centre'. My assignment from General Ely to set up the CCI indicated that it was to carry out 'ground intelligence for the benefit of operational units'. I had 400 officers under my command. Colonel Germain's SDECE, which you know about, was represented in it, as well as Colonel Decorse's 11th Shock Troops. Colonel Ruat commanded the operational half-brigade, and Colonel Parizot 'straight intelligence', intelligence proper.[23]

Let us be more precise. Colonel Clément Ruat directed an operational intelligence service made up of stations adapted to army corps, or stations adapted to needs. There was thus systematic coverage. A team of intelligence officers, for example, served covertly in the 157th Infantry Regiment at Constantine, or in the 61st at Oran. In Algiers and Hydra the CCI chose as its cover the 58th Infantry Battalion, and then a civilian firm, SODEP. There were some strong personalities in the team, such as Louis Bertolini, the initiator of anti-terrorist commando groups, like Jo Rizza's, made up of 'pieds-noirs' (white colonists in Algeria). Its objective was to carry out attacks in the Casbah and elsewhere. Thanks to CCI records, Bertolini – later 'Benoît' of the OAS – was to provide targets for the commando groups of Lieutenant Degueldre. Benoît, recruited because of the good contacts he had with SDECE, was to take part in an OAS attack in 1961 against General de Gaulle, Operation 'Chamois'. On the other hand Captain René Crignola, who worked alongside Bertolini, was to follow a totally different, and much more prestigious, course in SDECE. Having been head of station in Prague and Tokyo, he was not to leave his post as head of the Research Branch in Africa until the Left took power in 1981. Thus during the Algerian war we find very different types of men in these services.

Section A – for Action – of the CCI grouped together the special teams that carried out raids and individual operations. They participated directly in missions to deceive or penetrate the enemy, which were wholly successful, such as – as we shall see – 'Blueitis' or 'Force K'. Thirdly, Colonel Teyssère's technical services played a central role, in particular in radio direction-finding to locate the enemy's transmissions; using fixed and mobile posts, and the T26 direction-finding planes, the radioelectronic communications units (GCR) intercepted, transcribed and decoded. Finally the monitoring services, under the orders of Captain Mattéï, an SDECE man based in the Rue Michelet, met with real successes. In fact, the FLN put out its messages in French. The reason for this was simple: its leaders had never been able to come to an agreement as to which language to adopt, Arabic or

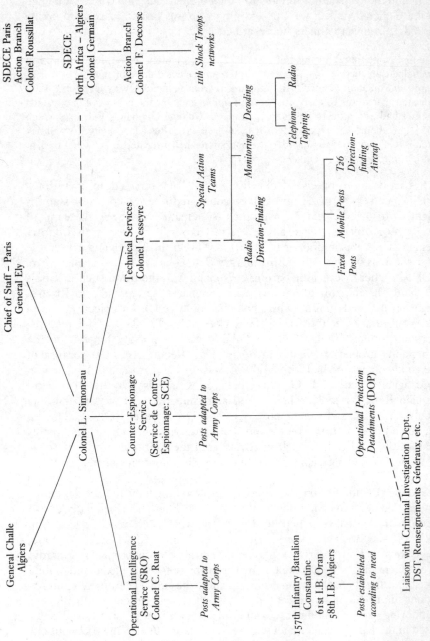

Figure 6.1 *The Inter-Army Coordination Centre (CCI) in Algeria (1957–1960)*

Berber. At the demand of Robert Lacoste, Captain Mattéï was dismissed. In the summer of 1957 it emerged that he had been falsifying the monitoring reports in favour of activists under surveillance.

The structure of the CCI remains engraved on everybody's memory, at least in Algeria, in particular the Operational Detachments for Protection (DOP), in charge of the 'interrogation of prisoners'. 'I can't let it be said,' declared Colonel Simoneau, taking the bull by the horns, 'that intelligence was obtained by massacring people.' He was aware of the accusations made against the CCI and the DOP.[24] 'To these mixed units consisting of specialist officers I had attached police officers and gendarmes to supervise the legality of the interrogations!'[25] Honoré Gévaudan was one of the men from the criminal investigation department given the job of liaising with the CCI. (In fact, he kept a close eye on the interrogations of the communist Yveton, who had placed a bomb in a gas works.)

Covertly, during the Algerian war, and then afterwards openly, a number of works appeared concerning torture. Names of Indo-China veterans, members of SDECE and the paratroop units, and practitioners of counter-subversive warfare in circles close to Colonels Godard and Trinquier, have been published, often rightly so. Yet in several cases that the present authors were able to check, they were published with ulterior motives that related more to the war of words than to respect for historical truth. To defend the honour of an officer wrongfully accused is not our business, nor to feed the fire by giving the names of those whom we are quite certain have committed crimes. The fact remains that the historian will have to explain the disappearance of some 4,000 Algerians during the battle for Algiers, a figure computed by Paul Teitgen, the secretary-general of the Prefecture, who had signed the order for the internment of these suspects when they were handed over to members of the DOP.[26]

To cite one example, General Bigeard confirmed to the present authors that the head of the armed FLN force in Algiers, Larbi Ben M'Hidi, arrested by the General's paratroops on 23 February 1957, had not committed suicide in his cell – the official version – but had been tortured and then murdered by the special services: 'For ten days, nothing happened to him. We had a mutual esteem for each other. Then, upon the order of the government – the instruction came from Lacoste – we transferred him to the special services, to men who were working for General Massu.'[27]

In his book *La Vraie Bataille d'Alger*, Massu describes why he ordered the transfer of Ben M'Hidi, and how the latter hanged himself using electric wire, as soon as he arrived at the headquarters of Marcel Bigeard. As commander of the Tenth Paratroop Division, let us leave him to expound his philosophy and his description of the DOP methods:

Then, in practice, if it was necessary to rough someone up a bit to make him talk, the interrogators inflicted physical pain on the suspect, gradually increasing it in order to arrive at a confession. Certainly there were risks, and accidents did occur. But all the same it was only physical pressure, even if violent, used to procure immediate intelligence, and it did not degrade the individual.

Obviously this was very much where the moral sense and cool head of the interrogator came in. The procedure most commonly employed, besides beating, was to use electricity from the radio generators ('la gégène'), and apply electrodes to different parts of the body. I tried it out on myself in my office at Hydra at the beginning of 1957, and most of my officers did the same.

The setting up of a special unit, the CCI, maintaining its own operational protection detachments, the DOP, specialists in the interrogation of suspects who refused to talk, corresponded to the desire of the high command to entrust this task only to tried and tested cadres.[28]

Captain Léger's 'Blueitis'

Another testimony, and a weighty one, comes from Captain Léger:

There was a little FLN cell at Belcourt. In it was a girl called Tadjer Zora. She hadn't done very much. Afterwards I learnt that she had made a flag. Just in case, I sent out a search order. She had fled to Bordj Menaïel. Two or three days later the local intelligence officer telephoned me: 'Your girl, we've copped her. She was going to take to the hills – she's all yours.'

I went there with my assistant, the former head of Algiers Sector III. My practice was always the same. Every time I confronted a rebel, I discussed matters and 'turned' him or her. At the time, you know, that was not difficult; you only had to say that the war was a civil war, and it was Frenchmen fighting Frenchmen . . . that I made no distinction as between a Mohammed and a Dupont. There was no problem. Apart from the few, the committed, who clung absolutely to the independence of Algeria.

So I went to see this girl, and I proposed that she worked in my group concerned with intelligence and its exploitation. And she accepted. . . But in my opinion she accepted too readily. Because, you know, the kind of mission that I was suggesting to her was disproportionate to what she had done. Yes, she accepted too quickly. Anyway I brought her back to Algiers, but on the return journey I arranged to take her around a bit, so that she should be seen in my car, and I took her home to my house at El Biar. There I explained what she had to do: 'You must go back to your mother. You're to telephone me every week, and then, one day, perhaps I shall have a mission to send you on.'

I had prepared the ground because I suspected something. She asked too many questions. She asked me, 'Who is working with us, are there some nationalists too?' I replied, 'Of course.' I possessed false letters, with official stamps (coming from 'KJ 27', the previous operation) signed by an FLN captain who had written to me that the 'operation' had gone off very well and that he – the fellow who had signed the letter – had absented himself from the command post while the operation was taking place, and had laid all the blame on the unfortunate Ahmed Sabri, who had been condemned to death.

At that moment Colonel Godard telephoned me – the telephone was in the passage. The girl was in my office and the letters were there on the table. Through the door, which was ajar, I watched her. She got up and went to look at the letters. She read them through and examined the signatures, etc. I said nothing, without thinking for a moment about what might happen later. I had done this just in case; it really was a 'try-on'.

Then she went home to her mother. The following week she telephoned me for the first time. Afterwards, nothing more . . . I sent someone to find out what was happening. Her mother said she had gone and had not been seen since: I said to myself: 'There's no problem, she's gone to the FLN.' When she joined up with them she fell in with a man called Mayhouz Hacène, a captain in Zone II, who was a brute nicknamed 'Hacène the Torturer'. He said to her, 'You've been seen with Léger in his car.' 'Right,' she said, 'he suggested I should work for him, and I agreed' . . . 'You've betrayed us' . . . 'If you're looking for traitors, just look around you, there's a lot.'

And she told him the story, with the names. The FLN grilled her, put her through the mill, what they called 'the Helicopter'. She confessed a lot of nonsense. I read her interrogation two months later – it was terrifying. And that was how 'blueitis' began.

The Algerians arrested people and tortured them. The poor fellows said anything, gave away names they knew, confessed that they were indeed working for me. Under torture they made up all kinds of stories. And it went right up to Amirouche, to Wilaya [area] IV. Clearly suspicion fell upon people from Algiers, generally students, militants with more education than the simple Fellahin from Kabylia. That's how a massacre of officers, or those who later might have become officers, began. Some 4,000 of them. We found heaps of corpses.'[29]

Captain Léger, who described in clinically minute detail the origin of 'blueitis', was well aware that he had played the part of the sorcerer's apprentice. Today, at least, he notes that he was surprised by the scale of the thing. This onetime FFL parachutist had specialized in covert warfare since 1946 in Indo-China – using infiltration and deception, and rallying prisoners to his side. At the beginning of 1953 Léger became an instructor at the GCMA's school of guerrilla warfare at Cape Saint-Jacques, run by Captain Daniel Pradère-Niquet. From 1955 to 1957 he was assigned to the North Africa section of SDECE.

From 1957 onwards Paul Léger undertook to put his Indo-China experience to good use in Algeria. Under the aegis of Colonel Trinquier he was posted to the Group for Intelligence and Intelligence Exploitation (Groupe de Renseignement et d'Exploitation: GRE). The GRE, a small organization, comprised three sectors: an intelligence branch proper, with 70 agents, a branch for exploitation and action, and, above all, the branch for the organization of civilians run by Captain Allain. This last sector was the originator of the 'blueitis' type operations. Indeed, it excelled in 'turning' the other side. Former FLN members who had come over to the French henceforth worked against their ex-comrades: they were the so-called 'blue boiler suits' – hence 'blueitis'.[30] Their activity in the Algiers Casbah and elsewhere kept up a fear in the ranks of the FLN of defection, on which

Captain Léger relied to launch his deception operations, such as the one just described in minute detail. It was to paralyse the activities of Wilaya III, commanded by Amirouche.

The success of the French secret services in the psychological war was indisputable. The general staff decided to extend it, giving carte blanche to a completely new service, the Bureau for Studies and Liaison (BEL).

The Deception Operations of Jacquin the Legionnaire

The former chief of the Deuxième Bureau on the Algiers staff, Colonel Henri Jacquin, took command of BEL in 1959. A Foreign Legion officer and a graduate of Saint-Cyr, he had participated since the 1930s in every 'pacification' campaign in Indo-China and North Africa. During the Second World War he had participated in the resistance against the Japanese.

Head of the secret services of the Foreign Legion, the enigmatic 'Statistical Bureau', he cultivated an air of mystery. So inflated was the legend about him that in Algeria they said that Henri Jacquin had fought in the International Brigade in Spain. In short, he was the traditional type of officer, a skilled practitioner of covert warfare, and an original thinker in the field of psychological action. With BEL – in which Léger's team was incorporated – they went overboard for deception and disinformation. As General Jacquin himself emphasized, the creation of BEL permitted a more flexible tactical use of pursuit units. He summed up his mission as follows:

BEL had access to the operations room of the inter-armies general staff, where, within minutes of their occurring, all incidents, no matter how minor, were registered. In this war no detail was negligible. The operations room also took detailed note of all the intelligence concerning the enemy emanating from the Deuxième Bureau: the ALN battle order, where it had established itself, the messages exchanged between the GPRA and the Wilayas, the state of stores depots in Libya, Morocco and Tunisia, and the correspondence between the rebel leaders and their accomplices in France itself, or abroad – the intelligence provided by the traditional intelligence services, or from other sources that BEL directly contrived for itself.

Around Henri Jacquin were assembled

a small team of officers coming from the most diverse backgrounds, often already initiated into the mysteries of intelligence and clandestine warfare: Captains Léger and La Bourdonnaye, former assistants to Colonel Godard during the battle for Algiers, Commandant Cathala, formerly of the Leclerc Division, Captain Planet, an escapee from the Vietminh 're-education' camps, Commandant Chamagne, a veteran of the Chinese 'Long March' in 1945, and Captain Heux, who had captured Ben Bella at the Maison-Blanche aerodrome.[31]

This Captain Pierre Heux was to be at the centre of one of the controversies of this war. In 1959, copying Léger's methods, he weakened Wilaya IV by carrying out 'contamination' operations. An atmosphere of mistrust was created between the leaders of this Wilaya and the GPRA, the Provisional Government of the Algerian Republic. In June 1960, answering the 'Appeal for a Peace of the Brave' that de Gaulle had just launched, the former envisaged negotiations with the French. After numerous unforeseen events – in the framework of the ultra-secret operation 'Tilsitt' – on 10 June 1960 an astonishing meeting took place at the Elysée Palace. Si Salah, Si Mohammed and Si Lakhdar met the General. He informed them that he was ready to negotiate with the Wilayas, but on condition that contact was at the same time made with those outside Algeria, the GPRA. In fact, at the end of June discussions were to be started at Melun between the GPRA and the French. But meanwhile, as early as 18 June, a meeting took place between various French spokesmen, among them Colonel Jacquin and Si Salah, who was accompanied by Si Lakhdar. Its object was to prepare for the former's trip to the leaders of Wilaya IV, in order to propose that they too should accept the 'Peace of the Brave'.

The situation became complicated. Learning of the terms of the Melun meeting, Si Mohammed decided to break with Paris. He arranged for the arrest, and then execution, of Si Lakhdar and Si Abdellatif. Si Saleh in his turn was arrested. In 1961 the GPRA demanded that he be escorted to Tunisia. But on 20 July a pursuit unit intercepted the convoy: Si Saleh was killed. And the killing was not over. At Blida on 8 August a commando unit of the 11th Shock Troops led by Commandant Prévôt executed Si Mohammed, the last witness to the 'Tilsitt' affair.[32] Thus this supreme attempt at a separate peace was aborted.

All the missions of BEL cannot be set out here in detail. However, we must mention the activities of its Bureau for psychological warfare, under Captain Delorme. The object remained the same: to sow disunity in the enemy camp. Thus, for example, there was the dispatch of hundreds of letters to known ALN fighters in Tunisia exhorting them to return to Algeria, which would gladden the hearts of their families. But this form of deception was to obtain only limited results.

A more successful operation was that of the false *Moudjahid. El Moudjahid*, the FLN newspaper, was typeset in Rabat, but was printed in Tunis. Its printing-blocks came through Algiers in an Air France plane. They were spirited away on several occasions, and agents of the BEL psychological action group, in particular Captains Dubois and Perdon, succeeded in altering various articles. Sometimes it was enough to preserve the general drift of the article but to alter some key words that would sow doubt; at other times, whole articles were drastically changed. Thus in May 1960, for the local canton elections, while Ferhat Abbas, in the name of the GPRA, was recommending a boycott, BEL ferreted out an old article by the chemist from Sétif, in which he called upon Muslims to participate in elections in order to exercise their democratic rights. The GPRA was forced to use the radio to denounce these forgeries published in its own newspaper and widely distributed before the fraud was discovered.

BEL successes became a cause for concern to the traditional secret services. Thus Colonel Simoneau, the head of CCI for a little while longer, was to complain to his colleague Jacquin that BEL's disinformation operations had stirred up such an atmosphere of suspicion among the Algerian fighters that infiltration missions had been made more difficult. There is no possible doubt that some Arab agents of CCI or SDECE were liquidated in certain Wilayas, carried off by the wind of insane suspicion that BEL had set in motion.

Rise and Fall of the 11th Shock Troops

The 'maid of all work' service, the spearhead of the secret war in Algeria from 1954 to 1962, was clearly the 11th Paratroop Shock Battalion. From 1952 onwards, when Colonel Yves Godard handed over command to Colonel François Decorse, the 11th Shock Troops passed entirely under the control of Action Branch of SDECE. As we have seen, its units were available both to the Action group of Colonel Germain and to the CCI under Colonel Simoneau. They were to intervene in Algeria one month after the All Saints' Day insurrection.

By December 1954, 300 men and officers of the 11th Shock Troops had arrived in Kabylia. The cover-name of this operational detachment was the 'Marching Group'. Decorse ('Anatole') installed his units in the south, at Dra El Mizan and Tizi Remiff. The cadres had had experience of subversive warfare in Indo-China, mainly in the Mixed Airborne Commando Groups (GCMA) or in the foreign paratroop battalions.[33] The unit was divided into two subgroups, each made up of two 'hundreds' – the equivalent of two infantry companies – and then split up into small commando groups that ranged throughout Kabylia. Their mission was a formidable one, although simple to express – at least at the beginning. They began by cutting the communication and supply lines of the Fellagha and creating a constant state of insecurity. A first observation was that, steeped in the principles of guerrilla warfare, the Fellagha avoided confrontation to such an extent that for a time it could be said that 'order reigned in Kabylia'.

'What is needed is to organize counter-guerrilla warfare.' At HQ in Paris Colonel Morlanne did not mince his words: 'Sow terror in the FLN ranks!' During the war the 'Blue Berets', scattered between Fort-de-l'Eau, Colomb-Béchar, Tipaza, Oran and Bone, were led in succession by three station heads of Action Branch. They had all been with the GCMA in Indo-China. Captain Thébault ('Pat') had been trained in Annam by operations against the Hre tribes and commando operations against Vietminh lines of communication. Captain Duvivier had been a member of Colonel Trinquier's staff in the GCMA. Finally, Captain Erouard, a former soldier in de Lattre de Tassigny's army, directed the operations for infiltration and destruction in central Annam before becoming chief instructor in the Ty Wan school of guerrilla warfare.

Upon arriving in Algeria Erouard first became commanding officer of one of the Light Intervention Groups (Groupements Légers d'Intervention: GLI), which were 'super-commandos' attached to the 11th Shock Troops for special missions. The idea for this structure came from Captain René Krotoff, who in December 1955 joined the 11th Shock Troops in Algeria to set up this GLI, with a strength of some 40 in all. Krotoff, in SDECE legend, was the most 'hairy' of them all. He commanded the 'school centre', the training school of Action Branch at Cercottes in the Loiret.

This team was to strike the first hard blows against the FLN. Liaison between the GLI and Action Branch (with Morlanne in Paris, and Germain in Algiers) was maintained by Michel Badaire, the future television journalist. According to an instructor in Action Branch at the time, these units were then carrying out some 30 missions a month – one a day. But gradually they became reserved for large-scale strikes. For example, in March 1956, the GLI attempted to destroy the headquarters of Wilaya I, which was led in the Aurès by Mostefa Ben Boulaïd. Captain Krotoff was killed in an ambush on 15 March. He was given the finest burial within the memory of any secret agent, at the Invalides.

He had a posthumous revenge: shortly afterwards a trap that he himself had set up snapped tight. An SCR 694 radio, booby-trapped by 'Jerry', one of the ace explosive experts at Cercottes, was parachuted into the Aurès by a Junkers from Persan-Beaumont. And, on 27 March, Mostefa Ben Boulaïd was blown to pieces when the radio set exploded. But SDECE did not find this out until August. Through the report of a French agent they learnt that at the FLN Soumam's congress it was mentioned in an address that 'Brother Ben Boulaïd Mostefa has fallen on the field on honour'.

Captain Hentic, a Breton, had a somewhat Asiatic physiognomy, as if, by imitating them, he had come to resemble those he had fought in Indo-China, where he had been assistant to Captain Belleux, the head of SDECE. He was well versed in how to 'turn' insurgents, and rally national minorities to the French army. If he had succeeded on the high plateaux of Indo-China, why should he not repeat his success in the Aurès? In fact he led GLI2, which was modelled on the super-commando group created by Krotoff. His 30 'leopards', based at Tigzirt, near the sea, were professionals. He decided to throw them into Kabylia. Hence the name 'Force K' (or more poetically, 'Blue Bird') to designate his mission.

His objective was to play upon the traditional hostility between Arabs and Kabyles. The anthropologist Jean Servier, entrusted by the Government-General with special missions, was a valuable adviser: he knew Kabylia through and through, and spoke all its dialects. For such operations it is important to study the psychology of the local people, their practices and customs, their family and social structures, and their beliefs. Captain Hentic's GLI2 was to enlist hundreds of the native inhabitants of Greater Kabylia to fight against Krim Belcacem's guerillas. They were provided with arms, ammunition and means of communication. But appearances were deceptive. From the very beginning these units were penetrated by the ALN, and one fine day 600 men made off to join the Algerian insurgents with their arms and baggage. Here was one shock that rebounded.

Was there some error in handling them? Undoubtedly. The most considerable national minority in Algeria, the Kabyles were totally won over to the idea of independence. The minority did not yet know that it would have difficulty in having its national rights recognized, once the new Algeria had been born. In their defence it must be said that the 11th Shock Troops and SDECE were not alone in committing a blunder of this kind. General Jacquin's BEL was to experience similar difficulties. In October 1956 – whilst Ben Bella was being kidnapped – Superintendent Lassabe of the DST believed he could raise a counter-insurgency group in the Orléansville area, thanks to one of his informants (known as 'Kobus', although his real name was Derviche). He was given help to recruit former insurgents. At the beginning of 1957 they numbered 400 and acted under the supervision of Captain Pierre Heux of BEL. But, unbeknown to Heux, Omar Oussedik, the dynamic leader responsible for the information and liaison branch of Wilaya IV of the ALN, had already recruited them. The result was that the 'Liberation Army' gained both arms and fighters. Kobus – the double agent is always the loser – was executed by his new allies.

One can understand the position of Colonel Germain. To undermine the ALN, having taken into account previous failures, he preferred to recruit counter-insurgents outside the FLN. The Algerian Nationalist Movement (Mouvement Nationaliste Algérien: MNA) of Messali Hadj afforded him an opportunity to do so. In the beginning the Movement was opposed to armed insurrection. SDECE always played on the rivalry between the MNA and the FLN, and was particularly successful in Europe, where the two organizations fought each other for influence over the Algerian community in France proper.

The head of the MNA in Kabylia was Mohammed Bellounis. He created the 'Messalist' insurgent group against the FLN, but the latter crushed them in 1955. Bellounis withdrew with the rest of his troops to the southern Sahara. He was ready to make a pact with the 'Devil' – the French Army. Colonel Germain despatched to him an Indo-China veteran, Captain Rocolle,[34] head of a 'hundred' in the 11th Shock Troops, supported by Captain Freddy Bauer of Action Branch. The idea was to create a 'third force'. From Paris Jacques Chaban-Delmas, Minister of National Defence, gave his support to Operation 'Olivier'. Catastrophe ensued. Obsessed by the sense of his own importance, Bellounis twisted and turned, demanding that France give him considerably more support, and proclaiming that after the war there could be no return to the former status that linked France proper to its colony: in short, 'General' Bellounis became an embarrassment, who would have to be got rid of. In May 1958, a few days after de Gaulle had returned to power, Bellounis was killed. His army broke up: one section joined the FLN, the other the French Army, and finally others melted into thin air. To say the least, Operation Olivier was not a success.

Let us leave Roger Wybot, the head of the DST, to draw the moral of the story:

Did the military show less skill and professionalism in the difficult and delicate operation of manipulation? The fact was that Bellounis tended to elude them. He became ever more demanding vis-à-vis the authorities in Algiers, arrogant and sure of himself, conducting himself like a war lord. The military command then gave the order to liquidate him, purely and simply, along with his men. The mission was to be carried out by Colonel Trinquier. In this way we finally succeeded in destroying an operation that was getting out of hand. Trinquier, Bellounis's 'executioner', himself deplored this in his report: 'The disappearance of the Bellounis system creates a vacuum. This runs a danger of being filled by the FLN, reinforced by those bands of Bellounis troops that have escaped our operation.'[35]

It was also the swan song for the 11th Shock Troops. It was May 1958.

At the time when de Gaulle took over power, 800 parachutists of the 11th Shock were bivouacked at Corte and Calvi, in Corsica. Their leaders, Captains Ignace Mantéi and Freddy Bauer, requested that they should not intervene.[36] But politics soon divided them. In 1961 many of them were to choose French Algeria and the OAS. They followed the example of Colonel Godard, who for a long time had been their leader. Former comrades in battle tore one another apart. The government mistrusted them. The ground was slipping from under their feet. Some of them realized this and, from 1960 onwards, they began to leave Algeria and the army, thus avoiding a painful choice. Captains La Bourdonnaye-Montluc, Faulques, Badaire, Egé, and many others, went their way, to go and fight in Katanga with Moïse Tschombe's mercenaries, the 'Affreux'. Naturally these men did not cut the umbilical cord that linked them to SDECE. Still under its aegis, they were to go and fight alongside the royalists in the Yemen, only too happy to strike a blow against Nasser's policy in the region.

In July 1962 those of their comrades who had remained in the 11th Shock Troops regrouped in Corsica, both the cadres and the junior NCOs dispiritedly awaiting the reshaping that Paris had imposed. After ten years of command Colonel François Decorse, deemed too close to his men, had been placed on the promotion list, and thus eased out. Officially the 11th 'Half-brigade of the Parachute Shock Troops' was kept on, but it was no more than a shadow of its former self. Lieutenant-Colonel Albert Merglen, the Gaullist officer given the job of pulling it together again, and his aides,

Commandants Bauge and Barthez, set it on a new course. Rid of its surplus 'fat', the 11th DBPC constituted a nucleus of cadres for the commando training of regular units, giving rise to the National Centres for Commando Training (Centres Nationaux d'Entraînement Commando: CNEC). Henceforth, as they chivvied poorly motivated conscripts across 'monkey bridges' and other risky obstacle courses, these aces of 'hairy' operations would recall with nostalgia the days when they pitted their wits against the 'Viets' and the 'Fellouzes'. Others, deemed politically more reliable or technically irreplaceable, were posted to form the backbone of the 13th Dragoons Parachute Regiment, in the Moselle department, a unit that still carries out strategic intelligence missions. Many were shown the door and went off to make their way in 'Civvy Street'.[37] Others were to become soldiers of fortune in the four corners of the earth. Certain others occasionally agreed to give advice to today's recruits, the greenhorns of Action Branch.

But the 'Shock spirit' endures, and so does its solidarity. Each first Friday in the month, the veterans of 'Shock' and 'Action' gather around Colonel Sassi, President of the Bagheera Association at a restaurant in the Paris area that (symbolically) overlooks a magnificent Olympic swimming pool. They meet to help one another and to relive memories already fading into the past.

PART III
The Gaullist Republic

7

Grossin's 'Firm'

'What have you been doing?' asked de Gaulle.

'This and that,' came General Grossin's reply.

'But have you information about the Russians and the Americans?' persisted the head of state.

'Well,' faltered the head of SDECE, 'we are mainly fighting the arms traffickers in Algeria.'

De Gaulle grunted. These minor police matters scarcely interested him. Upon his return to power in 1958, he had summoned General Paul Grossin, the director of the secret services – who reported this dialogue – in order to find out how French intelligence was faring. Ever since London and the BCRA of Colonel Passy, the head of Free France had dreamed of a great secret service on the lines of the British Intelligence Service.

De Gaulle wanted to give French intelligence a universal perspective. It is true that there was a need to reinforce activities aimed against the Eastern bloc – the people in Moscow were devising the first 'insulated chamber' to make eavesdropping impossible;[1] but there was also a need to obtain technological and scientific information about the United States and the other Western countries. As early as July 1958 the General assembled the Higher Council for Intelligence.[2] This was a major event: in the whole history of the Fourth and Fifth Republics it was the first and last time that it was summoned. During this meeting, all, or almost all, the ministers remained silent. Only Maurice Couve de Murville, who had inherited the Foreign Affairs portfolio, put forward a few prudent suggestions. For his ministry he would like to obtain intelligence 'à la carte'. 'What does that mean?' de Gaulle asked his minister ironically. Exasperated by the general banality of the discussion, the General rapidly closed the meeting. He had realized that intelligence could not be an inter-departmental affair.

From then on it was he in person who ran the secret services – either directly, or through his prime minister, Michel Debré, or Jacques Foccart, his Secretary-General for African and Madagascan affairs. The reform of the Constitution and the election of the President of the Republic by universal suffrage were to reinforce this tendency to consider SDECE as a tool or a weapon in the service of the Elysée Palace.

If on certain occasions de Gaulle appeared to hesitate in making up his mind, it was for purely tactical reasons. Throughout the war in Algeria he entrusted to Michel Debré and his adviser Constantin Melnik,[3] a former member of the secret services, the task of mounting operations against the FLN. On the prime minister's orders SDECE was given the particular job of handing out 68 million francs to arm the insurgents that had been 'turned' by the French. In the regular army it had been put about that it was the Israelis who were parachuting in weapons. When at last he learnt the truth, General Paul Ely, chief of the general staff, protested to Louis Joxe, the Minister for Algeria. The latter, in his turn, complained to de Gaulle who, simulating astonishment, called an inter-ministerial meeting with Louis Joxe and Michel Debré. The Minister for Algeria immediately set about criticizing the activities of the French services. Michel Debré remained silent and de Gaulle asked him no questions. Painfully and laboriously, General Grossin had to justify the activities of his services. Amused, General de Gaulle terminated the meeting on a lordly note: 'All that is very well, but it must stop.' The ministers and the head of SDECE departed. Louis Joxe was convinced that his point of view had triumphed with the great man. And General Grossin, congratulated upon his actions, was close to thinking the same thing.

To obtain industrial or scientific information SDECE now required the help of civilian personnel, top civil servants less easily detected than its agents stationed inside embassies. For this de Gaulle wanted the cooperation of the great departments of state, but his entourage jibbed at this. When the head of SDECE, accompanied by Colonel Passy, paid a visit to Georges Pompidou, the head of the General's Private Office, the latter amiably sent his visitors on their way. The future President understood nothing of the secret services and did not wish to hear about them. The idea of 'loaning' some top civil servants to SDECE revolted him. In France a technocrat (a graduate from the Ecole Nationale d'Administration) could not become a *barbouze*. The noble 'profession of intelligence', so cherished by the English and Americans, had a bad reputation in France. Upon de Gaulle's advice, General Grossin tried his luck once more with Pierre Guillaumat, the Minister of Defence, who had been the director of the Atomic Energy Commission (Commissariat à l'Energie Atomique: CEA), and requested the attachment to his services of several engineers. There was a total lack of understanding between the two men, and Pierre Guillaumat was scandalized at the request.

Lacking both the men and the means, SDECE obtained only indifferent results in its new mission. At the consulate in New York Colonel Hervé, given the task of heading a small scientific group in the United States, was suffering from a grievous lack of informants. After canvassing the great departments of state, SDECE had ended up by getting hold of two scientists who were brand-new graduates of the *grandes écoles*, but the Quai d'Orsay then appointed one of them to Washington as assistant press attaché. A terrible muddle: since he did not belong to the scientific services of the embassy, the young engineer had absolutely no contact with his transatlantic colleagues. A blow had been struck in vain.

Sometimes 'allied' espionage ended in outright catastrophe. At the time of the first plans for a Franco-German tank, in 1960, SDECE, through a secretary of the Bundestag defence committee, obtained a copy of the summary report drawn up by the German authorities. Its tenor was clear. In spite of the assurances given by Franz Joseph Strauss, the Minister of Defence, to his counterpart, Pierre Messmer, the Federal Republic refused to collaborate with the French. Official circles in Paris were so incensed that they divulged the famous report. And the investigation that was immediately set in train in Bonn traced the leak. The SDECE agent, an Alsatian, to whom the secretary had handed over the precious documents, had only just time to leave the German capital and cross over the frontier. The Franco-German tank was buried for good.

A Very Political General

'The best head of SDECE.' 'The most competent and the most political, which is not without its usefulness in this post.' All the testimonies agree. General Paul Grossin was a 'great' director of the French secret services. Born in Oran in January 1901, the young secondary schoolboy of Casablanca soon discovered his military vocation. He continued his studies at the Lycée Chaptal in Paris, taking a baccalaureate in science. He then enlisted in the Army, rising in rank very creditably and regularly. Having been made a lieutenant at the age of 31, in 1942 he was a lieutenant-colonel in Algeria, then a brigadier-general, and finally a major-general in 1949.

It was at this time, amid the upheavals of the Fourth Republic, that Paul Grossin finished his 'apprenticeship'. The Socialist President Vincent Auriol summoned this fresh-faced soldier and appointed him military secretary-general. The struggles between the parties were at their height. Scandals followed one after the other. At the Elysée Paul Grossin was seen as the republican general who defended the options fixed by the government. From this time dated his socialist reputation. Nor did Grossin hide his links with freemasonry, which evidently helped him to pick his way more skilfully through the maze of politics. In February 1956 he was appointed general commanding the 9th Military Region at Marseilles, but he became bored. Thus it was with eagerness that a year later he responded to the summons of the new prime minister, Maurice Bourgès-Maunoury. As he recalled:

I went to see Bourgès in Paris. When I arrived the prime minister said to me: 'Hang on, I want to give you SDECE. But wait a moment. I must find that wretched speech I had prepared for this evening.' Around the prime minister, everybody was rushing about. They searched under the tables, they rummaged through the offices, even the dustbins were turned out. And finally the famous speech was found. But Bourgès was late. He had to leave for his political meeting, and told me, 'Come back and see me tomorrow morning.' The next day he explained to me that he really did want to appoint me as head of the secret services, and I was to provide him with a detailed organizational plan. His entourage insisted that Pierre Fourcaud[4] and Louis Mangin[5] should figure on it. So I included them as advisers to the Director. But that was not good enough. Abel Thomas[6] came to see me to tell me that Louis Mangin could be nothing less than the assistant director. I refused, because that upset my whole organizational plan, and finally he gave way.[7]

As head of SDECE Paul Grossin embarked upon a cautious reorganization, aimed at placing the services under the sole aegis of the prime minister's Office. Under the Fourth Republic the habit had gradually grown up of confusing SDECE with a kind of junk room for storing all the whims of the ministries – this or that head of a minister's office asked it for advice, another recommended a friend, etc. The services themselves were very divided between Socialists and Gaullists, civilians and military personnel, and General Grossin had to work hard to introduce some order into them. The coming to power of General de Gaulle was to make things easier. Paul Grossin had known the General in 1939, at the declaration of war, when he was part of the Fourth Bureau of the Fifth Army under General Bourret, whose command post was installed at Wangenbourg in Alsace. During the 'phoney war' Colonel de Gaulle commanded the cavalry unit in that army, and loved organizing full-scale war games. Exercises cost dear. But Commandant Grossin discreetly provided de Gaulle with fuel so that he could carry out these exercises. Since then the two men, in spite of their political differences, had maintained a friendly relationship.

Nevertheless, had General Grossin helped de Gaulle's return to power? Had he participated, as had many military leaders, in the many plots that beset the dying Fourth Republic? In SDECE some claimed this was the case. In May 1958 some of them, including Louis Mouchon, even dispatched a short note to the Interior Minister, Jules Moch, alleging that, under the benevolent eye of their director, arms had been distributed to reservists so as to facilitate action on the part of the paratroops of Algiers.

'In fact,' affirms General Paul Grossin today, 'I had actually asked all the senior officers in the secret services to arm themselves, but had given a definite instruction: "We must not get mixed up in politics. Whoever they may be, whatever their political complexion, I order you to fire on any group that might try to gain entrance to Mortier barracks." In each of the three barrack buildings I had designated the most senior in service and rank and passed on the instruction to them. To cap it all, certain SDECE personnel afterwards wrote to Foccart that I was a puppet of the Socialists.'[8]

In any case, Paul Grossin the Republican demonstrated that he could put up very well with a change of government. The SDECE director served the new Gaullist government without any soul-searching. It could even be said that he spared no pains in giving it his support. In 1959 it was aircraft of Action Branch that carried the posters about the referendum to all the regions of France. Moreover, on this occasion the SDECE director agreed to lend some of his special funds to Jacques Soustelle, the new Minister of Information.

On the other hand, General Grossin did not give up hope of seeing the reform of the secret services. He had handed over a bulky dossier to Constantin Melnik, the adviser of Michel Debré, the prime minister. 'The recruitment of personnel was going very badly,' he explained. 'After the War there were up to 14,000 men in the services. Fortunately, we had dismissed most of them. But there remained a large number of drivers, typists, odd-job men, cleaning women, etc., in short, people who carried out no intelligence work at all. All these people were protected by SDECE's statute regarding civilian personnel. I therefore requested that this statute be abolished. It wasn't easy. Some of the civilian personnel appealed to the Conseil d'Etat, which finally found in my favour.'

Grossin's demands did not stop there. Since taking over he had deplored the absence of a real intelligence school in France. The officers that arrived at SDECE were certainly willing, but they were sadly short of training. 'In this,' the general concluded, 'I must confess that I was not successful. The most I obtained were a few courses lasting three months, to knock the rough edges off. They took place in Mortier barracks under the direction of Henri Trautmann. But it was still not sufficient.'[9]

General Grossin, having reached the age limit, was due to take retirement in 1962. De Gaulle hesitated to let him go, although, in his struggle against the OAS, he was going to need men on whom he could rely, and Paul Grossin, a soldier above all else, did not wish to participate in that struggle, against officers who might have been his fellow cadets.

The Boarders at the Gambetta

Domestic, quiet and comfortable – one almost put on slippers so as not to sully the polished parquet floor – such was the Pension Verdin, at 102 Avenue Victor Hugo. Up to 1953 SDECE officers stayed there when they passed through Paris, and even lived there, until the 'Dairy'[10] moved: from then on SDECE cadres whose identity did not need to be concealed spent the night at the Grand Hotel Gambetta, Avenue de Père Lachaise, ten minutes' walk from headquarters.[11] This arrangement mainly affected bachelors and officers coming from abroad or from the provinces. It is hard to imagine the problems of daily life that secret agents have to face.

Men of importance were to be found at the hotel, those who made up the management team of the 'Grossin firm': for example, his right-hand man,

Colonel Jean Auriol, a former head of the colonial intelligence service who had specially concentrated on Indo-Chinese sects. Colonel 'Jeannot' Auriol had an original mind, and occasionally tended to complain that the 'DG' (Director-General) did not allow enough scope for military personnel. The criticism was unjustified. In the 1960s the proportion of 60 per cent civilians at headquarters was to be reversed. But the 'big boss' still wanted to spread his net widely, broadening the recruiting field for future SDECE officers, and drawing upon the universities.

It has been a perpetual disadvantage for the French secret service not to be able to recruit scientists, economists and linguists on the university campus, as the British and Americans do. The lightning passage of officers who spent two years in SDECE before becoming military attachés, and then returned for a time to an Army unit, often proved disastrous. It was a question of security, pleaded Colonel Lionnet; it was a question of learning the job, complained 'Admiral' Trautmann, who in 1958 had just left his post in the Research Directorate in order to take on the training of agents.

He relinquished his post to Lieutenant-Colonel Maurice Dumont, undoubtedly one of the most accomplished of the leading lights in the history of SDECE. Dominique Loisel ('Domino'), a specialist in Soviet affairs, was at his side. Even in the middle of the Algerian war, the Eastern Europe networks were being strengthened. The Research Directorate indicated the direction of external action, defined 'intelligence objectives', and coordinated the work of station heads, in the Eastern bloc often officially 'assistant military attachés'.

On the fringes of the Communist world, in Vienna, Lieutenant-Colonel Humm, the former head of the Resistance network 'Uranus', had to unravel the threads of Soviet penetration in the most dangerous station of all. In Istanbul Lieutenant-Commander René Taro had very recently emerged from the top-secret submarine operations of Action Branch against the Algerian FLN. Another great name in Action Branch, Lieutenant-Colonel Louis L'Helgouach, explored the mysteries of Hungary. In Prague Commandant René Crignola, destined in the distant future to succeed his chief Dumont, arrived from Algiers: he knew the hidden links between the Czechs and Algeria, then almost independent. In Sofia Jacques Levacher, the 'commercial attaché', perceived a reality that today is self-evident: the Bulgarians merely constitute an unofficial Soviet Republic, simply lacking the name. Truculent Nikita Khrushchev should have been wary of Captain Albert Labbens. His SDECE station extended over Finland and Poland, and uncovered infiltrations even within the French Embassy in Moscow. Finally, Colonel Dumont did not scrimp on the 'honourable correspondents': who can say what secrets the great actress Marie Bell gleaned during her tours of the Eastern bloc?[12]

Sometimes the work was delicate. The Quai d'Orsay hardly made things easy: it afforded a diplomatic 'cover' to SDECE agents that allowed their holders to be identified immediately. Thus in the Cameroons the unfortunate Bounier presented himself as an 'assistant press attaché', when there was no press service at the embassy!

'Yes, but the people in Intelligence Branch are go-getters, men who serve as bait, who are set up so that our rivals in the East may attempt to recruit them.' The speaker, René Delseny,[13] was head of Counter-Espionage under General Grossin. A former head of military security from 1944, in Italy and then Germany, he became the counter-espionage chief in Indo-China. 'To carry out intelligence,' he asserted, 'is easier than to carry out counter-espionage. We only arrive at results after a lot of work. Counter-espionage provides intelligence; the converse is not true.' Indeed, following this logic, an intelligence officer sends off information. This is 'processed', summarized and exploited. But the counter-espionage man – at that time he was inside an embassy (as 'vice-consul', 'assistant consul', 'commercial attaché') – must cross-check it, verify whether the sources are sound, protect the vulnerable intelligence post, and organize the penetration of the enemy's set-up.

Through the section dealing with the traffic in arms, directed first by Albert Camp and then Paul Zigmant, Delseny's Counter-Espionage was at the centre of the struggle against the FLN during the Algerian war. His branch still controlled communications intercepts, through the GCR. Nor was this all: Counter-Espionage headed the internal stations in France. The Paris base, under the command of Colonel Roger Kessler and located at the Invalides, provided logistic support for SDECE and the agents in the capital, but also for activities directed against embassies that had been 'targeted', principally those of the Eastern bloc, as well as against representatives of African states visiting the capital.

Colonel Kessler was likewise responsible for the 'honourable correspondents': for example, a construction company carried out a contract at Tashkent in the USSR, and provided an opportunity to gain precious information. The same held good for the foreign relations branch of the Thomson company, managed by Paul Richard. Other SDECE stations functioned on French territory, aimed at neighbouring countries: from Strasbourg, Colonel Marcel Bernier worked on Germany; from Nice, Henri Géniès on Italy.

Until then the TOTEM sector had been organized by an agent named Ramier, who would send on material to Lieutenant-Colonel Marcel Mercier. TOTEM was the 'intelligence exchange', the link with foreign intelligence services. 'When I arrived,' said General Grossin, 'we had connections with other foreign services (Italy, USA, Great Britain, the German Federal Republic, and Belgium). But these remained too informal and were limited in scope. I set up a real organization, which I entrusted to Mercier: from then on we had links with the Danes, the Turks, the Greeks, the Spanish, the Japanese and the South Africans. It was a kind of barter system which, it must be said, never brought us much. The British did not always play the game and often passed on to us intelligence of no interest.[14]

This was also the opinion of Colonel Delseny, the head of Counter-Espionage Branch:

On China we had only mediocre intelligence. We sought it from the Americans and linked up with them in Taiwan. The Japanese? They came to see us at Mortier HQ. They brought with them a paymaster. I didn't understand much of their rigmarole. They thought only of one thing: getting drunk. Hong Kong was a jungle for spies. With the British and the Americans we swapped lists of crooked spies. The German BND [Bundesnachrichtendienst], Gehlen's 'firm', produced a lot. It handed over to us a mass of documents, but in general they were from published sources. Contrary to legend, I never had the impression that they did excellent intelligence work.

General Grossin's SDECE could, moreover, have kept control of the telephone monitoring service; his philosophy decreed otherwise. In 1959 the monitoring service was detached from SDECE, and the Inter-ministerial Communications Group (Groupement Interministériel des Communications: GIC) was set up. It was headed by the best technician in the 'Firm', Colonel Eugène Caillot, who had been detached for this purpose. He was from the Morvan region and of peasant stock; he had distinguished himself in Corsica during the War. A signals specialist who had joined SDECE when it started, his rise had been meteoric – first in Morocco, then at headquarters. His salary, it was said, was that of a brigadier-general. About 50 years old, going grey, wearing glasses and a hat – sometimes tilted back, even in the office – Caillot was a hot-blooded type. He was nicknamed 'Gégène' because of his outbursts of temper.[15] At 2 bis, Avenue de Tourville, from where he operated – the former HQ of the pre-war intelligence service – scores of technicians drawn from Renseignements Généraux and the DST, even temporary staff coming from French Railways, were busy.[16] Through the PTT (Postes, Télégraphes et Téléphones) they recorded or listened in 'live' to suspected sympathizers of the Algerian FLN or the Soviet KGB – and political opponents of the Gaullist government. This was the reason why General Grossin was delighted when the monitoring services passed under the control of the prime minister. But the 'chief' still amused himself – at noon, every day – by reading the monitoring reports that SDECE had ordered. For, as one might suspect, the service was well represented there. Eugène Caillot was to remain head of GIC for 15 years, and other technicians from the SDECE were to follow on after him.

An X-Ray Picture of SDECE

Under the general direction of Paul Grossin, Colonel Roger Fournier, an escapee from the Indo-China resistance, devoted himself to a 'permanent review of staff' – in other words, modifying recruitment with a view to greater 'militarization'.

The 1960 figures are public knowledge, so it is possible to form a fairly accurate idea of the organization of the service.[17] A total of 1,652 agents, civil servants and officers, could essentially be divided into three categories. On the one hand, there were 755 permanent civilian staff at headquarters, from directors to office personnel, senior clerks, telephonists and secretaries. For the classic tasks of intelligence and counter-espionage, directors, deputy directors and section heads ruled over the whole, whilst at the heart of the operation were the 'heads of Studies' ('exceptional', 'unclassified' or 'first class'), 'delegates', 'expert analysts', 'coders', 'documentation secretaries', and a whole spectrum of technical personnel, from laboratory technicians to locksmiths. To this established personnel must be added 54 members of the analysis staff (in reality, on detachment from the GCR), and two agents on contract.

Still at headquarters, a second contingent was made up of 244 officers and 260 NCOs. Of the 1,335 staff in the Boulevard Mortier and its annexes 62 per cent were therefore civilians. In a number of cases military personnel might perform the same role as civilians. This is why the SDECE directorate devised a table of equivalence between a status based on that of civil servants and a military one. Thus the heads of Studies in the 'exceptional' class were colonels, and the 'expert analysts' lieutenant-colonels. Conversely civilians were accorded a military rank for use outside.

A third group made up the 'external services', which officially comprised 317 people, both civilian and military personnel. They manned the intelligence and counter-espionage stations throughout the world.

Who were these men and women? The study of a sample of 80 biographies undertaken by the authors (5 per cent of the staff at the time of General Grossin) provides a number of pointers. Selected mainly from the 'top team' of SDECE, they all ended their career before the 1980s. The presence in this sample of only one woman at a level of high responsibility – a directorate secretary – is not as arbitrary as it may appear. In Mortier barracks women played a subordinate role, at best being analysts, but mainly shorthand-typists.

Our group comprised 30 per cent of civilians, all with fictitious ranks and subject to various regulations identical to those in the civil service, except for trade union rights – which were non-existent. Seventy per cent were military men: this is not truly representative of SDECE as General Grossin found it upon his arrival, but reflects the tendency that was accentuated after his departure, and became the rule later, especially after 1966, when SDECE passed from the prime minister's jurisdiction to that of the Ministry of Defence. This is how this sample population breaks down:

Working at Headquarters or its annexes	70 per cent
In external posts or with the 11th Shock Troops	30 per cent

At the time of the Algerian war covert action necessitated heavy deployment in external posts. The distribution between the services was:

Counter-Espionage (CE)	16.25 per cent
Intelligence (SR)	36.25 per cent
Action Branch (SA)	21.25 per cent
Administrative and technical services	26.25 per cent

Cross-postings occurred. Agents changed their branch or service. Thus, as we saw, Colonel Maurice Dumont, head of Counter-Espionage, became head of Intelligence Branch upon the arrival of General Grossin. And Paul Zigmant left Action Branch to lead the section concerned with the traffic in arms. Their origins were:

Former members of Resistance networks	56 per cent
Former members of the traditional SR/CE (including pre-war members)	32 per cent
From de Gaulle's BCRA	30 per cent
From other networks, especially the Socialists of Libération-Nord	38 per cent

Here one notes the phenomenon styled 'Neapolitan slices' within SDECE. For a long time yet – up to the end of the 1970s – the Resistance matrix would be the determining one. Needless to say, survivors of the Communist resisters in the Francs-Tireurs et Partisans were non-existent.

Participants in the Indo-China war	32 per cent

It was essentially former members of the BCRA who participated in that war as members of the secret services. The BCRA was the only one to possess an Action Branch, hastily refurbished under the auspices of Colonel Fourcaud, Morlanne and Aussaresses. The 'old' intelligence service did not really possess an Action Branch. The experience and average age of its cadres rather led them to work at headquarters or in stations directed against the Eastern bloc.

Participants in the Algerian war	38 per cent

Essentially these consisted of former participants in the Indo-China war, but also some younger staff – although the former Counter-Espionage group, in particular that of the CCI under Colonel Simoneau, were represented.

Length of Career

5 years or less	3.75 per cent
5–10 years	7.25 per cent
10–20 years	27.50 per cent
20–30 years	40.00 per cent
30–40 years	18.75 per cent
Over 40 years	2.75 per cent

The 30–40 years group came, of course, from the Resistance 'pool'. In

future recruitment was to be modified; although military personnel became the majority, their presence in SDECE was often interrupted by periods of command in the regular Army. The doyen of this sample, Captain Trautmann, began in 1924 in naval intelligence and was to finish his career in 1967 as Head of Training at SDECE.

Transfers out of the service   29 per cent

These left SDECE to enter another administrative department or, more frequently, to go into civilian life (often as security heads of big firms); the employment they chose corresponded to the expertise they had acquired (arms sales, analysis of future prospects, computer technology).

Careers abruptly terminated   25 per cent

Half of these were due to political reasons, such as belonging to the OAS or the Service for Civil Action (Service d'Action Civique), or participation in political, financial or other scandals. There remain five cases of persons suspected of relations with a foreign secret service; one case of assassination by an enemy service; one suicide; one case of insanity; one fatal accident during a mission; one agent condemned for the murder of his wife.

Geographically, Bretons and Corsicans were numerous in Action Branch and in SDECE as a whole. Many officers were natives of eastern France: Lorrainers and Alsatians recruited before or during the War. They were to be found in Counter-Espionage.

Socially, SDECE leaders came from the upper reaches of French society. More than 20 per cent belonged to the nobility and more than a third figure prominently in the *Bottin Mondain* (Social Register) or *Who's Who* – without of course their exact occupation being mentioned. However, that statement must be modified: contrary to the practice in the English-speaking countries, members of the elite who had graduated from the *grandes écoles* and entered SDECE as analysts, economists or information technologists were poorly rewarded financially for their decision to join SDECE. Likewise officers frequently considered, not without reason, that a spell in the secret services hindered rather than accelerated their promotion in the Army. Contrary to legend, a good dose of patriotism or the spirit of adventure was required to branch off into this path.

Dr Morali and Mr Daninos

Just beyond the mess, in the first building on the left in Mortier barracks, was the medical service. A man from Service 7 was just getting ready to leave. But the good doctor detained him for a moment: 'Wait, I've forgotten to make a note of your first vaccination.' Somewhat astonished, the head of the section dealing with the traffic in arms in the 'Firm' retraced his steps, provided the information and again made towards the door. 'One moment; where have we put your father's date of birth?' cried the doctor. Exasperated, the officer turned round, proffered a few swear-words regarding the medical profession, and left. 'Very good,' Morali-Daninos called after him. 'Fortunately, you ended up by rebelling.'

At SDECE such scenes were a daily occurrence. The psychiatric doctor was a formidable person. Behind the thick glasses, André Morali-Daninos had a piercing gaze – sparkling eyes that scrutinized and undressed you. From 1944 to 1971 all the directors of SDECE had complete confidence in this dry little man, weighed down with diplomas (in biology and psychology), with his satisfied smile.

In contrast to Michel Bommelaer, the ordinary doctor of the services, 'decorated with epidemics', André Morali-Daninos was concerned exclusively with the mental health of the little world of intelligence. 'If I needed stimulants or tranquillizers,' said a former safe-breaker, 'I would go and see Bommelaer. With him, it was all right. But I hated being psychoanalysed by Morali, who was a funny kind of chap. Frequently he had forgotten the key of his drugs chest and I was obliged to open it up for him.'

The room in which the psychiatrist receives us today is in an extraordinary muddle. On a small pedestal table stands a majestic wooden ship, surrounded by many photos of seascapes. The American and British colours, and the little flag of Williamsburg, fly over his desk. 'As a naval lieutenant,' our interviewee explains, 'I was in Algiers at the end of the war. Jacques Soustelle, then head of the DGSS, asked me to become the head of the psychology service. I accepted, and moved into a little room that had been requisitioned for me at Claridge's. Then Jacques Chaban-Delmas generously gave me one of the numerous apartments that had been requisitioned for him on the Place des Etats-Unis [Algiers]. I was able to bring my family and – for reasons of discretion – I employed my wife as my assistant. At that time I went to London a lot, and worked for their anti-submarine school.'

André Morali-Daninos stops his story for a moment and then continues, his face shining: 'One day I greatly astonished the British. I was then sitting on the Selection Board of the British War Ministry. Under the chairmanship of a colonel, there were present an expert in military testing, a psychologist and a doctor. It was exactly as in *The Jungle Book*: Bagheera, the panther (the expert), the bear (the psychologist), and the serpent (the medical virtues). I remarked to the British that it seemed like a re-run . . . They had never considered the matter like that.'

Forty years later, the psychiatrist still laughed at that joke, which was a diversion from the humdrum monotony of the services. In fact, the methods of the psychiatrist have nothing revolutionary about them. 'A spy,' said André Morali-Daninos, 'may be defined according to his capacity for adapting to different and hostile environments. He must also be fascinated by secret matters and be able, in all circumstances, to refrain from expressing an opinion.'[18] Fortified with this elementary common sense, the psychiatrist inflicted upon all the 'Firm's' agents a series of tests (which were at the time applied in other departments of state, such as the Ministry of Labour, and related to perception, and spatial and verbal intelligence). But above all Morali-Daninos was a specialist in 'inkblots' – the most famous method, that of Rorschach, consists of interpreting a dozen plates showing black or multicoloured blots.

The psychiatrist also had available instruments of greater accuracy, such as the lie detector. The first machine was introduced at Mortier during Pierre Boursicot's directorship.[19] Other detectors of a more sophisticated kind have replaced it. 'The most sensitive improvement,' explained the experts, 'was the introduction of the painless subcutaneous connection'. For his part Morali-Daninos mistrusted innovations – he was basically a traditionalist. It is true that this convinced Gaullist was to go on courses at the CIA, in the United States, in 1951 and 1962, but this did not make him forsake the good old methods. 'One must always,' he asserted, 'get as close as possible to real-life events. For example, when a candidate chooses a knave of hearts rather than another card, a face card rather than a number card, this is already an indication. The most anodyne questions are capable of revealing character, such as your attitude towards the British national colours. Or whether you prefer a flag or an ensign.'

Within the services André Morali-Daninos was respected, but opinions about him were nevertheless divided. The socialist clique of 'Morvan', rationalists to the *n*th degree, did not look upon all these 'interrogations' with a very favourable eye. On the other hand, the technicians were enthusiastic. 'An excellent specialist', General Grossin declared. 'His reports,' said Colonel Lionnet, head of security, going one better, 'were very useful. I always re-read them before an interview. They were very precise.' 'A terrific chap,' confirmed General Paul Aussaresses. 'Colonel Morlanne was a great friend of Morali-Daninos. In 1947 he suggested to him that the first 500 men enrolled in the 11th Shock Troops should undergo tests. At the same time Morlanne asked the military hierarchy to mark the men according to the usual cumbersome procedure. Then he compared the results. They differed in only one case – and that was regarding a man working in the officer's bar. Son of an air force colonel, he was a brilliant fellow, but very lazy . . . In short, in one day Morali-Daninos had arrived at results that were comparable to those we had obtained over several months.'[20]

The 'Invisible Images'

As soon as he was appointed to Mortier HQ General Grossin discovered a 'Top Secret' file. Only Bourgès-Maunoury had wind of this extraordinary affair. Each month SDECE paid over a million francs to a body that was studying a revolutionary photographic process. And the secret services were not the sole 'godfathers' of this invention, since the research was also financed by SEITA – the French state tobacco monopoly. This was the key point: the latest fashion, coming from the United States, was to perfect a 'psychological cinema', inspired by the first great advertising campaigns. Since it had been shown that a slogan could make a product sell, why should it not be possible to modify human political behaviour in a similar way?

The Director of SDECE, very interested in this, summoned the scientific genius behind it to him. His first disappointment was that Gilbert Cohen-Séat had not invented anything at all.[21] He was an academic, the head of the Centre for Film Studies at the Sorbonne, and the author of numerous research studies on the impact of the cinema, and he was merely proposing testing so-called 'subliminal images'. The idea was scarcely very complex. Normally a film is projected at 24 frames per second. The Americans thought up the idea of introducing a 25th image, which the spectator did not see, but which was registered all the same in the subconscious – these additions were christened 'invisible images'. When this process was invented in the 1950s, many thought that it would open up new paths. Some doctors prided themselves on having succeeded, through film, in appreciably modifying the condition of certain kinds of psychopath. These initial results made it possible to envisage manipulating the masses.

When he had finished explaining, the general questioned Gilbert Cohen-Séat: 'If I understand you rightly, you claim, if your experiments are successful, to be able to rally the battalions of the CGT and the Communist to the Gaullist ranks.' 'Precisely,' replied the professor with a laugh, 'but we have a long way to go yet. Our studies have hardly begun and will require time. We do not even know whether the procedure is really valid.'

Months passed, and the SDECE Director heard nothing further. In the secret services more tangible results are preferred. General Grossin decided to dispatch André Morali-Daninos, the psychiatric doctor of the 'Firm', to attend one of these celebrated experiments. The doctor returned unconvinced by what he had observed. The Director of SDECE in turn went to the scene of the research – a large apartment in the 7th *arrondissement*, entirely empty save for an immense screen. The master spy did not understand exactly what it was intended to prove to him, and remained perplexed. The first encephalograms recorded from viewers of the 'invisible images' did not make him any more enthusiastic. Today François Cohen-Séat explains: 'My father did not believe that this process was reliable either. But he wanted to be absolutely sure, by carrying out in-depth research: if they were successful, subliminal images really did open up unbelievable prospects. They knew how to make explosive charges, but not how they would explode in people's heads. In fact, all the experiments turned out to be negative, and so my father called a halt.'[22]

Without waiting for the experimental results General Grossin determined to get rid of this burdensome file that was costing his services so dear. But it was not so easy. Circles around Félix Gaillard, the new prime minister, remained favourably inclined towards the studies being undertaken by the professor and his team from the Centre for Film Studies; the head of his Private Office, Maurice Aicardi, was a vehement supporter of the project. On the arrival of Félix Gaillard's successor, Pierre Pflimlin, the head of SDECE made a fresh approach. But once again the head of the prime minister's Private Office – now Michel Poniatowski – explained to him that the objective remained one of the highest importance. When de Gaulle entered the Elysée, General Grossin thought that at last his troubles were over. Not at all. The 'invisible images' were still in favour in the higher reaches of the State. However, out of prudence, ten members of the Institut de France were brought together to ensure that the research was proceeding smoothly. The learned experts were very impressed by the statement made by Gilbert Cohen-Séat. 'I do not doubt,' expostulated the Director of SDECE, 'that the process is very interesting and full of promise, but I do not see why the research money should come from SDECE funds.'

It was finally decided to withdraw the file from the secret services. But, when the Centre for Film Studies obtained no other subsidy, it threatened to take SDECE and General Grossin to court for breach of contract. 'The decision taken by Michel Debré to stop all subsidies,' the academic's son observed with equanimity, 'killed the Centre for Film Studies. What a pity!'

Service 7: Cinema and Publicity

The opening of diplomatic bags often brings surprises. The Japanese pouch yielded an enormous amount of intelligence regarding political options in Tokyo, its economic spying and its links with the CIA. Then, one day, there was nothing. Naicho, the Japanese counter-espionage service, had discovered the SDECE intrusion into its private papers. It therefore preferred to direct SDECE's attention to a more enlightening form of literature: from then on the SDECE cover agents continually found bulky memoranda concerning Communist China! It was as good a way as any of honouring the TOTEM agreements concerning the exchange of intelligence between Paris and Tokyo.

Another time, Service 7 – nicknamed familiarly 'Cinema and Publicity' in the 'Firm' – opened a pouch belonging to the Egyptian Embassy. At the beginning of the Algerian war, this was target No 1. An astonishing find was made: a report from the head of Egyptian intelligence in London, Zacharria Ouftigouma, congratulating himself on having succeeded in intercepting the French diplomatic pouch in Great Britain!

The activities of Service 7, which came under the Intelligence Directorate, certainly were not commonplace. Since the 1950s it had grown solidly. 'Morvan', the head of the former 'Service 25 2/4' (which became '7' on the arrival of Paul Grossin), had gained a dynamic assistant, an ex-member of his Resistance network in Brittany, Marcel Le Roy, known as 'Finville', formerly employed in Supply. Occasionally Finville was criticized for taking an unfair advantage and claiming the credit for exploits carried out collectively. In reality Service 7 was one of the most flexible structures in SDECE: above all, it was a team entirely made up of civilians.

Its objective was to ferret out documents using every kind of covert means. Microphones were installed, mail was intercepted, diplomatic bags were opened – in short, activities went on that no government in the world would acknowledge. To do this – and this was what was unusual about it – Service 7 intervened even within France, whether the DST liked it or not. Foreigners passing through France were 'legitimate' targets, as were diplomatic missions or airlines and commercial companies of the Eastern bloc – which were often covers for communist espionage. Immediately frontiers, airports and certain railway stations became the happy hunting grounds of Service 7.

'Every day microfilms of documents seized from diplomatic bags were evaluated in the geographical sections of Intelligence Branch,' stated a former principal in Service 7. 'But, to be honest, 90 per cent of the information turned out to be unimportant. It was of stuff like: the Belgian ambassador requests so many rubber erasers and so many pencils from his ministry.' Le Roy and his assistant, Jean-Pierre Lenoir, supervised the teams of 'operational' agents and 'plumbers', always alert, always on the move in order to snatch documents, photograph them and then return them, unbeknown to the enemy. It was a mad race against time.

At the centre of the set-up there was a small team. In the camouflaged laboratories, Veuve, the technician, supervised the photographing. Then they proceeded to the 'distribution'. The analysts, sitting in a very small room in Mortier HQ, each covered a geographical zone. There were two former members of Renseignements Généraux: Marcel Nicolas took care of the 'free world' (America and Europe) and Pierre Catherine, a Norman, was responsible for the Eastern bloc countries (he was also a man of action, who succeeded in spiriting away a prototype of the Tupolev jet engine from the Russians). Michel Couvert, a Breton, followed the Far East. Louis Mouchon, a former head of the political sector, specialized in black Africa. Marcel Chaussée, a onetime administrative secretary, dealt with Arab questions, which were particularly vital during the Algerian war.[23] Guy Duboÿs, unfairly deprived of the post of deputy director, was the administrator and manager. Finally, Service 7 possessed its own security system, under Jean Tropel.[24]

But the wealth, the 'jewel' of Service 7, just as much as its 'safe-breakers', was its broad panoply of 'honourable correspondents', men and women to whom it could turn from time to time in order to carry out an operation. They acted out of sympathy, out of memories of the Resistance, or a passion for this secret world, or patriotism . . . There were hundreds of them. Chaussée had recruited an elite from the most advanced industries: for instance, the international relations department of Thomson, and many others. With René Kannengiesser, Commandant Chaumette directed the aeronautical section, and they recruited numerous 'honourable correspondents' in this field, which was both sensitive and decisive for any secret service. Under their influence, certain captains of Air France agreed to take considerable risks by departing from their flight plan over communist countries in order to photograph forbidden areas.[25]

Marcel Chaumien, an aviation specialist, whom we have already met in connection with operations in the Eastern bloc countries with the MINOS group, had likewise joined Service 7. He recruited 'honourable correspondents' in Air France and UTA, whose director of external relations was constantly lending a helping hand to SDECE. But Morvan, Finville and their men still recruited in all sectors of society. Two contrasting examples may be cited: the former motoring correspondent of *L'Aurore*, who became a reporter for French television news, Daniel Pouget; or – and this is a less delicate matter – the gangster Raymond Meunier, called 'Les Grosses Paluches' ('Big Mitts'). One day Finville enlisted the deputy head of the passenger service at Orly airport, Antoine Lopez. Through him, SDECE was to be deeply involved in the Ben Barka affair, and Service 7 to be reduced to nothing.

Jean Violet: A System of Influence

'Do you know the point of indecision, that moment when everything can tilt in one direction or in the other?' The speaker spoke slowly, but in assured tones. His dark eyes sparkled, fixing you like those of a hypnotist. 'It's upon that, upon those uncertainties,' continued the little bald-headed man, 'that I have built up my system of influence in the economic, military and political fields.'[26]

One morning in 1969 in Paris a vehicle belonging to the secret services stopped abruptly at 46, Rue de Provence. General Eugène Guibaud, the new head of SDECE,[27] and Colonel François Bistos got out of the vehicle. They entered the house of Jean Violet, the lawyer, to ceremonially invest him with the rosette of the Legion of Honour (Military Division). What were the meritorious services that such a distinction was rewarding? It was in 1951 that Jean Violet, an international lawyer in Paris, had made the acquaintance of Antoine Pinay, then prime minister. Jean Violet told the story: 'A Geneva firm during the war had been deprived of the services of a special metallurgy firm it had set up on German soil. As I am an international lawyer, Prime

Minister Pinay had got in touch with me in order to help one of his friends, a Swiss lawyer, sort out the affair. Going to discuss matters with the Germans, I quickly discovered that the requisition order the firm had produced in order to justify its claim was a forgery. As illegal appropriation had in fact occurred, I advised the prime minister not to get mixed up in the affair any further.'

Antoine Pinay had been very impressed by the personality of Jean Violet. He recommended him to Pierre Boursicot, the head of SDECE. Thereafter Jean Violet gave free advice to the services. 'Many people,' he explained, 'give a part of their time free of charge to causes of general interest, such as political parties and large-scale charities . . . Aware that I could be of some use to my country, through my international professional status, I opted to work for France through SDECE.'[28]

In 1957, after the arrival of General Grossin as head of the services, the personality of Jean Violet was to take on an added dimension at SDECE. The Director-General, in spite of the protests of various fiefdoms at Mortier HQ, employed him on political missions of great importance. The lawyer was entrusted with some of the contacts with the East. At the time of the Suez affair, at the very moment when Lebanon was preparing to join the small group of Arab countries which favoured breaking off relations with France, Jean Violet was sent to Beirut. Picking his way through a maze of religious brotherhoods, the lawyer managed to have a brief note passed to the Lebanese president. 'The point of indecision,' he smilingly claims today. 'The Lebanese had great interests in French-speaking Africa. If they were to persist in their attitude, I pointed out to them, those interests would be directly threatened.' It was a gigantic bluff, but in fact everything was totally restored to normal with Lebanon. Then the lawyer was dispatched to the United Nations and attempted to prevent that international forum from condemning French policy in Algeria.

At that time Jean Violet, who used an office close to the General Directorate, was accountable for his actions only to General Grossin himself. His sphere of influence continued to expand under the reigns of Generals Jacquier and Guibaud. Then Jean Violet applied his talents to other continents. He turned up in Brazil and Venezuela, where he won important contracts for the French Army. And also, it was said, in Switzerland, where his connections in ecclesiastical circles helped Marcel Dassault to sell his first Mirage planes. In so doing, the networks set up by Jean Violet had swollen in numbers and were costing the services more and more. Rumour had it that the lawyer was the most expensive 'honourable correspondent' in the whole of SDECE. This is one of the reasons for his eviction in 1970, when Alexandre de Marenches in his turn took over the direction of the 'Firm'. The new head had built up his own 'sphere of influence', and impinged on Jean Violet's. This was why it was impossible for the two men to get on together.

No Scandal at the United Nations

With his 'preaching friar' manner, Yves-Marc Dubois inspired confidence in his flock. He recruited them on every continent, and more especially in South America. At the United Nations Dubois, the Dominican father, was a member of the papal delegation, and it was in that capacity that he assiduously frequented the immense glass building on New York's 42nd Street. When he was not living in the house of his order in Paris, at 222, Rue du Faubourg Saint-Honoré, he was pacing the corridors of the United Nations in search of souls to be converted. But the font and the blessings aside, Dubois also tried to be a 'patriot'.[29] For him France was a second religion. And naturally he had been recruited by SDECE as an 'honourable correspondent'.

At the time of the Algerian war, he was often to be seen in the well-lit precincts of the United Nations, accompanied by an old acquaintance, Jean Violet the lawyer, accredited to the French delegation to the United Nations. The two men had little in common. If the reverend father liked his libations, particularly when they concluded with a brandy, the lawyer, his senior in age, liked to cultivate an ascetic side. This said, when it came to gathering intelligence, or 'manipulating' on an international scale, the two companions were inseparable. At Mortier HQ it was General Grossin who personally 'controlled' the two men. Their mission was no ordinary one. From 1955 to 1960, throughout the Algerian war, France was on trial in the court of international opinion. Jean Violet and Father Dubois had to fight this view, by every means. Before each session of the UN, the Director of SDECE invited them to dine, in order to work out a new plan of action.

From the time of its creation, the UN had become the platform for anti-colonialist struggles, which annoyed the 'builders of empire'. The Algerian affair appeared on the agenda for the first time on 30 September 1955. Immediately the French delegation, led by Antoine Pinay, left New York. In Paris the 'Friends of France' were alerted. In *Combat*, the daily newspaper, Raoul Fernandès, first the ambassador and then the foreign minister of Brazil, published a virulent article under the heading 'United Nations intervention in the Algerian affair would be unlawful.'[30] Even our most zealous diplomats would not have dared to employ such strident tones, for however good a cause. On the banks of the East River, the UN finally adopted a moderate resolution, which spoke of 'a peaceful solution, democratic and just, arrived at by the appropriate means and in conformity with the principles of the United Nations Charter'. But some years later the supporters of Algerian independence won their first vote. The 'Afro-Asian bloc', as they were beginning to be called, which grouped together most of the 'progressive' countries of Africa and Asia, in December 1958 almost attained the requisite two-thirds majority. Only one vote saved France from being condemned.

De Gaulle was very upset. He had never liked the UN 'thingummy'. But he feared the consequences of a widely adopted resolution. From the Quai d'Orsay every ambassador was ordered to promote in foreign newspapers a campaign favourable to French interests. 'The aim,' wrote Professor Alfred Grosser, 'was to prevent an accumulation of hostile votes in New York . . . And they were obliged to restrict the work of French representatives in a number of capitals to exerting pressure in favour of a non-hostile vote by the General Assembly.'[31]

The year 1959 threatened to be even worse than its predecessor. Observers at the UN predicted that several countries, such as Brazil and Chile, up to then favourably disposed towards France, would abstain when a fresh vote was taken. The Elysée wanted at all costs to avoid a fresh scandal.[32] In September de Gaulle dispatched André Malraux, the Minister of Cultural Affairs, to Latin America, in order to attempt to gather the lost sheep. The attitude of the Latin American countries would be decisive in the vote. SDECE was also on the alert. In New York, where they had set up their headquarters, Father Dubois and Jean Violet were in continuous contact with Colonel Hervé, their head of station. The fourteenth session of the United Nations opened in December in a tense atmosphere.

In the betting stakes France was always tipped to lose. Was it not even rumoured that generalissimo Rafael Trujillo, the director of the Dominican Republic, 'friend' of the French and a picturesque figure at the UN, might come out against Paris? That case was quickly settled in France's favour. But Father Dubois learnt, in the hushed atmosphere of the UN corridors, that Brazil in its turn would tip the scales against France. That very morning its delegation had met the representatives of the provisional Algerian government. First things first. In Rio de Janeiro Jean Violet was instructed to exert his 'system of influence'. What did the lawyer promise to the people he approached? That remains a mystery. The fact is that, a few hours before the vote, President Kubitschek sent a telegram to his delegation requiring them to vote in favour of France.

There was another source of satisfaction: Peru, which had wavered for a long while and had abstained in 1958, swung in the right direction. From Paris General Grossin personally followed the repercussions of the UN debates. Throughout the voting, which was taken clause by clause, Nicaragua and Paraguay continually raised the stakes. Now they would support a part of the Afro-Asian motion, now they abstained, or did not take part in the voting. Father Dubois spared no efforts in propagating his Gaullist faith. He beat a tattoo of powerful arguments. At the moment of the final vote Nicaragua and Paraguay rallied to the French side. Against all predictions, the two-thirds majority had not been reached. France emerged from the hornet's nest unscathed.

Three months earlier de Gaulle had received at the Elysée Dag Hammarskjöld, the Swedish secretary-general of the United Nations. Coldly, and not without arrogance, the General had told him that 'no other country could do as much for Algeria as could France', and that the carrying out of the French plan required that 'her hands should be left free'. From December 1959 onwards France regained that freedom. She owed it in part to the secret services, and their curious ways.

The Church of Silence

In spite of the Algerian war France did not give up its attempts to penetrate the Eastern bloc countries. Active as they were at the United Nations, the Violet–Dubois pair were mainly occupied with the communist world. Every month they received from General Grossin 500,000 francs to fund the 'Church of Silence' and its publications beyond the Iron Curtain. In exchange the two men submitted to SDECE information concerning the Soviet satellite countries.

What was the Church of Silence? Since the beginning of the Cold War this generic term has covered various operations of the Western secret services under cover of the Catholic Church.[33] It all began with the call of Pius XII for a holy war against communism: 'No one,' said the Pope, 'can be a good Catholic and at the same time a true socialist.' In no circumstances 'could socialism be reconciled with the profession of Catholicism'. The Americans pledged themselves to encourage this new crusade. An agreement, known as 'Plan X', was even signed between the Holy See and the State Department. 'Since the era of Constantine,' James Burnham, Truman's adviser, was to explain, 'the Church has known how to employ the secular arm, and it can bring its remarkable resources to bear through intelligence, persuasion, plans and organization.'[34]

Naturally it was in Rome that these new missionaries were trained. Training took place in three centres: the Russicum, or Russian Pontifical College, the Oriental Pontifical Institute and the Jesuit Novitiate. As the communist Roger Garaudy, not as yet defrocked, observed at the time, 'The fighting methods employed by the Jesuits are various. They work at the training of their agents and collaborators, whom they drill in military-style colleges.'[35]

In its Christmas 1949 issue the *Giornale della sera*, the clerical evening daily of Rome, described in full detail the activities of the Russicum. The author of the article noted:

The Institute is at present directed by Father Wetter, a young Austrian who in 1930 entered the Russicum voluntarily – as do all the students. The missionaries who graduate from the Russicum must have a perfect knowledge of Russia both before and after the Revolution, must be well up in sociology and be able to talk fluently and persuasively. This is what Father Wetter told me. But he did not wish to tell me anything about the very well-equipped gymnasia in the Institute, nor about the exhausting physical preparation that students undergo in order to face up to any circumstances. Wrestling, athletics, boxing, firearms practice and perhaps parachuting, are not minor subjects, but essential to the training of the missionaries of the Russicum. Nor did he talk to me about the physics, chemistry and mechanics laboratories, and the very diverse activities that the students undertake, so that they leave the Institute with a training that is not only apostolic, but also scientific and craft-based, in order to be able to face up to any event and play any role.

Each year a score of graduates from the course, such as Father Vandelino Javorka, made their way to Russia. In Rome these men were familiarly called 'the black parachutists'. Ever since the late 1940s, the meeting-place for all journeys towards the East has been Fribourg in Switzerland. One of the great centres of Catholicism, the town houses a very large number of religious orders. Its university is a breeding ground for secret agents. When the Cold War was over, the journeys overland or by parachute became rarer. But the town of Fribourg remains the best source for intelligence about the East.

Father Yves-Marc Dubois had a friend on Swiss soil, Canon Marmier, who happened to work in the bishop's palace at Fribourg. It was through these channels that SDECE, which had become increasingly wary of the organizations for émigrés from the East, which were numerous in Paris, was henceforth to obtain its intelligence – all the more so because Father Dubois also had the benefit of much support in the Vatican from Cardinals Benelli, Oddi, Siri and Villot.[36]

What was the value of that source in 1958? 'It varied considerably,' concluded a former high official of SDECE. 'But generally we had the impression that the best things were not passed on to us, but were reserved for others.' Hence, no great results in the East. In Paris the SDECE chiefs were only moderately worried. The obsession remained the struggle in Algeria.

8

Signed: The 'Red Hand'

Leon Trotsky founded the Fourth International in 1938. In 1960 this small organization had as its leader a legendary figure, the Greek revolutionary Michel Raptis, nicknamed 'Pablo'. Well versed in the art of covert activities, he committed his forces to support the FLN. Here they carried bags, there they helped prisoners to escape, elsewhere they built a clandestine arms factory.[1] For SDECE Pablo remained a permanent target, and on 10 June 1960 he was caught in the trap. To help the Algerians Pablo had set up a team specializing in the printing of forged French banknotes. The system functioned jointly between Holland, where the presses were, and Osnabrück in Germany, where Oeldrich, the photo-engraver, worked. Thanks to a Dutch informant, SDECE knew all about it. In order to emphasize the importance he attached to this capture, General Grossin went personally to Germany to persuade the counter-espionage service of the Federal Republic, the Bundesamt für Verfassungsschutz, to arrest Oeldrich. At the same moment Pablo and a Dutch Trotskyist leader, Sal Santen, were being questioned by the Dutch Internal Security Service (Binnenlandse Veiligheidsdienst: BVD) in Amsterdam. Locked away, then sentenced to prison until the Algerian war was over, after a much publicized trial Pablo could count his blessings. 'You're lucky to be in prison. You should be wary of the French, they're capable of anything,' he was warned by the prison governor, Tajconis. 'Them and their damned "Red Hand" . . .'

Pablo grasped very clearly what the Dutchman meant. One day near Bonn, the car in which he was travelling had been sprayed by a burst of submachine gun fire from a Mercedes. And a very recent event came to his mind. His wife often made the trip coming from Germany to Amsterdam to visit him in prison. One day on the return journey she found herself alone in the compartment. A man in a trench coat entered. He was cold and distant, as if he were not present. He had no cases. He simply took out of his pocket a detective novel, half-opened it, and stuck the cover under the eyes of the woman, who gave a start when she read the title: *The Red Hand*. Pale with fear, Mme 'Pablo' spent the rest of the journey ready to spring to the emergency alarm.[2]

The 'Hand of the Fathma'

Outside the Arab countries the Algerian war also wrought havoc. Starting in 1956, mysterious attacks struck down arms traffickers, their ships and cargo. Scores of Algerian leaders all over Europe fell under the assassin's bullet. Sympathizers with the Algerian cause, almost always Left-wingers, received threats, and occasionally even booby-trapped parcels. Each time, they bore the imprint of the 'Red Hand'. Journalists investigated.[3] In the press, different hypotheses were put forward. According to some, it was a clandestine organization made up of counter-terrorist groups, fanatical supporters of the French presence in Algeria, forerunners to a certain extent of the Secret Army Organization (Organisation de l'Armée Secrète: OAS).

It had, moreover, already struck at the Arab nationalists. As early as 1952, in Tunisia, the 'Red Hand' had liquidated the trade union leader Ferhad Hached. In 1955, at Casablanca, the director of the Lesieur oil company and of the newspaper *Maroc-presse*, Jacques Lemaigre-Dubreuil, a supporter of Moroccan independence, was assassinated. The assassination bore the mark of the 'Red Hand'.

Various mysterious individuals, identified as the authors of the attacks, were not reluctant to give an account of themselves. One such was Christian Durieux, a notorious member of the 'Red Hand'. A young teacher from Corsica – he was nicknamed 'Napoleon' – he taught mathematics at the Collège Albert-de-Mun, at Nogent-sur-Marne near Paris. He led a chequered life. It was said that his absences for illness coincided with escapades in Germany, where he shot down selected targets. At the end of November 1959 Durieux met Michael Jacobson, the British correspondent of the *Daily Mail* in Paris. The Frenchman pretended to confess:

I am an active member of the 'Red Hand', the secret organization that was founded in North Africa to pay back the terrorists in kind. Our activities have extended to Belgium, West Germany, Italy, Switzerland, and even to Britain – everywhere that agents of the FLN are to be found. If today I agree to make this statement, it is in order to re-establish accuracy of information about our movement. A tremendous number of falsehoods have been told about it – in particular, that we are Fascists who like violence for its own sake. The 'Red Hand' is neither a cranky nor a racist organization. It emerged because of the existence of terrorism. Its emblem was chosen as an allusion to the 'hand of the Fathma', the Muslim good-luck talisman, which is generally represented in gold or in black. Ours is red, standing for blood. Although up to now no French official has dared to admit our existence, the newspapers and the public have recognized us as the authors of numerous counter-terrorist exploits. We are not fanatical about violence. We claim the distinction of having put an end to the activities of certain arms traffickers.[4]

In April 1960 a hand-picked group of journalists were invited to a press conference at Versailles. It was held in secret. A one-armed colonel welcomed them, as the spokesman for a rival organization to the 'Red Hand', the 'Catena'. Taken prisoner at Dien Bien Phu, wounded in Algeria in 1956, attached to the Fifth Bureau (psychological warfare, they were assured), the colonel had left the army because of a disagreement, but also to devote himself to the 'Catena', the purpose of which was a whole programme in itself. He wished, he said, 'to prevent the Christian West being engulfed by the Barbarians'![5]

There was no need to fear an outburst of rivalry between the 'Red Hand' and the 'Catena' because, a few months later the connections between these two outfits were revealed in a report published in book form under the title *The Red Hand*. It was certainly not a bestseller, but its circulation was none the less astonishing. Since then, hardly a book has been written about espionage or the Algerian war that has not to some extent made use of 'information' contained in the text. The report was taken from a long interview with one of the presumed leaders of the 'Red Hand', and written up by the spy novelist Pierre Genève.[6] The highly coloured account related the various activities of the 'hit group' and of members already known through the press. The book fully reinforced the idea that the 'Red Hand' was an independent entity, even if it occasionally exchanged titbits of information with the celebrated 'Colonel Mercier' of the Deuxième Bureau – whilst of course justifying the attacks.

Why this publication? It was clearly to put up a smoke screen. Every line of it was based – and this was its strength – on the mistakes committed by the journalists who took it seriously.

What was its provenance? The publisher of *The Red Hand* was Jacques Latour, a bachelor born in June 1929 at Saint-Maur, where he was still living in 1960. His publishing firm, Nord–Sud, which was on a corner at 97, Rue de Richelieu and 25, Passage des Princes, was put on the Paris Commercial Register on 2 January 1960, and changed its name on 18 July, before ceasing its activities on 31 December 1963. As a publishing house Nord–Sud published only one work – *The Red Hand*!

But Jacques Latour himself had been a genuine French army officer, employed in the secret services.[7] His house, not far from the town hall of Saint-Maur-des-Fossés, was only a quarter of an hour's walk along the Avenue de Marinville, from the ruins of the abbey in the old quarter of Saint-Maur and the Tour Rabelais. What was the significance of this? Doubtless only a minor detail, but 23, Rue de l'Abbaye was then the home of Marcel Mercier, the SDECE colonel who had recourse to the processes of psychological warfare.[8]

In fact everything about this story was a matter of psychology. For instance the 'Catena' never existed, as was confirmed for us by one of the heads of SDECE's Action Branch at the time. The idea had simply come from an officer in the secret services with a lively mind, Dominique Loisel. The 'Red Hand'? 'The One-Armed Man'? Durieux's statements? A huge deception!

Today we can disclose that the 'Red Hand' was purely an SDECE creation. 'We guided this affair by remote control from beginning to end,' stated a former director, 'We had given Action Branch the job of playing the part. So the "One-Armed Man" had opened an office in Versailles, quite openly. But every time a newspaper requested an interview with the "Red Hand", everything was first concocted on the Boulevard Mortier.'

A False Scent: Colonel Mercier

Colonel Mercier was the *deus ex machina* of the 'Red Hand' – or was he? Was he the man who established links between the activists opposed to the independence of the Maghreb countries and SDECE? Whether he was or not, legend attributes both these burdensome offspring to him. Every arms trafficker who died owed his death to Mercier. The man was everywhere. 'Colonel Mercier, of French Intelligence, one of the finest and noblest figures of the post-war French services,' wrote Pierre Genève, 'one of those to whom France owes its most celebrated feats, remained in constant touch with us [the 'Red Hand'] and we often exchanged information.'

As one might suspect, the truth was somewhat different. The man called 'Little Mercier' or 'Von Kluck',[9] Marcel-André Mercier, was born on 24 November 1911 at Belfort. Recruited by Colonel Germain – who had kidnapped Ben Bella – during the War Mercier became the head of the 'Camélia' network in covert counter-espionage (the 'Travaux Ruraux' – 'Rural Works'), which, from Clermont-Ferrand, covered Central France. His ability to insert agents to penetrate the enemy set-up made him the 'Number Two' of Counter-Espionage in Occupied France, the deputy to Colonel Verneuil.[10] Alas, not for long! In June the Gestapo unleashed a terrible wave of repression. He escaped, but his wife's family and a number of his comrades were arrested. The net closed in. Arrested at Roanne in December, detained in Fresnes under the name of 'Robert Debenoist', he managed to have a report smuggled out explaining how his network had been rolled up. 'Little Mercier' was deported from June 1944 to May 1945, first to Dachau and then to Allach.[11]

Thick-set, 1.70 m in height, brown hair, slightly greying after leaving the camps, very dark chestnut-coloured eyes, this resolute intelligence officer, trained in the old school, was, like many others, astonished by the atmosphere of disorder that reigned in the DGER in 1945. Against every expectation, in SDECE he did not rejoin Counter-Espionage Branch under Colonel Verneuil, but was drawn towards Research. In 1952 he was in Switzerland. It was then that the legend began to emerge, which was later to dog him – that of his double, the 'terrible' Mercier of the 'Red Hand'.

Officially a commercial attaché, Mercier's work essentially concerned the Communist bloc. He, the deportee from Dachau, through Swiss Intelligence in Berne, made the first links with the former head of Nazi counter-espionage in the East, Reinhard Gehlen, the future head of the secret services of the new Germany. In 1954 the Algerian insurrection broke out. The SDECE organization in Switzerland took a different direction. His job was to learn about FLN contacts with the East, to trace the bank deposits of the 'rebel' faction – the financial donations made by the various Arab countries – and to sabotage budding Algerian diplomacy. Marcel Mercier excelled at it.

But in autumn 1956 awkward rumours began to spread. High officials in Switzerland were alleged to be agents of French espionage. Swiss neutrality was shaken. The threat rumbled on. The scandal was not long in breaking out. Mercier had recruited a Swiss secret agent, Inspector Ulrich of BUPO, the Swiss secret service, and (more notably) the public prosecutor of the Swiss Confederation, René Dubois. The latter, well versed in intelligence, provided hundreds of documents to SDECE. At Mercier's request, he facilitated the expulsion in June 1956 of Moulay Merbah, the secretary-general of the Algerian nationalist movement. Even more serious, he allowed SDECE interception of telephone communications between the Egyptian Legation in Berne and Cairo.

Ulrich was arrested and Dubois, the public prosecutor, put a bullet through his head on 24 March 1957. The press exploded. Max Ulrich was sentenced to two and a half years' imprisonment for 'political espionage', since it was also learnt that he had been providing Mercier with information about the Swiss political parties. 'M. Marcel Mercier,' the Federal Political Department announced on 20 May, 'who has been involved in the affair of leaks in the Swiss Civil Service, no longer belongs to the staff of the French Embassy. M. Mercier has left Switzerland for good.'

For almost 15 years BUPO, the Swiss secret service, was to carry on its campaign of revenge against SDECE, with the result that in August 1960 two other embassy attachés, Robert Cardi and Eugène Genot, as well as a Swiss woman, Mercier's former secretary, were in their turn accused of espionage. 'After these various affairs,' said Colonel Delseny, the then head of Counter-Espionage, 'until my departure in 1969, the Swiss would have nothing more to do with us. We did indeed once hand over information concerning a Russian network on their territory, through the military, but this did not put us back in contact with them. As for Genot, we never saw him again in our services.'[12]

In short, Mercier was 'blown'. Henceforth the press hounded him. It was said that he was organizing the 'Red Hand' attacks in Germany. This was not correct, but not entirely false. We find him again in Munich, enjoying consular cover. He established contacts for SDECE with General Gehlen's BND. He was an old friend of Gehlen. In exchange a BND officer was attached to Mortier HQ. Mercier's role was to exchange information, but also to ensure that the BND shut its eyes – and even give a little help – to the attacks carried out by the 'Red Hand', that is SDECE, in Germany. As headquarters feared for his life – during the Algerian war his name appeared constantly in the press – an officer from Counter-Espionage was dispatched. General Gehlen reassured him: 'I'll protect Philippe (Mercier's code name) like the apple of my eye. Never fear.'

And in fact, without naming him, the old Nazi spy in his *Memoirs* was to pay a resounding tribute to the secret agent, the former deportee:

My cooperation with SDECE continued, during the ensuing years, in close liaison with Franco-German rapprochement. In this connection, I must insist here on expressing my gratitude – notwithstanding his modesty and his well-known discretion – to the St-Cyr graduate, the officer who became my friend, who for more than 20 years became my interlocutor, with the full confidence of his successive chiefs and the French government. Hardly had he emerged from the horror of the Nazi concentration camps to which his activities in the Resistance had led him, together with his father, his mother-in-law, and two female cousins, not to mention numerous comrades in the network for which he worked – hardly had he been released than he had overcome his bitterness and become an enlightened, firm and effective worker for the reconciliation of our two countries. A passionate defender of his country's interests, acting with loyalty, dynamism and courage, in my eyes he represents an exemplary picture of the French intelligence officer, too often disparaged in his own country.[13]

Everyone had understood. After the Algerian war Colonel Mercier returned to Paris. From then on, until the end of the 1960s, under the name of 'Mareuil', he was to head the TOTEM section in SDECE, the 'information exchange' between the Western secret services. So it was not 'Little Mercier' who organized SDECE's sporadic operations under the 'flag of convenience' of the 'Red Hand'. But if it was not Mercier, who was it?

Operations 'Homo' and 'Arma'

Two men conceived, and then protected, the SDECE operations. As early as 1956 the socialist Director-General of SDECE, Pierre Boursicot, and his deputy Louis Lalanne, provided the impetus for this monumental deception operation. Boursicot, Henri Ribière's successor, was a former official of the Indirect Taxation Department, and a member of the Resistance up to the end of the War. In August 1944, as regional commissioner of the Republic at Limoges, he had his differences with the local Resisters, the Francs-Tireurs et Partisans led by the 'Tito of the Limousin', Georges Guingouin. Nevertheless two years later, with the coming to power of the SFIO, he was appointed Director-General of the Sûreté Nationale. Lalanne, a lawyer from Biarritz, was his assistant. There followed a short period as a prefect, and in May 1951 Pierre Boursicot was appointed Director of SDECE. Louis Lalanne became the head of his office. Former members of SDECE remember him as a man of character, hard-working, but occasionally adventurous – but all in all a good director 'for a civilian appointed by a political party'.

Faced with the upheavals in the Maghreb, it was necessary to retaliate. A secret cell was created, nicknamed, out of partiality for the Americans, the 'Braintrust' (*sic*). Under cover of the 'Red Hand' it was to fund very special operations: the assassination of leaders opposed to French policy, and to begin with not only those who supported the FLN. There were also Moroccans such as Allal El Fassi or Medhi Ben Barka; the Tunisian, Habib Bourguiba (who in the end was to be taken off the list); and, later on, Algerian leaders such as Aït Ahcene and Hafid Keramane, and German arms traffickers such as Georg Puchert, Marcel Leopold and Otto Schlütter.

The leaders of SDECE got together with representatives of the different ministries. From SDECE there were firstly Counter-Espionage Branch and Research, occasionally Service 7, and above all Action Branch. The last was the 'secular arm' of 'Braintrust', the real powerhouse of the 'Red Hand'. From numerous statements by witnesses the authors have been able to piece together the way 'Braintrust' worked. Let us take a simple example: Captain Paul Léger, before organizing the most devastating of all the 'contamination' operations of the Algerian war, Operation 'Blueitis', was posted to SDECE from July 1955 to March 1957, first to the 11th Shock Troops, and then to headquarters as a case officer, where he found a number of his former colleagues from the Indo-China War. Léger then took part in the operations designated as being the work of the 'Red Hand'. 'Naturally,' he confirmed, 'the "Red Hand" was a myth.'

His description of the operations conducted from beginning to end by SDECE – in particular that concerning the attack on the sloop *Bruja roja*, which he himself witnessed – could not be clearer:

With the approval of Guy Mollet, the prime minister, SDECE took the decision to carry out a one-off operation against ships due to arrive in Tangiers. I was put in charge of it. This is what normally occurred: a case officer was given a mission that did not involve others. He had available the resources of Intelligence Branch and the material means that he deemed necessary; then he elaborated his plan, which was presented before what was called the 'Braintrust' – representatives of Intelligence, Action Branch, etc., in the 'Firm' – SDECE. The operation was discussed, approved and presented to the prime minister's Office, which, in general, ratified it. The case officer then began his operation.[14]

All the resources of the 'Firm' were brought to bear. At the very beginning Colonel Morlanne, the head of Action Branch, even resorted to criminals. 'We'll use Jo Attia from Tangiers,' he said to Bob Maloubier, who recruited Attia as an 'honourable correspondent' for the Mediterranean. The mission was to assassinate Allal El Fassi, the leader of the Moroccan nationalist party, the Istiqlâl. There was no doubt that Attia was a gangster. This former soldier of the 'Joyeux', the African battalions, was also brave; nobody

disputed his distinction in the Resistance, still less his heroism in the camp at
Mauthausen. Big-hearted and loud-mouthed, he had nevertheless been
mixed up in all post-war crime, starting with the saga of the gang led by
Pierre Loutrel – 'Pierrot le Fou'. What is more he was remarkably
incompetent. In January 1956, accompanied by Gaston Despierres of
SDECE, he had attempted to blow up the Dersa Hotel in Tetouan in order
to kill El Fassi. It was a fiasco, and he was arrested by the Spanish.[15] His
friends in Paris succeeded in getting him charged with another crime, the
double murder at Monfort-l'Amaury, a dirty affair in which another of
SDECE's 'honourable correspondents', Francis Bodenan, was implicated.[16]
They achieved their aim: Attia was extradited to France, but at the cost of
enormous publicity, which SDECE could have done without.

Pierre Boursicot was furious. Morlanne gave way under the recriminations
and expected to be shown the door. In fact, he was to remain as head of
Action Branch for a further two years before being replaced by his deputy,
Colonel Roussillat. Maloubier was exiled to Gabon, where he was employed
by a cheese factory. The lesson went home. In the 'Red Hand' operations
there was no longer any question of using the Attias and their ilk. Only the
small teams of Action Branch, disciplined, mobile, perfectly isolated from
one another, were authorized to act. At Cercottes, in the jargon of the
branch, they set up the 'Homo' (homicide) and 'Arma' (arms) operations. In
numerous cases the objectives were revised, since it was a matter of putting a
stop to the traffic, firstly by destroying the shipments, and if then necessary
by executing the gunrunner himself.

The Arms Traffic Section

Georg Puchert, the head of Astramar Import–Export in Hamburg, was
supplying the FLN with weapons. The first time he was warned by SDECE.
The Counter-Espionage representative in Tangiers, Lieutenant Boureau-
Mitrecey, even met him early in 1957 and said: 'M. Puchert, you should stop
selling arms to the Algerians. You are letting yourself in for serious trouble.'
Herr Puchert stood his ground. Then on 18 and 21 July two ships, the *Bruja
roja* and the *Typhon*, were blown up in the port of Tangiers. Puchert, whose
gang had been infiltrated by SDECE, thought he could withdraw to
Hamburg. In the night of 30 September/1 October 1958, the frogmen of
Action Branch struck once more: the *Atlas* was sunk, and was a total loss.
Since he had still not got the message, Georg Puchert was blown up in his
booby-trapped car in Frankfurt, in March 1959.

One may disapprove of this, but one certainly cannot criticize SDECE for
acting blindly and unthinkingly. Otto Schlütter, another gunrunner (who
later supplied the IRA), abandoned the game.

In tracking down, detecting and pinpointing the traffic in arms, the central role was played by Colonel Delseny's counter-espionage section. In Tangiers, Bourreau; in Hamburg, Nadal; in Berne, Genot; in Brussels, Fichard and Gaspard; in Beirut, Geniès – these were the remarkable 'vice-consuls' who kept watch, together with a few others who, day after day, observed the smallest transactions that might help to replenish FLN supplies. As soon as the insurrection began in 1954, an arms traffic section was set up in SDECE. It centralized all the intelligence that the various services could gather. One of its former leaders stated:

During the Algerian war the struggle against the supply of war materials to the FLN was the essential part of our work. It was through this new 'specialization' that we learnt the methods to follow, the scents to trace back, the financial dealings, the names of the traffickers and the principal middlemen. After having tracked down and pinpointed the gunrunners and their different networks, the General Directorate had to be informed through memoranda, syntheses and files, and it was the Directorate which decided whether we should to follow something up. From what I knew of it, our favourite informant was the Navy, which very often intercepted ships transporting arms and equipment for the FLN. If Action Branch was entrusted with isolated operations, the arms traffic section was not informed. Secrecy between units remained strict. Only the General Directorate made decisions.

In these matters, the role of the 'honourable correspondents' was vital. Thus Paul Richard, the chairman of the Thomson firm, used to warn SDECE when he had wind of shipments of arms to be sold clandestinly. He bought them, and SDECE reimbursed him. One day he called headquarters and said: 'A supply of arms, particularly bazookas, is up for sale in Stockholm!' Even before Paris had made up its mind, the SDECE station in Beirut reported that two Lebanese planes of Middle East Airlines had taken off without their destination being announced. On the return journey, on its stops at Basel, Genoa and La Seynia, the plane with its cargo of bazookas came to a halt at the end of the runway and was never searched. SDECE finally had it intercepted when it was over Oran.

Action Branch also mobilized its 'honourable correspondents' for one-off operations. Although it was a fairly small number of men who actually carried out the attacks attributed to the 'Red Hand', the logistic support was considerable. With Colonel Roussillat, his assistants, Zahm and Lehmann, trained the agents at Cercottes and chose the ones to be assigned to armed operations. Colonel Jacques Zahm, deputy commander of the 11th Shock Troops, in charge of intelligence and training at Cercottes, had nine lives. A former member of the BCRA, he was deported to Auschwitz in 1944, but succeeded in reaching the Soviet lines at the beginning of 1945. After repatriation he joined the DGER, then the Legion in Indo-China. In April 1952 he was in command of a company of Legionnaires whose position was suddenly raked by mortar and bazooka fire. It was a massacre. Wounded by a burst of fire, but one of the few survivors, Lieutenant Zahm was questioned by the Vietminh about any arms caches he might know of. He refused to talk.

The political commissar had him lashed to a post, walked up to him and fired a bullet into his neck. A flash – but nothing happened. Then Zahm broke free whilst the hut was burning, crawled along the ground and plunged into a swamp. Picked up by a French medical team, he recovered.[17]

It was also he who brought to Cercottes the 'Aztec Wizard', Captain Jeannou Lacaze, the great explosives expert. 'Red Hand' operations also meant special weapons, such as the celebrated long blowpipe equipped with a poisoned dart, which was used for the assassination of Marcel Leopold, another German arms trafficker, at Geneva in 1959. Similarly, pen-shaped pistols were perfected by a goldsmith, the Polytechnique engineer Henri Deruelle, who had already invented the MAT 49 submachine gun. The powerhouse for one-off operations was section B3 of Action Branch, where they were planned.

Then there were the means of communication: at the time SDECE possessed its own air squadron, with Hurel-Dubois planes that needed only a short landing strip in order to put down men clandestinely. Above all, the Navy made available to SDECE a small submarine and two minesweepers. The figure of René-Charles Taro dominated all the naval operations of the service, particularly those involving sabotage. Taro, a lieutenant commander of about 40, who had undergone training as a paratroop commando, could take credit for having sunk 14 yachts, freighters and coasters, and sent to the bottom 2,000 tonnes of arms intended for the Algerians.

Thus the 'Red Hand', manipulated from beginning to end by SDECE, was anything but a man-hunt organized by a handful of fanatics. Nor was it the only SDECE operation outside Algeria.

'Kléber', the SDECE Radio Station

His name in the Resistance was 'Colonel Franck'. He organized the 'Andalusia' network, one of the most important escape and intelligence networks in the south-west. After the War he became responsible for SDECE counter-espionage in Spain and Latin America. Although he had married a colleague of Colonel Passy, he was none the less a friend of Jacques Soustelle, Passy's predecessor as head of the services. His real name was François Bistos, and he was to have a long career in SDECE.[18]

In July 1958 he headed an astonishing operation, which has remained unknown up to the present day. Officially Bistos was then a technical adviser attached to Jacques Soustelle, at that time Minister of Information. Through a private company, Vigie Immobilière, SDECE bought the magnificent estate of La Chintraie, at Jouy-sur-Eure, near Chartres, where it planned to establish a radio station for programmes in Arabic and Kabyle. SDECE was granted a budget of 120 million francs. The 'sponsors' were the Ministry for Foreign Affairs (35 million), and the directorate for Algerian Affairs (15 million), and it was supported by the Ministry of Information as well as

Radiodiffusion Télévision Française (RTF). The population of Jouy was amazed. In August the estate was guarded by a colonial parachute section that had come up from Pau. Electrified barbed wire and mines round the outskirts of the park protected the villa. Christened 'Studio Kléber', the transmission centre was linked to RTF's Studio Christophe Colomb, which specialized in Arabic and Kabyle programmes.

Christian Chavanon, the RTF director-general, himself paid a visit to the Jouy centre, which broadcast on low frequency through the Studio Christophe Colomb (whose staff allegedly did not know that the broadcasts had been pre-recorded at Kléber). The idea was to spread 'black propaganda', in other words, deception material, on the short-wave in the 17, 19 and 25 metre band, and only in the evening.

Fourteen Arab and Kabyle announcers and their families lived tucked away in the Kléber centre, maintained by means of 200 million francs made available from the Quai d'Orsay and its Middle East desk. Under François Bistos, a troika of specialist officers ran this 'black' radio station: Captain Langella, expelled from Tunisia; Commandant Colonne, an officer for Native Affairs who in Paris was concerned with broadcasts in Arabic and Kabyle; and finally, Lieutenant Franco, a former censor with Moroccan radio, who was forbidden to reside in Morocco.

Jouy 'manufactured' both false variety shows and political reports modelled on the 'Voice of the Arabs' or the 'Voice of Free Algeria'. The principle was the same as that employed for the bogus newspapers pirated in Algiers by General Jacquin's Bureau of Studies and Liaison. Jamming of broadcasts allegedly relayed from Radio Lebanon or Radio Free Algeria was simulated through transmitters not far from the Tunisian frontier. The announcers, natives of the Maghreb, the Mashrek and the Middle East, imitating the special style of the FLN, modified the content in order to cause disquiet among its supporters. It was nothing like the open propaganda broadcast to the Arab countries from Cyprus, through Radio Somera.[19]

With the exception of a handful of RTF technicians who were doing their military service at the Kléber centre, the presence of Arabs and paratroops gave rise to incidents with the inhabitants of the small village, who numbered fewer than a thousand. This is not to mention the improper behaviour of certain officers with regard to the very few women attached to the centre. Yet if the Studio was finally doomed to disappear, it was above all because of the rivalries that surfaced after 1961. The protection exercised by Jacques Soustelle over the Kléber centre demonstrated that the former head of the secret services had from 1945 preserved a certain influence in the field. But Soustelle picked an ever increasing number of quarrels with Constantin Melnik, the adviser in this matter to Michel Debré, and hardly endeared himself to the SDECE chiefs. Privately he even averred that its director should be replaced, and whispered the names of possible candidates, among them that of Colonel Fourcaud. The problem was only completely resolved on the day when Soustelle opted to side with those who were unconditionally for a French Algeria. His friend, François Bistos, was to rejoin SDECE, from which he had been temporarily detached, and soon became the head of General Jacquier's office.

The 'Magenta' Disaster

Pierre Gondolo was a model employee. In his fifties, he was married, but with no children. Born in the Var department in 1908, at the age of 20 he settled in Tunisia and made his career in the PTT. In 1955, at Independence, he became section head at the central telephone exchange of Tunis and, like many other Europeans, agreed to remain and work for the new state, within the framework of technical cooperation. But on the morning of 10 February 1959 Pierre Gondolo fell out of the fourth floor window of a building belonging to the Tunis security services. Their head, Ali M'Rad had no reputation for soft-heartedness, but this was certainly going too far. The broken body of the technician was still warm when Taïeb Mehiri, the Minister of the Interior, organized a resounding press conference, at which he said:

A serious crime has just been uncovered by the [Tunisian] Sûreté Nationale and the services of the PTT. French civil servants, recruited through the [French] cooperation agency, employed to give technical assistance and paid by the Tunisian government, are responsible, with others, for this crime. Remarkable for their technical perfection and attention to detail, the incriminating activities are unique in nature. We know of no previous example in the history of espionage, a field where ingenuity has rarely led to so many vile actions.

Pierre Gondolo had been one of a group of 14 French citizens arrested the previous day for espionage.[20] His 'suicide' had been a 'deplorable accident', but he had preferred to kill himself rather than confess to his activities, declared Taïeb Mehiri. Hubert Dubois, officially a 'technical assistance adviser,' was alleged to have been servicing the activities of the network. The journalist Guy Sitbon, who was the correspondent for *Le Monde*, wrote:

The [Tunisian] Secretary of State for the Interior then set out in detail the results of the enquiry, which, he said, had gone on for two whole years. The networks covered the whole of the Tunisian Republic. They were run by SDECE under the code name 'Magenta'. 'Magenta', M. Mehiri indicated, was run by Commandant Conty (who had recently been recalled to France) and was split up into various sections. One, directed by Commandant Jean Geoffray, was in charge of providing intelligence about Libya, the Middle East and oil supplies. Another, continued M. Mehiri, gathered information about Tunisian political activity, that of the FLN and of foreign embassies in Tunis. It had powerful resources as its disposal. One part of the network – that of telecommunications – especially attracted attention.

The Secretary of State for the Interior gave the names of the French technicians who were in charge of the different sectors and who had developed original systems of interception, the plans for which, signed by their authors, were presented to journalists during the press conference. According to the minister, the centre of this network in 1947 was in the premises of the French Red Cross, in 1955 in the Casbah barracks and, since 1956, in the French Embassy in Tunis (in the 'penthouse' on the third floor of the embassy).[21]

It was a harsh blow to the SDECE set-up in Tunisia, all the more so because the 'Magenta' network had carried out some memorable feats: even the private telephone of President Habib Bourguiba had been tapped. However, René Delseny, the head of SDECE Counter-Espionage at the time, asserted, 'No, it was not a setback for our services. In this kind of undertaking one takes risks. That's normal. The mistake was to have left these people on the job for so long.'[22]

This statement could also be applied to Commandant Paul Conty, the head of the network. Shortly before the round-up of the 'Magenta' network, Conty was closely 'tailed' by the Tunisians, and his home was under surveillance day and night. He succeeded in shaking off this tough surveillance and in getting back to France. Paul Conty, a Tunisian-born officer trained at Saint-Maixent, had spent a long career in North African intelligence, first at the Military Security Bureau in Constantine at the Liberation, and then in 1956 he had been made assistant to Colonel Germain in the Tunis counter-espionage section. This big, stout, balding officer, had been too long in Tunis not to acquire habits or to fall into a certain routine, and thus was constantly followed by the services of Ali M'Rad, who was backed up by the CIA and the West German BND, playing against their French 'allies'.[23]

Nevertheless, this having been said, Commandant Conty had organized a vast apparatus that allowed numerous agents to escape being rounded up.[24] Such was the case of Armand Belvisi, who said: 'The secret service in the French Embassy for which I had been working for four years advised me to leave Tunisia and seek refuge in France. My work as an intelligence agent was over. So were my investigations into FLN bases in Tunisia, the training camps, the supply centres and covert printing presses ... All that was over ... I was no longer useful.' In 1961 Belvisi was to become a member of an OAS network. He was arrested, but freed in June. On 24 June he blew up the Paris bookshop of François Maspero. In August he organized the attempt on de Gaulle's life at Pont-sur-Seine.

Other agents of Commandant Conty succeeded in avoiding the great round-up of February 1958. Claude Bachelard, of the 'Magenta' network, got away in time. He was to be found a year later taking part in the special operation against Sékou-Touré's Guinea. Jean-Jacques Leroy, a Public Works engineer attached to the Bey's palace, became the friend of President Bourguiba. But, recruited by Laurent Pace, photographer to Georges Gorse, the ambassador, he took part in various isolated operations of SDECE and was to be expelled from Tunisia in 1960.

Thus the 'Magenta' network faded away. SDECE was never to build up such an effective organization except during the colonial war. At the time, the 'Magenta' affair, which happened just when General de Gaulle was on a visit to Algeria, provided Bourguiba's Tunisia with the opportunity to give forthright expression to its support for the FLN.

The Mattei Rumour

On 27 October 1962, Enrico Mattei, the Italian oil magnate, and a journalist from *Time* magazine, died in an aeroplane accident in northern Italy. The twin-jet Morane-Saunier 760B, Mattei's personal plane, crashed at Bascape, near Pavia. According to the commission of enquiry that was set up immediately, the accident was due to bad visibility as well as pilot error. But the magistrates did not rule out the possibility of some sort of hidden destructive device. The hypothesis of an assassination was not completely rejected.

Thus the Mattei legend was born. And there were clues enough to implicate SDECE. For several years Mortier headquarters had indeed taken a close interest in the head of ENI (Ente Nazionale Idrocarburi). For Mattei was no ordinary manager. After the war he had endowed his country with an impressive petroleum industry, covering Italy with 4,000 kilometres of pipelines. But he needed crude oil. Defying the monopoly of the powerful US multinationals, Enrico Mattei succeeded in negotiating with the Russians and the Shah of Iran. A convinced anticolonialist, he supported the young Algerian revolution as soon as war broke out – not without ulterior motives. Much information reaching Paris at the time dealt with transactions between Mattei and the Arab leaders. In exchange for material support the Algerian leaders promised him a future monopoly in oil prospecting in the Sahara. SDECE even managed to obtain the contract signed between Ferhat Abbas and Mattei. In this document the Italian magnate pledged himself to supply large consignments of arms to the 'rebels'. The French secret services therefore had reason to bear him a grudge. And it is true that General Grossin gave orders to his agents to watch Mattei's comings and goings – to keep an eye on him, but not to kill him.

The Italian industrialist was not a professional arms trafficker, like those whom Action Branch usually took as its prey. He was a politician, popular in his own country and throughout the Third World. A former head of SDECE reported: 'We never received an order to execute him. Mattei was in any case well protected, and we never made any attempt upon his life.' However, the rumour grew. Captain Henri Trautmann, by then retired, made some startling revelations on the subject. In the process of knocking the rough edges off the young recruits to the Boulevard Mortier, this former director of Research at SDECE had fallen into the habit of romanticizing about the history of the secret services. Thus when the 'Admiral' decided to pass on a few confidences to three journalists,[25] he embroidered the truth a little. For example, in order to illustrate the role of Action Branch during the Algerian war, he quoted the case of the execution of a 'big shot' in the oil business, who was linked up with the Algerian 'rebels'. By coincidence, two years later Thyraud de Vosjoli, a former member of SDECE who had taken refuge in the United States, accused the Gaullist regime of having had Enrico Mattei assassinated.[26]

'It wasn't SDECE, I am convinced.' The authors received this assurance from one of the leaders of Action Branch at the time of these events. 'Besides, by October 1962, the Algerian war was over, and the OAS people who had actually sworn to kill him [Mattei] were either in prison or had fled. As for Thyraud de Vosjoli and the others who say that, using some sort of special computer technology, SDECE had decided to assassinate Mattei, they made it all up. They knew nothing about this story, because of the compartmentalization that is the rule in our services.'

Who was it then? 'The Americans,' our interviewee from Action Branch replied without hesitation. This was a hypothesis recently taken up by the Soviet secret services, who accused the CIA of having put the assassination out to contract, via the Mafia.[27] The sudden disappearance of the Italian journalist Mauro di Mauro on 16 September 1970, in any case confirmed the part played by the Mafia in the affair. For the purposes of his film *The Mattei Affair*, the film director Francesco Rossi had asked Mauro to reconstitute hour by hour the timetable of the Italian magnate in the course of his final journey in Sicily. To a few of his cronies the journalist had confided a few days before his death that he had gathered information about the Mafia that would 'blow the Italian political world apart'. A mysterious death – disappearance without trace – was the reward for his efforts.

SDECE Ignores the OAS

'I'm against the OAS. But I don't want to hunt down officers like ourselves. That's the cops' job, not ours. We mustn't make the "Firm" blow itself up!' This was the main objection put forward by General Grossin in 1961 to all those who asked him to launch the commandos of Action Branch against those of the Secret Army Organization (OAS). The rumour was circulating that the arms traffic section had been changed into an anti-OAS section. In reality the Director-General did not want the Tourelles barracks changed into a kind of medieval tilting-ground for the settling of old scores. He had more than one argument up his sleeve: that the OAS was a matter for home affairs and verged on civil war (this was true, but so did the FLN uprising, in official eyes); or, that whole networks would run the risk of being wiped out, and SDECE would survive for a long time after the clash of arms had died away in Algeria.

A few officers, such as Philippe de Massey, were prosecuted for their activities on behalf of the OAS. Others joined a combined group, with Military Security, in the struggle against the OAS. Jacques Foccart was its founder. Contrary to legend, he did not recommend recourse to the *barbouzes*, the covert commandos, but the use of men of the regular services. And yet Commandants Poste and Rançon of Military Security were assassinated in Algiers, and Louis Soliveau, nicknamed 'Jacques', an SDECE agent, was killed by a bullet through the head near Aix-en-Provence whilst he was investigating their deaths.[28] Foccart gave up, and the *barbouzes* took over, working with the Action Association of the brothers Le Tac or Ponchardier, and with Lucien Bitterlin and his Movement for the Community (Mouvement pour la Communauté) – in short, with a whole bunch of riff-raff recruited by the lawyer Pierre Lemarchand or by Roger Frey, who had been brought together because of their affinities and their loyalty to Gaullism. Personnel taken from the various police services were to lead the intelligence battle against OAS. SDECE turned its gaze elsewhere, a little farther south. In black Africa too a page of history was being turned.

9

The Colonies are Finished

It was a modest office on the third floor of the central building in the Tourelles. On the wall was a map of Africa, already out of date. A handful of files were scattered across two tables, at one of which a functionary was laboriously filling in a record card. That was SDECE's Africa service before 1958 – a few pen-pushers, 'Benedictines', as they were called in the 'Firm', lacking resources. The archives were still littered with files dealing with Collaboration and the Resistance, and very little shelf space was devoted to African affairs. The paucity of resources and the poor quality of the intelligence collected considerably limited the credibility of the SDECE synopses destined for the government authorities.

France was then at the height of the Algerian war. Colonel Tristan Richard, who directed the Africa–Middle East division, only knew the northern part of the continent. The rest could wait. On the ground the situation was hardly any different. In the whole of Africa, leaving out the Maghreb countries, SDECE had only five stations: Addis Ababa in Ethiopia, Abidjan on the Ivory Coast, Dakar in Senegal, Brazzaville in the Congo and Tananarive in Madagascar. Curiously, all these stations, set up in the 1950s, were run by Counter-Espionage. This was because, at Mortier headquarters, one man was at the height of his power: Colonel Verneuil, head of Counter-Espionage. On the other hand, the 'honourable correspondents' were legion. Service 7, given the task of recruiting them, did not stint on its enrolments.

SDECE agents were enlisted by any means available. 'I had recruited a friendly trader of Port-Etienne,' said Maurice Robert, ex-head of the Dakar station. 'One day he insisted on introducing two lobster fishermen to me, who, he said, might be useful. One of them was none other than Georg Puchert, the notorious arms trafficker,[1] who concealed his activities by trading in fishing nets. But my correspondent did not know this.'[2]

In short, 'subsector' Africa amounted to an amiable joke. Paradoxically, it was during the period of decolonization that the French secret services became intent on playing a major role there. After his return to power de Gaulle confided to Malraux: 'The colonies are finished.' On 23 August 1958, in his celebrated speech at Brazzaville, the General set in train the process of decolonization. His plan for a 'community' – a confederation of African countries linked to France – was only an intermediate stage. From 1960 onwards most of the former colonies became independent. Two years later, it was the turn of Algeria, and the French Empire no longer existed. Gabon, the Congo (Brazzaville), Oubangui-Chari (Central African Republic), Chad, Senegal, Ivory Coast, Dahomey (Benin), Guinea, Upper Volta, Mauretania, Niger, Togo, Cameroon and Madagascar became sovereign states. New forms of cooperation replaced the old system. In de Gaulle's mind, these territories remained irrevocably attached to France. He considered that the historical, sentimental and economic ties uniting the former Metropolitan country, France, to the French-speaking African countries justified this interactive process.

Independence, by all means – but on condition that it did not run counter to the interests of Paris. The surveillance of Africa was all the easier because these young nations were very vulnerable. They possessed no military weapons and appealed to France in building up their armies. Bilateral or multilateral agreements were signed, depending upon the situation. It was often former black officers of the French Army who occupied the key posts in the new national units. Through Technical Military Assistance (Assistance Militaire Technique: AMT), within the geographically strategic triangle formed by Dakar, Pointe-Noire and Fort-Lamy, France trained the forces of its former possessions.

Under the Leadership of Colonel Foccart

In Luzarches he is still called 'the Minister for Foreign Affairs'. In this little market town in the department of Val-d'Oise, Jacques Foccart did not need to be a municipal councillor in order to become the champion of twinning with foreign towns. And Luzarches, a modest commune on the outskirts of the Paris area, has the rare privilege of being twinned with the new capital of the Ivory Coast, Yamassoukro, the village where Houphouët-Boigny was born. This is symbolic. Behind the wrought-iron gates of his Villa Charlotte Jacques Foccart is still a work-horse. His gaze is still turned towards Africa, to which he has devoted his life, and where he maintains financial interests. Even today Jacques Foccart remains the head of the French Import and Export Co. (SAFIEX), a family business specializing in trade with overseas countries which he started in 1946, just after the War. At the same time, from his Paris office, he keeps an eye on two Ivory Coast firms, Gonfreville Etablissements, a textile firm, and SITAF, of which he is a director.

The very name of Jacques Foccart is legendary. Over two decades this agent of the shadows, hiding a real timidity behind his large half-tinted glasses, cultivated an air of mystery. What is there left to be said about this prematurely bald, tubby little man? What conspiracies did the press not attribute to this eminence grise with the stern manner and severe dress? There was not a single African 'exploit' perpetrated during the 15 years he was in the Elysée Palace, first with de Gaulle, and then with Pompidou, whose authorship was not credited to him, even down to the sinister assassination of Ben Barka in 1965, characterized in the famous phrase, 'that smells of Foccart'. In vain he attempted to mount a counter-offensive against the media by inviting the great names of the press to dine at his table.[3]

He was wasting his time: the myth had been born. It even clouded his past with the rumour that he was the illegitimate son of a nun. The truth was more straightforward. Jacques Foccart saw the light of day at Ambrières-le-Grand, in Mayenne, on 31 August 1918. His family was well known in the area, having been established there for several generations. His great-grandfather, Guillaume-Louis Koch, had married a Foccart. His father went off to make his fortune in Guadeloupe by the export of bananas; he owned an estate there at Goubeyre, and became mayor of the town. He married a girl from Creole high society, Elmire de Courtemanche de la Clémandière. Little Jacques divided his childhood between the French West Indies and Mayenne.

After having served as an infantry sergeant-major in 1939–40, Foccart retired to his native heath, where he set up a charcoal business for gas-driven vehicles. He was very impressed by the 'Appeal of 18 June' launched by de Gaulle, and in 1942 established contact with London and was enlisted in the services of the BCRA. His Resistance name was 'Binot' – a misspelt reference to the main boulevard of Neuilly, where Foccart had lived before the war. In Mayenne his burgeoning network showed itself very active. His Action group had a reputation for being tremendously efficient. On 27 April Foccart narrowly escaped death. At the wheel of a Renault he rammed a road block set up by the Feldgendarmerie. Roger Le Guerncy, his assistant, died, shielding him with his own body. A month later most of the members of the network were arrested by the Gestapo. Foccart was not discouraged and set up a new group. In London Passy had nothing but praise for the services he rendered. He was promoted to the rank of lieutenant-colonel. In the jargon of the Gaullist secret services he was a 'P2 agent'. In contrast to 'Po' (occasional) agents and 'P1s' (semi-permanent) agents, P2s were permanent and were paid.

At the time of the Normandy landings Jacques Foccart was put in charge of executing the celebrated 'Tortoise Plan'. This was designed to slow down the passage of German armour to the Normandy front. 'Mission successful,' was the judgement of the BCRA leaders. In October 1944 Jacques Foccart left for London to join the Allied special services. We have seen how he mounted an operation to liberate some POW and concentration camps. Once the war was over, he officially left the secret services and resumed his commercial activities.[4]

Nevertheless, he did not abandon politics. As soon as the RPF was formed, de Gaulle turned to him to establish the party in the north and west of France. From then onwards he made his career in de Gaulle's organization. A member of the National Council of the RPF, then deputy secretary-general, in 1964 he replaced Louis Terrenoire at the head of the movement. For a time this faithful servant of the General also had charge of the service that maintained order for the organization. Between 1948 and 1955, he was often to be seen at Persan-Beaumont (Val d'Oise) undergoing a short refresher course with Action Branch.[5] These courses permitted the former BCRA lieutenant-colonel, who had become a captain in SDECE, to rise to the rank of colonel in the secret services.

De Gaulle also made him responsible for the party overseas: he was the national delegate of the RPF for Overseas Departments and Territories (DOM-TOM), and in 1952 was co-opted by the Gaullist party to be its adviser for the French Union. Through a small, roneoed publication, *Lettre à l'Union Française*, he was already corresponding with the four corners of the globe, and he became an indefatigable traveller, spreading the Gaullist message in person. Maurice Robert, the future head of the Africa section at SDECE recalled: 'I saw him set up the first RPF branch in Mauretania, at Port-Etienne, at a trading station lent by a business man. The whole French colony – about a hundred people – attended the meeting.'[6]

In Africa Foccart established close links with the business sector, and founded his first semi-official intelligence networks. At this time, with a few former members of BCRA, he set up a host of small businesses specializing in imports and exports. Greatly helped by this coverage, the Gaullist political machine was occasionally better informed about the situation in Africa than the governments of the Fourth Republic. But Foccart did not break the bonds that united him to SDECE. Right up to 1958, through the good offices of Colonel Morlanne, the head of Intelligence Branch, he passed on many items of information. He remained an 'honourable correspondent' of great value.

What then did Foccart think about the first signs of African emancipation? If he remained an unconditional supporter of the maintenance of order in the colonies – as all the votes he cast in the Assembly of the French Union show – he was not hostile either to the new relationships being established between Metropolitan France and its protégés. He was personally in contact with African leaders who did not hide their progressive aims. During the tour made by de Gaulle in 1953 through 18 African countries, which he had organized, Foccart met Félix Houphouët-Boigny, whose liberal ideas were upsetting the government in Paris at the time. But above all Foccart was a loyal supporter. As regards Africa, he unhesitatingly endorsed every fluctuation in Gaullist policy.

In June 1958, after his return to power, de Gaulle naturally called upon him to take up the post of technical adviser in the prime minister's office at the Hôtel Matignon, in charge of African affairs. Because of the confidence the General placed in him, and his numerous acquaintances on the dark continent, in March 1960 he succeeded Raymond Janot as Secretary General for African and Madagascan Affairs. He was assisted first by Alain Plantey, and then by René Journiac. From his office, first in the Rue de l'Elysée and then the Rue de Grenelle, Jacques Foccart was no longer content merely to maintain a link with SDECE. Henceforth he supervised the French special services. Every Wednesday he had a long meeting with General Grossin, the SDECE director, in order to pass on the instructions from the Elysée regarding Africa. In the middle of the decolonization process the task was an especially delicate one. In de Gaulle's mind, every French retreat in Africa would leave a gap to be filled by the activities of the 'Soviets', coupled with those of Communist China. Thus the USSR must be prevented from controlling permanently any zones of influence on that continent. In extreme cases de Gaulle ordered the secret services to react with force.

Thus, when Guinea, now independent, seemed to draw closer to the USSR and Czechoslovakia, the French head of state undertook to overthrow the regime of Sékou Touré. After several plots had failed, those around the General attempted to spread the idea that de Gaulle had been personally opposed to them. This version of events was scarcely credible. General Grossin had regular private meetings with de Gaulle, and would not have taken the risk of launching certain actions without the explicit go-ahead of the Elysée. It may be true that the French leader later regretted his attitude. The fact remains that in the beginning he did try to get rid of Sékou Touré.

In the event, Foccart, as always, was merely the faithful interpreter of the General's wishes. His role as adviser has often been exaggerated, and that of his master played down. The Secretary-General for African and Madagascan Affairs, however, drew his power from a simple source: his daily meeting with de Gaulle. Every evening the 'man of 18 June' received Foccart for about 20 minutes. No minister enjoyed such a privilege. Jacques Foccart declared: 'Every morning all the telegrams and cables were seen by me and one of my collaborators. We picked out the important documents, because we clearly could not submit all of them to the General. During the evening interview, if there was a point that had attracted his attention the General spoke about it, indicating what should be done. Very often also he would annotate the documents. Then it was up to us to make known the line to be followed.'[7]

In the margin of the summaries drawn up by Jacques Foccart was the fine handwriting of his chief, vigilant and attentive to detail. For example, Foccart was asked why the French ambassador in Mauretania did not reside in Nouakchott, the capital. Or a note would say: 'You will remind me to tell the Prime Minister not to touch the budget of Réunion.' Never so much as under de Gaulle has Africa been the special preserve of the President of the Republic.

If Foccart caused the powerful men of the Fifth Republic to tremble – even the celebrated 'barons' – it was less because of his charisma than because he was his leader's shadow. In the presence of de Gaulle he manifested an almost sickening reserve. 'He would not willingly have risked the General's frown,' said his friend Roger Barberot ironically.[8] Faced with the accusations levelled against him, this privileged adviser was wont to justify himself as follows: 'For 23 years I remained at General de Gaulle's side. He was not naive and knew full well how his colleagues behaved; he certainly would not have put up for 24 hours with anyone who acted in any way maliciously.'[9] It is certain that when Jacques Foccart interfered in the internal politics of African countries, even going so far as to meddle in local political quarrels, he was carrying out orders. France continually intervened on the dark continent, in a succession of acts, sometimes guided by its immediate economic interests. Through the functions he performed Foccart was an omnipresent figure.

From the 1960s the secretary-general fulfilled several tasks. In fact, he wore two hats. Besides heading African affairs, for which he had available the intelligence services, he was given the title of 'political adviser' by de Gaulle, and was able to act freely within the Gaullist party. Jacques Foccart explained:

I was part of the Private Office of General de Gaulle. Essentially I was entrusted with Africa and the DOM-TOM. In addition, the General asked me to maintain contacts with the Gaullists: the UNR (Union pour la Nouvelle République) (later the UDR: Union des Démocrates pour la République), the UJP (Union des Jeunes pour le Progrès), the Association for supporting their activities, and naturally the Service for Civil Action (Service d'Action Civique: SAC). Bear in mind that I was the last secretary-general of the RPF. Now, since the RPF had ceased all its activities in 1954–5, those who had belonged to its service for the maintenance of order stayed together as a group and formed the SAC in 1958.[10]

This testimony is valuable because it explains clearly the bonds of friendship that linked Jacques Foccart with the principal SAC leaders ever since the days of the RPF. Afterwards the secretary-general always defended himself against the charge of having used Gaullist *barbouzes* in his African policy. But can he really assert that he never yielded to a few former Resistance colleagues, who had moved from the BCRA to the Gaullist service for the maintenance of order? Was it not sometimes more convenient to have recourse to these militants, who, although they were certainly unruly, were entirely devoted to the person of the General, rather than go through official channels? Jacques Foccart would not answer. However, it is certain that several operations in Africa were mounted with the approval of de Gaulle, without calling in SDECE. This was particularly so in the cases of the successful escape in 1964 of the former president of the Congo

PLATE 1   The DGSE Headquarters in Paris, 'La Piscine'. 10 August 1985.

PLATE 2   General Paul Aussaresses, founder of the Action Branch
11th Shock Troops started up again after the *Rainbow Warrior* scandal.

PLATE 3   The first photograph ever to be published of Colonel
Germain, who organized Ben Bella's kidnapping in 1956.

PLATE 4   (far right) Alexandre de Marenches, Director-General of
SDECE, with (centre) the French president, Georges Pompidou. 3
January 1972.

PLATE 5   Breton Colonel Georges Barazer de Lannurien, mole hunter in the 1960s, during an interview with Roger Faligot.

PLATE 6   Reunion at the French Ministry of Defence with (left to right) General Jeannou Lacaze, Chief of Staff and former head of DGSE Action Branch, the head of DGSE, Pierre Marion and Charles Hernu, Minister of Defence. In the background is co-author Pascal Krop. 10 July 1981.

PLATE 7 General Michel Fleutiaux (second from left), head of French Military Intelligence in 1988, here as a UN observer in the Lebanon. 17 April 1984.

PLATE 8   Admiral Lacoste, head of DGSE during the *Rainbow Warrior* scandal. September 1976.

PLATE 9   Airforce General François Mermet, from 1985 the head of the French nuclear experimentation centres, which include the weapons-testing site on Mururoa Atoll in the South Pacific; he became Director of DGSE from 1 January 1987.

PLATE 10   French President, François Mitterrand (left), and Minister of Defence, Charles Hernu (right), during a meeting at Camp Canjuers in October 1982.

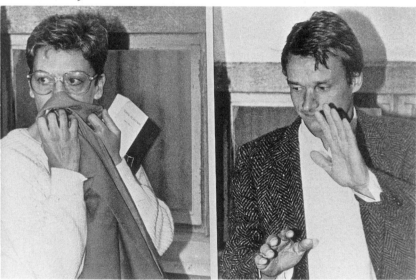

PLATE 11   (left) Dominique Prieur alias Mme Sophie-Claire Turenge and (right) Alain Mafart alias Alain-Jacques Turenge, the two DGSE agents involved in the sabotaging of the Greenpeace vessel *Rainbow Warrior*. Auckland, August 1985.

PLATE 12 On 10 July 1985, the sloop *Rainbow Warrior* of the environmental organization Greenpeace was sabotaged in the Port of Auckland causing the death of a Portuguese photographer.

PLATE 13 Policemen working in the hole caused by the second explosion which sank the *Rainbow Warrior*. 25 August 1985.

(Brazzaville), Fulbert Youlou, and of French help to Biafra by means of mercenaries. All this was to give Foccart a very bad reputation. His name remains forever associated with the 'barbouzeries', the dirty tricks of the Fifth Republic.

After the resignation of the General in 1969, the President of the Senate took over as interim President, and stripped Jacques Foccart of all his functions, replacing him by Daniel Pépy, a Conseiller d'Etat. He was accused of having equipped his office at the Elysée with a superb system for monitoring telephone conversations. The matter turned to farce. Immediately after his victory President Pompidou reinstated him as Secretary for African and Madagascan Affairs. But his role from then on was limited to this. He no longer held sway over the secret services.[11] If Foccart was the *eminence grise* of the African policy of the General, his executant on the ground, his faithful right-hand man, also deserves some attention.

Maurice Robert, the 'Little Lieutenant'

'A business for rogues, carried out by honest people. We kill only for reasons of state.' Behind his thick-lensed glasses Maurice Robert's gaze suddenly turned fixed and hard. This contrasted with the calm appearance of this small, jolly man. We might imagine him in the luxurious atmosphere of a provincial drawing-room rather than in the heart of the African savannahs.

And yet his was no ordinary career, but of a Gaullist soldier moulded by the War and colonial skirmishes. In 1939, at the age of 20, he was called up. At first a cadet officer at Saint-Maixent, he then joined the 150th Infantry Regiment in Lot-et-Garonne. In September 1940 he was stationed on the demarcation line between the occupied and unoccupied zones of France, at Saint-Pierre-de-Mons, in the Gironde. 'Up to March 1941,' Maurice Robert recalled, 'I succeeded in smuggling across a fair number of escapees. Because of my height the local people had nicknamed me the "Little Lieutenant". But on 13 March the Germans arrested me on the road to Bazas. They made me get back into my vehicle and mounted the running-board. When we arrived at the local *Kommandantur*, on the Place de Langon, they made the stupid mistake of getting off the running-board. I stepped on the accelerator, telling my passengers, "Keep your heads down," and succeeded in reaching the unoccupied zone.'[12]

Maurice Robert was forced to leave the area. Soon afterwards the army sent him to Dakar, then Casablanca, and afterwards to Mauretania. He was to finish the War in the 'pocket' round Royan, in Battalion 14, which came from Chad. Transferred to the Marines, shortly afterwards he was posted overseas, firstly to Port-Etienne in Mauretania, then to Saint-Louis in Senegal, where he ran the school for soldiers' children. Two future heads of state were among his pupils: Mathieu Kerekou, from Benin, who was to become his country's leader in 1972, and Seybi Kountché, who seized power in Niger in 1974.

After his return to Paris, in 1949 Lieutenant Robert studied at the Centre for the Study of African and Asian Affairs. Next came a posting to Tonkin, in Indo-China, where he was given the task of training a Vietnam unit alongside the Bamboo Canal. 'Commando Robert' – 60 strong – operated with other paratroop units under General Fourcade. Maurice Robert's unit was No. 3, and was sent to Thai Binh in the region of Tonkin.

All the Vietnam commandos trained by French officers were liable to be infiltrated. The most famous, those of Vandenberghe and Rusconi, were to be decimated in this way. Maurice Robert described how he escaped assassination by a hair's breadth:

A fortnight after Vandenberghe's death the same thing happened to my unit. As a precautionary measure I had shut my staff up in a pagoda. At two o'clock in the morning, the Vietnamese radio operator came knocking at the door. I invited him in to drink tea, and at the same moment we heard the whistle of bullets outside. It was the signal for the attack. I learnt afterwards that the radio operator was the organizer of the plot. Detained by me, he had been unable to issue instructions, and, having no precise orders, the men had not moved. Such changes of side were inevitable, since our commandos were themselves made up of former Vietminh who had been 'turned'. The next morning I called for the help of the counter-espionage service at Thai Binh. And by the evening three-quarters of my commando unit were under lock and key. I was forced to rebuild the unit.[13]

At the end of 1952 'Commando Robert' was incorporated into the Naval Commando Group in North Vietnam. Under the orders of Captain René Bichelot, it was used for special operations in North Annam. On the island of Hon Mhé – the base for operational commandos – Captain Robert struck up a friendship with a young Army film producer, Pierre Schoendorffer.

Twice wounded – once seriously in December 1953 – Maurice Robert returned to Paris at the beginning of the following year. In Indo-China he had met Captain René-Louis Bardet. This SDECE officer, a former station head in Poland, recommended him warmly to Henri Trautmann, the head of Research Branch. This system of co-optation was then frequent in the services. 'You are of interest to us,' the 'Admiral' told the young naval officer. Maurice Robert agreed to join SDECE. He was to remain in it for 20 years.

Dakar was his first posting. There he succeeded Commandant Caron. As we have seen, the African sector was in a very primitive state. A methodical official, Maurice Robert applied himself to remedying this. He set up the first infrastructure in West Africa, both French- and English-speaking. But under the Fourth Republic the resources made available for the African stations were derisory. Gaston Defferre, the Minister for the Colonies, took scarcely any interest in the secret services. After the coming to power of General de Gaulle, the African sector really took off. Recalled to Paris in

1959, Maurice Robert, a Gaullist officer, was appointed to head the sector. He was in contact with most of the African heads of state, in particular Léopold Sédar Senghor, whom he knew well. His new responsibilities also broadened his horizons. At the time of the secession of Katanga, he went to the Congo to supervise the special operations. There he met the mercenary Robert Denard. 'A good fellow,' was his opinion. The two men became friends. In 1962 Commandant Robert also struck up a friendship with a young Gabonese official, Bernard-Albert Bongo. After the death of Léon M'ba in 1967 this new president of Gabon was frequently to consult the head of the Africa service concerning security matters.

At Mortier headquarters Maurice Robert continued his ascent. Head of the Analysis and Production Branch, then deputy to the director of Research, with the rank of colonel, he nevertheless abruptly left the services at the end of 1973. 'In order to begin a new career in civilian life,' he asserted, but doubtless also because of the personal enmity between him and the new Director.[14] The latter planned to give preference to sectors other than Africa, and so the dissatisfied Gaullist colonel banged the door behind him.

This former soldier did not need to fear unemployment. For five years he was to work for Elf-Aquitaine, in charge of relations with the petroleum-producing countries of Africa and Asia. In the autumn of 1979 he was finally appointed to be French ambassador in Gabon. This new promotion aroused some astonishment at the Quai d'Orsay. The colonel had not followed a diplomatic career, and had not even been in the former overseas administration. 'I had in my favour,' retorted Maurice Robert, 'the fact that I knew Bongo well, and was familiar with questions of intelligence and oil problems, which were very important in Gabon.' The presence of the ex-SDECE agent at Libreville was in any case to stir up some fine arguments. The ambassador was criticized for not having kept his distance from the Gabon regime and for having covered up its crimes.[15] 'Can you see an ambassador of France acting in such a way?' says an astonished Maurice Robert today. 'The accusation is untrue. I did nothing save serve my country.' In 1981, with the coming to power of the Left, he was to be peremptorily dismissed, after 22 years' good and loyal services in the Africa sector. Maurice Robert had had the 'good luck' to take over the dark continent precisely at the moment when, under the impulsion of General de Gaulle, it became a venture of prime importance.

Liaison and Intelligence Stations

By 1958 the restructuring of SDECE was on the agenda. The plan for a 'Community' put forward by de Gaulle, forced General Grossin to review the whole intelligence organization in Africa. As Colonel Maurice Robert related:

I was called to Dakar in 1959. I was asked to establish liaison and intelligence stations (Postes de Liaison et de Renseignement: PLR) to function with all the countries of the Community, that is to offer them technical aid in the field of intelligence. When in 1960 the Africa service became an autonomous sector, I became its head. I met most of the African leaders in order to explain to them what the stations were and to propose setting them up. This was to enable me to forge very favourable relationships in all the French-speaking countries of Africa.[16]

From then on the Africa service, which at the beginning of the 1960s comprised some 150 agents, including those stationed on the dark continent itself, became one of the key sectors in Mortier headquarters. Maurice Robert gathered round him policemen on detachment from their original services. His deputy was divisional superintendent Roussel. The department also employed two chief superintendents, Henri Anglès and Paul Vergès, who had had colonial experience in Madagascar. These two were to be more especially posted to 'Bison Base', which Maurice Robert set up as soon as he arrived. This small group, located within the precincts of the Invalides, had the task of establishing contacts with African leaders passing through Paris. Later, in 1967, Bison Base was to lose its specifically African orientation and was in fact to be attached to the SDECE directorate.

At the top, it was now the Secretary-General for African and Madagascan Affairs, Jacques Foccart, who supervised the intelligence bodies. He communicated directly with embassies, without going through the Foreign Ministry. His secretariat possessed the 'code' and used the diplomatic pouch. Foccart also received a copy of all documents sent by representatives of France abroad, as well as the reports from agents of the secret services. What was most important, in Jacques Foccart's estimation, 'was the fact that I was available. At any hour of the day or night I could be at the end of a telephone if there was a problem. The care paid to the transaction of business created a climate of great confidence, at least I profoundly believe so.'[17]

As we have seen, Jacques Foccart met General Grossin, the SDECE director, regularly. He was also in direct touch with Maurice Robert. But nothing was undertaken without the Élysée and Matignon being informed. 'We functioned,' asserted Colonel Robert, 'under this double guarantee. It was impossible for de Gaulle not to know about the operations we were carrying out. Officially the head of SDECE passed the orders on to me, and after that I worked in liaison with Jacques Foccart.'[18] We are a long way here from the superficial but widespread judgement that the French secret services were 'out of control'.

However, the Africa file was not solely in the hands of Jacques Foccart. In the early years of de Gaulle's regime, Michel Debré, who headed the General's Private Office and was later prime minister, played a large part in this field. Officially SDECE fell under the authority of Matignon. Several African affairs concerning the Cameroon and Guinea were to be dealt with directly by Michel Debré and his advisers Constantin Melnik and Robert Delmas.

The Francophile Circle

In Africa the liaison and intelligence stations (PLR) were the foundation stone of the new system, in accordance with Gaullist doctrine. After the shock of decolonization France had to be able to count on firm friends in Africa. There should be a kind of Francophile circle: this was formed with Léopold Sédar Senghor in Senegal, Houphouët-Boigny in the Ivory Coast, Philibert Tsiranana in Madagascar, and first Léon M'ba then Bernard-Albert Bongo in Gabon. These were relationships of trust, involving relatively stable regimes to which de Gaulle was ready to grant the necessary support.

In particular, SDECE, through the PLRs, provided useful information. Contact with the officers of the very young African armies was all the easier because the officers had only just left French schools. In 1961 Maurice Robert organized the first PLR courses at Dakar. From then on SDECE received some three to ten officers a year as trainees. The courses were held in Mortier barracks. At the outset there was a PLR in each of the French-speaking African states. But through lack of funds, certain of these were quickly closed down, such as those in Upper Volta, Niger and Togo. The SDECE directorate averred that they were not of 'capital importance'. Colonel Robert nevertheless esteemed that it was detrimental to the coherence of his African network.

In exchange for such 'technical' aid these countries allowed SDECE to keep a watch over French interests on the spot. The Madagascar post, for example, was used to maintain surveillance on Mauritius and Réunion. Paul Perrier, the former head of the Special Branch, the secret service of Mauritius, has retailed to the authors how coordination was effected with the French:

We were under a Regional Liaison Office (RLO) of the British MI5, directed from Kenya by John Thompson. We were working against subversive activities by the communist countries. From 1963, after an agreement between the French prefect on Réunion and the British governor of Mauritius, we decided upon a common line of action. In 1966 one of our preoccupations was Maoist penetration, particularly among the Chinese community of Mauritius. Thus I frequently used to meet with Commandant Boulle of the French services on Réunion, in liaison with the station in Madagascar. He asked me to watch the manoeuvres of Paul Vergès, the head of the Communist Party on Réunion, who was passing through Mauritius, and in exchange I suggested to him that Paul Berenger, the founder of the militant Mauritian Movement, should be followed.[19]

In different circumstances, the PLRs were useful antennae for SDECE, allowing developments in different countries to be followed. Paris had some reason to be wary of unstable regimes. Between 1960 and 1967 one *coup d'état* followed another in Africa. In Togo, Sylvanus Olympio was assassinated; Nicholas Grunitzky, who replaced him, was himself overthrown by Colonel Etienne Eyadema. At Ouagadougou, in Upper Volta, Colonel Sangoulé Lamazina replaced Maurice Yaméogo. In the Central African Republic, finally, Colonel Bokassa seized power from David Dacko. SDECE agents informed Paris about the preparations for these plots, but France did not intervene, for the 'waltz of the presidents', which could be explained by purely internal factors, scarcely affected French interests.

The situation was different when SDECE perceived in a change of regime the seeds of outside intervention. The Soviet threat was the main preoccupation of the service. 'Since the Tsars and since Lenin,' affirmed Colonel Maurice Robert, 'the Soviets have always pursued three major objectives: to control the Indian Ocean, to isolate South Africa and above all to cut off Africa from Europe. Between 1955 and 1960 communist penetration was greatly feared. It was thought, for example, that the Russians were going to establish a base in Uganda. But they were very ham-fisted, in both Benin and Mali, and also in Equatorial Guinea. We contented ourselves with neutralizing individuals who might have been taken over by the USSR.'[20]

The prospect of a lasting Soviet presence in Africa was the background to all the analyses made at the time.[21] SDECE then envisaged collaborating with South Africa. As Colonel Georges Barazer de Lannurien reported: 'Accompanying Maurice Robert, I left for South Africa in order to strengthen the links with BOSS, the secret service of that country. The South Africans complained that they had nowhere to withdraw to, and that, like the French settlers born in Algeria, they had their backs to the wall. An alliance with them was feasible. Only our report would not have been accepted by the politicians.'[22] The phobia about the Reds also led the Gaullist government to detect the 'hand of Moscow' here, there and everywhere, and brutally to put down trade unions and progressive movements – all the more so because France allowed itself an extremely wide field of action in Africa. In an article published in the *Revue de défense nationale* in May 1963 Pierre Messmer, the Minister for the Armed Forces, defended French military policy in the following terms: 'Internal security is a matter for the local authorities. Upon the express request of the latter, however, France may exceptionally lend assistance in this sphere.' The minister added: 'The French armed forces have the joint task of global defence and technical cooperation. They can provide an additional means of action in case of local aggression or subversive operations.'

In August 1963 the crowd demonstrated in Brazzaville against the regime of Fulbert Youlou. In Paris the corruption that reigned in Congo

(Brazzaville) was perfectly well known but de Gaulle feared that revolutionary elements less favourably disposed to France might seize power. The head of state personally gave instructions to General Kergaravat, the commander of the troops on the spot, to intervene in favour of Father Youlou. The latter preferred in the end to step down rather than to give the order to open fire. The Elysée was later to entrust to Jean Mauricheau-Beaupré, a specialist in delicate missions, the task of effecting his escape from his Congo prison.

The same scenario was repeated in February 1964 at Libreville. The Gabonese president, Léon M'ba was overthrown by a handful of military leaders, without a drop of blood being shed. The Army then handed over power to Jean-Hilaire Aubame, the leader of the opposition. At SDECE in Paris Colonel Robert was worried because he could not get hold of any news. His correspondent, Commandant Haulin, had stupidly got himself shut up in the presidential palace, having gone to seek information. When he was finally informed, de Gaulle decided once again to use force. Gabon was at the heart of the French 'circuit', and the former colonial power still retained powerful interests there, among them an oil company. The Americans or the Russians might take advantage of the disarray to gain a foothold themselves in the country. In the eyes of the Elysée, everything favoured swift intervention. A company of paratroops was sent to Brazzaville to 'clear the ground'. From Dakar a DC8 brought in another company of reinforcements. Colonel Maurice Robert, head of the Africa service at SDECE, was on board the plane.[23] With the military authorities on the spot he directed the attack on the camp at Lalala, where numerous Gabonese soldiers were killed. Léon M'Ba was restored to the presidency.

Five years later came the intervention in Chad. The nepotism of President François Tombalbaye's regime was being undermined by the numerous regional revolts inspired by the Chad Liberation Front. There again, and in spite of his initial reservations, General de Gaulle agreed to send in the 1st Overseas Parachute Regiment (Régiment Etranger Parachutiste: REP) to restore the situation. At Ndjamena (Fort-Lamy), the capital, the United States was threatening to take over from France. And in Paris there was a desire to stifle at birth the new Libyan influence that was emerging in the north of the country.

During all these military operations, officially justified because of attempts at foreign intervention, the liaison and intelligence stations (PLR) were no longer merely information exchanges. SDECE officers gave technical assistance to African services which unfortunately were also serving the local police. And under the pretext of fighting Soviet machinations, France soiled its hands by taking part in the repression of purely local opponents. This was the case in Gabon and Chad, and Cameroon is another example. When his country first became independent, Fochidé, a Cameroon police officer, had come to Paris to train under the auspices of the PLRs. Having returned to Cameroon, he set up a Service of Documentation and Studies for

Cameroon Security (Service de Documentation et d'Etudes de la Sécurité Camerounaise (SDESC),[24] a carbon copy of SDECE. The difference was merely that in the building where Fochidé operated, close to the municipal lake at Yaoundé, torture was routine. In the capital the PLR, for its part, continued to function normally. Was this not playing the sorcerer's apprentice? One would like to be certain that no information concerning the Cameroon opposition in France was ever passed to the services of Fochidé, the policeman, all the more so because, during 30 years, Cameroon patriots have already paid very heavy tribute to the French secret services.

A 'Thriller Series' in Cameroon

The prime minister was upset. Revolt was brewing once more in southern Cameroon, in the Bamiléké country. He summoned the SDECE director to Matignon. Irritably, he questioned him: 'Have you any intelligence about Cameroon? Something should be done!' The master spy replied: 'With them, because of the way the tribe is organized, if you deal with the chief, everything is settled. The chief is Félix Moumié, and he is in Europe. We can get rid of him.'

This scene is neither an invention nor a caricature. On a gloomy day in the autumn of 1960, the visit to Matignon did indeed take place. How long will it be before the principal actors of the Fifth Republic write their true memoirs? Can one claim to be writing history if one cuts out the violence and the blood? To look back briefly into the past: since 1955 Cameroon had been beset by serious troubles. In the south of the country, the Bamiléké were demanding independence. The opposition, represented by the Union of the Populations of Cameroon (UPC), was one of the most active in Africa. Pierre Messmer, the high commissioner and a Companion of the Liberation, tried to establish links with Um Nyobé, the leader of the UPC. He failed. The 'Black Crab' – the magnificent emblem of Cameroon – then broke out in rebellion. Maurice Delauney, commanding the region, favoured extremely radical measures. In his book he recalls: 'The most spectacular operation was the one that allowed me utterly to destroy the UPC headquarters at Bamenda (British Cameroon). One fine night, a few determined men, both French and Cameroon, all volunteers, crossed the British frontier, arrived in Bamenda, entered the HQ of the UPC, burnt all the buildings, and put out of harm's way some of the party's leaders. Moumié, unfortunately, was not there that day.'[25]

In the Bamiléké country, justice was summary to say the least. In September 1958, soldiers assassinated Ruben Um Nyobé in cold blood, near his native village of Boumnyebel. In his *Carnets secrets de la colonisation* the journalist Georges Chaffart tells how the leader of the UPC was killed by men under Captain Agostini, an intelligence officer: 'Suddenly the Sara

(Chad) infantrymen flushed out four men crouching in the undergrowth, who ran away. One of them was carrying a big briefcase. In his oral report the sergeant-major told how he had immediately identified him as an "intellectual", and how he had made the challenges laid down by regulations. And since all the fugitives continued to run away, he gave the order to fire. All were hit, and fell.'[26] A fine piece of work! Lieutenant-Colonel Jean-Marie Lamberton, former head of the Deuxième Bureau in the Far East land forces, then stationed in Cameroon, did not condemn the actions of his subordinate. Nor was there a word of reproach from Daniel Doustin, the future head of the DST, the high commissioner for South Cameroon. The way was henceforth clear for the French candidate, Ahmadou Ahidjo, a Muslim from the North, trained under the colonial administration. But the new president was scarcely popular in the country.

The new head of the UPC, Félix Moumié, a 32-year-old doctor, was steadily gaining ground. Soon Ahidjo no longer controlled South Cameroon. He was forced to ask for help from France. Even before gaining independence Cameroon had signed a top-secret agreement on military cooperation with France. This enabled Ahidjo officially to request support from Paris. It was Jacques Foccart – whom he had known when they had both sat on the benches of the Assembly of the French Union – who pleaded the case to de Gaulle. Although nothing obliged him to do so (at the time France had made no automatic commitment to intervene militarily), the General agreed. In South Cameroon Colonel du Crest de Villeneuve, a former member of the intelligence service during the War, was deemed too timorous, and was replaced by General Briand. In the army it was said of the latter that he was 'a real Viking'. He was a fair-haired, blue-eyed giant, who had arrived straight from the Algerian inferno. In Indo-China he had commanded the 22nd Colonial Infantry Regiment – whose reputation was far from angelic. In the early months of 1960 five battalions combed the forests of the Sanaga and brutally suppressed the rebels. Several dozen villages were set on fire and razed to the ground. Many officers were later to admit that such a bloodbath could have been avoided.

That left Félix Moumié, who had miraculously escaped the repression. SDECE now had the green light from the top to mount a 'Homo' operation, a term much in vogue in Action Branch since the beginning of the war in Algeria.[27] Exiled from Cameroon, the leader of the UPC divided his time between Accra in Ghana and Conakry in Guinea. Since he travelled a lot in Africa and Europe, he was an ideal target for the secret services.[28] His tumultuous private life – Moumié had a weakness for women – was to allow him to be drawn into a trap. For this delicate mission Colonel Roussillat, head of Action Branch, had selected an 'honourable correspondent' with an adventurous past. 'An ace operator, and quite a card,' was the view of his former colleagues. 'He looked like a wild animal, with his great mop of unruly ginger hair,' according to one officer of Action Branch. 'In '53 and

'54, when he was almost sixty, he was still coming to Cercottes to make a few more parachute drops.'

Born in Epinal, 'Big Bill' had been a courageous member of the Resistance.[29] He belonged to the 'Sussex' intelligence network, which was linked to the British Intelligence Service. After the War he could not settle down again to civilian life. He was noticed from time to time in the office of his friend Pierre Fourcaud, the fiery deputy director of SDECE. Then the old warrior went to Indo-China with the 'Conus' commando, which was run by the secret services.[30] Later he joined the Simca firm, where he was entrusted with the maintenance of security against the CGT. At the same time he kept up contact with the services, continuing to train for and willingly lend a hand to Action Branch in the struggle against the FLN.

In 1960 'Big Bill' carried a press card as his cover. Installed in Geneva, he worked for the Acmé agency. He came and went between his Paris home at 68, Rue Vercingétorix, and a rented apartment in the Swiss town at 42, Grande-Rue. His visits to Africa were frequent, but he wrote very few articles.

One 'Pastis' Too Many

Thus the scene was set, the actors were ready, and the tragedy of Félix Moumié could begin. SDECE has its own version of the assassination, which was very technical and very brutal, and is told here for the first time. A high-ranking officer in the secret services spoke about it:

We used 'Big Bill', posing as a Swiss journalist. In August 1960 he went to see Félix Moumié in Accra, using this cover. The two men got on well together, and he proposed to the Cameroon leader that he should come to Geneva to receive treatment for a liver disorder. Our journalist said that he knew some excellent doctors. Three months elapsed, but Moumié still had not come to Switzerland. We were beginning to despair. But one day in October 1960, he contacted our agent, announced that he was in Geneva, and suggested they meet.

Felix Moumié had arrived in Geneva on 2 October. Was he a little wary of 'Big Bill'? No doubt. He had waited until the 10th, in fact, before getting in touch with him. At first he had planned to go back to Africa on 9 October, but had been unable to get a seat on the plane. He had to wait a few more days. In Geneva he was bored, so he rang 'Big Bill'.

Our agent invited him to dine on Saturday, 15 October, in a restaurant in the old town in Geneva, the Plat d'Argent. Moumié went there with a Cameroonian studying in Clermont-Ferrand, Jean-Martin Tchaptchaët.[31] They had hardly arrived when Moumié was called to the telephone. He was surprised, since no one knew that he was at the restaurant, but he went to the telephone. The journalist distracted the attention of the student by showing him some confidential documents about his country, and discreetly poured a little thallium into Moumié's Ricard. The

The Colonies are Finished

Cameroon leader returned to the table, grumbling that there had been nobody on the line. Moumié talked a lot, but did not drink his aperitif, which he put to one side on the table. Our agent therefore repeated his trick with the wine. The operation was dangerous, because both men were there. Finally Moumié drank his wine. This was perfect. He would go off to die in Conakry, where not a single doctor would be able to diagnose that he had been poisoned. Sékou Touré would be accused of the murder. But suddenly catastrophe struck. When the meal was finishing with coffee, Moumié retrieved his Ricard and drank it. The game was up. The dose that had been meticulously prepared at Mortier HQ was now a double one, too strong, and Moumié was taken into hospital in Geneva the following night. The agent had made a mistake. He should have knocked over the Ricard.

After dinner, Félix Moumié went back to his hotel. At dawn he was seized with violent stomach pains and rushed to the Geneva regional hospital. A doctor by profession, the militant leader said perfectly lucidly to those around him, 'I have been poisoned with thallium, I shall suffocate, it's the "Red Hand".' The white-coated doctors did not believe him. Félix Moumié died in terrible pain. The Swiss authorities waited two long weeks, the time it took to secure the results from their laboratory in Zurich, before deciding to support the poisoning theory. Finally, on 29 October the Swiss police issued an international warrant for the arrest of 'Big Bill', who had taken flight long before. On the other hand, the police overlooked another SDECE agent, who a few days before had put up at a big Geneva hotel. He was the man who had telephoned Moumié at the restaurant. He was there to cover for the 'journalist' in the event of a slip-up. As for the charges levelled against 'Big Bill', they were overwhelming. Jean-Francis Held, a journalist on *Libération*, carried out an on-the-spot enquiry in Geneva.[32] After having met the Swiss legal authorities he informed them that a mass of documents had been found in 'Big Bill's' home, including a notebook, which was a kind of diary relating to the Indo-China war and, among other things, contained a list of the different ways of killing a man without leaving clues, as well as plans and projects for an attack on a public figure in Berne, and above all, fragments of thallium in the pocket of one of the jackets he had so precipitately abandoned. Swiss justice did not succeed in getting its hands on 'Big Bill'. And for good reason. After the assassination the SDECE man had taken refuge in a house rented by the French secret services on the Riviera. Soon General Grossin contrived to have him struck off the list of persons wanted by the police and he could therefore travel freely in France.

But the adventurer liked to be on the move and often went abroad. He was arrested in Belgium and in 1975 extradited to Switzerland, where he was charged with first-degree homicide. The French authorities exerted discreet pressure to gain an acquittal. At the end of 1980 he was given the benefit of the doubt and acquitted. By freeing the tired old man the Swiss authorities did not suspect that they were undoubtedly avoiding another weird episode. For several months his friends had been planning to attack the prison where he was being held. A helicopter had already been hired to carry out this spectacular exploit.

'Big Bill' – we must recall – had been a genuine Resister. The officials of the 'Sussex' old comrades' association and the 50 or so survivors of the networks unanimously acknowledged this was so. When he was imprisoned his friends, motivated by feelings of solidarity, sought to save him. In the bar they frequented on the Rue de Tournefort in Paris (the same spot that had served them as a meeting-place during the War), they hatched up various different plans to get him out of gaol. The clemency of Swiss justice forestalled them.

'Big Bill', whose real name was William Bechtell, died a very old and lonely man in the summer of 1988.

10

Secret Missions on the Dark Continent

On 27 August 1958 the President's Superstar aircraft, bearing the cross of Lorraine, landed at Conakry, capital of Guinea. The General was paying a visit to Sékou Touré, the popular leader of the Democratic Party of Guinea (Partie Démocratique de Guinée: PDG), in order to explain to him his plan for a Franco-African Community. The welcome was a spectacular one, noisy and extraordinarily colourful. The men had put on their best clothes, and the women wore the same style of dress, the *moumou*. On the road leading from the airport to the town over 500,000 people had gathered to acclaim the French head of state. Shortly before de Gaulle's arrival, immense posters had been stuck up all over Conakry, showing an elephant adorned with a cross of Lorraine. The elephant is the emblem of Guinea. In the vernacular, the word is 'Sili'. In the stormy period of decolonization the term quite naturally designated Sékou Touré. Deceived by the poster and ill-informed by obsequious officials, de Gaulle was for a time to think that 'Sili' meant himself. The General was all smiles.

'Sili', the Obstinate Elephant

That same evening, however, the wind of history was to sweep away the old Franco-Guinean friendship. Even today Jacques Foccart retains bitter memories of it. Here is what he says:

The rift with Guinea happened an hour and a half later, at the meeting of the Territorial Assembly, when Sékou Touré, in a harsh and brutal tone peculiarly his own, gave a stern speech that was hardly justified, because the General had already taken a stand that reckoned with the possibility of states attaining their independence. Sékou Touré's curt tone was reinforced by the fact that, apart from the few people accompanying the General, the gathering was made up of party officials, who with extraordinary violence acclaimed his words.[1]

But the Guinean leader had not been trying to catch de Gaulle unawares. At Abidjan, the last stopover before Conakry, an emissary of Sékou had handed the text of the speech to Jacques Foccart. The latter, deeming it to be somewhat outspoken, passed it on to Bernard Cornut-Gentille, the Minister for the Associated States. He, however, did not pass it on to de Gaulle, who was sleeping on the plane.

Sékou's declarations were in any case nothing very new. Draped in his white robe, with the traditional African fez, the Guinea leader restated positions that he had already expressed many times: 'We intend to exert our sovereign right to independence, but we intend to preserve our links with France. In that association with France, we shall become a people that is proud, free and sovereign.' But, in the overheated conference hall, these generally moderate statements sounded like a challenge. The clamour in the hall, which punctuated each of 'Sili's' words, quickly transformed this speech into a violent diatribe. Huddled in his chair, pale and clearly tired, de Gaulle was deeply irritated. But it was in a voice of some melancholy that he replied to Sékou: 'There has been talk of independence. I say here even more loudly than elsewhere that independence is available for Guinea. It can take it on 28 September by saying "no" to the proposal that has been made to it.'

The die was cast. For de Gaulle, the insult had been proffered. He was never to forgive Sékou Touré. From then on France heaped one vexation after another upon the head of the Guinean leader. Pierre Bas, the colonial administrator, was given the task of informing Sékou that his presence was undesirable on the presidential aircraft that was taking de Gaulle on to Dakar the next day. For his part, Cornut-Gentille, the minister, tried, in the name of an old friendship, to persuade Sékou to apologize to the General. Gaullist-style decolonization was not without a somewhat old-fashioned paternalism.

During a government conference General Grossin, the SDECE director, was more direct. 'What is being done about Guinea?' he asked. Bernard Cornut-Gentille reassured him. He was looking after the Sékou affair. He knew the Guinean leader well, and, with the help of Houphouët-Boigny of the Ivory Coast, guaranteed to bring him round to reason. For a long while France had provided Sékou Touré with subsidies. What Cornut-Gentille was forgetting, on the other hand, was that, instead of making himself rich like many other leaders, Sékou had used this money to develop his own party. The man had integrity. And Guineans adored 'Sili', the stubborn elephant. The French administration tried to build up a 'yes' front. In Paris, the Minister for France Overseas personally contacted the leaders of the African Bloc of Guinea, a small party consisting mainly of parliamentarians, in order to persuade them to support the Gaullist plan. In Guinea itself Colonel Pelicier assembled all the officers at Mangin Camp, in Conakry, in order to persuade them to cast a 'yes' vote at the referendum. He was wasting his breath! 'Sili' swept all obstacles aside. On 28 September, the 'no' recommended by Sékou Touré gained 1,136,324 votes, as against 56,901 'yes' votes. On 2 October, Guinea's independence was proclaimed at Conakry. Sékou Touré became head of the government. On 5 October the USSR recognized the new state. The next day it was China's turn to ratify the birth of an independent Guinea.

De Gaulle versus Sékou Touré

'Guinea today appears to be a striking example of how communists can take over a country without a blow being struck, and one might fear its being caught up in so many ties that it could not disengage itself even if it wished.'[2] Thus in a few words the *Revue de défense nationale* summed up the Gaullist view of the Guinea regime.

France waited until 2 January 1960 before recognizing the new Guinea. Meanwhile, it was no time for diplomatic exchanges. General de Gaulle gave the go-ahead for a comprehensive destabilization operation. For 20 years plots followed one after another on Guinea's territory. The French secret services, though they gradually gave way to the German BND, the CIA and the Portuguese PIDE, were never to let go of their prey completely. The French press gradually slipped into the habit of describing Sékou Touré as a dangerous mythomaniac, afflicted with 'spy mania'. Indeed, that is what he became. The Guinean leader had pitted against him the whole of Western intelligence. But at the beginning the young leader of the 1960s, trained in the school of trade unionism, had none of the features of the bloody dictator he was later to become. Was not this metamorphosis hastened by the series of plots? In any case, 'Sili' unfortunately made the slogan 'For permanent conspiracy, permanent terror' his own.

As soon as the results of the 1958 referendum were known, Guinea became an 'objective' for SDECE. Colonel Tristan Richard, responsible for the Africa–Middle East sector, installed three agents in Guinea. Maurice Robert, station head in Dakar, enlisted a dozen 'honourable correspondents'. The idea was to establish a new intelligence network able to keep the French government speedily informed about policy trends in Guinea. Bangouri Karim, the moving spirit of the African Bloc of Guinea (Bloc Africain de Guinée: BAG), who then became Guinea's Secretary of State for Mines and Industry, stated: 'I was recruited by the French services through Jacques Périer, who represented the former French trading stations in India. In July 1959 I met him at his home in the Avenue Raymond Poincaré to make my first report. The secret instruction to the French services at the time was to enter the government of union and the administration, and to carry on the work for French dominance in every sphere, particularly in the economic, cultural and political areas.'[3]

'It was the military supply officer Arens who recruited me,' admitted also Keita Noumandian, the combined chief of staff. 'The first contacts were

established by Captain Boureau, in 1960 officially press attaché at the
French Embassy. From time to time Captain Boureau came to my home to
pick up intelligence about the army, troop morale, and the army's
relationship with the government.'[4]

The French services paid particular attention to the economic agreements
that Guinea might conclude with the Eastern bloc countries. Considerable
sums of money were paid out to counter Soviet and Yugoslav plans, and to
promote the presence of French firms. From this, general corruption spread
throughout Guinea.

At the same time the French secret services disorganized the country's
finances. It happened that Guinea had just withdrawn from the franc area.
Sékou Touré instituted the national bank and the Guinea franc (= 0.0225
Fr. francs). At first he nevertheless thought of using the reserves of CFA
banknotes that he still possessed in order to pay for his purchases in other
African countries.[5] Paris did not leave him time to do so. At a single stroke
the Bank of France decided to cancel all former CFA notes. To make
matters worse, SDECE was ordered to print false currency. Colonel
Beaumont was given the task of supervising the printing, in the secret
services' Mortier HQ, of these notes 'made in SDECE'. 'The result,'
according to one of the senior officers of SDECE, 'exceeded all our
expectations. Our notes were of much better quality than their own. Panic
broke out in Conakry.' The Guinea franc became a kind of 'toy' money, kept
going by the CFA. This was all compounded because Paris stepped up
operations designed to heap ridicule on the Conakry regime. Thus ex-
servicemen were paid twice: once in Guinean 'toy' money, and a second time
– in order to emphasize the difference – in real CFA francs.

De Gaulle was not satisfied merely with this destabilization operation.
Discreetly SDECE sabotaged a journey to London by Sékou Touré. Then it
was decided to strike a major blow: to eliminate Sékou Touré and install a
new regime by force in Conakry. The onetime colonial power used a former
overseas administrator in Guinea as adviser to the operation. Action Branch
delegated a first-class soldier from the 11th Shock Troops to lead the men.
In the Guinean capital Captain Boureau-Mitrecey, a former counter-
espionage agent in Tangiers, was to act as the link with the internal
opponents of the regime. Jacques Achard, as Counsellor attached to
ambassador Yves Guéna, came from Abidjan in the Ivory Coast to the
frontier, to follow the preparations that were going on. The Dakar station,
headed by Maurice Robert, served logically as the rear base.

In Guinea harassment began. 'Dubois', the SDECE radio operator,
established contact with insurgent groups that had been positioned in the
mountains of Foutah Djalon, a region traditionally opposed to the Conakry
regime. Captain Marie, garrisoned in the neighbourhood of Dakar, carried
out frequent incursions into Guinean territory. In Conakry itself SDECE
could now count upon a whole network of traders and industrialists. By the

end of 1959 everything was ready. But at the very last moment Colonel Tristan Richard received the order from Paris to halt the operation. Leaks had occurred. Sékou Touré, helped by his Czech experts, knew about it. What had happened? According to a senior officer of SDECE, the operation had been very badly prepared. 'Because of a shortage of resources the service had recruited officers from among troops stationed in neighbouring African countries. And in Dakar the rumour quickly spread that the French were up to something.'

In April 1960 a fresh attempt was made. It was the same operation, but this time commando raids were to be launched from the frontiers of Ivory Coast and Senegal. The troops for the rebellion were for the most part made up of Fulani or Peul émigrés, a people critical of Sékou Touré. What SDECE did not know was that at the same time another plot was being hatched by a group of Guinea leaders in Conakry. This second operation was unmasked by Sékou Touré's security services. Straight away the prominent men that were accused denounced one another. Throughout the country opponents, believing they had been uncovered, took flight in a veritable panic. Stocks of arms were discovered at Beyla, Dinn Defelou, Bakouaka and Dindi Fello, on the frontiers with the Ivory Coast and Senegal. France was accused. Several of its nationals were arrested, but Sékou Touré, anxious to preserve links with the former Metropolitan country, if only for economic reasons, did not wish to break off diplomatic relations. After the operation only one single Frenchman was in fact charged, Pierre Rossignol, a chemist, who was accused of having covered for the activities of one of his employees who was suspected of belonging to SDECE. In Paris the affair caused a rumpus and France, after a prolific press campaign, was to secure the release of the chemist.

In November 1965 the lightning struck again. From the podium of the United Nations Achkar Marouf, the Guinea delegate, once again accused France of wishing to topple the Conakry regime. He spoke of a 'permanent conspiracy' against his country, and accused Raymond Triboulet, the French Minister for Cooperation, and Louis Jacquinot, a minister of state. At a gigantic mass meeting Sékou Touré publicly denounced Jacques Foccart as the *deus ex machina* of this umpteenth plot. The Secretary-General for African and Madagascan Affairs protested his innocence. Whereupon a Conakry business man, Mamadou Touré, tried to form an opposition party. With the agreement of several ministers, among them Fodéba Keita, the creator of the famous Africa Ballet, the removal of Sékou Touré was planned. The attempt failed, unleashing a merciless repression. This time it would appear that the French secret services had not directly instigated the affair. On the other hand SDECE had given its approval to the opposition in Guinea. At the French Embassy Lieutenant Henri Moutin had on several occasions met 'Little Touré', one of the conspirators. The SDECE officer had also made numerous contacts in Conakry. Feeling that he was blown, he was replaced, a few weeks before the operation was launched, by Captain Lanquetin, another officer in the secret services.

The constant ferment stirred up by French circles was sufficient for Sékou Touré to take energetic measures. In November 1965 he expelled all the members of the French Embassy. This signalled the breaking off of diplomatic relations between the two countries. In 1969 and 1970, the CIA and the West German BND, as well as the Portuguese PIDE, were each in turn to launch several armed operations. But Paris, having learnt prudence, was content to give timid logistic support. At SDECE it took the arrival of a new head, Alexandre de Marenches, to incite Paris to make preparations for a raid in 1974, and so resume its unrelenting struggle against Sékou Touré.

A year before his death in 1983, 'Sili' discreetly received Jacques Foccart in Conakry. The former Secretary-General for African Affairs continued to fascinate Sékou. Indeed the fascination was mutual. Houphouët-Boigny served as go-between for this meeting. The President of Ivory Coast had received a personal assurance that the invitation given by the Guinea leader contained no hidden trap, and placed one of his personal planes at Foccart's disposal. 'Let us not speak of the past,' declared Sékou Touré. 'On the contrary, let us have some explanations,' retorted Jacques Foccart. 'Tell me the reason for your attack on General de Gaulle.' 'At that time,' Sékou replied, 'France's attitude was outrageous. Why did it knowingly leave consignments of food intended for my people to rot in the port of Marseilles? Not to mention the conspiracies . . .'

Horoscopes and 'Marabouts'

The room was nondescript and smoky. One could hardly make out the poor gouache seascape by the Breton Le Corre, the stock painter at Mortier HQ. Colonel Maurice Robert puffed cheroot after cheroot, thumbing through the pages of the periodical *Horoscope* as he did so.[6] He was extremely annoyed. For several years this magazine, published in France and very widely read in Africa, had intrigued him. His agents on the spot had indicated to him that the African section of *Horoscope* never lacked biased news. It disclosed political changes at opportune moments. This was tantamount to saying that at SDECE the magazine was suspected of being funded by an intelligence service. At first this was thought to be the CIA, and then the Russians. But on that day Colonel Maurice Robert had to admit that the various enquiries had led nowhere.

In Africa very often heads of state themselves provide the main national daily with their personal horoscope. Bernard-Albert Bongo, the president of Gabon, was an old hand at this practice. One never knows: on the African continent religious beliefs, backed up by a definite predilection for magic, remain very strong. And certain heads of state feel their regime to be so shaky that a bad omen might cause it to crumble. But in the present case, there was nothing like that.

Colonel Robert went back to his source. It was Jean Viaud, living in Arcachon, who provided the African section. Enquiries having been made, it appeared that the man was a kind of astrologer, very expert in his own field. The advertising ran: 'The astrologer of several heads of state, of *Horoscope* and *Détective*, the only one to have warned Kennedy of his assassination.' On African questions Jean Viaud was even more precise; shortly before the Claustre affair he wrote: 'An acute state of tension between Ndjamena and Paris could soon reach a critical point.'[7] He did not hesitate to blame Foccart for the troubles in Cameroon: 'There, as in Chad, Guinea and elsewhere, the *éminence grise* of the Élysée will be blamed for all misfortunes.'[8] Occasionally Jean Viaud also took on a threatening tone: 'An African head of state might well regret having taken a new ideological path in 1973.'[9] All these predictions might have been laughable if they had not been so widely known in the countries concerned.

Maurice Robert therefore considered employing this super-clairvoyant in SDECE. Jean Viaud the astrologer would only have to slip in a few titbits of information prepared by the secret services for France to reign supreme over rumours in Africa. Immediately the head of the Africa department despatched an officer to Bordeaux. But 'Mr Viaud' remained impervious to the offers made to him. It was really impossible to persuade him 'to work for his country'; even when envelopes containing the Republic's money were slipped to him, he disdainfully rejected them! At Mortier HQ this was definitely not understood. Several months had to pass before the secret services finally discovered that the Bordeaux astrologer was in cahoots with several African heads of state and preferred to carry on business in his own way.

It was not the first time that SDECE had lent its attention to divine matters. Under de Gaulle the Africa department had systematically manipulated the various religious brotherhoods. For example, on 26 August 1958 the General had been welcomed in Dakar by thousands bearing placards demanding independence. The atmosphere was especially heated. Within the Senegalese Progressive Union (Union Progressiste Sénégalaise: UPS), which was the dominant party, many recommended that the Franco-African Community proposed by de Gaulle should be rejected. Léopold Sédar Senghor, the future president of Senegal, and Mamadou Dia, then its prime minister, were away from Dakar. Faced with this political vacuum, the French administration put its money on the 'marabouts', the priests. In Dakar Governor Lamy and Captain Maître, in charge of Muslim affairs, maintained frequent contacts with them. During his visit to Dakar General de Gaulle gave long audiences to the main Muslim leaders. According to Jacques Foccart, 'The marabouts wrote to the General to encourage him, to give him advice and to assure him of their spiritual support. And in fact, during the stay in Dakar they came to tell me: "Be assured that what you have seen is not the whole of Senegal. We can guarantee that the vote will be in favour, the General should know that he need have no fears about Senegal, the groundswell of opinion is with him and for him." '10

In Senegal the heads of the religious brotherhoods formed an elite who had absolute control over the growing of the groundnut crop. Protected by the French administration, they had everything to lose if there were a sudden break with metropolitan France. This was even more true because the progressive leaders did not conceal their fierce hostility towards them. Their Guinean neighbours were hardly more friendly. Sayfoulaye Diallo, the party's national secretary, had just launched a campaign in Conakry directed against 'marabout rule'. And in Senegal itself, Abdou Diouf, then president, denounced 'the feudalism and obscurantism of the marabouts'. The religious leaders were thus openly backing the French option. Shortly before the referendum on the Community most of the 'marabouts' – Ibrahima Diop, the customary chieftain of Dakar and guide of the Lébous of Cap Vert, Falilou M'Backe, the Khalifa of the Mourides, and Abdoul Aziz Sy, the Tidjane Khalifa – joined the Association for the Fifth Republic (Association pour la Ve République). The declarations in favour of the Gaullist plan became more forceful, until in the end the UPS was obliged to pronounce in favour of accepting it. The referendum results delighted them. The 'yes' vote triumphed overwhelmingly.

After this success, the 'marabouts' attempted to found a Muslim Gaullist movement: the Party of Senegalese Solidarity (Parti de la Solidarité Sénégalaise: PSS). The French administration did not believe in this attempt, which ran the risk of setting Paris against the new Senegalese authorities. In Dakar SDECE refused any material aid to the movement. Beaten in the 1959 elections, the PSS disappeared, not without having attempted a final appeal to de Gaulle. 'According to one of our informants,' revealed Christian Coulon, an African specialist at the National Centre for Scientific Research (Centre National de Recherche Scientifique: CNRS), 'Sheik Tidiane Sy, after his electoral failure, was alleged to have met de Gaulle in Paris to inform him about a possible plan for an armed coup against the Senegalese government. The French President is supposed merely to have placated him.'11

The French secret services nevertheless continued actively to collaborate with the Muslim brotherhoods. For over 20 years SDECE made liberal payments to two of the most popular 'marabouts' in Senegal for information concerning the links between the Senegalese Muslim movements and Saudi Arabia and Morocco. These contacts continue even today, as can be established by examining the finances of the very active Islamic sects in Senegal in recent years.

In Guinea SDECE encouraged the initiatives of El Hadj Barry Diawadou, before independence one of the founders of the African Bloc of Guinea

(BAG), and then Sékou Touré's ambassador in Cairo. A devout Muslim, Barry went frequently to Saudi Arabia and dreamed of establishing an Islamic republic in Guinea. After his return to Conakry this opponent of the Sékou Touré regime had a mosque built in Ratona. With the help of the Peul Imams of Conakry, he published in French translation thousands of copies of the Koran. Barry's reasoning was very simple: if he succeeded in winning over the head of a family he could, because of the homogeneity of the African family unit, rally several persons to his cause. SDECE, which had relied for a long time on the Peuls to mount its plots against Sékou Touré, encouraged this attempt at sedition. It was a failure.

'Monsieur Jean'

One evening in 1965 a dug-out canoe was making its way along the meandering Zaïre River. In the boat a white man was giving orders to several blacks disguised as guards. Arriving at the river bank, the little band examined several aerial photographs, consulted together for a moment, and then determinedly made its way towards the prison at Brazzaville. Taken in by the garb of the daring kidnappers, the warders were to allow the escape of Father Fulbert Youlou, the former president of Congo (Brazzaville).

Jean Mauricheau-Beaupré had pulled off a fresh exploit. De Gaulle would be pleased. For 'Charlot', as he called the General, 'Monsieur Jean' would do anything. But did he at least possess an official order for the assignment? No. Was he attached to SDECE or to any other service? Again, no. But Jean Mauricheau-Beaupré was fanatical about secrecy. His name did not figure in *Who's Who* or in any directory. He belonged to no official body, not even to the secret services. Indeed, in his own right he justified the rumours about the notorious 'Foccart' networks. Publicly, he occupied an office in the Secretariat-General for African and Madagascan Affairs. But he was never to be found there. Officially he was also said to be technical adviser to the president of the Ivory Coast, Felix Houphouët-Boigny. But in Abidjan they had no trace of him.

It was during the War that Jean Mauricheau-Beaupré acquired a taste for intelligence work. He joined the Resistance very early on. Attached to the 'Kléber' network, he then became the head of the 'France-Sud' group, attached to Air Intelligence. 'Even in those days he was a colourful personality,' said his friends. 'He was already very well connected in fine art circles. Since at the time he was lodging in the attic of the Louvre, he arranged all his meetings at the Tuileries.'

A dedicated Gaullist, after the War Jean Mauricheau-Beaupré opted to enter journalism. But his pen could not endure moderation, and he very quickly became chief editor of the celebrated *Courrier de la colère*, founded by Michel Debré. It was a vitriolic paper – partisan to the nth degree – and strengthened his desire for action. When Michel Debré entered the Hôtel Matignon in 1959 'Monsieur Jean' hoped to become his adviser on secret matters. But in the end it was another intelligence specialist, Constantin Melnik, who stole the position from him. Mauricheau-Beaupré, for his part, joined the Private Office of Father Fulbert Youlou in Brazzaville.

Africa was not unknown to him: it was in his blood. Before the War his father (who was the curator at Versailles) had received a visit from Haile Selassie, the Emperor of Ethiopia. From 1960 onwards 'Monsieur Jean' found himself involved in all the disturbances on the black continent. Everywhere that France hesitated to intervene officially, where SDECE was too easily identifiable, there loomed the silhouette of Mauricheau-Beaupré. A friend of Debré and Foccart, he even met the General: there was no question of curbing the actions of such a man. On the ground, the French diplomatic representatives as well as the local heads of SDECE had orders to give him all necessary assistance. 'Monsieur Jean' was seen with Delarue, the former policeman, in the Kasaï region, and then in Katanga with Faulques and Denard. He was present in Ghana when the CIA toppled the nationalist regime of Nkrumah. And when Biafra seceded, it was again he who coordinated the transportation of arms to the rebels.

Relations between Mauricheau-Beaupré and SDECE were not always easy. The officers of the secret services too often had the impression that they were being 'short-circuited' by this dynamic man of action. Maurice Robert, then head of the Africa department, disliked the initiatives taken by 'Monsieur Jean'. For military men, it was all too disorderly, muddled and even dangerous: elementary security rules were not respected.

Among Mauricheau-Beaupré's friends, conversely, the apathy and lack of imagination of SDECE were attacked. For the escape of Fulbert Youlou, Mortier HQ had in fact planned several possible scenarios. But because the means were lacking, nothing had been attempted. It was then that 'Monsieur Jean' had taken the matter in hand. Helped by Moïse Tschombe, who had just returned to power in Léopoldville, he recruited a few black mercenaries – which oddly enough, SDECE never did, for security reasons – among them the priest's former driver. After a few reconnaissance flights Mauricheau-Beaupré launched his operation. He freed Father Fulbert Youlou. At SDECE they pulled a sour face.

Katanga, the Land of Mercenaries

'Look here, Grossin,' rapped General de Gaulle as he accompanied the SDECE director to the door of his office, 'this Tschombe, this Moïse, he's good, he speaks out – we should help him.' 'We are doing that through Father Fulbert Youlou,' replied General Grossin. 'Fine, that's good,' de Gaulle grunted. The Katangan adventure began on 30 June 1960, the day when the former Belgian Congo gained its independence. Katanga, the richest area in the country, a big producer of copper, cobalt and manganese, proclaimed its secession. A colourful and quite popular figure, Moïse Tschombe, took over control of the new state, supported by Belgium and the Union Minière.

Without Katanga, its economic lung, Congo could not live. The prime minister of the country, Patrice Lumumba, whose progressive ideas disturbed all the Western capitals, threatened to retake Katanga by force. The USSR, which counted on Lumumba to increase its influence in Africa, was generous with material aid. The UN and its Secretary-General, Dag Hammarskjöld, likewise supported the central authorities in Leopoldville. The United States also threw its hat into the ring. In the autumn of 1960, Colonel Mobutu, supported by the CIA, which had placed him at the head of the Congolese national army, had Patrice Lumumba arrested. A few days earlier Lawrence Raymond Devlin, the CIA station head at Leopoldville, had telegraphed to its GHQ at Langley House: 'Station head advice: Lumumba in opposition is almost as dangerous as in power. Congolese politician has made known he understands situation and implies could physically eliminate Lumumba.'[12]

Joseph Mobutu was to fulfil his task for the United States. On 7 January, 1961 Patrice Lumumba, half-dead after being horribly tortured, was dispatched to Elisabethville, capital of Katanga. Lumumba was seen no more and, with him, the USSR disappeared from the Congo scene. During all these events France was not idle. In Paris, too, interest centred on the mineral wealth that Katanga contained. 'In 1947,' recalled the diplomat Boris Eliacheff, 'I was a commercial counsellor in black Africa. I had managed to get hold of a piece of uranium from the deposits being mined by the large Belgian company, Union Minière of Katanga, which had a 25-year contract with the United States. Unable to buy the precious metal, the people responsible for our economy, which was beginning to pick up, at that time at least wanted to know what its characteristics were.'[13]

These economic considerations were not the only ones. In 1960, after the Belgian withdrawal, the British Federation of Rhodesia and Nyasaland asserted its claim to Katanga. This was more than de Gaulle could bear. 'The position of France,' the General once said, 'depends upon the honour of its flag and not on the growth of its GNP.' In the spring Maurice Couve de Murville, the Minister of Foreign Affairs, informed the Belgian Ambassador, Marcel-Henri Jaspar, that France also laid claim to this Congolese province. According to the old agreements between Leopold II and Jules Ferry, made on 23–4 April 1883, in the event of Belgian withdrawal Paris retained a pre-emptive right to the Congolese territory. And this was precisely what had happened.

Meanwhile, in Elisabethville, Moïse Tschombe was desperately seeking support. He appealed to Paris. The French government was divided: some of its members rightly remarked that the regime of 'Mr Cash-Drawer', Tschombe's nickname, was decidedly too corrupt. But de Gaulle resolved to give substantial aid. So through Fulbert Youlou, the President of Congo (Brazzaville), SDECE provided Katanga with arms, ammunition and even money.

At the same time Moïse Tschombe made contact in France with several officers who had been disappointed by the turn that events had taken in Algeria. De Gaulle had prudently removed those soldiers from the scene of operations. Colonel Trinquier, the head of the Mixed Airborne Commandos (GCMA) in Indo-China, was languishing in the military sub-area of Nice. Together with several others, among them Commandant Roger Faulques, he gladly accepted the invitation to launch a new crusade against communism in Africa. These officers, who were still on the active list, asked their minister to allow them to go ahead. In Pierre Messmer's Private Office it was Captain Pierre Dabezies who was given the task of following up the Katanga affair. A score of French military men were authorized to 'make themselves available'. In Katanga they were to be named *Les Affreux*, 'the terrible ones', and this nickname stuck to these hardened veterans, who had become specialists in subversive warfare in Algeria. Among them were two former members of the 11th Shock Troops, Captain Yves de la Bourdonnaye-Montluc, the head of the Fifth Bureau, who was in charge of psychological warfare in Katanga, and Joseph B. Captains Ege, Ropagnol, Lasimone and de Clary were also tempted to embark upon the adventure. Another Frenchman, Lieutenant Tony de Saint-Paul, had stolen a march upon his comrades by reaching Katanga in the autumn of 1960.

On the spot, difficulties quickly arose. The Belgian officers still at Tschombe's side – although their government supported the secession of Katanga with increasingly timidity – refused to entrust Trinquier with the command of the army. Moïse gave way to them, and the French colonel, after two brief stays in Leopoldville, went back to Paris. However, the mercenaries remained in the Katangan capital, where they enjoyed the active assistance of the French consul-general, Joseph Lambroschini, a former member of the BCRA (the famous 'Colonel Nizier' of the maquis on the Glières plateau).

In Elisabethville Tschombe continued to waver. In August 1961, hoping to win clemency from the United Nations, he sought to hand over his mercenaries, but they got wind of it and escaped. There was a fresh turn of events in September, when the central government in Leopoldville, backed by United Nations troops, decided to attack Tschombe's capital. At the head of some 30 men and the Katangan gendarmerie, trained by the former Belgian administration, Roger Faulques resisted a veritable army. The 'blue helmets' launched their final attack in December 1962, with an incredible deployment of force: the UN battalions included no fewer than 22 nationalities. The mercenary Bob Denard, a former quartermaster in the

Indo-China war, who had turned mercenary as much for financial reasons as by inclination, held his ground for several days, helped by a few dozen men. Then, in good order and with his equipment, he retreated to Kolwezi and Angola. In January 1963 Tschombe reached Europe, and waited for another day.

It was not slow in coming. On 26 June 1964, Moïse Tschombe again landed in Leopoldville, where he was welcomed by a joyful crowd. What had happened? For several months the Congo had once again been a prey to internecine strife. Three Marxist leaders, Pierre Mulelé, Gaston Soumialot and Christophe Gbenye, had held the central government in check. Anxious about the future of the mines, the American and Belgian governments sent for Tschombe. Going one better than Katanga, they offered 'Mr Cash-Drawer' the whole of the Congo.

That kind of barter did not satisfy de Gaulle. In spite of its first resounding failure, Paris still had confidence in the Katangan leader – but on condition that he did not become the pawn of the United States! This was all the more the case, because although the General had supported the secession of Katanga from the beginning, he had little taste for the sordid manoeuvrings of the CIA, and in particular for the assassination of Patrice Lumumba. 'It is more than a crime, it is a mistake,' de Gaulle was to say, turning a famous slogan to his own use. From now on *Realpolitik* guided the French moves in the Congo. The siege of Stanleyville, occupied by the rebels, was a striking illustration of this: whilst Belgium and the United States were putting the finishing touches to an airborne operation in cooperation with Mobutu's Congolese Army, in order to save those of their nationals who had not been massacred, France, for its part, negotiated with the 'simbas' occupying the town. 'Was the basic interest of France,' demanded Jacques Kosciusko-Morizet, a former ambassador to the Congo, 'threatened by the fact that a part of the Congo had fallen under the domination of those so-called rebels, "Mulélistes", "Lumumbistes", etc.? Clearly not. No French interest was directly threatened . . . I believe that de Gaulle, perhaps having learnt from the mistakes committed in Guinea, had a very clear idea that at that moment there was no possibility or interest that might cause us to intervene.'[14] In any case no French citizen was affected. The Congo adventure was almost over. In October 1965, Moïse Tschombe was overthrown by Colonel Mobutu, who gave the Congo the name Zaïre. Having gone back to Europe, the Katangan leader was already preparing his return. But the new Zaïre president, supported by the CIA, was on the watch.

SDECE versus the CIA

'A bad blow!' Jacques Foccart was furious. Yet he had warned Moïse Tschombe. For several months the Secretary-General for African affairs had had wind of a plot by the CIA and Zaïre Security. In spite of these warnings the Katangan leader had trusted the former convict Francis Bodenan. Already mixed up in the murder of two iron dealers near Montfort-l'Amaury – an affair that had caused a scandal in France – Francis Bodenan had switched to commerce. It was under this cover that he had got to know Belgian industrialists close to Tschombe, and then the Katangan leader himself, still in exile in Madrid. He had proposed that he should become the 'front man' of a mystical African social movement that would be financed by the United States.

On 29 June 1967 Francis Bodenan arrived in Palma from Geneva, via Rome. He was the sole passenger on board the Hawker Siddeley 125 hired by SODEFI, his Swiss company. That evening he dined with Tschombe at the Hotel Del Mar, and suggested to him that the following day they should go on an excursion: 'The big American boss is only arriving tomorrow. We could take a trip to Ibiza in my company's plane.' Incautiously, the Katangan leader accepted. On 30 June, on the way back from Ibiza, Francis Bodenan stood up suddenly, facing Tschombe and the few companions travelling with him and said: 'I am a secret agent! And a killer! Look out, because I aim straight and I have precise instructions.' And, to the two British pilots he gave the order: 'Set course for Algiers, Algiers as priority! Have you got it?'

At the military airport of Boufarik the Algerian police were awaiting their cargo. Roughly interrogated by the security services of President Boumedienne, the Katangan leader was brought to court in July. At his trial Tschombe made rather a good impression, as he tried to justify the secession of Katanga. The Supreme Court finally ordered his extradition to Zaïre. But the order was not carried out, and the former Katangan president died in prison in June 1969. Francis Bodenan, for his part, was soon released. At the time SDECE was accused of the abduction. Had not some well-known *barbouzes* been spotted among Tschombe's entourage? But today, almost 20 years later, tongues have been loosened. Francis Bodenan did no more than obey the orders of Mobutu and of the CIA agent Lawrence Raymond Devlin, who became the personal adviser to the Zaïre president. Several former ministers of Mobutu have recently given their testimony in the Belgian press: 'Bodenan was in the service of Zaïre Security,' said Nguza Karl I Bond, the former prime minister of Zaïre, on 29 January 1982. After Tschombe's death the president of Zaïre received Bodenan in a Tunis hotel and, before a witness, handed over to him a reward of 1 million dollars.'[15] Mungul Diak, who was the Zaïre Ambassador in Brussels and one of the chief protagonists in the affair, stated: 'I was summoned to President Mobutu on 30 June 1967, when the news of the abduction became known. There were present Bomboko, the Minister of Foreign Affairs, Singa, the Minister of Justice, Tshisekedi, the Minister of the Interior, and myself. The president was exultant; he ordered bottles of champagne to be opened, and wanted to confer Zaïre nationality upon Bodenan in order to thank him.'[16]

The mercenary himself has on many an occasion admitted that it was Mungul Diak who directly passed Mobutu's orders on to him.

The French secret services were not at all involved in this plot. In 1967 Paris was continuing to play the Tschombe card in the Congo. The Katangan leader enjoyed the personal support of Jacques Foccart. The two men had met and approved of each other. 'When the news of the abduction reached Paris, Jacques Foccart flew into a rage. Gaullist diplomacy no longer had any pawn to promote in Katanga and for a long while it abandoned the field to the Americans,' recalled one of the close companions of the Secretary-General for African and Madagascan Affairs.

It was not the first time that France had a bone to pick with Washington concerning African affairs. On several occasions SDECE had made it plain to the CIA that it would not tolerate American agents carrying on recruitment in the heart of Paris. René Delseny, the head of French Counter-Espionage, was adamant on this point. In spite of repeated warnings Charlie Lester, the person responsible for liaison between the CIA and SDECE in Paris, did just as he liked. At 115, Boulevard Saint-Michel, the headquarters of the Federation of Black Students in France, the inspectors of Renseignements Généraux given the job of surveillance of progressive movements frequently reported the presence of American agents.

But there was something even more serious. According to Robert Lemoine, the former Resistance member who had become an auxiliary of Action branch:

In Paris, the CIA bought up former brothels kept by Arabs. They modernized these hotels, leaving an immigrant behind as the owner, having forced him to sign an enormous IOU, to prevent him from leaving the network. Then the CIA told him: 'We are going to send you some guys from Black Africa, who are coming to train. At the beginning you will only ask them for a modest sum to cover the room and food. But every time they need money for women, drugs, etc., you will lend it to them and make them sign IOUs.' These IOUs were then handed over to the CIA. When the students returned to Africa, American headquarters could ask them to do whatever it wanted. It had got them in its clutches. SDECE stumbled across this affair and broke it up.[17]

Through an Albanian immigrant, Robert Lemoine learnt the name of one of these hotels, the Pavillon d'Alger, which was controlled by the Americans. It was at the beginning of the 1960s, and the SDECE directorate was getting less and less happy about the anti-French machinations of the CIA in Algeria. There was no question now of allowing the US headquarters to trespass on the French preserve in Africa. This was the beginning of the so-called 'Francophonie' movement. On the US side Charles Lester had entrusted the control of the hotels to an agent by the name of Hechberg. On behalf of SDECE, Action Branch received orders to retrieve all the IOUs from the African students. During the operation Robert Lemoine broke into the Paris apartment of Hechberg and found himself face to face with him. The two men took a shot at each other. The American agent was seriously wounded, and eventually had to have his leg amputated.

Robert Lemoine found himself before the courts. In the witness box Hechberg claimed to be working for NASA. 'Is it customary for NASA engineers to carry firearms and believe that they are out in the Wild West?' the judge asked. 'As a matter of fact,' replied the American, 'I belong to NASA security.' 'Or the FBI or CIA,' the judge corrected him. In the dock Robert Lemoine burst out laughing. The judge turned towards him: 'As for you, Lemoine, I know you only too well, I advise you to take care.'[18] Finally Robert Lemoine was sentenced to six months in prison. A few days later he was freed.

'Biafra: A Brave Little People'

'A brave little people, Foccart, something should be done.' General de Gaulle felt an instinctive sympathy for the Biafran people. In July 1966, the northern Nigerians, belonging to the Hausa tribe, massacred 50,000 Ibos living in the south of the country. Lieutenant-Colonel Ojukwu, who at the time posed as the leader of the Ibos, proclaimed the independence of the eastern region of Nigeria, under the name of the Republic of Biafra. From Lagos, the Nigerian capital, General Gowon, who belonged to a different ethnic grouping, a very small minority in the country, rejected partition. It was war – and in the form of genocide: it was to cause 2 million deaths. To start with, the federal government in Lagos had available decisive means of support: the military aid of the USSR and Great Britain. From the outset of the conflict the Soviets sent MIG aircraft and Ilyushins. As for the British, anxious about their oil interests – Shell and BP – in the region, they dispatched John Peters, a former SAS corporal, to recruit mercenaries for the Lagos government.

In Paris, even although de Gaulle declared his sympathy for Biafra, prudence was the order of the day. It is true that the General had not forgiven Nigeria for having in January 1961 expelled Raymond Offroy, his ambassador, in protest against the third atomic test explosion at Reggane, in the Sahara. But the French government had also to take into account the fact that most of its interests lay in the Nigerian areas.

On the other hand, factors of a purely geographical nature pleaded in favour of the secession of Biafra. The *Revue de défense nationale* wrote: 'The crisis in Nigeria, which history has placed at the heart of the French colonial area, could not leave France indifferent: four French-speaking states surround the Federation, and considerable minorities are to be found in them: the Yoruba in Dahomey, the Hausa in Niger, the Ibo in East Cameroon.'[19] However, in the name of the sacrosanct principle of the inviolability of the frontiers inherited from the colonial empire, most of the countries of Africa sided with Lagos. Only four presidents, Houphouët-Boigny (Ivory Coast), Bongo (Gabon), Nyerere (Tanzania) and Kaunda (Zambia) personally intervened with aid to Biafra. De Gaulle had to take all these factors into account.

As in Katanga, France could not involve SDECE openly in this affair. Throughout the conflict the only contribution of the French secret services was to arrange the delivery of arms; but at no time was Action Branch present on the ground. Paris insisted on keeping its room for manoeuvre. Its attitude was not without its contradictions: in 1967 France delivered 21 Panhard machine guns to Nigeria, whereas semi-officially it supported the Republic of Lieutenant-Colonel Ojukwu.

At the same time, using the cover of the Biafra Historical Research Centre, which had been given permission to establish itself in Paris, the Ibos were on the look-out for their first mercenaries. In the capital, as it had been for Katanga, it was Commandant Faulques and also Robert Denard who were given the job of recruitment. They had available a lot of money (coming from the French government, so they said). The former Foreign Legionary Rolf Steiner, who had known Faulques in Indo-China, and then in Algeria in the OAS, tells of his encounter with him: 'Without telling me explicitly, he gave me to understand that he was indeed semi-officially mandated by de Gaulle. He explained to me that his mission was not to fight, but to help the young Biafran army to get itself organized.'[20]

Via Lisbon, some 150 mercenaries made the journey to Biafra. They were not to make much impression. Ill-prepared for the fight, the majority left the country as early as the summer of 1968. Only Rolf Steiner, at the head of his famous 'Black Legion' of 4,000 men, who left for battle singing the 'Marseillaise', kept his word. From September 1968 in constant touch with Philippe Le Terron, called 'Monsieur Philippe', who was SDECE's man in Libreville and ensured his supplies, this 'war maniac' for a while held his own against the Nigerian troops.

In Paris things were moving fast. On 31 July 1968, a communiqué from the French government for the first time asserted the right of self-determination for the Biafran people. And on 9 September, the General gave a press conference. For the General, the struggle of the 'Ibosses', as he pronounced their name, was a just one. It amounted to a struggle for national liberation.[21] The head of state exclaimed:

Why should the Ibos, who are mostly Christians, live their own life in the South, and have their own language – why should they depend on another ethnic grouping in the Federation? For this is what it comes down to. As soon as the colonial power had withdrawn its authority, in an artificial federation it was one ethnic element imposing its authority upon the others . . . in this affair France has helped Biafra within the limits of what is feasible. It has not carried out the act that would be decisive: the recognition of the Biafra Republic. For it believes that the birth of Africa is, above all, a matter for Africans.[22]

From then onwards French assistance was no longer restricted to the recruitment of mercenaries. In September 1968 an 'air bridge' was established between Paris, Libreville and Biafra. Jean-Claude Brouillet, the director of the Transgabon and SDECE station head in Libreville, was in charge of it. Officially it was designed for the dispatch of medicines and foodstuffs, but now and again the barrel of a machine gun stuck out from among the pills and serums. The French services had thought up the idea of using this 'air bridge' to dispatch weapons. In Libreville their task was made easy because the military attaché was also the local president of the Red Cross. Humanitarian organizations at the time constituted the safest cover for all secret services. But occasionally it was at their own wish that certain religious orders called upon these very special missionaries. Count Carl Gustav von Rosen figured among the recruits. It was under the aegis of Caritas Internationalis that this extremely wealthy Swedish aristocrat became involved in Biafra. He formed a small squadron of Malmö MFI9Bs: the special feature of these tiny planes, which were very vulnerable, was that they were equipped under their wings with rocket-launchers. The von Rosen squadron was to succeed in destroying some ten Soviet MIGs on the ground.

In all, Biafra received each week 350 tonnes of arms, from the autumn of 1968 onwards.[23] Apart from the official supplies of arms, the French government closed its eyes to the tens of thousands of weapons that left French factories directly for Biafra. It was with the approval of the highest authority that Jean Mauricheau-Beaupré, alias 'Monsieur Jean', was actively involved in the arms traffic to the Ibos. A journalist on *Paris-match*, for his part, sought new volunteers to replace the mercenaries who had taken to their heels.

And SDECE? It did not remain inactive, although it had received strict orders not to involve any of its officers in the fighting. At the end of 1968 it was no longer Jacques Foccart who was supervising operations. Pierre Messmer, the Army Minister, had taken over from him. SDECE still kept a watch on the overall arrangements for aid to Biafra. Maurice Robert, the head of the Africa department, regularly dispatched missions on the spot. In October 1968, Colonel Fournier, accompanied by three officers of SDECE, arrived to appraise the military situation. But these hasty visits – of roughly two months – hardly gave enough time to arrive at an opinion. The mission of SDECE was therefore very often limited to covering operations from afar and – should the need arise – to 'retrieving' any over-enterprising mercenaries. For their part, the official representatives of France had received instructions from Michel Debré, then Minister of Foreign Affairs, to support French operations. In Libreville Maurice Delauney, the ambassador, helped by Colonel Merle, the military attaché, did not lag behind. They facilitated the task of the mercenaries.

General de Gaulle was to assist the secession of Biafra right to the end. The last cabinet meeting that he presided over, on 23 April 1969, unambiguously reaffirmed the right of self-determination for the Biafran people. The accession of Georges Pompidou to power heralded a change in policy. Military aid gradually ceased. In January 1970 the defeated Colonel Ojukwu abandoned the struggle and departed to a lengthy exile in the Ivory Coast. It was the end of the Biafran war. 'The mistake,' asserted a high official in SDECE bitterly, 'lay in a lack of political will. We were behind the secession of Biafra. Afterwards, we should have involved ourselves up to the hilt, and not done things half-heartedly.'

I I

The Hunt for Moles

The chapel of Keramanac'h in Brittany is a magnificent edifice that was a staging-post for the Knights Templar in the fifteenth century. *Manac'h* means 'monk' in Breton, and it was doubtless as much the amusing homonym as a liking for old stones – he lived in a house once occupied by Gauguin – that impelled Etienne Manac'h, director of the Asia–Oceania department at the Quai d'Orsay, to pause there one fine day in 1963. The family paid a visit to the chapel bordering the RN12, halfway between Morlaix and Guingamp, and then set off once more. They did not notice the camouflaged, unmarked car that stopped shortly afterwards.

'This proves it! It's a dead-letter box for the Russians!' In Paris, in the Russian division of the DST, the fever mounted. André Guérin, its head, nicknamed 'Toto', was jubilant. Chalet, the divisional commissioner, was dealing with the Manac'h file directly with Jean Bozzi, the head of the Private Office of Roger Frey, the Minister of the Interior. He gave the go-ahead. During the night the Brest team of the DST went to the site of the Templars. And into the small hours of the morning the security crusaders examined each stone under a magnifying-glass, in order to discover some secret message that would establish the diplomat's treason.

In vain. In all the time DST had been watching Etienne Manac'h, they had found nothing. What did the DST have against the future ambassador to China? The fact that in 1941 he had represented Free France in Turkey and had perhaps met Georges Pâques there, under the auspices of the National Committee for Free France in Algiers. Pâques had been unmasked in 1963: for 20 years he had spied for the Russians. Since that time a poisonous atmosphere had prevailed, and a number of historically well-known Gaullists became suspect in the eyes of the DST.[1]

The Golytzin Source

Since the Cold War Vienna had remained the hub of espionage activities on the borders of the Soviet bloc. SDECE maintained a solidly based station there for research and counter-espionage. Maurice Clément, the 'vice-consul', in reality responsible for the counter-espionage network, succeeded in bringing about a few 'defections' at the end of the 1950s. But for the most part it was to the Anglo-Americans that defectors to the West gave themselves up. The CIA possessed many escape routes of one sort and another, large resources, and reception centres in the Federal Republic as well as in the USA.

It was indeed with the Americans that, on 15 February 1954, Piotr Deriabin, a leading light in Soviet military intelligence, the GRU, 'chose liberty', as the saying goes in such cases. His entrance into the American GHQ in Vienna made a resounding impression.[2] Amazed, the CIA men stared at the Russian as he dashed off a list of potential turncoats, men who would willingly change sides, provided they were assisted to do so. The list was headed by a 'big fish': one of his colleagues in Vienna, Anatoly Alexandrovich Golytzin, a counter-espionage specialist. He was unstable, detested by his subordinates, and notorious for his marital problems. His wife Svetlana was his weak point, the one that might cause him to cross the Rubicon, thought the CIA experts. Yes, but . . . Suddenly Golytzin was recalled to Moscow. For six years he was to work in Dzerzhinsky Square, in the chief directorate of the KGB, in the Anglo-American section.

He languished there, in the paper-chasing mediocrity of a state bureaucracy, amid the petty rivalries of the *Apparatchiks*, and the dazzling memories, during evenings spent by the samovar, of a turbulent Vienna and an unfaithful wife. In short, Golytzin had sworn to himself to cross over to the West when the time was ripe. So he noted and recorded the names of officers operating in Europe and America, copied organizational diagrams, memorized operations in progress or completed, with all the more minuteness because he was transferred to a special unit for directing Soviet infiltration into NATO. Finally, in 1960 he was appointed to the embassy in Helsinki and skipped over the fence.

The CIA station head listened with astonishment to the first revelations by Golytzin. If the United States welcomed him, he would tell all: how the KGB, for 20 years, had succeeded in hiding itself away in the very heart of the Western special services, in Britain, Sweden, Canada, the Federal Republic, and even in the USA and France! To prove his sincerity, Golytzin supplied the KGB order of battle in Finland, and promised to identify all the Soviet 'illegals' that he knew throughout the world. After passing through the CIA's European centre in Frankfurt, he was transferred to a reception base of the American headquarters, Ashford Farm.

James Jesus Angleton

In the CIA Golytzin was known as AE/LADLE. It was unnecessary to reveal his true identity, even to the Allies. The man charged with 'debriefing' him, and questioning him relentlessly, was the head of counter-espionage himself, and a colourful personality. James Jesus Angleton was born in Idaho in 1917 of a Mexican mother and a US father, an officer famous for having remorselessly hunted down Pancho Villa, the Mexican revolutionary. In 1940, at Yale, he threw himself into poetry, and came into contact with outstanding writers such as Dylan Thomas and Ezra Pound. Very much later he was to win competitions for growing orchids. One has to be patient, meticulous, even obsessive to take an interest in certain varieties that flower only once every seven years. Meanwhile Angleton worked in London in 1942 for OSS, the forerunner of the CIA, liaising with the British SIS. Among them he met Kim Philby, then deputy head of counter-espionage. Four years later he was representing the American special services in Rome. Finally, from 1949 onwards, he took part in starting up the CIA's Office of Special Operations (OSO), before assuming the post of director of counter-espionage.

With his assistants, Newton Miller and Raymond Rocca, shortly afterwards posted to Paris, Angleton therefore recorded the revelations of the Russian defector. To tell the truth, these were not very precise: a Swedish colonel in the air force was working for the Russians, as were some British intelligence officers, and an important member of General de Gaulle's entourage. This is what Golytzin said in substance. For month after month Angleton's team prepared dossiers for each of the countries concerned. There then began the great game of musical chairs as experts of each nation came, at the invitation of the CIA, to hear Golytzin's confession.

The British first of all – *noblesse oblige*. For them he was called 'KAGO'. He revealed the extent of Soviet penetration into Great Britain, especially confirming the guilt of Kim Philby, a Soviet agent who since the 1930s had risen to the highest level in the Secret Intelligence Service. 'KAGO' also enabled them to identify Sir Anthony Blunt, the Surveyor of the Queen's Pictures, as a Soviet 'mole';[3] and also the spy John Vassall at the Admiralty.

Occasionally the revelations of the Soviet agent left something to be desired. Whether he is honest, or, on the contrary, an agent sent by the other side to 'contaminate', a defector always has a tendency to 'pile it on', to increase the value of his statements in the eyes of his hosts. Stig Wennerström, the Swedish air force colonel, was arrested on 20 June 1963 by SAPO, his country's counter-espionage service. At Langley, the CIA headquarters, Angleton was jubilant. But at the same time *his* defector committed a gaffe concerning Scandinavia. At Golytzin's instigation, Ingeborg Lygren, the secretary of Colonel Wilhelm Evang, the head of Norwegian military intelligence, was 'given the works'. She was recognized as being totally innocent, but she lost her job – the Parliament in Oslo was to vote her a sum for damages and compensation.

The witness's sagacity seemed to work with greater success in Germany. General Gehlen's BND was shaken in its turn. The head of counter-espionage against the Soviet bloc, Heinz Felfe, was unmasked. Golytzin appeared to be the inspirer of this important capture. But in reality the defector was only providing confirmation of the game that Felfe had been playing. For the latter had been arrested on 6 November 1961, just before Golytzin had crossed to the West. The 'mole' was already in the trap.

Now the inevitable happened. One day Golytzin announced to his American friends that they should clean up their own front yard; in the CIA too the moles had burrowed tunnels.[4] From 1963 onwards the CIA divided into two camps: the pro- and anti-Golytzin. The wisest among them wondered if, in the end, the whole saga did not primarily benefit Moscow. Inevitably some posed themselves the question: might not Angleton himself be the Russian spy Number One in headquarters?

Moreover, the affair grew extraordinarily more complicated. In June 1962 another defector chose the West. Yury Nossenko, a KGB officer, a member of the Soviet delegation to the Geneva disarmament conference, changed sides. His revelations cracked the pillars of the temple. According to him Golytzin had been sent by Moscow to bring the secret services of the Atlantic Alliance to a standstill, and to create a psychosis. Moreover, he added, the agents identified by Golytzin had all been 'blown'. Moscow had had a fine time by throwing them to the lions in order to cast discredit upon others who were really innocent. This hypothesis suited Angleton's opponents, both in the CIA and in the Allied services, who had been bewildered by the investigations that had been unleashed upon them. But shortly afterwards Nossenko disappeared. It was he who had been Moscow's envoy, sent to discredit Golytzin. At the CIA this episode confirmed it: it was agreed that it was decidedly necessary to cleanse the Augean stables. And, the bulkiest dossier put together by Angleton was that concerning Soviet moles in the French secret services – even in the entourage of General de Gaulle.

The French Called him 'Martel'

To follow the sequence of events it is essential to go back a little. In December 1961, then, Anatoly Golytzin changed sides. Two months later SDECE changed its director. The air force general Paul Jacquier replaced General Grossin. The intelligence specialist gave way to an amateur, chosen essentially because of his fidelity to Gaullism. Hardly had he been installed on the Boulevard Mortier than he had to confront the storm.

For the French everything began with the spring. John Fitzgerald Kennedy sent a special courier to the Elysée. De Gaulle, whose mistrust of the United States had been exacerbated during the Algerian crisis, thus learnt that an important Soviet informer had made some frightening revelations to the CIA: his secret services, and even his government, had been penetrated by Russian agents. The French head of state dispatched to Washington a man he could trust, General Jean-Louis du Temple de Rougemont, who knew the Anglo-American world well: a former military attaché in London, then the representative of the NATO standing committee in Washington, in 1962 he was director of the Intelligence division of the general staff in the Ministry of National Defence. 'They make me sick with this story,' de Gaulle said to him, convinced that it was a put-up job to discredit his policy. Who were 'they'? Either the Americans or the Russians, who might be trying to exploit Franco-American rivalries.

But, having had a long confrontation with Golytzin, Temple de Rougemont formed a different opinion. Back in Paris, he confided to Etienne Burin des Roziers, Secretary-General of the President's Office: 'It's serious!' And to General de Gaulle he declared: 'A genuine Soviet defector. He knows a great deal. There are grounds for ordering an enquiry!'

In May 1962 counter-espionage experts from the DST (Daniel Doustin, Marcel Chalet and Louis Niquet) and SDECE crossed the Atlantic.[5] Colonel Delseny, who was also on the trip, complained: 'As usual, the Americans were in no hurry to reveal this source to us. That had happened before with another defector, Oleg Penkovsky.' Golytzin, whom the French called 'Martel', was a small, skinny, nervous man. For weeks on end he revealed what he knew about Russian infiltrations into France. Martel did not know precise names – in the KGB he mainly directed the Anglo-American bureau – but he was positive: firstly, various ministries had been infiltrated, and an influential Frenchman was working at NATO for the KGB. Secondly, important Gaullist civil servants, some in the entourage of the General himself, were informants for Moscow. Thirdly, a network of Soviet agents, given the name 'Sapphire', was operating inside SDECE. On this last point Golytzin was more precise. According to him, General Sakharovsky, head of KGB clandestine operations, was congratulating himself in 1959 that he possessed all the plans for the reorganization of SDECE drawn up by General Grossin. He boasted of receiving the main SDECE summary reports in Moscow three days after their distribution. And what was more serious, Martel said, was that the KGB had learnt that a special section for scientific intelligence, targeted at the USA, was to be set up by SDECE at the request of General de Gaulle. Now, this section did in fact come under the aegis of Colonel Jacques Hervé, in the summer of 1962, almost six months after Golytzin's statement. The operation was entitled 'Big Ben'.

Upon their return to Paris the counter-espionage experts set to work. And results were not slow in coming. On 10 August 1963, Georges Pâques, the head of NATO's press service, was arrested whilst meeting a KGB officer. In the Rue des Saussaies he admitted that the Russians had recruited him in Algiers in 1944. Immediately the DST set about tracking down Gaullists who might have met him among the Free French in 1944. A malicious rumour, taken up later by the press, accused Jacques Foccart, responsible for French policy in Africa. The origin of this intrigue lay across the Atlantic.

Among the Gaullists whose biographies were scrutinized by the DST were numerous diplomats, in accordance with Martel's suggestions. We have already encountered one of them – Etienne Manac'h. The scrutiny also extended to Georges Gorse, who in 1943 had carried out missions to the USSR, before becoming an ambassador, notably in Tunisia; and also to Louis Joxe, the secretary-general of the Committee of National Liberation, then ambassador to the USSR, and since 1959 a minister of General de Gaulle.[6]

The French Ambassador in Moscow

The 'case' of ambassador Maurice Dejean was even more disturbing. It all started with the story of another defector who had crossed over to the West. On 2 September 1963, Yury Vassilievich Krotkov, on a visit to London, presented himself to the British security services: 'I used to work for the KGB. I was given the job of ensnaring the French ambassador in Moscow. The order came directly from Khrushchev . . .' was the substance of what he said.[7]

Political adviser to the French Committee of National Liberation, then a minister plenipotentiary accredited to the Allied governments in London in 1944, Maurice Dejean afterwards embarked upon a diplomatic career, which, in December 1955, took him to Moscow. He was to be ambassador there for nine years, until 1964. Yet this seasoned diplomat was no novice as regards espionage. Before the War he had been one of the rare members of the intelligence service for whom the Quai d'Orsay had agreed to afford diplomatic cover (it was in Berlin in 1935, and Dejean was fighting the Nazis).

So there he was, at the end of the 1950s, ambassador in Moscow, where one of the high officials in the KGB, Lieutenant-General Oleg Gribanov, worked out a very sophisticated plan. A film-maker, Yury Krotkov, was selected for this purpose by the KGB. His aim was not to seduce Marie-Claire, the ambassador's wife, but to make friends with Dejean, so as to start up a network of social relationships selected by the KGB. All this would contribute, when the time was ripe, to shaping the trap set for Ambassador Dejean.

He was already under close surveillance: Marie-Claire Dejean's chamber-maid and her husband's chauffeur were in the pay of the KGB.[8] In order to get a hold over the ambassador, said a to be a *bon vivant*, the KGB thought up a comedy worthy of Feydeau. After several fruitless attempts, Krotkov introduced to Dejean a charming actress who had been given the job of seducing him, Lara Kronberg-Sobolevskaya. In the summer of 1958 the idyll began. The date was crucial: first, the ambassador's wife was taking a holiday in France, and, most important, General de Gaulle had returned to power. According to the KGB, Dejean was liable to be recalled to Paris, in order to play an important role at the General's side. His recruitment had to be speeded up.

One afternoon, in Lara's studio, the lovers' embraces were interrupted by a red tornado. 'Good heavens, my husband!' A gigantic Mongol burst in, hit his 'wife', and attacked the ambassador, shouting that he would have the law on both of them. Scandal! 'We'll fix that, never you mind, old chap,' the shaken Dejean was assured by one of his new friends, a Russian general, to whom he had been introduced a few months previously by the nice Krotkov. No prizes for guessing that the general was Gribanov, of the KGB! There was no question at that moment of blackmailing the ambassador, nor even of asking him to reveal state secrets. As an agent possessing influence he might render much greater service, and constitute a long-term investment.

But the KGB had wanted to get too much out of it. At the same time it tried to recruit the assistant air attaché, Colonel Louis Guibaud. Also compromised by a woman, he could not stand being blackmailed and committed suicide. Immediately Krotkov, doubtless sickened by the whole operation, crossed over to the West, and recounted Dejean's story to the British. Recalled to Paris in 1964, the ambassador was interrogated by Counter-Espionage and then retired into private life.[9] In the end he had done France no harm. In any case SDECE was on its guard. Through the Moscow station directed by a naval officer, Commander Labbens, General Grossin had learnt about the diplomat's escapade. During an audience at the Elysée he had asked for the recall of Dejean but it had not been granted. Meanwhile he had placed the latter under close surveillance.

Thus Golytzin had indeed identified Dejean. But he was not the 'mole of the century' for which the Americans had hoped. Nevertheless, a last instalment of 'Martel's' revelations was taken very seriously: it concerned the infiltration of SDECE itself.

The 'Sapphire' Network

Martel was categorical. According to him, there was a network of Soviet agents, called the 'Sapphire' network, inside SDECE. It was just at a time when the French secret services were embarking upon a reorganization. General Jacquier decided to place the whole of his organization under a specialist. Former BCRA members suggested to him the name of a man who ten years earlier had directed Research Branch in SDECE, Colonel Léonard Hounau. In the meantime he had been returned to army duties. But Hounau strangely resembled one of those moles whose photofit picture Martel had sketched out.

A graduate of the Polytechnique, class of 1933, member of the 'Martial' Resistance network, leader of the irregular forces of the Tulle region, which he had liberated in 1944, Hounau was invited to join first the DGER and then SDECE by his fellow graduate of 1933, Colonel Passy. A warm, humorous personality, and a *bon vivant*, Hounau, together with Fourcaud, Trautmann and Verneuil – in short, the 'old hands' – presided over the creation of SDECE. The rivalries between the various factions had grown from year to year, and in 1952 Hounau left the Research directorate of SDECE to become military attaché in Prague. What had happened in the Czech capital? Did the Czech STB attempt, as in the case of his predecessor, Colonel Gastaldo, or Maurice Dejean, to compromise him in some affair with a woman? Those responsible for security had long since formed an opinion on this matter. The officer had not been blackmailed. In their view, Hounau, the courageous Resistance leader, was incapable of betraying his country. But the rumour persisted. Today, for the first time, Colonel Hounau answers his detractors: 'The whole story was invented by the Americans. Angleton was a madman and an alcoholic. He was trying to set us against one another.'[10]

Yet in 1963 the Directorate for Surveillance of the National Territory (DST) decided to study Léonard Hounau's dossier more closely. At the time it was impossible to ask General Jacquier to open an enquiry: he did not really believe in the Martel source, and moreover he had himself chosen Colonel Hounau as his deputy.[11] Daniel Doustin, the head of the DST, had only one man he could trust at SDECE: this was Colonel de Lannurien, the Number Three in the 'Firm'. He recommended the latter to the prime minister. The situation was undoubtedly unique: Georges Pompidou met de Lannurien to talk over the Hounau case, although Hounau was de Lannurien's superior in SDECE. He went further: he gave him the task of clearing up the mystery, particularly because the rumour was spreading. A former senior official of SDECE, François Saar Demichel, was also deemed suspect. He was a friend of Jacques Foccart. Under the Occupation he had been, as we have seen, a member of the 'Gallia network'. Afterwards, under the name 'Coriolan', he led the Fighting and Intelligence Unit (Unité de Combat et de Renseignement: UCR) of General Hounau. After the War we met him in Italy, as the head of the 'Calvary' mission, then at SDECE's Vienna station, and finally as director of Political Action section. He had finally left SDECE in 1949 and had gone into business trading with certain Eastern bloc countries, a fact that clearly obliged Counter-Espionage to take a certain interest in him.[12] Today he gives a frank explanation:

I was accused by certain newspapers of being, with Jacques Foccart, a Soviet agent. That is ridiculous. I had an export business in raw materials and we dealt a lot with Eastern Europe. I know the Russians very well. I saw Khrushchev and Kosygin on several occasions. Doubtless among the people I met there were some who belonged to the KGB. How could one know? I was doing business, that's all. Can you imagine a KGB agent who would show up at Deauville or Cannes, as I did, with my acquaintances from the Eastern bloc? De Gaulle entrusted me with important missions of a diplomatic nature. I was in charge of funds during his years in the wildnerness'.[13]

All the same, at the time the French government took the affair very seriously. With the blessing of the highest state authorities Colonel de Lannurien flew off to Washington.

'My Reports were Handed over to the Russians'

When his plane landed at Washington on 22 November 1963, panic reigned at the CIA. President Kennedy had just been assassinated. The deputy director of intelligence, Richard Helms, welcomed him in perfect French, but his mind was elsewhere. De Lannurien, with the help of the man who was to take over as head of the Washington station, Michel Laporte, intended to carry out a thorough enquiry into Soviet infiltrations of SDECE. In Angleton's presence he interrogated Martel. The result was devastating: a dozen SDECE men were allegedly working for the 'Sapphire' network of the KGB. Upon his return to Paris, General Jacquier was put in the picture. Seized with doubt, the Director-General decided to part company with Hounau, but with him alone, in compliance with an order emanating from Georges Pompidou.[14] He was to be replaced as head of Research Branch by Colonel Beaumont, a choice that was later to raise other storms.

For the moment, the situation became even more complex. Colonel de Lannurien, to whom the enquiry had been entrusted, was grilled in his turn. More rumour: his Resistance activities in Slovakia at the end of the War were suspect. This time, however, it was clear that the manoeuvre was intended to discredit a man anxious to restore order within the 'Firm'. He therefore decided to leave SDECE: 'I wrote a report on these facts and listed the numerous infiltrations since the War, by the services of the other side, before leaving in May 1964. My reports have disappeared. I am convinced that they were handed over to the Russians. I know by whom. Later, Michel Debré asked me for them, since they were no longer to be found at headquarters.[15]

But the temporary defeat of Colonel de Lannurien and his investigation inside SDECE was also linked with the second mission entrusted to him at the time of his visit to Washington, namely to bring back SDECE's head of station in the USA. This man held centre stage in a controversy that embittered Franco-American relations just as seriously as the Golytzin affair.

The Dossier of Thyraud de Vosjoli

Head of the Washington station for 12 years, Philippe Thyraud – who called himself 'de Vosjoli' – was born in 1920. He took part in various Resistance operations in his native region of Romorantin – his brother, the lawyer and Senator Jacques Thyraud, is still its mayor. At the end of the War, first at the BCRA and then at the DGER, he formed part of a skeleton section for Far East intelligence directed by Commandant Revol. In May 1947, Philippe Thyraud was given a promotion in SDECE that satisfied his ambitions: he was appointed head of Henri Ribière's office.

In January 1951, when Pierre Boursicot replaced Ribière, his socialist comrade, as head of SDECE, it was Thyraud who was in charge of the handover of power. Furthermore, he organized a meeting between Stewart Menzies, the head of SIS, and the SDECE directorate, in order to improve Franco-British relations (they were tense, particularly because of the affair of the generals). The French were also interested in setting up an SDECE liaison post in Washington, which had been lacking since the War. The CIA did not see it in this light, agreeing to a liaison mission, but only in Paris! Finally, in April 1951, Philippe Thyraud de Vosjoli landed up at the French consulate in Washington and settled in there, officially as a 'counsellor', but semi-officially, under the code-name 'Lamia', as the SDECE representative. His assignment read as follows:

République Française

Prime Minister's Office	SDECE
Ref. (please quote): 289/11.1.	Paris, 7 April 1951.

Letter of Appointment

Monsieur de VOSJOLI, the representative of the Director General of SDECE in Washington, is entrusted with:
(1) Ensuring a permanent liaison with the directorate of the CIA, in accordance with instructions that will be forwarded to him.
(2) Carrying out, under the technical control of '23',[16] any special missions that the General Directorate may entrust to him.

The Director-General
P. BOURSICOT

It was a dangerous liaison. For gradually on the Boulevard Mortier a disturbing question began to be asked: Could 'Lamia' have become the agent of his American hosts?

'You have to understand Thyraud's position: as head of station he did not do very much,' recalled Colonel de Lannurien. 'Liaison with the CIA, of course. But he also organized the visits of directors, ensuring that all went smoothly as regards their accommodation, buying flowers for the chief's wife or those of his deputies that went to the United States. So, inevitably, even those who criticized him behind his back were very pleased to be treated like princes in Washington, and so they kept quiet.'[17]

The FBI, American counter-espionage, which liaised in New York with Colonel Hervé, let it be known that Thyraud had been recruited by its great rival, the CIA, and by Angleton personally. For the 'allies' of the Agency, this would be advantageous, because the SDECE station in the USA gathered a lot of intelligence. However, when in the spring of 1958 Boursicot's successor, General Grossin, met the head of the American Agency, Allen Dulles, it was agreed that Lamia should work still more closely with the CIA.

Thyraud willingly accepted this involvement, but did his objectives really coincide with French interests? For example, Andrew Tully, the first historian of the CIA, writes: 'On 7 December 1960 there was a secret lunch given by the head of French intelligence in Washington. There were present Jacques Soustelle, the onetime fervent Gaullist who had come out against the General because of his Algerian policy, and Richard Bissell, Jnr., director of the Operations section of CIA. The lunch went on long into the afternoon, and Soustelle spent the time indoctrinating Bissell, who in the CIA had control of air missions, guerrilla operations, and propaganda.'[18]

Five years later, the ambiguities in the situation showed up more clearly: did 'Lamia' represent the French with the Americans, or the Americans with the French? Take the case of intelligence in Latin America: in large part it was under the SDECE station in Washington. Thyraud organized networks in the southern tip and in the Caribbean, particularly in Haiti and Cuba. The SDECE contribution to the American organization was not inconsiderable: indeed in the communist order of battle, and even after the dissolution of the Cominform, the French and Italian communist parties had responsibility for Latin America. Thus the journeys of party members such as Jacques Denis and Georges Fournial were followed with interest. The eye of the storm was Cuba. Thyraud declared that he had set up a network there, and in August 1962 he reported that the Soviets were landing missiles on the island.

Death of an Agent in Havana

In SDECE the intelligence provided by 'Lamia' was taken less and less seriously. He was summoned to Paris at the end of 1962 to be ticked off. In his book Thyraud has given his own version of the interview:

Mareuil was in charge of SDECE liaison with foreign intelligence services. He made two extraordinary proposals to me. First, I should hand over to a certain officer the names of my informants in Cuba. Next, I should organize in the United States a covert intelligence network designed to gather information about military installations in the United States, and about scientific research. The Americans, Mareuil said, had refused to help us to set up our atomic strike force. We had to gather the necessary intelligence to allow us to act using our own resources. General de Gaulle had decided this.[19]

In February 1963 it was General Jacquier himself, who, after a fresh report on Cuba, required 'Lamia' to give Paris HQ the name of his informant. According to Thyraud the latter was shortly afterwards arrested and shot in Cuba. This could be seen as proof that the KGB 'Sapphire' network inside SDECE had passed on the information. 'Not at all,' retorted Thyraud's critics, who were becoming more and more numerous at Mortier HQ. 'In reality, "Lamia" never had a network in Cuba! His informant was never given away, let alone shot, because he never existed.[20] He contented himself with serving the French with warmed-up dishes provided by the CIA.' Besides the Cuban affair, Thyraud jibbed at setting up a scientific intelligence unit in the USA. This brought about his disgrace.

The break between Thyraud de Vosjoli and SDECE was certainly very abrupt. On 16 September 1963 he received a cable announcing that his duties would terminate on 18 October. On that day Thyraud de Vosjoli submitted his resignation to SDECE. According to him, he would in fact have gone back to Paris on 22 November 1963, the day when Colonel de Lannurien was arriving in the USA, if 'a well-wisher' had not warned him that as soon as he returned to Paris SDECE would have him executed.[21]

The Thyraud de Vosjoli affair might have remained hidden away in the archives of the secret services. But in 1967 the writer Leon Uris, the author of the bestseller *Exodus*, published a new mass-circulation novel, *Topaz*. 'Topaz' is clearly 'Sapphire'. Thyraud inspired its plot, which was very simple: an SDECE officer, André Dereveaux (alias Thyraud), tries to warn President La Croix (de Gaulle) that his government has been infiltrated. The defector Boris Kuznetzov (Golytzin) has alerted him, and among the moles there figures a very close adviser to the president, Jacques Grandville (clearly Jacques Foccart, the *bête noire* of the Americans in Africa).

Then Thyraud de Vosjoli published his book, *Lamia – l'antibarbouze*, in which he recounts his career and gives his version of his eviction from SDECE, also disclosing the names of officers in the service suspected of being moles.[22]

For those in charge of Security Branch, this period, the most troubled in the history of SDECE, can be summed up as follows:

Golytzin was a true defector: the Americans did not exaggerate. He belonged to the KGB, but did not know about its French section. He only revealed vague matters, the rudiments . . . The CIA then made up small parcels of information for the British, the Germans, the Swedes, and then for us. We worked on it, and ten agents that had infiltrated did indeed confess, but the biggest one got away. They had been warned about the suspicion that hung over them. And, above all, Thyraud torpedoed our work with his book. We needed time, but this way these fellows were alerted. In my opinion, Thyraud had ended up by becoming an American agent recruited by Angleton, undoubtedly a good chap, but warped by his counter-espionage work.

A few archivists were to leave SDECE, as did Colonel Hounau. Others escaped general suspicion. This caused Colonel de Lannurien, upon his departure in May 1964, to say to his Security colleague: 'Carry on, Lionnet, you must persevere! Carry on, old chap!' It was in Colonel Lionnet's nature to persevere. For a long while he pursued his hunt for moles.

Two Defectors Die

The Poles helped the architects who rebuilt Warsaw after 1945 to reconstitute exact replicas of the old city by collecting thousands of pre-war postcards and photos. This signifies that they have a sense of detail. So did their spies. The latter made a list of all the buildings in Paris with two entrances. This allowed them to detect if they were being followed and to lose the 'tail', throwing counter-espionage investigations off the scent. Thus the church of Saint-Louis-d'Antin in Paris was for a some time a favoured meeting-spot for agents of the Eastern bloc. They entered the building from the Rue du Havre, and there would contact a colleague. The DST men would wait for them to come out again. But to the left of the altar there is an exit which gives on to a narrow passage leading to the Rue Caumartin, under a 'Prénatal' shop sign.

The Czechs were another headache for the DST. They thought up 'the "First Class" trick'. The resident agent of the STB, the Czech secret service, travelled outside the rush hours. He would dive into the Métro station of La Motte-Picquet, a stone's throw from the embassy, take the line to the Gare d'Austerlitz, and always choose the middle car, the first-class one. To follow him the DST 'tail' would do likewise. It was easy to scrutinize the faces of the passengers, very few in the afternoon. At the Emile Zola station the Czech would change cars and get into a second-class one. Who, unless he were following someone, would decide to travel second class with him, when he had a first class ticket in his pocket?

At the same period, in Prague, whenever a vehicle went careering out of the French Embassy at 2, Velkoprevorske Namesti and it turned off to the right, by a stroke of bad luck the lights would turn red. In fact, a policeman was given the job of hand-operating the red light, as soon as he was told by radio that a car was coming out of the French Embassy. The slow-down allowed the STB car to pick up the trail: 'It's Commandant Crignola of SDECE, let's go!' was the ritual announcement made by the squad leader, whilst his Volga-Zis took off on its wheel-rims in order not to lose the French. It took years for SDECE to catch on to the trick; then they would drive a vehicle as bait towards the famous traffic lights, whilst their men made off on foot in the opposite direction.

These tricks of the trade used by Communist agents were learnt by the DST and Counter-Espionage Branch of SDECE essentially through defectors. First there was a Pole. Wladislaw Mroz was an 'illegal'. Provided with false French papers, and having a perfect knowledge of the society into which he melted, he installed himself at Epinay-sur-Seine, married and became a father, and carried on his business as a photographer. In reality, he was running a spy network that his predecessor had 'passed on' to him. But Mroz decided to break with communism.

One day in 1960, he went into 11, Rue des Saussaies, and revealed everything to the DST – his network, and the methods of the Polish secret services. He was to teach his interrogators about the buildings with two entrances, so that the section concerned with following suspects hit upon the happy idea of making up a huge file index, a sort of alphabetical directory of the public buildings and places of this type in Paris. He also revealed the special methods for the protection of covert rendezvous and for using 'conspiratorial apartments' (see figure 11.1).

'And then,' Mroz added with a smile, 'I can even inform you that a photograph of M. Guérin is pinned up in the office of the head of our French section in Warsaw!' Commissioner André Gucrin, called 'Toto', was

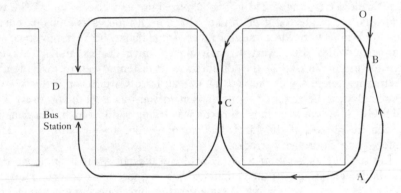

Figure 11.1 Eastern bloc agents: how rendezvous are kept

Key: O   Point of departure for Control Officer
      A   Point of departure for Agent
      At B: O and A pass by each other for a first time in order to recognize each
            other and to check that neither is being followed.
      At C: They cross for a second time behind the complex of buildings in the
            neighbouring street in order to ensure their rendezvous is protected.
      At D: A bus station. O and A meet each other.

Note: This method was revealed for the first time to the DST by Mroz, the Polish defector.

the head of the Soviet section of the DST. Mroz was undoubtedly the best Polish defector that the French secret services were ever able to 'debrief'. But, and this was the nightmare of the Eastern bloc refugees who were welcomed into France, he was very badly protected. Since he wanted to rebuild his life, an occupation and an apartment were sought for him. He was even put at the top of the waiting list for cheap accommodation ('Habitations à loyer modéré' – HLM) at the local housing office. He got his home in ten days, whereas normally it took seven months. Through their French agents the Poles finally discovered him. In October 1960, near Argenteuil, the police discovered the little Pole who wanted to live in the West in the back of a 403 car – with a bullet in the back of his neck.

The Czechs also had their 'renegades'. Another defector turned up. Kondek, an STB officer installed in Switzerland to organize illegal operations on French territory, had squandered all the funds entrusted to him. Penniless, he went to the French Embassy and confessed to his secret activities. Then the Czechs were shaken once again, by the arrest of Pierre Cardot, one of their illegal agents in France.

Cardot presented himself to the French consular authorities with a very plausible cover-story: he was born of a French mother, Thérèse Cardot, in Czechoslovakia. Prague did not recognize him as a Czech, and so he was stateless. He requested French naturalization. Enquiries as to his parentage found no objection. He came to France. Immediately he began to engage in covert activities. But every French citizen must do his military service: Cardot found himself at the air force radio listening centre in Baden, in Germany. Then, having served his time, Pierre Cardot – and this was an extremely rare occurrence – put himself forward as a candidate to work in SDECE! How could a translator who was trilingual in French, Russian and Czech be refused if the DST had no objection? In September 1962 he entered the Tourelles barracks.

In the Czech section of SDECE its head did not speak a single word of the language of the country that he was supposed to 'cover'. Thus his deputy, Simon, a senior NCO, steered the ship. This Simon was a little eccentric. For example, he had a very cut and dried theory about the CIA's having sabotaged Marcel Cerdan's plane over the Azores in 1949, in order to prevent him retrieving his world title from Jack La Motta! But he was a hard worker. One day he came across an article in the *Gazette de Lausanne* that recounted the story of a spy arrested by Swiss Security, and who got into Switzerland by passing himself off as the illegitimate son of a citizen of that country who had died in Prague during the war.[23]

It was self-evident, he realized: Prague regularly employed this stratagem. On 14 November 1962 the DST arrested Cardot in Paris, in the 7th *arrondissement*. A radio transmitter and white carbon paper were found at his home. It was the 'tailing' operation, carried out at the request of Simon, that brought about his arrest. There then occurred a fantastic incident, which, to this very day, those in the Rue des Saussaies are reluctant to boast about. The former head of DST operations in Algeria, back in Paris, decided to confront Kondek, the defector, face to face with Cardot, the captured spy. In May 1963 Cardot was exchanged for a French student arrested in Prague on a charge of espionage. He reported to his headquarters. Was it a coincidence? Shortly afterwards Kondek's body was found: he had apparently been asphyxiated by a leak from a faulty gas pipe! It is understandable that defectors from the East, given these circumstances, prefer to knock on the door of the CIA or the British SIS.

It should be added that in the 1960s SDECE had no reason to be envious of the DST. The latter kept backing losers. First, there was the affair of 'widow Chauvière' – again the 'Cardot method' of getting into France. Mme Chauvière lived in Normandy. The son she had had by a Czech husband rang her doorbell and wanted to settle in France, using her name. The brigade commissioner for surveillance of the Rennes area was given the task of following up the affair, but instead of trapping this important agent of the STB, he became his mother's lover. During this period a commissioner in Paris asked to be transferred to Public Security, deploring the fact that a conscience clause did not exist, because the Soviet section (KARU) of the DST proposed to assist a secretary in the Russian Embassy in obtaining an abortion, provided that she came over to the West. Finally, in 1962 the head of the DST network in West Berlin was arrested, having compromised himself with the East German secret services. Naturally one cannot generalize. The DST remained a dynamic force. It dismantled several Romanian networks. But, whilst it was demanding a little more order within SDECE, it was itself not above criticism.

'It was Rousseau's Fault'

The Eugène Rousseau affair has caused a lot of ink to flow. In his defence Gilles Perrault published an astonishing book, demonstrating both his innocence and certain very special methods used by Colonel André Camus, of SDECE Security.[24] Eugène Rousseau, born on 26 January 1907, was given a permanent appointment at SDECE on 1 May 1955 as a 'chief clerk', and became secretary to the station head in Belgrade in 1956, and then in Bucharest in 1962. In Bône (Algeria) in 1965 his cover title was 'vice-consul'. In 1968 he was an SDECE 'group leader' in Mortier barracks, responsible for Middle East Section I, namely Iraq. On 2 July 1969, he entered the office of Colonel Lionnet, the head of Security, and was informed that he was thought to be a spy of the UDBA, the Yugoslav secret service.

Fifteen years later, the version of the accusation given by the Security branch of SDECE was as follows: Eugène Rousseau, who was a man of very strict principles, took his daughter Monique with him when he was officially appointed as 'secretary to the assistant military attaché' in Belgrade. Monique fell in love with an attractive Yugoslav, a UDBA agent. They threatened to show her father compromising films of her. She agreed to pass on information concerning the SDECE station where her father was working, and where he had arranged to have her taken on as a secretary, in order better to keep an eye on her. She then married a cook who took her off to the USA.

It was there that in 1968 men of the SDECE Security service, accompanied by watchdogs of the FBI, knocked on her door: 'I have been expecting you for ten years,' she is alleged to have said, and confessed to everything. When interrogated the following year her father confessed: when he was working in the central registry he was already passing on secrets to the Yugoslavs. Later he was to go back on his confession.

Two opposing hypotheses were possible: either Rousseau was innocent, and his repeated admissions, made to SDECE and the DST (and then retracted), were merely aimed at protecting his daughter; or he really had passed on information to the Yugoslavs because he had been odiously blackmailed. But even if this latter hypothesis is accepted, the SDECE agents freely admit that a professional with so little experience in intelligence abroad should never have been appointed at a 'sensitive' level. Moreover, to employ his own daughter in SDECE's Belgrade station constituted a serious error. The fact remains that Eugène Rousseau was sentenced to 15 years in prison, and then, 18 months later, pardoned by President Pompidou.[25]

SDECE's head of counter-espionage, who as it happened retired in 1969, let it be known that it was standard practice to think of agents posted to the Eastern bloc as bait for sophisticated 'turning round' or infiltration operations. Was Rousseau, the little SDECE official, at the centre of an elaborate scheme that went far beyond him and was aimed at someone higher? For example, was it aimed at Colonel Beaumont, an officer who served in Yugoslavia and was then one of the directors of French intelligence?

In 1971 two men, both well versed in intelligence matters, exchanged some edifying thoughts on this theme. They were Gilles Perrault, a writer who had just published a book in defence of Rousseau; and Jean Planchais, a journalist on *Le Monde*, who was an expert on SDECE problems:[26]

G.P.: M. de Marenches liquidated a certain number of officers of the rank of colonel who were directing important departments in SDECE, such as Beaumont, at the head of Research Branch, an essential service. Beaumont fell into the 'top brass' category . . .

J.P.: The 'top brass' play a complicated role, but one that is completely ineffectual: the game of double or triple agents, whether these agents know it or not, is a game of concealment. Rousseau perhaps played the role of the stupid decoy . . .

G.P.: According to your hypothesis the chap was posted abroad, they allowed him to be recruited, and to act as a traitor, putting him on ice: it might always come in handy. I don't see what good could come of the operation . . .

J.P.: The operation may have been a camouflage for other complicated operations. If it comes to a public trial, it is really because a public trial is needed.

Beyond little Rousseau, the victim of an internal settling of accounts within SDECE, it was indeed another target that was aimed at.

'Colonel Beaumont' Accused

'La Piscine' had never so well deserved its name. They wallowed in it. Hardly had they got over the Ben Barka affair than the French secret services had a series of failures in the East. In October 1969 Colonel Cheyron de Beaumont d'Abzac de La Douze, head of the centre for exploiting intelligence in the Eastern bloc countries, was killed in a traffic accident in Romania, engineered by the local secret services. 'He has made the supreme sacrifice!' was the assurance given by Colonel Paul Bourgogne, the head of the Deuxième Bureau.[27]

Whereupon a new scandal broke, similar to that of the Rousseau affair: Sergeant-Major Jacques Blaret, in 1967 secretary to the SDECE station head in Prague, was arrested on a charge of spying for the STB. In 1968 Pavel Sidorin, a Czech agent of SDECE, was questioned, transferred to the USSR and shot at Kharkov. This time the rumour became persistent. Like a fish, SDECE was rotting from the head downwards. And here Golytzin's allegations come up again.

It was René Bertrand, 'Colonel Beaumont', director of Research at SDECE since June 1964, who was put on the spot. The whole post-war career of this former flyer, a Polytechnicien who had graduated in the same year as Colonels Passy and Hounau, had been spent in SDECE, first in the MINOS unit assigned to parachuting émigrés into the Eastern bloc countries at the beginning of the 1950s, then as head of the scientific section, responsible for computer decoding equipment, in the following decade, until his appointment as Number Two in the 'Firm'. It was inevitably a high-risk post, but one that was highly coveted. The head of Research Branch was exposed to all the pitfalls inherent in controlling agents and, as we have seen, to all the traps of enemy counter-espionage. That was why his detractors were many: 'Beaumont was not a member of the Resistance, but was very well in with Philippe Henriot in Vichy. At the Liberation he had to appear before a "purging" committee. He was in the Air Ministry when Charles Tillon, the Communist, was its minister. He was a miliary attaché in Yugoslavia. He joined SDECE, and was responsible for some unfortunate missions.'[28] The name of the MINOS unit was never uttered, but they insisted on the fact that 'Yugoslav parachutists' had been sent to certain death, because Belgrade had been forewarned.

This view of the matter largely cross-checked with the admissions made by Eugène Rousseau who, worn down, ended up by accusing his boss, who was also branded 'a UDBA agent'. We have seen that Beaumont had worked under Charles Tillon. Was not the latter a communist dissident who, after having commanded the Francs-Tireurs et Partisans in the Resistance, was alleged to have more sympathy with Tito than with Stalin?

Finally, in 1969, when the Markovic affair broke (named after Alain Delon's bodyguard, who was found murdered), Section 6, the 'Base Bison' of SDECE, learnt that scandalous revelations might implicate the first lady of France, Mme Claude Pompidou. Research Branch, headed by Beaumont, asked for the matter to be investigated. Beaumont's enemies said that he wished to feed this ridiculous rumour, and give substance to a conspiracy in which the Yugoslavs – yet again – were said to be involved.

One can understand that, sooner or later, Colonel Beaumont was bound to be dismissed. This is what happened in 1970.[29] Marthe Bertrand, his widow, stated:

When my husband was kicked out of the secret services we left Paris and sought refuge in the Ardèche. It was the worst period of his life; he was very unhappy, a broken man, and may have died of grief. Alexandre de Marenches, who hunted him out of SDECE, certainly did not know what he was doing; he did not have the same experience in intelligence. Up to then my husband had not tried to make any earth-shattering revelations, out of respect for a department of the state. At the end of his life, only a few threads were missing that would have enabled him to unravel the whole skein.

It is true that the story of his life was greatly distorted by his accusers, such as General Billotte and Roger Barberot. Mme Bertrand briefly recalled this:

He was a Polytechnicien, a graduate of the class of 1933, with Léonard Hounau. A flyer, and captain at the age of 26, before the War he was posted to the base at Bricy-Orléans, under the orders of Colonel de Perronet. During the war he worked in the Secretariat of State for Aviation, still under Perronet's orders. At the end of the war my husband left for Yugoslavia as a member of Perronet's military mission. He stayed there 14 months. The fighting was still going on. He was present when Tito took over power. I was without news for six months. When he returned he told me he had been sickened by what he had seen. His profound anti-communism dated from this time. He could not stomach the fact that a communist, Charles Tillon, was running the Air Ministry. He resigned from the forces. Then he joined the secret services, at the end of 1948, slightly by chance. It was his fellow-graduate, Colonel Hounau, who suggested that he should join SDECE.[30]

If they considered that SDECE was thoroughly penetrated by Communist espionage, even those most convinced of his guilt could not put forward anything more than an inner conviction based on the study of the files. Others considered that Beaumont, the Polytechnicien, wanted to build up over-complicated strategies, admirable on paper, but in practice the source of endless muddles. Finally, there were those who believed essentially that these matters, reinforced by the then prevalent paranoia, had their origin in foreign secret services who were happy to see General de Gaulle's secret services deteriorate.

In the doubt that existed, in order to put an end to this detestable atmosphere, there was hardly any other solution open than that adopted by the new director-general, Alexandre de Marenches: to make a clean sweep.[31]

12

In the Turbulence

The CIA big, ginger-haired Irishman usually worked with precision. But this time, as he was boring a hole to install a microphone above the Cuban ambassador's desk, the vibrating played a trick on him and a piece of plaster came crashing down. He fitted the microphone all the same. The next day Harold Gramatges, the diplomat in question, threw a memorable tantrum: he hated the house-work to be badly done.

The aim of the operation, carried out in the mid-1960s, was to listen in on the preparations for a meeting between Castro's representative and General de Gaulle. The plan was simple: the CIA station in Paris, anxious to 'bug' the Cuban Embassy in the Rue de la Faisanderie, turned to the DST. Could it be helped to get into the building? This was possible, through the many different contacts among the concierges and security guards for the block. Thus the DST, in the very heart of Paris, was covering a CIA operation. But there was a significant difference: the operation was in everybody's interest. General de Gaulle wanted to know how the Cubans regarded the coming interview and what would be the crucial points in the discussion; the CIA wanted to know what de Gaulle and Castro were cooking up together. So the Americans transcribed the conversations between Señor Gramatges and his 'First Counsellor' (in reality, the head of the Dirección General de Intelligencia). A copy of the report on the 'bugging', somewhat watered down, was handed to the DST liaison officer, normally Alain Montarras. And the latter provided a 'rewrite' – the Americanism is appropriate – in summary form for de Gaulle's secretariat.

The procedure seems an extraordinary one. But it worked in the same way with the North Vietnamese delegation, on the Rue Leverrier, whose adviser, Tran Viet Dung, reckoned to be a master spy, was closely tailed. And again, in 1965, Stent, the FBI representative at the American Embassy, contacted the head of Daniel Doustin's office to obtain news of the travels of Régis Debray – they might perhaps lead to Che Guevara. The Americans cross-checked their information on Latin America with SDECE's, and that gleaned by the DST from left-wing revolutionary circles in Paris. 'The DST has become a branch of the CIA,' certain DST inspectors used to complain at the time.

In fact, the DST nevertheless kept their 'American friends' under surveillance. Proof of this is the 'work-sheet' below made out at the request of the technical secretariat of Montarras-Deshereau – a kind of assignment order (RO.1164) regarding the microphones hidden in 'the Embassy of the United States, 2, Avenue Gabriel, Paris. Tel: ANJOU 34-60.' Monitoring began on 3 February 1965, and the grounds for it were given as follows: 'It is necessary to uncover possible suspect contacts made by the CIA station in Paris.' The instructions ran:[1]

Contacts with the DST or SDECE will be either summarized or merely referred to. The identification of other possible correspondents might prove interesting:
KNOWN PERSONS:
– GOURLAY, Larry, diplomat ⎫
                            ⎬ Liaison officers with DST and SDECE.
– LESTER, Charles ⎭

The DST set up certain solo 'counter-intervention' operations, for example those directed against the French Communist Party. In 1964 it succeeded in introducing a microphone into the room on the Place Kossuth where the Central Committee of the PCF usually met. Finally, it was going to be able to follow 'live' the deliberations of the communist leadership and note the speeches made by its 'big guns' – Thorez, Duclos and the others. But from its very first meeting, the ears of the DST were assaulted by a gigantic roar – the Niagara Falls, Force 10. It was easy to identify what it was – a lavatory flushing. The PCF's security service had discovered the microphone and, not without a sense of humour, had installed it in the lavatories.

But there is nothing to laugh about. The gap between Gaullist policy and the practices of the intelligence services, and the friction between the French and American services provided enough material for a newspaper serial, and this was to have repercussions in the Ben Barka affair, which shook the Fifth Republic.

Ben Barka: 'Above All, Do Nothing!'

Her sole costume, a bunch of bananas. The image still enchants: 'J'ai deux amours' – Paris and Cuba. At the beginning of January 1966 Josephine Baker was the radiant star of a show in Havana. The Cubans have music in their blood. Their counter-espionage service would not dare to remind them that Josephine was an 'honourable correspondent' of the French secret services. It was Fidel Castro who had personally invited her. But the show was above all political: the delegates of the 'revolutionary' forces of the Third World converged on Cuba. A meeting, the most important since the Bandung Conference, was set up, under the title of the 'Tricontinental' – a gathering of three continents in ferment: Africa, Asia and America.

The real star was missing. The man who had thought up, conceived, and hoped for this assembly – of which he was to be the secretary-general – was Mehdi Ben Barka, the Moroccan abducted in the heart of Paris three months earlier. After 29 October 1965 he was never seen again. The scenario is now well known: a group of criminals, shady policemen and men half in the pay of the secret services had kidnapped him at the instigation of the Moroccans. Ben Barka, the former tutor of King Hassan II, had many enemies. Chief among them were General Oufkir and Colonel Dlimi, the chiefs of Moroccan security, who foresaw with apprehension the possibility of a reconciliation between the Moroccan opposition leader and his sovereign. Moreover, the Americans of the CIA contemplated with horror the formation of a federation of Third World liberation movements, the 'Tricontinental'.

At the heart of this political and police imbroglio was SDECE. There was Antoine Lopez, the former Air France manager at Tangiers. In 1965 he was doing the same job for Air France but at Orly airport. His dream was to become Director of Royal Air Maroc. General Oufkir, his friend, encouraged him in this dream. Lopez had rendered him very great services. Nor had his key position at the Paris airport escaped the attention of the secret agents of Service 7. Through him SDECE could follow the movements of certain passengers, and temporarily spirit away their baggage, or the diplomatic bags, in order to photograph their contents. Thus Marcel Le Roy (called 'Finville'), the new head of Service 7, had long since recruited him as an 'honourable correspondent'. They had become very close. Who would have believed that this modest 'honourable correspondent' was to stir up one of the gravest crises that SDECE had ever known, and even shake the Republic to its foundations?

At the time SDECE comprised some 1,500 permanent staff, 500 station or network heads and several thousand 'honourable correspondents', about a thousand of whom were attached to Service 7. When he departed in 1963 to run the Esterel motorway, General Grossin left behind him an SDECE in perfect working order. His successor was to leave nothing but ruin and desolation. Paul Jacquier, an air force general with 5,000 hours of flying time, was undoubtedly very competent in aviation, his branch of the forces, but the realm of the secret services was foreign to him. Why in the world had he been put forward to head SDECE? To tell the truth, Jacques Foccart had earmarked this delicate post for Paul Jacquier's brother. But Colonel Henri Jacquier had turned it down. What was important for Jacques Foccart and his friends – at a time when a 'policy on all fronts' was being launched – was that the new chief of SDECE and his subordinates should play along with Gaullist strategy. There was no problem. Paul Jacquier was a deeply committed Gaullist.

He needed an effective adviser. Guy Marienne ('Morvan') was a friend of his brother: he would do nicely. Up to then Morvan had directed Service 7 –

which once again found itself with no leader, although Finville, his deputy, was delighted to take over from him. He was a man of action, a go-getter, and not an intellectual like Morvan. He liked to 'strike a blow'. His teams, made up of covert agents and safe-breakers, achieved good results. But Finville was engaged in carving out a little empire for himself, a service within the service, a state within a state. He became fascinated by the game. In Research, to which Service 7 was attached, the situation went out of control.

But Lopez, his correspondent, was himself uncontrollable. The Moroccans were also manipulating him. According to Le Roy Finville:

More than being an honourable correspondent of SDECE or a 'grass' for the Vice Squad or even the attentive servant of his Moroccan friends, Lopez (called 'Savonnette') was the criminals' man. The villains kept a hold over him, manipulated him, used him for their business in and out of Orly. They were no common or garden rogues; at the time they were more powerful than Roger Frey, the Minister of the Interior, Papon, the Prefect of Police, General Jacquier, or the King of Morocco. They were loaded with passes of all kinds, and were up to all manner of tricks. They claimed to have worked for SDECE, and this was true of some, such as Jo Attia, Boucheseiche and Renucci, who were used for operations that failed miserably, but gave them lasting kudos.[2]

In these circumstances, why had not the links with Lopez been severed? It was because he was very useful to Le Roy. This was proved when, on 17 May 1965, the head of Service 7 dispatched to his counterpart in Section 3/A, Colonel Tristan Richard, of the Arabian department, a note that was formulated as follows:

Subject: Morocco
For your information I am pleased to forward herewith the report by Lopez, dated 12.5.65, on a journey he made to Rabat. Taking into account the quality of the contacts of this agent, who has to return frequently to Morocco, I think that we might draw up a questionnaire for him. I will remind you briefly that Lopez:
– was manager of Air France at Tangiers, and is now manager at Orly;
– is a friend of Oufkir (he acts as the Paris guardian for Oufkir's children when they are staying in France);
– has just attended his wedding;
– is well in at Court;
– and is being sought after by Royal Air Maroc to run its external relations department.

Lopez's report on his journey followed. From it these two remarks may be extracted: (1) 'The general has confirmed to me his plan to get Ben Barka back, but he must await the results of His Majesty's statement concerning a government of national unity.' (2) 'He did not hesitate to confide to me the desire of the Moroccan leaders to *put an end to the position* of Ben Barka, using unorthodox procedures.'

On 17 May 1965, Finville therefore warned the unit concerned, Research

Branch's Arab department, that the Moroccans were hatching up something concerning Ben Barka. Did this note, addressed to Colonel Richard, remain tucked away in a drawer without being passed up through the usual channels? It is highly unlikely. In fact, in a summary drawn up on 22 December 1965 (No. 5140/DG/CAB) for Louis Zollinger, the examining judge in charge of the case, General Jacquier, the director of SDECE, explicitly referred to the note and assumed responsibility for it. He wrote to the judge: 'Following up your request, I am pleased to forward to you the information concerning the Ben Barka affair that was communicated to the service by M. Finville, as a result of his meetings and conversations with M. Lopez between 12 May 1965 and 12 October 1965.'

There follows a lengthy extract from the note. At no time did the head of the secret services deny knowledge of this memorandum. If, for whatever reason, General Jacquier had not been warned in time of the intelligence passed on by Finville, it is plain that two months after the abduction, in a letter destined for the legal authorities, he would have taken good care to absolve himself from blame. We are therefore obliged to acknowledge that SDECE, five months before the leader of the opposition in Morocco was ambushed at the St Germain drugstore, knew of 'the desire of the Moroccan leaders to put an end to the position of Ben Barka, using unorthodox procedures'.

Nor is this all. On 22 September 1965 Finville wrote a second note which clearly shows that 'the process of approaching Ben Barka' was under way. Here again, the directorate of the secret services was put in the picture, since General Jacquier also quoted this document in his summary of 22 December, intended for Judge Zollinger. Finville wrote:

According to M. Lopez, General Oufkir, the Moroccan Minister of the Interior, has asked Dlimi, the Director-General of the Moroccan National Security, to prepare an attack on Ben Barka, the Opposition leader, at present staying in Geneva.

In order to accomplish this, on 2 September he sent to Cairo a special team whose mission was to contact Ben Barka, then attending a preliminary meeting for the 'three continents' conference to be held in Cuba in January 1966.

The team was made up as follows:

– CHTOUKI, Larbi, born in Rabat, a Moroccan, holding an official service passport, representative of the Moroccan government;

– BERNIER, Philippe, born 1 or 17 August 1920 at Bois-Colombes, French, a journalist residing at 21, Rue Lalande;

– FIGON, Georges-Auguste, born 21 October 1926 in Paris (14th *arrondissement*), French, an industrial chemist, residing at 14, Rue Pierre.

Bernier was to introduce Figon to Ben Barka as a film producer. Figon was to submit to Ben Barka a plan for a film dealing with 'Revolutions', using shots filmed during the Casablanca incidents [the riots of March 1965].

The trap was worked out. Through Lopez SDECE kept close observation on all the steps taken by Oufkir, even if doubts persisted about the real intentions of the Moroccans. In fact, Finville made it clear:

M. Lopez, according to what he says, in spite of the conversations he has had with the trio, has been unable to determine precisely the reasons for this mission, which is controlled at a distance by Oufkir. Is it merely the desire of the Minister of the Interior to ascertain precisely the present activities of the leader of the UNFP, or in fact, to home in as closely as possible on a permanent 'objective'?

If we recall the confidences whispered in Lopez's ear in May by General Oufkir, such a question seems extremely disingenuous – all the more so because Finville, a fortnight before the abduction, had passed on the gist of a conversation between Lopez and Figon. The latter confided to his questioner: 'I have the impression that my journey to Cairo with Chtouki and Bernier conceals something else. If they want to play a dirty trick on Ben Barka, I want the money immediately, otherwise I'll spill the beans to the newspapers. And since you're so well in with the Moroccans, warn them about this.'

Thus the SDECE directorate had known since May that Oufkir wanted to 'snatch' Ben Barka. It knew in September that the manoeuvres to get near him, using the film project as a pretext, were under way. It knew in October that one of the 'half-pay' operatives being manipulated suspected that they wanted to use him as bait 'to play a dirty trick on Ben Barka'. And in spite of all this information the head of SDECE, who was aware, hour by hour, of the movements on French soil of the prime movers in this affair, wrote to the examining judge on 2 December, as the conclusion to his memorandum: 'In these circumstances the service had no grounds for thinking that the abduction of Ben Barka might take place in France.' At the very least, this may be termed incompetence.

A few days after the abduction Finville sent a note to the Director of Research which read: 'On several occasions I have been able to draw the attention of 3/A to the intention of General Oufkir to neutralize Ben Barka (my note VII/1912/R of 22.9.65). This information was passed on to us by our correspondent (Lopez), who was able, in particular, to detect how Dlimi, the Director of the Moroccan National Security, tried to establish contact with Ben Barka during the latter's stay in Cairo.' Between these assertions by Finville and the 'absence of grounds for thinking' of General Jacquier, the divergence of views is, to say the least, surprising. The head of Service 7, for his part, seemed to have scarcely any doubts. And he was right: a week or so before the abduction a strange incident occurred in Service 7. Marcel Chaussée, the official in charge of Arab affairs, received from Finville, his chief, a note on which four names figured: Oufkir, Dlimi, Chtouki and El Mahi. 'They are coming to Paris,' he said, 'to contact Ben Barka in order to discuss the possible formation of a government of national unity, which the King of Morocco desires. Write me a minute about it.'

Three-quarters of an hour later Finville came back: 'I rather think the Moroccans are coming to Paris to get Ben Barka. That changes everything. Do nothing. I'll look into it.' The head of Service 7 retrieved his note.[3] Immediately after the kidnapping of Ben Barka, Colonel Lionnet, of Security Branch, opened his investigation and Chaussée told him about this statement, which proved that Finville knew what was going to happen to Ben Barka. Michel Couvert, the head of the Far East department, who was present at the time of the incident, confirmed his colleague's assertion. Finville was suspended, accused, and finally cleared.

On 29 October 1965 Lopez is actually alleged to have telephoned headquarters on the direct line (NOR-92-40), and delivered a message, 'from Don Pedro to Thomas' (that is, from Lopez to Le Roy), announcing that the abduction had taken place. But Finville was not there. Lopez evidently had telephoned in order to compromise him, in case the affair should misfire.

On 7 February 1966 General Guibaud reported on the internal enquiry into whether Finville had indeed received a telephone call from Lopez informing him of Ben Barka's abduction. He wrote to Pierre Messmer, the Army Minister:

The staff of Service 7, statements from whom were taken on 21 January 1966 and who were questioned again on 7 February by SDECE's own security service, confirm that they have no recollection of any communication from Lopez between 15 and 31 October 1965, except for what appears on a Service 7 document dated 22 October 1965, when this informant called M. Finville, who was absent.[4]

There followed a memorandum from Colonel Lionnet, who was in charge of security, certifying that no telephone call had been recorded in the office log book. One of the staff of Service 7, Jacques Boitel, was, however, to contradict this under interrogation. Before the judges he confirmed that he had indeed recorded a message for Finville on 29 October. 'What I am saying,' he declared, 'is that the message mentioned a rendezvous at a given place.' Moreover, Finville had received another call from Lopez, on 31 October. What did the latter say during this telephone conversation, which lasted 20 minutes? 'Everything,' claimed Lopez. 'Almost nothing at all,' was the substance of Le Roy's reply.[5] As for the various statements by the senior officials of SDECE, they were aimed above all at protecting the service.

The enquiry proceeded. Figon, the shady character who had drawn Ben Barka into the trap, 'committed suicide'. The press suggested that the secret services wanted to get him out of the way, and alluded to the role of the various 'SDECE killers' – in particular Roger Lentz, nicknamed 'Poupon le Stéphanois', and Christian David, who cropped up again as a drug trafficker in Latin America and an 'honourable correspondent' of SDECE.[6] Other names, those of a Corsican gangster working for military security, and a 'journalist' close to Figon, have been mentioned to the authors. In addition, several men mixed up in the Ben Barka affair belonged to networks of anti-OAS *barbouzes* connected with the lawyer Pierre Lemarchand.

Public opinion wondered what role might have been played by SDECE. 'What happened was simply vulgar and third-rate,' General de Gaulle replied during a notable press conference on 21 February 1966. He could not for a moment imagine that Jacques Foccart, who, it was said, was in the know, and General Jacquier, head of SDECE, had actively taken part in the abduction. These Gaullists, numbered among the faithful, knew that the President was due to receive Ben Barka for a private audience on 30 October 1965.[7]

SDECE turned into a madhouse. The senior officials no longer knew what to do. On 3 November 1965, Colonel Beaumont, Director of Research, sent a note 'for the attention of M. Finville': 'Do nothing in the Ben Barka affair (take no initiative). Report on any intelligence information gathered, but without revealing our sources in detail.'

Fearing that Finville had compromised SDECE, either by covering the steps taken by Lopez, his agent, to enable the Moroccans to kidnap Ben Barka, or purely and simply by his naivety, General Jacquier undertook a series of initiatives. Firstly, to 'freeze' all the activities of Service 7, which had been placed in the dock. Secondly, to undertake an enquiry in order to understand why SDECE was implicated. Finally – and this was serious, although understandable – to arm SDECE against the criticisms that would inevitably flood in on it when the news became public, and when trials began.

All the current operations of Service 7 were interrupted. One of the former heads of Action Branch recalls: 'It was panic in Service 7. Certain of its members – Paul Zigmant, Aldo Boccone and Robert Caillaud – came to see me to tell me that the "Firm" was in danger of collapsing.' In fact, the suspect branch was lopped off. It was soon replaced by a covert operations service headed by Colonel Hervé. But the heart had gone out of it. More than ten years' work had been wiped out. Several agents were 'blown' for good, because they had to come out into the open at the trial: among them were Jean-Pierre Lenoir, Jacques Boitel and Marcel Chaussée.

Since an enquiry had been ordered, all the 'Firm's' bloodhounds were called in. Even former agents, such as Robert Lemoine, were summoned to the rescue.[8] On 1 November 1965 a plane – a Morane Saulnier Paris-2 – took off from the Persan-Beaumont base bound for Rabat, via Ajaccio, with three SDECE officers on board, entrusted with gathering information about the abduction of Ben Barka.[9] In 1966 an SDECE officer was found murdered in Morocco. Yves Allain, a former attaché in the Prague embassy, the correspondent in New York of ORTF (the radio and TV service) – in fact, the representative of SDECE – was liquidated whilst he was working on the affair.

Paul Jacquier, the Director-General, was sacked. He was replaced by

General Eugène Guibaud. This former officer in the Marines, a man of integrity, had to manage a service that was to suffer many vicissitudes between 1966 and 1970. His experience of intelligence work was not undisputed. A former head of the Deuxième Bureau in Indo-China at the time of the Dien Bien Phu ambush, he greatly underestimated the Vietminh forces, as his reports proved. Twenty years later, the former chief of the general staff in Indo-China, General Henri Navarre, himself a former member of Intelligence branch, was still complaining about it.[10] This was tantamount to saying that Guibaud had been overwhelmed by events. In the Ben Barka affair he adopted the same line of defence as Jacquier: to 'cover' the service so as to keep it afloat. Many thought at the time that the secret services of the Great Powers – both the CIA and the KGB – had every interest in discrediting French Intelligence.

A decision of the utmost importance was taken. Furious with Prime Minister Georges Pompidou, as if he were responsible for the Ben Barka episode, General de Gaulle relieved him of his duty to oversee SDECE. Henceforth, by a decree of 19 January 1966, the secret services were attached to the Ministry of Defence. But the repercussions of the Ben Barka affair were to weigh heavily on the internal life of SDECE for several years to come.

SDECE Saves Sihanouk

In the autumn of 1966, whilst in France the Ben Barka trial flared up again with the appearance of Dlimi in the dock, General de Gaulle started on a world tour, during which he set out in forcible terms his international policy on the Third World. His final destination was Cambodia. His speech at Phnom Penh dealt with the quest for a 'third way', outside those of the two great blocs, Soviet and American. The General supported Norodom Sihanouk, the little neutralist prince, and demanded that the United States withdraw its troops from Vietnam.

The French President knew that he was going to hit the bullseye, and thereby alienate the Americans a little more. In March 1966 the French had withdrawn from NATO. De Gaulle had excellent reasons for fearing action by the CIA, to whom he attributed various hostile manoeuvres during the Algerian crisis, the affair of the 'moles', and the abduction of Ben Barka.

SDECE had prepared for the journey to Phnom Penh. It was a question of knowing what would be the reaction of the population to de Gaulle's words, and of assessing US influence in the country. The SDECE station, manned by Captain Touzelet, was under close surveillance. So Colonel Beaumont, head of Research Branch, opted to send in a team which, ironically, was infiltrated by a Czech agent.

However, it gathered excellent results. Thyraud de Vosjoli was categorical on this point: 'In the end, we did not suffer from the blackmail exercised by the Czechs upon one of our correspondents. His intelligence about Cambodia was good, and I am convinced that it will be used by General de Gaulle during the speech that he is to pronounce at Phnom Penh.'[11]

As a matter of fact, SDECE had already proved its worth in Cambodia. Eight years earlier, it had saved Sihanouk's skin. In 1958 the CIA decided to attack neutral Cambodia, particularly because, at the end of the year, upon his return from Peking, the hereditary prince opened diplomatic relations with the People's Republic of China. In Saigon, William Colby, the CIA's head of station, was on the alert. At his side there was an old acquaintance of the French, a man whom Marshal de Lattre had expelled from Indo-China during the colonial war: General Edward Landsdale.

When the old Khmer king Suramarit died, Landsdale stirred up a plot, with the help of the right-wing Issarak Khmers. Its object was to overturn the new ruler, Sihanouk. At Phnom Penh, from within the US Embassy, a strange figure was pulling the strings for the CIA: Victor Masao Matsui. Of Japanese origin, he had gone through his training in military intelligence, the G-2 branch. He was preparing a putsch in the capital. But he was shadowed day and night, his movements and contacts were noted, and his intentions divined. The 'shadowers' belonged to the SDECE and the Te Wu – Chinese Intelligence. French and Chinese secret agents even exchanged information. Captain Husson, head of SDECE in Phnom Penh, given the green light by his boss in Paris, General Grossin, decided to warn his Cambodian colleagues.

Matsui was expelled for espionage.[12] The CIA putsch failed. It was denounced publicly by Prince Sihanouk on 13 January 1959. He was to acknowledge later the assistance he had been given: 'In general, our intelligence service did rather well, and we had the good fortune to possess good friends in various diplomatic services. Thus we were informed not only by our own services, but also by those of the People's Republic of China and France of the fact that something was brewing.'[13]

'Vive le Québec Libre'

Pierre de Menthon, French consul in Quebec; Robert Pilquet, first counsellor at the French Embassy in Ottawa; Jean Troché, commercial counsellor; Jean-Claude Corbel, scientific counsellor; Jacques Flaud, cultural counsellor, also in Ottawa . . .

These were the men that members of the counter-espionage section of the RCMP followed day and night. The files grew thicker. Their slightest moves were spied upon, photographed and analysed with as much care as in an Eastern bloc country.

For John Starnes, the head of the security service – intelligence and counter-espionage – of the RCMP, there was no possible doubt: French secret agents were swarming around, and using a thousand different ploys to sustain Quebec subversion against the Canadian federal authorities – from the training of the Quebec Liberation Front (in cahoots with the Cubans) to the secret financing of René Lévêque's Parti Québecois. The French were doing everything to promote independence: this was the feeling of the Ottawa authorities and of their friends in London and Washington.

Who has forgotten the triumphant journey of General de Gaulle to Quebec, and his resounding call in Montreal on 24 July 1967: 'Vive le Québec libre'? Certainly not the people of Quebec, nor Canadian counter-espionage. This is why the RCMP watched the French diplomats closely, whilst the FLQ (Front de Libération du Québec: Quebec Liberation Front) were organizing their attacks. After the abduction of James Cross, the British commercial counsellor, and Pierre Laporte, the Quebec Minister of Labour, in October 1970, a state of siege existed in Quebec. Did the French play a part in all this? The question is a delicate one. Pierre Elliott Trudeau, the Canadian Prime Minister, summoned John Starnes, the head of his secret service, to Ottawa: 'Is it true that you have mounted a surveillance operation against the French embassy?' The other silently agreed. 'All right, but if you're caught out, I shall have to deny that I have been informed,' continued the prime minister.[14]

However, in 1968 the RCMP became convinced that Philippe Rossillon, one of the organizers of General de Gaulle's visit, was working to promote Quebec independence. On 12 September, during a press conference, Trudeau publicly denounced France. General de Gaulle's government was accused of having sent a 'more or less secret agent' to act in a 'clandestine and surreptitious' manner with the French-speaking authorities in Manitoba. Philippe Rossillon, the general spokesman of the High Commission for the Defence of the French Language, and a counsellor attached to the office of Georges Pompidou, the French Prime Minister, was suspected of being an SDECE agent, and was then expelled from Canada and forbidden to return for five years.[15] Today Philippe Rossillon no longer has anything to hide:

It is true that, within the framework of aid and cooperation programmes, we assisted associations of a cultural nature. If my memory is accurate, the total amount of aid given was 4 million new francs. For the newspaper *L'Evangélique*, for example, we provided a printing press, a telex and a few small sums of money . . . According to my recollection, we contributed to the construction of a building for the Assomption insurance company at Monckton, which since then the Hotel Beauséjour has taken over. We also gave medicines, scholarships and books. All this aid was passed on through the Société Nationale des Entreprises de Presse (SNEP), set up in 1945, which was an instrument for French intervention.

But did Philippe Rossillon help the FLQ?

I never came into contact with them. Politically they were crackpots. To get mixed up with terrorist affairs in such a bourgeois setting one must be mad . . . In Quebec we needed more than anything a special cultural service, with films and periodicals, in order to carry out 'agit-prop'. But we did not even have the resources to do that. In my time there were only twenty permanent staff in Quebec. Now, I must acknowledge that I was able to help certain members of the Rassemblement pour l'Indépendance Nationale (RIN), which was a legal movement. I knew the secretary of the RIN, who was mixed up in a shady affair with the Black Panthers. As for the FLQ, it was completely infiltrated.[16]

Had our interlocutor been closely linked to Jacques Foccart, as has been suggested, or directly to SDECE, as the RCMP asserted?

Not only did I never receive any instructions from Jacques Foccart, but our contact, when we met at receptions, was always very limited. It was very conventional. I would say, 'Good day, M. le Secrétaire Général,' and he would reply, 'Good day, M. le Rapporteur Général.' About SDECE, I remember an amusing story: one day Raymond Bousquet, our ambassador in Ottawa, summoned me to ask whether I could not do anything to get a member of SDECE assigned to the embassy. He had never succeeded in obtaining an on the spot representative of the French secret services.[17]

Senior officials of the French secret services, questioned by the authors, confirmed Philippe Rossillon's version of events. However, they pointed out that certain members of SDECE, from the United States or France, were able to mount certain operations as 'travelling agents'. This is borne out by the saga of Vaillant, 'the Breton Canadian', as recounted by a former member of the DST:

René Vaillant was arrested in 1968 at the time of the first attacks made by the Breton Liberation Front (Front de Libération de la Bretagne: FLB). He was the leader of the Morbihan section of the FLB. Now the pamphlets printed by the FLB had been done on a machine that had also printed those of the FLQ in Quebec. Also, the explosives came from Canada. Vaillant, 'the Canadian', owned a small company in Quebec. There he supported the French cause against the English-speakers. Back in Brittany he supported the Breton autonomist cause against Paris. For him there was no contradiction: it was a case of the small nations against centralization. But, unbeknown to him, in Quebec his operation had been exploited by SDECE. We at the DST knew about this.

PART IV
From Pompidou to Mitterrand

13
De Marenches at SDECE

Occasionally, of an evening Georges Pompidou wept over the Marcovic affair. This was because a few people had sought to impugn the honour of his wife and, through her, to compromise him. And also because he would never have believed that the race to succeed de Gaulle could be so cut-throat as to induce certain people to stoop to such base methods.

This is the explanation – as Pompidou acknowledged – of the appointment of Count Alexandre de Marenches to head SDECE in 1970. As early as July 1969 François Castex (the husband of Claude Pompidou's sister), whom Marenches had known in the African Army, and with whom he co-chaired the Old Comrades Association of the French Expeditionary Corps in Italy, had put his candidacy forward to the President. Others also recommended him, among them Pierre Juillet, Pompidou's adviser, himself a former representative of SDECE in Brussels when working at the Opera Mundi press agency, before becoming the head of André Malraux's Private Office in 1958.

'You ought to serve the state,' Pompidou declared to de Marenches. The matter was settled. But 'serving the state', besides the running of SDECE itself, consisted first of all in playing Sherlock Holmes for the Elysée and unravelling the Marcovic affair. In whose interest had it been to highlight this sordid story of the murder of Alain Delon's bodyguard, against a background of wild parties attended by the great names in the arts and in politics? And, above all, in whose interest was it to implicate the woman who was to become the first lady of France? Who were the conspirators? The names of Maurice Couve de Murville, the prime minister, and of René Capitant, the leader of the Gaullist Left, were whispered.

The appointment of de Marenches to SDECE came at a crucial moment: Service 6, 'Bison Base' in Paris, which dealt with 'honourable correspondents', and the director of Research, Colonel Beaumont, were under investigation. They were accused of having sought out witnesses to the double life of Mme Pompidou. In his posthumously published memoirs Pompidou clearly makes this understood: 'Secretly, I had numerous proofs that they were continuing to look for documents or witnesses that could compromise us both, my wife and myself. SDECE agents here and there were playing some ill-defined role.'[1] In such an atmosphere, at Tourelles barracks a 'purge' was expected as soon as General Eugène Guibaud left his post as director-general.

Alexandre the Fortunate

On the Place de France in Tangiers stood a magnificent high fashion boutique, showing the latest models from Paris. Its proprietor, Mademoiselle, who was also called Rose, was in the habit of taking tea at the Villa Saint-Gilles, in the La Montagne quarter, with her friend Marguerite, the Countess of Marenches. They talked, of course, about clothes. But the fashion-shop owner also brought along sealed envelopes for the countess to hand over to her son Alexandre.

Mlle Rose acted as a 'letter-box' for the French secret services. As for M. Alexandre, his SDECE control officer, Colonel Fayolle, had christened him 'Pervenche' ('Periwinkle'). Allal El Fassi, the old Moroccan national leader – the very same one who had escaped from the 'Red Hand' – liked to recount this story, and concluded that it was always worthwhile to sniff out 'French spies'. But could he have foreseen that one day Alexandre would become the all-powerful head of SDECE? Moreover, when he was appointed nobody knew de Marenches – the witnesses interviewed by the authors have repeated this a hundred times over. Like the journalists, they rushed to the *Bottin mondain*, the society *Who's Who*, but only found five lines in it: a string of decorations, an address, the name of his wife and the Christian name of their son Anselme, who had since died. Seated in the D-G's chair, Alexandre de Marenches was to learn how to promote publicity for himself in the American style, like CIA senior officials, and how to get himself talked about, in contrast to all his predecessors who never got a public mention to chew over unless some indiscretion they had committed was revealed in the satirical weekly *Le Canard enchaîné*.

Today it is easy to draw the portrait of this SDECE leader, a lover of good food and wit, whose height and size (1.90m, 100 kilos) and the little moustache he wore brought him the nickname 'Porthos' in the press.

In 1918, when he was an aide-de-camp to Marshal Foch, Alexandre's father had met Marguerite Monahan, a beautiful American, an ambulance driver with Pershing's army, and married her. The couple set up house in the Château des Rotoirs, a 367-hectare estate at Saint-Aubin-sur-Gaillon, in the Eure department. Alexandre was born on 7 June 1921. His childhood was uneventful. In 1939, as a young man, he enlisted in the armoured corps at Dinan. After demobilization, he tried to reach Spain, and was interned there for several months. Finally he joined his mother, who had taken refuge in Tangiers. And in 1942 he became a second lieutenant in the Spahis, first in Morocco and then in Algeria. Remembering that his father had been a liaison officer during the First World War with the American general John Pershing – which was how he had met Marguerite – Marshal Alphonse Juin entrusted Alexandre with a similar mission, attaching him to the American and British general staffs in Italy until 1944.[2]

After a spell with the French Army in Austria, he shed his uniform in 1946, leaving with the rank of colonel, and entered the private sector. He became a financial adviser in a boiler-making company, the Société Générale Thermique, which some believe was an early cover for his activities as an 'honourable correspondent' of SDECE.

For a while Alexandre de Marenches ran an armaments firm linked to the Ministry of Defence, and, at the time of the RPF, he was frequently to be met in the company of Captain Guy, the aide-de-camp to General de Gaulle. Marshal Juin, who had become his friend, invited him in 1950 to accompany him to Indo-China to review the situation immediately after the defeat of Cao Bang. Four years came the disaster of Dien Bien Phu. In that year de Marenches married a Scotswoman, Lady Lilian Mary Witchell. It must be said that for 20 years he was very discreet. He travelled, and carried out intelligence missions for the secret services. He was hardly ever seen except at the Jockey Club and the Old Comrades Association of veterans of the Italian campaign. In 1967 there appeared in *Paris-match* a picture no one could identify, of the man that nobody knew, as he walked before the funeral bier of Marshal Juin. He had been selected to arrange the ceremonial for the national funeral. In January 1970 assiduous readers of the *Journal officiel* noted that Alexandre de Marenches had been promoted to the rank of Commander of the Legion of Honour for 'services to the government'. The Marcovic affair broke: what followed was even more shattering.

The Great Purge

Alexandre de Marenches's assumption of the post of head of SDECE in October 1970 was quite simply a heroic act, and will remain engraved in the annals of the secret services. This almost unidentified man set in train a notable purge. The agents who filed into the office of the D-G to learn that they had been sacked were dismissed for various reasons. There were those who, on the eve of a great reconciliation with the CIA, were considered as being too compromised by the anti-Americanism of de Gaulle's policies. There were those who were judged ineffective or parasitic. Finally, there were those who had compromised SDECE in the scandals that had marked the Ben Barka and Marcovic affairs.

On 10 November 1970, a whirlwind swept down upon the Tourelles barracks. Colonel René Bertrand ('Beaumont') was declared undesirable. He was astounded by it, but very much feared that the suspicion that he was 'an agent of the Eastern bloc' was the cause. He was replaced as the head of Research by Colonel Tristan Richard, who was himself dismissed in April 1971.[3] It was then the turn of Colonel Jacques Hervé, head of Counter-Espionage, the traditional officer type and a practising Catholic; for a long while he had been at the New York station, where he acted as liaison officer with the FBI and had married off his daughter to a scion of the Rockefeller family. Recalled to France, he was entrusted with the remnants of Service 7, which was in poor shape after the Ben Barka affair and the departure of Le Roy ('Finville'). The older members of this service did not take too kindly to the social graces of this officer, or to his lack of familiarity with clandestine operations. More used to embassy cocktail parties than covert activities, Colonel Hervé was therefore eased out. By way of revenge he published a satirical work in which he portrayed the ways of the secret services.[4]

Meanwhile, however, the drastic pruning continued at the end of 1970 and the beginning of 1971. Among others expelled were Colonel Paul Durand, the head of the office of the former director, General Guibaud; Benoît Jeantet, head of the 89th Battalion of Special Services; Colonel Bauchet, the commander of the military personnel; and the heads of the scientific section, the technical services and the telecommunications control service. Dozens of officers and NCOs left SDECE for ever.[5] François Bistos was also dismissed, as was his 'honourable correspondent' Jean Violet, who was deemed too expensive. The dismay among the members of SDECE was comprehensible. One officer wrote:

Since the end of October 1970, different measures have turned the somewhat hermetic world of intelligence upside down. Examining the officially known facts, it can be seen that the Director-General of SDECE, the head of his office (Colonel Durand), the director of Research Branch (M. Beaumont), the director of technical services (M. Callot), his deputy (M. Le Roy), and the director of Counter-Espionage (Colonel Hervé) have by one means or another all been relieved of their duties since M. de Marenches took command. It is quite certain that measures on this scale, which deprive the French secret services of almost all their principal staff, can only be the result of some enormous scandal. Indeed we must not forget that, after the Ben Barka affair, which in its own way had certain repercussions, at the senior level of command only General Jacquier, the Director-General, was punished (M. Le Roy Finville, for his part, was only a subordinate official, whatever has been said).[6]

If there was a scandal, Alexandre de Marenches was not involved in any way. He simply inherited a situation that had developed under the two preceding directors, and which had a final postscript in April 1971. On 5 April, US customs officers arrested a Frenchman, Roger Delouette, at Port Elizabeth, New Jersey, whilst he was taking delivery of 44 kilos of heroin that he had brought over himself from France in a minibus. Was this a new link in the chain of the notorious French Connection? Delouette caused a sensation. The substance of the reply he gave to the Federal Judge in Newark who interrogated him was: 'I am an SDECE agent. I was bringing in the drugs on behalf of that service, at the request of Colonel Fournier. I was to hand them over to Harold MacNab of the French Consulate in New York.' Delouette and Fournier were charged, and predictably SDECE denied any knowledge of them.

Colonel Fournier did indeed exist. A stout man with bushy eyebrows and a crew-cut, this son of Toulouse primary teachers had been in 'Rural Works', Commandant Paillole's counter-espionage section in Algeria during the Second World War. After having joined the DGER, he worked for the general documentation section, and then, in SDECE, on the implanting of networks in North Africa, continuing his activities in Intelligence Branch during the Algerian war. Finally he was taken on by Colonel Beaumont as his assistant, to cover the Far East and North and South America. It was in this post that he apparently had brushes with the Americans, when he was investigating their role in the opium traffic in Indo-China, a role similar to that played in the past by SDECE.[7]

However, at the time of Delouette's arrest Colonel Fournier was the head of Paris station, in other words of Service 6 in SDECE, mainly responsible for the 'honourable correspondents'. This base seemed ill-fated, since it had already been under suspicion a year earlier during the Marcovic affair. Its senior officials at the time, Colonel Maurice Pierson, Captain Paul Santenac, Jean-Charles Marchiani and Claude Pradier, had been thrown out in February and March 1970. In connection with the murder of Alain Delon's Yugoslav bodyguard, an 'honourable correspondent' (a woman journalist code-named 'Karamel') had informed them of the existence of compromising photos of Claude Pompidou, which they set out to find. The rumour spread all over Paris – everyone began with superb confidence to talk about these pictures that nobody had ever seen. But the poison had spread to the very heart of the state. There were rumours and counter-rumours. The instigators of this story were allegedly the Service for Civic Action (Service d'Action Civique: SAC), more precisely, Gaullists opposed to Pompidou, whom they reproached with having betrayed the General. Santenac, a supporter of the RPF in his youth, looked a likely enough conspirator. Service 6 was therefore purged.[8]

If these names resurfaced a year later, on the occasion of Delouette's arrest, it was because the latter was not lying when he said that he was in the service of SDECE. Since the War, in which he had been employed by the BCRA, Roger Delouette had remained an 'honourable correspondent'. During the Algerian crisis he had worked under an SDECE captain, Jean de Lannurien. His training as an agricultural technician led him to rediscover an old friend, Colonel Roger Barberot, whose secretary he married. Barberot, a left-wing Gaullist activist, was then presiding over the Office for the Development of Agricultural Production (Bureau pour le Développement de la Production Agricole: BDPA), one of the cover organizations used by SDECE for its missions abroad.

In 1968 the secret services decided to reinforce their foothold in Cuba. Fidel Castro was suspected of giving aid to French revolutionary groups; moreover, the head of the network, Jacques Levacher, who passed as a 'commercial attaché', had become the target of the Cuban services.[9] Using the cover of the BDPA, Delouette was sent there as an agricultural engineer. On 23 October 1968 Colonel Barberot went to Cuba, with a half a dozen industrialists and a 'publicity man' – Santenac. Naturally they met Delouette there. In the 'Report on the Barberot Mission' the following, in particular, appeared: 'Ambassador Barberot set out the results of the BDPA mission and the possibility of extending it. He expounded the problems raised regarding the events of May and June in France, which arose from the activities of irresponsible political groups. This was presented as a preliminary to possible developments in technical cooperation between Cuba and France.'[10] Delouette was to continue his clandestine activities using the BDPA cover, this time in Biafra, at the beginning of 1969; rechristened 'Roger Delore', he and Colonel Fournier of SDECE supervised the transfer of arms destined for the secessionists.

The following year he was dismissed from the service. In a detailed list of the sums paid to Delouette sent to Roussel, the investigating judge, Security Section of SDECE indicated that he had received 52,000 francs, 27,000 of which had been paid on 6 March 1970, as a gratuity upon dismissal. Thus he was no longer a member of the 'Firm' when he was arrested in the United States. But the situation grew more complicated, because the 'villain' who had enlisted his services to smuggle in the heroin, Dominique Mariani, was none other than the cousin of Jean-Charles Marchiani, one of the members of Service 6. In response to Delouette's statements, members of the service, questioned by the investigating judge, off-loaded the responsibility on Fournier, and asserted that SDECE was indeed engaged in drug trafficking. One repercussion of this was that Colonel Beaumont was implicated.

Pierson, the head of 'Bison Base', testified: 'I have to inform you that, at the working meetings I attended in Beaumont's office during the last quarter of 1969 and the first quarter of 1970 different means were examined of financing a mission in the United States. I am not certain that drug peddling was mentioned as a potential means of funding.'[11]

Santenac testified:

It was on 23 November 1971 that Colonel Pierson told me the following: he had attended a meeting to arrange the financing of an operation in the United States. According to Pierson, in that meeting Beaumont had reviewed various methods of financing it, among them drugs, counterfeit currency and a call-girl network. Colonel Pierson then told me categorically that the choice had fallen on drugs: I should make clear that Colonel Pierson told me all this in the presence of Pradier.[12]

As if to make the intrigue still more confused, Jacques Soustelle, Colonel Barberot and General Billotte demanded the closing down of SDECE.

Colonel Barberot went even further: he announced publicly that the reason for Beaumont's dismissal in October, rather than concerning the Delouette affair, related to activities that could be termed high treason. When Beaumont decided to sue him, Delouette's former boss retracted. The fact remains that this torrent of statements threw an unfavourable light on SDECE, where Alexandre de Marenches had just taken over as director.[13] To cap it all, accusations of drug trafficking came up once more in October 1971. A man called André Labay was arrested in France under the same circumstances as Delouette. Now, he had worked for a long time for SDECE in Africa, and in particular had organized the secret services of Cyrille Adoula, the Prime Minister of Congo (Kinshasa). In Haiti since 1966 he had been the friend of the dictator François Duvalier, the lover of Duvalier's daughter Marie-Denise, and the local head of SDECE. But he was suspected also of being in the pay of the CIA.[14]

Naturally, in the light of this series of unexpected events the question arose: across the Atlantic had somebody set out to discredit SDECE? The hypothesis was a doubtful one, because the arrival of Alexandre de Marenches at the head of the organization could only give satisfaction to the US services. If they had still not understood this, one of his friends, General Vernon Walters, who had just left his post as military attaché in Paris to become assistant director of the CIA, put them in the picture. A second explanation remained: the desire for revenge on the part of those dismissed from Service 6, and more generally of the left-wing Gaullists after the Marcovic affair, which they themselves had launched.

The Renewal

A former primary teacher, André Devigny could not bear the Nazi Occupation. Late in 1942 he crossed the frontier and presented himself at the British Consulate: 'I want to fight Hitler.' The British Secret Intelligence Service directed him to one of its agents, a refugee from Pétain's secret services, Colonel Georges Groussard. Under the latter's control he set up a network in France. But he was tracked down by the Gestapo. In Lyons he was arrested by the services of Klaus Barbie. As Colonel Groussard wrote:

He suffered terrible torture, but did not talk. Sentenced to death, he performed an extraordinary, even a unique, feat: he escaped from Montluc. One should read – all young people should read it – the story told in his book *Un Condamné à mort s'est échappé*, a book as pure and cold as a blade of steel. Some 15 years later the film producer Robert Bresson was to breathe fresh life into one of the noblest deeds of the clandestine war by bringing this fascinating tale to the screen. For this escape was the work of Devigny alone. Nobody, absolutely nobody, could help him. It is one of the finest examples of what can be achieved by willpower, and how, by an extraordinary effort, a man can surpass human potential. The escape made the Germans mad with anger.[15]

In 1964, this Resistance hero was asked to reorganize the Action Branch: 'I was given carte blanche. Indeed I found a very distressed service. The Algerian crisis had shaken it up. It had become undisciplined and disorganized. I got rid of some 800 "honorable correspondents" and agents. When the new director, Alexandre de Marenches, took over in 1971, he found a well-oiled military machine. But I disapproved of the way he disposed of good technicians such as Colonel Durand, Dr Bommelaer and M. Beaumont So after seven years leading Action Branch, I quit. One of the key mistakes amounted to subordinating this Section to the Intelligence Branch, headed by Colonels Richard and then Lacaze.'[16] Thus General Devigny made way for Count Alain Gaigneron de Marolles, a fierce anti-communist. In 1976, after his promotion to Director of Intelligence Branch, the latter handed on the torch to a man who was in his element, Colonel Georges Grillot ('Bruno'); Grillot had made his name in Algeria with his 'tracking' commandos, the famous 'Commandos Georges', who had hunted the 'Khatibas', the mobile fighting units of the FLN. Thus in ten years Action Branch was reborn from its ashes and ready for operations, particularly in the Arab countries and in Africa.

The inevitable consequence was that the Director-General reactivated the special squadron of SDECE, the Mixed Air Group, GAM 56 ('Vaucluse'). Partly giving up the Persan-Beaumont airfield, from now on GAM 56 used the base at Evreux.[17] The good old Hurel-Dubois planes were handed over to the National Geographical Institute, and short take-off and landing planes, Bréguet 941s, replaced them. Noratlas planes (F-RAXA/F-RAXZ) and Puma SA-330 (F-SCOA/F-SCOZ) helicopters were also used. From 1978 onwards the small 'Twin Otters' would allow for the rapid transportation of special units. Finally, having been split off from GAM 56, the electronic Squadron 51 ('Aubrac'), also based at Evreux, handled operations for the interception of communications in flight. As can be seen, SDECE modernized itself in the 1970s.

The official budget of SDECE for 1971 amounted to 25,656,156 new francs, a 10 per cent increase over the preceding year, not counting the 'special funds' of the various ministries and the Elysée. This considerable advance allowed departments to be computerized: through the purchase of a UNIVAC 9400 computer, Research Branch was able to centralize its intelligence. At the same time, having been converted to Anglo-American methods, SDECE hoped to recruit brainpower from the universities. Small advertisements appeared in *Le Figaro*, which was no mean breach opened in the traditional method of co-optation: usually, for example, Action Branch recruited the sons of its former members. The result was disappointing: in 1971 17 students agreed to have their scholarships funded by SDECE and, in exchange, to give it ten years of their career. In 1972 their number rose to 37. But essentially economists, engineers and information technologists preferred to work in the private sector – it was less chancy and better paid.

Thus in 1971 the structure of SDECE was clearly redefined.[18] The General Directorate was supplemented by a Counsellor from the Quai d'Orsay (M. des Closières), a psychological adviser (Dr Beccuau, who replaced Dr Morali-Daninos), and its own office.The head of this office, Didier Faure-Beaulieu, a man of action, was replaced in 1977 by a gendarmerie officer, Michel Roussin, a specialist in oriental languages and scientific research,[19] backed up by Ferré-Patin in charge of general organization. Two small but nonetheless essential sections were attached to the central directorate: Colonel Jacques de Lageneste, like Colonel Mercier previously, was in charge of relations with foreign secret services. Security section continued to be the province of Colonel Georges Lionnet, a veteran of SDECE.[20]

Next came two major directorates. That of Infrastructure and Resources included sections for 'military personnel', 'personnel and finance', 'training', 'equipment and infrastructure', and 'general services'. The Army's controller-

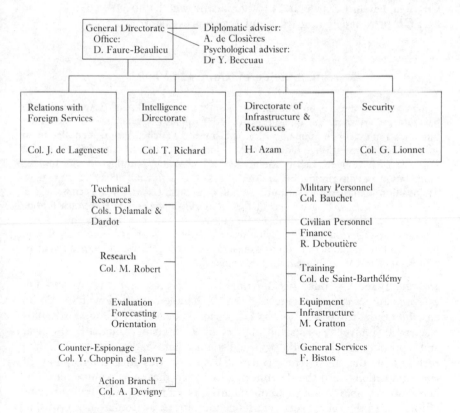

Figure 13.1 SDECE in 1971 under Alexandre de Marenches

general, Henri Azam, a doctor of law (his doctoral thesis was on the Foreign Legion, to which he had belonged after the War), commanded this directorate. There remained the heart of SDECE, the Intelligence Directorate: it weathered many changes under Alexandre de Marenches. Colonel Tristan Richard, an expert on the Arab countries, Colonel Jeannou Lacaze, 'the Wizard' of Action Branch, Colonel Bernard Grué, a former prisoner of the Vietminh, General René Candelier (from the gendarmerie), and finally General Jacques Sylla Fouilland, followed one another from 1970 to 1981. The 'waltz' of these Number Twos in SDECE undoubtedly demonstrates the instability that prevailed there (with the exception of Colonel Lacaze, who remained at his post for five years).

As for Research, the command fell to Colonel Maurice Robert, whose speciality was Africa. His own personal conception of intelligence, and the temperamental behaviour of the Director-General, caused him to resign in the summer of 1973. Colonel Deuve, who replaced him, was likewise an expert on Africa, but also on Asia.[21] Finally he gave way to Colonel René Crignola, whom we have met in Algeria, and who had been station head for SDECE in various countries, from Czechoslovakia to Japan.

The Suicide of 'Comrade Blanc'

I am at present on leave, but I think that as soon as I am back, on 16 August, there'll be a hue and cry about me, and a transfer order will also be awaiting me. I shall then find myself in exactly the same position as Comrade Touche. Although entitled to do so, I refused an invitation in January 1975 to join the permanent staff of SDECE, and since then I have been waiting for my fate to be decided, putting up with threats, intimidation and discrimination, and measures of harassment – all verbal, up to now. My position is intolerable, so much so that one must ask what has become of our democratic liberties. I have been in the GCR (Groupement de Contrôles Radio-électroniques) since 1941, that is for 35 years, and I served in the French expeditionary force in Italy (two citations), and then took part in the campaign in France and in Germany right up to Konstanz. I am 59 years old and have a son of 16 who is entering the 12th grade in September.[22]

Georges Blanc appended his signature to these lines on 9 August 1976. On 25 August he was found hanging from the handle of a window in his Berlin apartment, the city where he was GCR section head. The Group for Radio-electronic Controls was started in 1941 by Lieutenant-Colonel Paul Labat, and coordinated the work of the listening and radio direction-finding section for the Deuxième Bureau. Its task was the interception of communications, and the deciphering of coded messages, communications between an embassy and its home country, or any other radio transmissions of interest to the secret services. Its headquarters, at Boullay-les-Trous, in the Essonne department, mainly kept a watch on embassies. Fewer than a thousand civil servants were then working in the various GCR stations, spread around the centres of Alluets-Feucherolles (Yvelines), Velaine-en-Haye (Meurthe-et-Moselle) and Domme (Dordogne). The GCR erected its aerials and dishes from Berlin to Djibouti, and, using the cover of meteorological stations, from the island of Saint-Barthélémy (Guadeloupe) to Tromelin (Mauritius).

The GCR – which had always supplied information to SDECE – did not belong to it legally. The consequence was that its employees enjoyed civil service status and, for example, trade union rights. Blanc, like his friend Bernard Collin, the controller of the GCR in Berlin, who had been dismissed in 1979, belonged to the CGT. Colonel Yves Choppin de Janvry, the head of SDECE's Counter-Espionage Branch, complained that serious anomalies were occurring in the passing on of monitoring reports on the communist countries. To dispel this suspicion, it was decided to attach the GCR to SDECE from July 1970. Having refused to be assimilated into SDECE, Georges Blanc was the victim of somewhat brutal methods. As soon as he had returned from leave he was ordered to leave his flat in Berlin. He could not bear to do so. At the GCR centre at Domme, the same situation occurred: two agents committed suicide.[23]

Fresh Infiltrations

'Once, under de Marenches, I had to travel round the world in 17 days to repair the combination locks in our embassies in New Delhi, Canberra, Honolulu, Washington and Cairo, which strangely all failed on the same day,' said a former member of Service 7, who had remained in SDECE until 1976, after the service had been abolished.

After having been a safe-breaker, I worked for Security: the former poacher makes the best gamekeeper. After the Ben Barka affair I set up a small satellite unit within Colonel Lionnet's Security section. It was directly attached to the General Directorate, and not to Counter-Espionage. I went from one embassy to another, with six of the boys, to check on security. The first problem was to overcome the naivety of the ambassadors. Once I asked an ambassador accredited to a communist country to open his safe. He shut it again. I tried a new combination, and it opened: 'You've been had, Mr Ambassador,' I said. 'The Russians have been this way and opened all your safes.' I also ran courses to make important people visiting Eastern Europe aware of security problems: several times Valéry Giscard d'Estaing and some of his ministers attended them.

About this time, and for the first time in years, French counter-espionage, under Colonel de Janvry, welcomed an important defector from the East, who was able to give information on fresh communist infiltrations within SDECE.[24] What is certain is that in the mid-1970s counter-espionage assumed a growing importance, and was exclusively centred on the Soviet bloc. The mole hunt took off again, sometimes almost too enthusiastically. The Clément affair exemplifies this.

In 1943, at the age of 21, Maurice Clément took part in the creation of the Bureau of Investigation set up by the maquis groups. In August 1944 he was wounded during the struggle for the Liberation, on the Place Castellane in Marseilles. In 1946 SDECE opened its doors to this former grade P2 intelligence officer. He spent all his career in counter-espionage, first of all in Germany, then at the delicate post of Vienna, at the very beginning of the 1960s. As a 'vice-consul' – this was his cover as head of the counter-espionage network – he 'shadowed' and protected the work of the intelligence head, Colonel Humm. Clément succeeded in 'turning' a handful of Eastern bloc agents. But SDECE itself was 'contaminated', so much so that no one really knew who was infiltrating whom any more.

Upon his return to Paris in 1963 Maurice Clément was given the task of verification of sources at HQ, and especially of the records of 'honourable correspondents'. From June 1970 he became operational assistant to Colonel de Janvry, who six years later welcomed a defector from the East. On 29 June 1976, Clément was summoned to a rendezvous in a Paris flat. 'You have been a Soviet agent ever since Vienna, Clément, we want an immediate confession.' Such, without any other preliminaries, was the charge from his chief, who was accompanied by Commandant Camus (the man involved in the Rousseau affair), and others from the internal security section of Counter-Espionage.

Clément had to answer over 200 questions. He had to submit to a lie detection test administered by a doctor from the psychotechnical service. Then agents of Security and Action Branch hauled him off to a 'safe' house. Subjected to various threats and acts of violence, he signed on a scrap of paper a confession in which he acknowledged that he was being run by the Russians. It was a far cry from the polite but firm interrogations, with statements duly read back, carried out by Colonel Lionnet, who had retired a year earlier.

In such cases SDECE makes use of a privilege that distinguishes it from other departments. It can place an official on the retired list for up to five years, on half-pay, and force him to take retirement.[25] The head of the Director-General's office staff, Didier Faure-Beaulieu, requested Clément's resignation: he refused. The admissions had been extracted by force. He fiercely denied them. He was suspended. He decided to take SDECE to court. The latter had offered 150,000 francs as an indemnity payment, and the restoration of his pension rights, but no reinstatement. His own brother-in-law, Roger Duvernois, who was in charge of training, was dismissed in his turn.[26] And others followed. If SDECE believed Clément to be guilty, why was he offered compensation? If not, why not re-employ him? 'I consider that we should not have any doubts about our men,' replied Alexandre de Marenches. 'As soon as one arises, it is appropriate to get rid of him. For my part, at the time I was convinced that we had been penetrated. We had to react.'[27]

A Global Vision

'A real French Kissinger,' General Vernon Walters, for a long time the US military attaché in Paris, and then 'Number Two' in the CIA liked to say about his friend Alexandre de Marenches. The two men had got to know each other in 1944, in the Allied expeditionary corps in Italy. Walters spoke French fluently, and de Marenches admired the United States. So began a long friendship between these 'big names' in international intelligence. Walters was not wrong. At Mortier barracks the Director-General was even censured for his sudden disappearances, constant flights to pastures new, and neglect of his role as head of the secret services in the interests of turning himself into a Talleyrand of secret diplomacy. Giscard d'Estaing was annoyed: the head of SDECE liked to meet and give advice to many of the crowned heads and leaders of the Arab world. This was the origin of the 'Safari Club'.

At his instigation an ultra-secret agreement was signed on 1 September 1976 between Sheikh Kamal Addam, head of the Saudi Arabian secret services; General Nematollah Nassiri, head of Iran's SAVAK; the head of Egypt's Moukhabarat El-Amma; and, inevitably, Ahmed Dlimi, of the General Directorate and Documentation, the secret service of Hassan II. What was the reason for this pact? 'The recent events in Angola and other African countries have demonstrated that that continent has served as a theatre for revolutionary wars fomented and directed by the Soviet Union, which has been using individuals or organizations sympathetic to Marxist ideology, or already under the sway of that ideology.'[28] So an operational centre was set up designed to keep a close eye on African affairs. It was based in Cairo, and its programme included the preparation of synopses, forecasts and planning, but also operations. Communications equipment was supplied by SDECE. Summit meetings were held in Saudi Arabia, France and Egypt. The 'Safari Club' got results: in Somalia it persuaded Siad Barré to expel the Russians in exchange for arms. In Egypt it organized psychological and guerrilla warfare against Gadaffi. The Club played a part in Anwar al-Sadat's visit to Jerusalem in 1977. In fact its first setback resulted from this.,

Kamal Addam, a businessman of Turkish origin, and adviser to the Saudi king on security questions, was assigned by the CIA the task of passing on thousands of dollars to Sadat long before the latter became Nasser's successor. In 1977 the Saudi princes were furious: they learnt over the radio that Sadat was to meet Begin. Over the radio! Yet one of the leaders of the de Marenches Club was none other than their own adviser; and, furthermore, he was involved in the organization of the trip. As a reprisal Prince Turki Ben Faisal took over the direction of the Saudi secret services.

Major-General Ahmed Dlimi, director of the DGED in Morocco, was a faithful friend of Alexandre de Marenches. The Frenchman was very much at home in Morocco, and Hassan II displayed confidence in him – just as he did in Dlimi, until one day the latter met his death in a 'mysterious car accident'. In Iran too SDECE also relied on an old ally. Colonel Maudry had set up close links in the 1960s with SAVAK, before joining the secretariat of the Union Générale des Pétroles, which became Elf. General Nematollah Nassiri, who represented SAVAK there, was to be arrested during the Khomeini revolution. He had directed the Shah's secret police from 1966 to 1978, but he declared on television, before his execution, that he had never known about the torture and the political prisoners. Alexandre de Marenches, unlike his friends in the CIA, knew full well that a revolution was on the way. Being on good terms with Princess Ashraf, the twin sister of the Shah, he asked his services to enter into talks with the opposition. In January 1979, when he went to Switzerland to meet Parviz Khonsari, the Iranian ambassador, who was really the regional head of SAVAK in Western Europe, he was not unaware that the Iranian monarchy was at its last gasp.[29]

In 1979 some SDECE officers, particularly in Research Branch, complained that, under the influence of their Director-General, the French secret services were clearly the victims of political manicheism, and that in the Arab countries, the Middle East and the Levant they only maintained relationships with conservative regimes.[30] The fact remains that since the Algerian war SDECE had never been so well-informed about the Arab countries, as witness a 'scoop' that occurred in October 1973. It was alone among Western intelligence services in forecasting the exact date of the Yom Kippur war. Similarly, the French authorities were extremely well informed about the terrorist plans being hatched among the various Palestinian groups.

'The Blitz' Against 'Carlos'

Ilich Ramirez Sanchez, the international terrorist better known under the name of 'Carlos', was living in Algiers at the end of 1975. SDECE had 'winkled' him out and pinpointed his whereabouts. One of the places he dropped in at was the *Dar Salem*, the select restaurant frequented by Algerian high society, and owned by the brother of President Boumedienne himself. Carlos was under the protection of the secret services run by Colonel Kasdi Merbah, which had helped him to disappear from France. In the Rue Toullier in Paris he had shot down two DST investigators in June 1975. The previous September he had killed two passers-by and injured

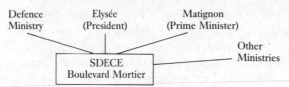

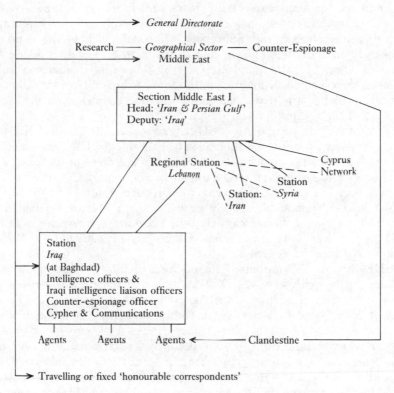

Figure 13.2 SDECE: The Intelligence Communication Chain (example: the Middle East)

some 30 people during a grenade attack on the St Germain drugstore. In January 1975 his commando group had failed in an attack at Orly on an aeroplane of El Al, the Israeli airline. Thus in the summer of 1975 the signal was given: 'Carlos must be liquidated.' The head of Action Branch put a team on his tail. These were men trained to kill, such as the one who bore the nickname 'The Blitz', at Neuilly and at Cercottes. The commando group filtered discreetly into Algeria, but came back empty-handed. For the head-hunters, the match was only postponed.

Alexandre de Marenches reported to the Elysée: 'We had the order to kill Carlos. We pinpointed his whereabouts a number of times, once in Algiers.

We went after him there, but we drew a blank.' Quite so. The long pursuit continued, whilst the terrorist slid like an eel through the meshes of the net and constantly changed his protector, from Iraq to Syria, or Libya. Carlos sensed the danger and even drew his philosophy from it: 'All that I know is that one day I shall be murdered. After all, this is what I live for. For us the only war that counts is between socialism and capitalism.'[31]

From the opening years of the 1970s anti-terrorism became a major preoccupation. An operational section was set up within Counter-Espionage, called 'Anti-terrorism and Subversion'. It owed much to the networks implanted in the Middle East, and to the help of Israelis working for Mossad. Later SDECE found itself side by side with the latter in a wider alliance, code-named 'Kilowatt', which served as a pool for information on terrorism, particularly that emanating from Arab countries, for the secret services of the Western powers.

Thus at the beginning of 1973 SDECE announced that Basil al-Kubaisi, of the Popular Front for the Liberation of Palestine (PFLP), was intending to install his headquarters in Paris. He was killed there on 5 April.[32] On 23 August the government received a further note on the 'activities of the Fedyahin in Europe', which foresaw a resurgence of attacks by the PFLP, based in the Netherlands. In the spring of 1974 SDECE submitted to Pompidou a file on the increasingly close relationship between the PFLP and the Japanese Red Army Faction. On 26 July 1974 the terrorist Yukata Furuya was arrested at Orly.

SDECE was often criticized for having increasingly intervened inside France, at the expense of the DST and the traditional police services, by invoking a 'right of pursuit' in the context of the anti-terrorist struggle. In fact, it participated in many liaison bodies, and many of its intelligence summaries went to swell the files of other services. For example, on 17 May 1972 a memorandum from SDECE destined for Raymond Marcellin, the then Minister of the Interior, described 'the Leftist activities linked to Cuba in south-west France' – intelligence gathered from a Cuban defector.

As for the unrest in the Basque country, a publisher of French grammar books in Barcelona was very frequently cited by the Spanish press as being the SDECE correspondent and acting as the link with anti-ETA commandos. As regards the Breton Liberation Front, the DST took the main role. Occasionally SDECE was able to provide technical aid, so that it could 'bug' the premises of suspected autonomists. A former intelligence colonel, who emerged from his retirement in Finistère in 1975, was chosen by SDECE because of his knowledge of Breton to go to Ireland, make contact with supporters of independence exiled there since the War, and assess whether they were playing any part in the attacks by the Breton Liberation Front.

Finally, how could SDECE not be tempted to intervene in Corsica, since it had installed one of the bases of Action Branch there?

SDECE in Corsica

'If they give us the green light we'll liquidate the Corsican National Liberation Front [Front de Libération Nationale Corse: FLNC] in a few weeks,' asserted an Action Branch frogman stationed at Aspretto in the Bay of Ajaccio. 'In fact, we are not intervening here, because it is French soil. For its part, FLNC has never attacked our base. Having said that, SDECE has in fact mounted a few operations against the Corsicans, but outside the island.'

Nevertheless it was certain that numerous members of Francia, the anti-independence movement, came from Action Branch – from which they had resigned. At the Training Centre for Volunteer Reservist Paratroops (Centre d'Instruction des Réservistes Volontaires Parachutistes: CIRVP) at Cercottes, 'destabilization courses' were being run towards the end of 1970. They taught how to carry out a 'rise through the structure', in other words an infiltration, a long-term penetration into a given organization – party, trade union, clandestine group. And also how to handle explosives or an Assemblat 6 × 6 camera.

In March 1978, at the invitation of Al-Fatah, three Corsican independence fighters went to its main Palestinian headquarters in Lebanon. SDECE's Action Branch photographed them from every angle. At Beirut, even if the agent Christian Dallaporta, nicknamed 'Qui de droit' ('Whom it May Concern') was a little too visible, SDECE had by then penetrated deeply into Lebanese circles. Its intelligence instigated the tailing, surveillance, and then the arrest in France of the Corsicans spotted in the Lebanon.

There was also a commando raid. Since 12 July 1960 Radio Corse Internationale had beamed programmes to Corsica from 6 a.m. to 10 p.m., from a transmitter installed on a mountain on the island of Elba, and linked by low frequency relay to a studio in Leghorn. The programmes were produced in Bastia by a team of journalists under Aimé Pietri. The station certainly did not favour independence, but its cultural programmes, its broadcasts in the local language and its reports sustained a general movement that strengthened Corsican identity. A team of frogmen from SDECE landed on the island on the morning of 14 August and blew up the station's transmitter.[33]

14

Coups d'état *in Africa*

'Commercial purpose: furnished house – provision of services', or: 'Furnished hotel – family pension'. In such terms the Paris Chamber of Commerce defined the social objects of high-class brothels, such as the Villa Montespan or the Villa des Marronniers. Numerous establishments of this kind, with very diverse clienteles, were of interest to the secret services, and particularly to SDECE, so frequently were they patronized by businessmen, political leaders and visiting diplomats. Fabienne Grunet, 'Madame Claude' ('Violette' to SDECE), had never hidden the fact that she supplied the Tourelles barracks with items of information gleaned by her 'girls' from 'pillow talk'.[1] Nor had Marie-Louise Roblot, 'Madame Billy', the proprietress in 1943 and in 1978 of the Etoile Kléber, one of the most famous brothels in Paris. In the same quarter a Russian bar, where the hostesses spoke various Slavonic languages, rendered great service to the Eastern countries section of SDECE and to military security.

To complete the picture, certain call-girls paid directly by SDECE enlivened the visits of Third World heads of state. One such was President Tombalbaye of Chad, whom the French had brought to power in 1960 immediately after independence. Fifteen years later the French no longer trusted him: might he not be trying, under American pressure, to move out of the French sphere of influence? To frighten Tombalbaye, some SDECE networks decided to brandish the threat of an offensive by the dissidents of the National Liberal Front (Front de Libération Nationale: Frolinat) led by Hissène Habré, who though he was prone to personal lapses had been an agent of the French for many years.

At the beginning of 1975 Tombalbaye paid a visit to France. Between two political meetings he spent several days in a villa at Grasse, in the company of two young French ladies, made available to him through the kindness of his hosts. In this way SDECE learnt that Tombalbaye was expecting to be rolling in money before long. By cross-checks at Mortier HQ, it was learnt that he was preparing to sell oil prospecting rights to a US company. In April a mutiny broke out in Chad. Tombalbaye was assassinated and replaced by General Malloum.

The Assassination of Dr Outel Bono

It was Sunday 26 August 1973. Dr Outel Bono climbed pensively into his DS, parked in the Rue de la Roquette in Paris. He was playing the trickiest game of his life. A doctor from Chad, and popular leader of the democratic opposition, he was at last returning to his country, after a series of complex negotiations with the French. Suddenly a mustard-coloured 2 CV pulled up sharply alongside him. A man opened fire with a 9mm pistol. Dr Bono died with two bullets in his head. The chance of a change of power from the Tombalbaye regime died with him.

It seemed a total mystery. Dr Bono's widow, a French teacher, was looked after by a singular character: Colonel Henri Bayonne, a former member of the BCRA, who for a long time had directed a building company in the Central African Republic, and who was no stranger to the secret services. Through Dinguibaï, the former Chad Minister of Planning, like himself a member of the national Grand Lodge of France, the colonel had met Outel Bono. Dinguibaï had suggested that, from the French point of view, the doctor, an honest man who had frequently been the victim of repression in Chad, was a card to be held in reserve.

Bayonne felt entitled to speak in the name of 'highly placed friends'. Bono could get his country out of the rut and set up a real democracy. Bono hesitated, because the idea of being brought to power by an act of force, even if the intention was liberal, did not greatly appeal to him. Finally he agreed, provided that a genuine popular vote and wide-ranging reforms ratified his action. In the months that followed, his programme was publicized in Chad, and a press conference was planned to announce his departure. But a week before the agreed date Dr Outel Bono was assassinated. Didn't this give the impression of a second-rate re-make of the Ben Barka scenario of ten years earlier?

Then the Claustre affair broke. The ethnologist Françoise Claustre was one of several hostages being held by Hissène Habré. The French government, which had worked miracles to get Habré out of his lair, sent emissaries to him, most notably Captain Pierre Galopin, a specialist from the secret services, who from 1963 to 1972 had operated in Chad, mostly against Frolinat (the National Liberation Front). The situation was even more complex because the experts in the Elysée and SDECE were hedging their bets. Thus officially France had supported Tombalbaye, and then, when he had strayed from the straight and narrow, General Malloum. Commandant Camille Gourvennec, a Frenchman, controlled the local authorities as head of the Centre for the Coordination and Exploitation of Intelligence, a sort of Chad branch of SDECE. For greater safety, from 1969 onwards the latter had infiltrated the Mission for Administrative Reform (Mission de Réforme Administrative: MRA), directed in 1974 by Pierre Claustre. Contrary to appearances, the latter did not belong to SDECE, even if he had sought its help to free his wife.[2]

At the same time the French services were seeking to neutralize the fraction of Frolinat supported by Gadaffi. Two investigators are categorical on this point, declaring: 'Charles Martini, a survivor of Bir Hakeim, officially "cultural attaché" at the French Embassy in Tripoli, took steps to contain the Frolinat opposition of Dr Abba Sidick, supported by Libya.'[3]

Finally, before setting out on a mission to Hissène Habré to obtain Mme Claustre's freedom, Galopin had opened talks with Frolinat's Second Army, supported by the Libyans to the north, and led by Habré's rival, Goukouni Oueddei. Was it not certain that to send Captain Galopin to Tibesti amounted to sentencing him to death? Yes, if the Toubous of Hissène Habré remembered that he had been the instigator of fierce repression in Chad. No, if Habré saw himself first as a former 'honourable correspondent' of the French secret services. The former theory prevailed: Captain Galopin, after suffering atrocious torture, was executed.

Shortly afterwards Thierry Desjardins, the *Figaro* reporter, was carrying out an investigation in Tibesti and met Hissène Habré. The latter made him listen to a tape recording, 'the confessions of Commandant Galopin'.[4] 'Outel Bono was assassinated by a man called "Leonardi", at the instigation of Commandant Gourvennec,' Galopin revealed. Even under torture, he could hardly have invented that name. In Paris, the lawyer representing the civil plaintiff, Maître Pierre Kaldor, demanded that Colonel Bayonne be heard on this new fact. Bayonne agreed to confirm the identity of the paid killer: 'Leonardi' was in reality 'Léon Hardy', a cover-name for Claude Bocquel, a former policeman at the Paris Prefecture.

Questioned by the examining magistrate, Bocquel averred that he had had nothing to do with Bono's death. Proof of this was the fact that Gourvennec had asked him to 'deal with' another Chad doctor, Abba Sidick, the head of Frolinat in Tripoli.[5]

The mystery persists. Was Outel Bono assassinated as a consequence of differences between various groups in the French secret services in Paris and in Fort Lamy (Ndjamena)? Above all, had he been condemned to die by those who feared the rise of an African leader of too independent a cast of mind? Camille Gourvennec, suspect No. 1, can no longer speak. Some say he died of cancer, others from poisoning. Françoise Claustre, who has been freed in exchange for arms shipments to Hissène Habré, has taken refuge in a profound and scholarly silence. Her jailer has once more become 'the friend of France'. The turmoil in Chad continues to make front-page news. Nadine Bono, who has now remarried and is a teacher in the south of France, waits for justice to be done. SDECE has closed the dossier.

Portugal: 'Mar Verde' and 'Safira'

In the autumn of 1974, a few months after the 'Carnation Revolution' in Portugal, a man fled his country, as did many others. But Agostinho Barbieri Cardoso had special reason to fear popular revenge. For a quarter of a century he was one of the senior officers of the PIDE (Policia Internationale de Defesa do Estado), which shared with the KGB the character of being both an intelligence service and a secret police. Under SDECE's protection, and that of the DST, he moved into a house in the Paris area.

Colonel Jacques Lageneste, SDECE's head of relations with foreign secret services, had provided him with what he needed. He knew the Portuguese very well. A year after the *coup d'état* of April 1974 one of its principal protagonists, General de Spinola, went over to active opposition, together with his covert organization, the Portuguese Liberation Army (ELP). In September 1975, to ward off the danger of a putsch from the extreme Left, SDECE, represented by Lageneste, organized a conference at the Sheraton Hotel in Paris of all the parties opposed to communism. as well as Spinola, there were present Freitas do Amaral, the head of the Christian Social Democrats (CDS), Manuel Allegre, a leader of the Portuguese Socialist Party, and men from the former colonies, Jorge Jardim, the millionaire from Mozambique, and the Paris representative of Unita from Angola.[6]

Agostinho Barbieri Cardoso had established contacts with SDECE that went back a long way. Having joined the PIDE in 1948, 15 years later he became its deputy director. In February 1965 he had organized the kidnapping and assassination of a celebrated opponent of Salazar, General Delgado, which had earned him promotion. He then became head of intelligence for the overseas territories.

To be in charge of African affairs was a poisoned gift. The wind was blowing in favour of the Marxist guerrilla movements active in Portugal's principal colonies: the Popular Movement for the Liberation of Angola (MPLA) under Agostinho Neto; the African Party for the Independence of Guinea and Cape Verde (PAIGC) under Amilcar Cabral; and the Mozambique Liberation front (Frelimo) under Samora Machel. Cardoso launched 'special operations' and travelled a lot with his deputy, Ernesto Lopes Ramos. He was seeking logistic support in Europe, and the French lent him an attentive ear. It must be remembered that Cabral's guerrilla forces in Guinea-Bissau had established a rear base in the other Guinea, at Conakry. Even if Sékou Touré was convinced of the contrary, SDECE, as we have seen, had given up trying to destabilize the country a decade previously. The matter had run its course. However, in 1970 there was agreement on one point: if the Portuguese wished to break up the PAIGC,

SDECE would not be averse to lending a hand, while at the same time delivering a side-swipe at Sékou Touré.

Cardoso fled from Portugal in April 1974, because a commission charged with dismantling the PIDE had seized the archives at his headquarters and begun to sift through them. The PIDE men had actually attempted to protect their archives, and this gave rise, on 25 April 1974, to the sole armed confrontation. The Portuguese are a peaceful people. But in these buildings they uncovered tons of documents revealing the secret mechanisms of the dictatorship, the names of informants, systematic records, torture. Many reports dealt with the relationships of PIDE with foreign secret services, in particular the French. This was borne out by the copies of the reports made by SDECE senior officials under diplomatic cover at Lisbon, such as Isidore Banon and Captain Gillier. These clearly proved the continual exchange of information between the PIDE, SDECE, the DST and Intelligence's Section 7 concerning Portuguese émigrés in France and various so-called 'subversive' groups. As for joint operations mounted in Africa, the archives allowed developments to be followed almost day by day.[7] So let us go back a little.

In 1970 – Salazar was dead and Caetano had replaced him – Cardoso proposed to SDECE a first large-scale operation to overthrow Sékou Touré, Operation 'Mar Verde' (Green Sea). Stillborn, it was succeeded by a second plan, named 'Safira'. Whereupon, on 20 January 1973, PIDE pulled off the assassination of Amilcar Cabral, the first leader of the PAIGC. The moment was ripe for provoking internal disunity in the movement, and incidentally the fall of Sékou Touré, whom SDECE would have liked to replace by Colonel Diallo, whose movement, the Rassemblement des Guinéens de l'Extérieur, was based in Gabon.

Among the PAIGC leaders whom PIDE had succeeded in recruiting were two agents whose code-names were 'Padre' and 'Anjo'. Cardoso thought up the idea of setting the Guinea émigrés against the representatives of Cape Verde, in order to destroy the alliance formed by Cabral. The minute drawn up by the PIDE and approved by SDECE stated categorically:

With the death of Amilcar Cabral, the gulf separating the Guineans from their Cape Verde allies has grown, and the idea of forming a new party, the PAIG (Parti Africain d'Indépendance Guinéenne) was forcefully expressed at the time of the proclamation of the 'State of Guinea-Bissau'.

Thus two ideological lines were defined:

that of the Guineans who followed a communist line or favoured Sékou Touré;
that of the pro-Western and anti-Sékou Touré group, who constituted a dissident faction, hoping to provoke a *coup d'état* within PAIGC.

PIDE and SDECE intended to widen the gap and planned to intervene at the end of June or in July 1974. Private capital from Brazil and Europe was invested. A division of labour was established: PIDE would manage its dissidents within PAIGC; SDECE would supervise the preparation of operations involving Sékou Touré. An SDECE report dated 4 April 1974 set out the final arrangements for the combined Franco-Portuguese intervention, dealing with the transportation of arms and personnel, and the organization of training camps and radio communications, and providing for an aircraft to fly the new government to Conakry to replace Sékou Touré.

According to SDECE specialists the 'Safira' plan would consist of the following stages:

16–23 April: Meeting in an African country of the Guineans (Republic of Guinea–Conakry), dissidents from the PAIGC, and the Senegalese, with 'C' (Calvao) and Aranha. Establishment of a plan for action.

22 April–5 May: Training of the leaders through our technicians stationed in Europe.

End of May–beginning of June: Installation of equipment; installation of personnel.

Second or third week in June: Training of personnel.

End of June–beginning of July: Operation receives the go-ahead.

The Safira mission did not come off, despite the fact that the plan was regulated like clockwork. One important detail put a spanner in the works – the 'Carnation Revolution', which broke out on 25 April in Portugal, just as the second phase was starting. Just like the CIA in Iran five years later, SDECE did not see it coming. This is the main drawback in cooperation between the Western secret services and their counterparts in any kind of dictatorship. The intelligence station on the spot went to sleep, paralysed by a routine that encouraged an easy existence. The SAVAK in Iran and the PIDE in Portugal provided files that were then passed on to Washington or Paris. It goes without saying that they never said anything to suggest that opposition was growing and would soon overturn the authorities in power. At the end of the day the PAIGC was to take control of Guinea–Bissau and Cape Verde. On the other side of the frontier Sékou Touré, ten years later, was to die peacefully in his bed.

Occupation: Reporter in Angola

It was November 1975. The Secretary-General of the Elysée, Claude Pierre-Brossolette, received a secret report about Cabinda, a small enclave in the north of Angola with borders on Congo and Zaïre. Both the French in Elf-Erap and the Americans in Gulf Oil coveted Cabinda because of its oil; SDECE and CIA agents would have liked to develop it into an abscess to bleed the Marxists of the MPLA. So the Front for the Liberation of the Cabinda Enclave (FLEC) was set up. From Zaïre in August 1975, its spokesman, Luis Ranque Franque, proclaimed 'the independence of Cabinda'.

But upon examination, the form of the FLEC did not appeal to the

French, who fomented a split led by Auguste Tchioufou, the former representative of Elf-Congo, a friend of Gabon and SDECE.[8] In August, however, the CIA and SDECE had made an agreement to work together. In particular the mercenary Bob Denard had served as an intermediary. 'The directors of French Intelligence had met the deputy director of the CIA, Vernon Walters,' recounts John Stockwell, the former head of operations for the American agency in Angola. 'SDECE received $250,000 from the CIA, but told it nothing about its own operation regarding the FLEC.'[9]

A France–Cabinda Association was founded in Paris, mercenaries were recruited, and Cabinda recruits began to train. The secret document that the Elysée received came from a journalist specializing in Africa, Michel Lambinet, a friend of Colonel Robert, who had recently retired from SDECE. This journalist, who ran *La Lettre d'Afrique*, was appointed in early November 1975 by Henrique Tiago Nzita, President of the FLEC, as the representative of his movement in Western Europe: 'M. Lambinet is authorized to solicit in the foremost circles of Western Europe – whether these be financial, economic, industrial and political, or diplomatic, humanitarian, cultural and governmental – all kinds of urgent help to directly assist our struggling people until the total liberation of our territory.'

In this capacity, from 8 to 12 November the journalist closely observed a 'lightning offensive' by the FLEC. It revealed the utter inefficiency of the 'liberation movement'.

By 1 p.m. it was clear that the planned lightning offensive could not succeed. Right at the frontier troops came across extensive minefields, some of which were several hundred metres deep. During the first half hour, losses were numerous (a score of dead and several dozen wounded), and above all it became apparent that the Cabinda troops were completely unreliable. In fact, from the beginning they fired wildly and continuously in all directions. . . . By 2 p.m. the Cabindans had already exhausted more than half their ammunition, but to no effect whatsoever. By the Saturday evening they had only penetrated 5 or 6 kilometres. Thus it was absolutely certain that it would be impossible to achieve the two main objectives that had been laid down: the capture of Tchiowa, the capital, and the oil wells farther to the north. During this first day, President Nzita was not seen once, either at the front or on the frontier. He remained in Lukula.

The rest of the description of the Cabinda offensive was just as extraordinary. Its author lucidly concluded:

1 The information about the internal situation in Cabinda did not correspond to the reality . . . ;
2 Nzita's claims about an alleged resistance in the north-west were equally false . . . ;
3 Thus one can say that Nzita's internal popularity, at least in the southern half of Cabinda, was almost nil;
4 Nzita's influence over the FLEC troops based at Tombo Yonga was also non-existent . . .
   To sum up, from both the civilian and the military viewpoint it was apparent that

absolutely no reliance could be placed on the Cabindans. The few trustworthy elements had been killed . . . On the political level, I would respectfully suggest that, as an immediate measure, Nzita be neutralized, as was done with Ranque Franque.[10]

It was realized that the official responsible for Angola in SDECE, Colonel Bordes, unnerved by this ridiculous situation, had to be replaced 'for personal reasons'. Nevertheless, the secret services did not give up. On 26 December 1975, the *Washington Post* announced: 'SDECE is cooperating with the CIA in supplying arms and funds to the National Front for the Liberation of Angola (FNLA). France is also providing direct support to the Front for the Liberation of the Cabinda Enclave.' The FNLA, also supported by the Chinese, collapsed. SDECE continued to sponsor the FLEC. Mercenaries such as Jean Kay came to its rescue.[11] A temporary member of SDECE's staff, Jean da Costa, undertook the training of two thousand men. Bob Denard and a certain 'Monsieur Charles' – not unknown to Michel Lambinet – continued the dispatch of mercenaries.[12]

In May 1977 the London *Sunday Times* announced the launching of Operation 'Cobra 77'. It was a new invasion of Angola on four fronts: from Cabinda, with the FLEC; from Zaïre; from Namibia; and by sea, thanks to ships that BOSS, the South African secret service, provided for Unita (whose code name was 'Cobra'). SDECE played a decisive role. The operation was organized 'from Senegal, whose pro-French president, Senghor, has refused to recognize the regime of President Agostinho Neto', the British paper noted.[13]

Over the next decade SDECE was mainly to support Jonas Savimbi's Unita. Here a flamboyant character appeared on the scene. He was another journalist, Dominique de Roux, writer, wild adventurer, the founder – with the publisher Alain Moreau – of the *Cahiers de l'Herne*, and author of numerous books. This scion of a noble family lived at an incredible pace. He died in March 1977 from a heart attack, at the age of 43. The Paris intelligentsia laid a few funeral wreaths around him: 'A highly cultured man and entirely lacking in prejudice,' wrote Bernard Poirot-Delpech in *Le Monde*, 'Dominique de Roux was all the more appealing a character because he could not be categorized, being unpredictable and imprudent.'[14]

Indeed, one of de Roux's articles devoted to Angola appeared posthumously in *Le Monde*: 'The Cubans are reported to be growing more and more isolated in Angola,' he wrote.[15] In fact de Roux had become the official adviser to Jonas Savimbi, the leader of Unita. He rendered numerous services to SDECE. 'Dominique de Roux,' noted an informed observer, 'took a wicked pleasure in carrying on covert agitation, and inventing clandestine operations, which he described in abundant detail in reports sent to SDECE and BOSS. He succeeded in making Colonel de Lignières and his superiors at Mortier HQ believe that he was playing a key role in southern Africa, but this was very overrated as compared to his real importance.'[16]

   This was so much the case that Gordon Winter, a BOSS officer, became intrigued by the role played by Dominique de Roux. This agent of the South African secret service asked Jack Kemp, his superior officer, for further details. He obtained them from Kemp:

'We know everything about him. He is on our files. He is an important French intelligence officer who uses journalism as his cover. He organizes the transfer of arms and munitions, which is important for Unita. Moreover, he reviews all Savimbi's war communiqués before passing them on to the Paris office of Unita, which publishes them' . . . I was really very impressed, and asked Jack Kemp how he knew so much about him. He smiled and explained that the logistic and psychological support for Savimbi and his Unita depended on a mutual agreement between SDECE, the CIA and South African military intelligence, in order to keep Savimbi's head above water until the MPLA was overturned.[17]

One might almost believe that the secret war in Africa was an affair of journalists.

Giscard's Brains Trust

In June 1974 René Journiac became the President's adviser on African affairs. He had a domed forehead and an unruly quiff of white hair, and gazed quizzically from behind tortoise-shell spectacles. Trained in the school of Jacques Foccart, this former lawyer had, as early as 1962, advised Prime Minister Georges Pompidou on the problems of the French-speaking countries and the economic ties with Africa. Journiac was therefore no unconditional Gaullist.
   At the time when he replaced Foccart and when the General Secretariat for African and Madagascan Affairs was wound up, the stance of the secret services towards Africa was being modified. For years the President's *éminence grise* for the dark continent had exercised authority over the secret services. Generals Jacquier and Guibaud were subject to the orders of the little office located at 2, Rue de l'Elysée. But from 1970 onwards, two men whose temperament and outlook were very different confronted each other: Foccart, the Gaullist, and Marenches, the 'Atlanticist', did not always get on well together. Their *modus vivendi* did not survive Pompidou. In 1974 Jacques Foccart was finally removed. A year earlier his friend Colonel Maurice Robert, Director of Research at SDECE and a specialist on Africa, had preferred to leave SDECE.
   The new President personally supervised operations in Africa. Journiac, his adviser, was more a messenger than a senior executive, as Foccart had been with de Gaulle. For his part, Marenches complained that Giscard's interest in the various African countries was too unevenly divided. From the

SDECE viewpoint a rapprochement with the Americans was undoubtedly due from 1974 onwards, in order 'to counter communist subversion in Africa'. From the government side, during the period of office of Valéry Giscard d'Estaing a number of important military and clandestine interventions were to take place.[18]

As we have seen, in 1975–6 SDECE, or mercenaries recruited at its instigation, were fighting the Marxist government of Agostinho Neto in Angola, with the agreement of the CIA, the British SIS and South Africa's BOSS.

On 16 January 1977, Operation 'Shrimp' was launched. Benin (formerly Dahomey), ruled by the Marxist–Leninist Mathieu Kérékou, figured on the 'black list' of regimes that were anathema to the French secret services. On several occasions armed coups were attempted and failed. René Journiac then called in Bob Denard, the most famous of the French mercenaries since the 1960s. At that time he was a technical adviser in the President's Office in Gabon. Denard, alias 'Colonel Bourgeaud', was in reality a 'sub-contractor' of SDECE. If an operation went wrong, he acted as the lightning-conductor; the lightning never struck the French State.

In the event, with the financial and logistic support of Hassan II of Morocco and Bernard-Albert (Omar) Bongo of Gabon, he recruited under a hundred mercenaries, dubbed 'the Foreign Intervention Group' (Groupe Etranger d'Intervention: GEI). The GEI trained mainly at the base at Benguerir, not far from Marrakesh, whose use was favoured by French shock troops. The objective was to land in Benin, overturn Kérékou, and bring to power the Front for the Rehabilitation of Dahomey (Front de Libération et de Réhabilitation de Dahomey: FLERD) under Gratien Pognon. The landing was a complete fiasco. There was utter chaos: the mercenaries fled, leaving behind them their weapons and baggage, and above all masses of documents setting out the details of the operation, which were quickly made public.[19] Those that got away still wonder how Denard and his associates were able to make so many mistakes.[20]

It was March 1978. SDECE got wind of a secret meeting held at Ouargla, in Algeria, between the National Front for the Liberation of the Congo, led by Nathanael Mbumba with the help of Cuban military men, and General Borissov, one of the Soviet Africa strategists, based in Ethiopia. At Easter 1977 the FLNC had made raids into the Shaba area, in southern Zaïre. President Mobutu had viewed this as an attempt to destabilize the former Katanga region and regain control over the area and its copper. On 6 April 1977, at the request of his Zaïre counterpart, Giscard d'Estaing launched Operation 'Verbena': Transall and DC8 aircraft transported military equipment and Moroccan soldiers to confront the Katangans. The 1st RPIMA from Bayonne and the 13th RDP from Dieuze, which were the regiments that provided Action troops for SDECE, served as reconnaissance forces.

The SDECE report on the talks at Ourgla between the Katangans and the Russians proved to be accurate. On 13 May Colonel Robert Larzul, the military attaché in Kinshasa, and Colonel Yves Gras, Mobutu's military adviser, announced in Paris that 'Katangan gendarmes' had made a raid on the Shaba area. Europeans were taken hostage at Kolwezi. On the morning of 19 May 1978 a 'crisis meeting' was held in the Elysée, to which were summoned the General Staff, Jean-François Poncet, the Minister for Foreign Affairs, René Journiac, and, naturally, Alexandre de Marenches. Sensing that the President was on the point of giving the go-ahead to Operation 'Bonito', the head of SDECE tried to take the heat out of the situation. Negotiations appeared to be beginning in Belgium. In substance, Marenches said: 'The Belgian Minister for Foreign Affairs, Henri Simonet, has begun to negotiate with Jean Tschombe.'[21] And he gloomily muttered, when the green light was given for intervention: 'If we want to play soldiers we'll have the whole of Europe on our backs . . .'

The Legion parachuted down over Kolwezi. Colonel Erulin's 2nd REP, preceded by elements of the 13th RDP under Colonel Bichon, took control of the town of Shaba. Two hundred European hostages were found murdered. Had this taken place before the intervention by the paratroops or because of it? The controversy continues. What is certain is that, reversing its policy of the 1960s, France had definitively turned its back on the Katanga dissidents in order to support Mobutu, the man whom the United States had installed in power.

The final airborne operation in which SDECE was closely involved was carried out in the Central African Republic. Throughout 1979 René Journiac and the African 'brains trust' had been trying to bring about the retirement of Emperor Bokassa, discredited – yet again – because of his mass execution of schoolchildren. Moreover, SDECE, through the CIA, had learnt that Bokassa – then on a brief visit to Libya, which he would have liked to make his ally – would not hesitate, if need arose, to make public certain documents detailing the gifts that he had presented to French leaders. His fate was sealed.

During the night of 20–21 September 1979 a Transall plane of SDECE took off from Villacoublay. On board was David Dacko, a former minister of Bokassa and the man who had been chosen to supplant him. About 11 p.m. the aircraft landed at Libreville in Gabon. David Dacko dived into a Hercules plane, protected by a detachment of the 1st RPIMA. An hour and a half later he arrived at Bangui: Operation 'Barracuda' had begun. Men of Action Branch, dressed in civilian clothes, were present. Jacques Duchemin, a former adviser of Bokassa, and an 'honourable correspondent' of SDECE's African section, greeted him. To forestall any possible reaction by Bokassa, who was still visiting Gadaffi, SDECE even made the operation public through the Trans-Continental Press Agency (Agence Transcontinentale de Presse: ATP).[22] In the six hours following Dacko's arrival in

Bangui ATP was the first news agency to pull off an exclusive interview with the new head of state.

Bokassa then tried to enter France. He was held up at the air base of Evreux, to which he had been diverted: this aerodrome was frequently used by the special squadron of SDECE, the Mixed Air Group (GAM 56 'Vaucluse'). Finally exiled to the Ivory Coast, the former emperor and his family were to eke out an existence at Abidjan, under the safe guard of SDECE, before returning to France.

Meanwhile incredible scenes were taking place in Bangui. Under the control of Colonel Degenne, the leader of Operation 'Barracuda' (he was under the command of Jeannou Lacaze, the former head of Intelligence of SDECE, then commanding the 11th Paratroop Division), and of Colonel Mazza, the local military attaché, the archives of Berengo Palace were removed by the paratroops. Today we know that they contained important information concerning Bokassa's gifts of precious stones to prominent figures in France and elsewhere. Operation 'Barracuda' was to tear to pieces the closing period of the President's term of office. Were the 'leaks' from these documents partly the result of a confrontation between various groupings within SDECE? This has been said. It is true that the African section was beset by various troubles at the end of 1979. Analysts, case officers and heads of departments disagreed over whether ties should be developed exclusively with the most conservative countries. Many also muttered that the French secret service was being used for personal ends, rather than the benefit of the State.

Finally, and this has never been disclosed, Operation 'Barracuda' started a serious dispute between SDECE and the regiment attached to it, the 1st RPIMA. A member of SDECE's Action Branch stated:

The 1st RPIMA broke with SDECE after its setback in the Central African Republic. It had failed in its mission. It was supposed to bring David Dacko to power without the French being identified as the authors of the coup against Bokassa. Instead of this, we saw the paratroops parading as if it were Bastille Day . . . There was a system of 'dual command' within the 1st RPIMA. The colonel of the regiment was answerable only to his superiors in the 11th Parachute Division. But, parallel to this, the leader of the group was under Action Branch of SDECE, which was commanded by Colonel Grillot – and these troops were intended to be completely clandestine. Instead, the 'clandestine' soldiers had shown themselves in full daylight. Afterwards Action Branch took Dacko completely under its wing. Our men put on regular paratroop uniform. Nobody understood this[23].

Target: Gadaffi

On 5 August 1980, 'D-Day', the Tobruk garrison in Cyrenaica rose in revolt. The conspiracy, organized by the head of military security,

Commmandant Driss Chehaibi, against Gadaffi, seems rapidly to have fizzled out. The rumours were contradictory. However, in Tobruk, 'life follows its normal course, in the beautiful summer atmosphere', the JANA press agency announced. SDECE gave out that Gadaffi had been wounded in the shoulder by a bullet.[24] Considerable sections of the Army had allegedly attempted to topple the 'Horseman of the Desert', with the support of Libyan opposition movements in exile in Cairo and Tunis, and of foreign secret services. But it was soon learnt that order reigned and that the coup had utterly failed.

At the end of August Count Alain Gaigneron de Marolles, SDECE's Director of Intelligence, asked to be relieved of his responsibilities 'for technical reasons'. Colonel de Marolles, the fifth Director of Intelligence to resign since the arrival of Alexandre de Marenches, was naturally at the centre of the Libyan affair. But it was not so much the failure in itself that explained his eviction. He had not been forgiven for having mounted the operation in direct collaboration with the Elysée, to the great wrath of the director of SDECE.

As early as 1974 the French secret service had considered the 'destabilization' of the Libyan leader. Alexandre de Marenches broached the matter with his counterpart William Colby, the head of the CIA. But the Americans were reluctant. For them Gadaffi was not yet 'the brains behind international terrorism'. SDECE therefore went it alone.[25]

In the summer of 1977 it launched its first operation. Its leader even then was Colonel de Marolles, but in his capacity as head of Action branch. He was supported by a great expert in Arab affairs, Colonel Charles de Lignières. In collusion with Hosni Mubarak, who controlled Egyptian intelligence, SDECE helped to form in Cairo the National Democratic Union, led by Mahmoud El Moghrebi, the first head of the Libyan government immediately after the seizure of power by Gadaffi in 1969. In July guerrilla warfare broke out on the frontier between Egypt and Libya. From Egypt Action Branch coordinated commando raids against the Libyans. It was a complete failure.

In Saudi Arabia late in 1979, Mecca was besieged by Muslim fundamentalists 'manipulated from abroad'. The Saudi Minister of the Interior, Nayef Ben Abdul Aziz, summoned his friend Alexandre de Marenches to the rescue. A team from SDECE, led by Colonel Genest Gillier, and another from the Intervention Group of the Gendarmerie Nationale (Groupement d'Intervention de la Gendarmerie Nationale: GIGN), under Captain Paul Barril, ensured the 'recapture' of the holy city in circumstances that remain obscure.

At the beginning of 1980 an uprising in Gafsa endangered the regime of the 'Supreme Tunisian Commander', Habib Bourguiba. It was bloodily put down. The mysterious 'Colonel Bruno' – in fact, Georges Grillot, the new head of SDECE's Action Branch – was sent to the scene. In this feverish atmosphere numerous attacks in Europe were laid at the door of Gadaffi, in particular, the murder of several of his opponents living in exile. SDECE, which can be diplomatic when it chooses, sent a senior officer to Tripoli in June 1980 to warn the the Libyan leader's cousin, Saif Kadaf-Adam, the head of Libya's secret services, that Paris would not tolerate an increase in acts of terrorism in France.

Finally, SDECE prepared for a full-scale operation. Colonel de Marolles, who had become Director of Intelligence Branch, received the go-ahead from the President's Office. His plan consisted of various preparatory psychological manoeuvres: a rumour about an attack on Gadaffi by June; manoeuvres against Libyan interests in Malta, which were carried out in conjunction with the British SIS and credit for which was claimed by a mysterious 'Maltese Liberation Front'. What was important (in this respect de Marolles tried out the same approach with the Afghan resistance) was to federate the various movements of Libyan exiles, and even to set up a provisional government in exile under Gadaffi's Minister of Foreign Affairs, whom SDECE hoped to rally to the cause.

But were the contacts established by the French secret services reliable? In the days that followed the failure of the coup, the leader of the mutiny started by the 9th Brigade of the Libyan Army at Tobruk, Commandant Chehaibi, was variously given out as 'killed', 'made prisoner', 'engaged in organizing a pocket of resistance', and, finally as being 'in exile in Cairo'. What was the reason for the debacle? The East German secret services, who allegedly participated in putting down the revolt, were also supposed to have 'bugged' the place where the conspirators were meeting.[26] Such an explanation hardly satisfied the general directorate of SDECE. As in the Nasser operation 20 years before, ill-fortune attended these plots, which were carefully worked out but too sophisticated. Far from striking at the front, they drove their adversary back to the last ditch.

In itself the failure was pardonable. Marolles fell because he maintained a relationship with the Elysée that short-circuited the chain of command; and this after he had undertaken, as head of Action Branch, to use his paratroops to retrieve the diamond archives of Bokassa at Bangui. Having been dismissed, and then a year later promoted to the rank of reserve brigadier-general, Count de Marolles was able to retire comfortably to his country house in Fercé in order to put down on paper his apocalyptic theories.[27]

15

Mitterrand's 'Specials'

It was February 1981. The base of Aspretto, near Ajaccio in Corsica, which housed the Frogman Training Centre (Centre d'Instruction de Nageurs de Combat: CINC), had smartened itself up to welcome its boss, Colonel Georges Grillot. As the head of Action Branch, he was coming to inspect the sailors of SDECE. He was a crusty but popular commanding officer. A former NCO at the Strasbourg School, after two tours of duty in Indo-China Georges Grillot had set up in Algeria the 'Commandos Georges', specialists in the struggle against subversion. Having been placed at the head of Action Branch by Alexandre de Marenches, he had certainly restored dynamism to the branch.

But Georges Grillot had not come to Aspretto that morning to speak to his men about new underwater techniques. His speech was to be political. In the secret services this was rare – sufficiently so for officers and NCOs to listen attentively to their superior officer. 'He came to tell us that our service was under grave threat,' an officer of Action Branch stated, 'that the Left was undoubtedly going to come to power. For him, this signified war. We had to carry out a scorched earth policy and leave nothing behind for them. Our "honourable correspondents" would become "sleepers". As for us, we should leave.' To completely convince his audience of the reality of the threat, Georges Grillot added that he had recently met General Jeannou Lacaze, the chief of the Army general staff, in order to explain his point of view. Apparently Lacaze had put up no objection.

Among the frogmen there was consternation. These were hardened soldiers, but they had fought in battles outside France and were scarcely accustomed to fighting 'the enemy within'. Moreover, certain NCOs clearly tended to favour the Left. They had been recruited into CINC for their physical qualities,[1] and because they had no political affiliations. They did not intend to become the mercenaries of any particular camp. In SDECE as a whole there were numerous agents who did not share the disgruntlement of their leaders. As soon as Grillot had left, some of the frogmen went to lodge a protest with Louis Dillais, the commanding officer of CINC. They received an icy welcome. The same indifference was shown by

Commandant Alain Mafart, the second-in-command. These officers were openly astounded that men of Action Branch could be prey to such soul-searching. From then onwards at Aspretto everybody awaited the result of the elections with a certain anxiety. On the evening of 10 May, when François Mitterrand was elected, there was no merrymaking among the leading ranks of the CINC.

If there was no celebration at the victory of the Socialist candidate, there were no resignations either in the days that followed. The 'Great Silent One' (the Army) remained mute. The accession to power of Charles Hernu reassured the military. This was why he had been appointed. The new Minister of Defence launched no large-scale reforms. The men of the 'ancien régime', including the three chiefs of staff, remained in their posts.

In Action Branch Colonel Georges Grillot himself did not give up his duties, as he had announced he would. Loyal to his post, he wished to try to safeguard what he considered to be the interests of the service. In all the offices of Action Branch, it was a time for cleaning up. The most compromising archives were burnt, particularly those that concerned spying on political parties or trade unions. More seriously, some of the technical reports of Action Branch were also destroyed. Officers in the branch were given the task of testing the protection of 'sensitive' military installations. Mock attacks on the base of Ile Longue, at Brest, the citadel of the French strategic force, had been organized on several occasions by SDECE, and had revealed grave defects in the area of security. These very useful exercises then served as object lessons for the instruction of officers in all the services.

No matter: all this had to disappear and not be handed over to the socialists. The Action Branch leaders also got rid of those officers who did not share their ideas. At Aspretto alone, 12 out of 34 NCOs had to leave.[2] In their offices the senior officers of CINC were to retain for several months – as an ultimate challenge – the portrait of Valéry Giscard d'Estaing that hung on the wall. Action Branch was not reconciled to the change, as its new leaders quickly learnt.

A Four-Man Committee of Socialists

For two decades the Socialists had been kept out of power. As the years went by, the former militants of the SFIO (Socialist Party) had disappeared from the key posts in the machinery of state. More than any other service, SDECE had been affected by this phenomonon. After the Ben Barka affair the French secret services had, moreover, been detached from the Hôtel Matignon and placed under the Ministry of Defence. The civilian agents of SDECE, often former members of the Resistance, and among whom the Socialists could count numerous friends, had gradually been replaced by military personnel.

Socialist leaders such as François Mitterrand no longer had any information about the world of intelligence. They listened, as did everyone else, to the rumours that circulated about these services. The Delouette affair, in which the CIA had for a time suspected SDECE of protecting drug trafficking, was still present in everybody's mind when Communists and Socialists sat down at the negotiating table to discuss a programme for government. From the outset the Communist Party, which ever since 1945 had been denouncing the existence of SDECE, proposed its abolition. The Socialists acquiesced without quite knowing what they were doing. On 27 June 1972, the Common Programme of the Socialist and Communist Parties was made public. It was under the heading 'Police' that one had to look for the passage concerning SDECE. It read: 'The criminal investigation department will be attached to the Ministry of Justice. The secret police organizations will be wound up. SDECE will be abolished.'

A few in the completely new Socialist Party set up at Epinay were indignant at the 'poverty' of such a text. They desired far-reaching reforms in the secret services, but did not believe that France could deprive itself overnight of the instrument of its Intelligence organization. But it was not until a Defence Committee was set up within the Socialist Party that the voice of this handful of 'realist' socialists was heard.[3]

In 1976 a small group was set up to reflect upon these questions. François de Grossouvre, during the 1950s a member of SDECE under the alias 'Monsieur Leduc', who had met François Mitterrand ten years later during a trip to China, was in charge of its work. He benefited from the valuable assistance of Louis Mouchon, who had just left the secret services after having spent over 20 years at Tourelles barracks. Charles Hernu and Jean-François Dubos, his adviser, also attended the meetings, which were held at the home of Louis Mouchon near the Esplanade des Invalides. On two occasions these experts submitted reports to Mitterrand. In their first review, the authors put forward a scheme for a reform of the secret services that would call upon people with 'open minds' about politics, economics and technology. Louis Mouchon, the author of the first report, wrote:

The structure of the world's intelligence services is identical. Differences in efficiency are dependent on financial and material resources, the quality of the agents, their love of their profession, and the ideology and faith that inspires them. SDECE structures have never been radically changed; mini-reforms have consisted in transferring a few senior officials and in switching the code numbers given the different services. If one assesses the efficiency of an intelligence service using the yardstick of the financial resources made available to it by government, France is the country among the Great Powers that spends the least (the CIA budget has been 150 to 200 times larger than that of SDECE, depending upon the period under consideration). When France was a member of NATO, SDECE was practically a creature of the CIA as regards its material and technical resources, its choice of objectives, and its possession of modern devices for speedy deciphering of documents in code and rapid translation from Asiatic and other difficult languages. It must be said frankly that intelligence regarding the Eastern bloc and China coming from SDECE sources was nowhere near as valuable as that obtained by the United States, Great Britain and the Federal German Republic.[4]

Was this a pessimistic view? Doubtless to some extent it was. Louis Mouchon, one of the political experts in SDECE, had been shocked by the massive influx of military personnel after the Ben Barka affair. He considered that many of them were not capable of carrying out intelligence work because of their lack of training. The second report of the Mouchon group, which, like the previous one, was handed over personally to François Mitterrand, aimed, predictably, to remedy this state of affairs. The Socialists set as their objective the splitting off of SDECE from the Armed Services Ministry. 'A body of this importance,' they said, 'can only come under the Elysée or the Matignon; all operations in progress, however minor they may be, should receive the approval of the head of state. An inter-ministerial control commission ought to exercise authority over all the secret services.' Such a 'demilitarization' would give dynamism to the services by allowing more civilians to be recruited from the industrial and scientific world. When François Mitterrand came to power, he attached François de Grossouvre to his office as his adviser, but he also listened to other experts who did not belong to the Socialist Party. All, or almost all, wished SDECE to be hived off from the Ministry of Defence.

Pierre Marion, or a Taste for the Theatrical

The telephone rang in a house in Washington. It was 5 p.m. there, and midnight in Paris. Pierre Marion, director of SNIAS for North America, answered it. He was just about to leave for a cocktail party for the small French community. 'Pierre, you must return to Paris immediately. I cannot tell you anything over the telephone.' Pierre Marion hesitated. Charles Hernu, the newly appointed Minister of Defence, was insistent.

The second act took place during the Le Bourget Air Show, some days later, at the beginning of June. It was there, among the military planes, that Charles Hernu officially invited Pierre Marion to become head of the French secret services. For this Polytechnicien whose whole career had been spent in aircraft companies, the offer was an attractive one. The world of secrecy had always tempted him. Pierre Marion loved anything theatrical. In Washington he acted regularly in the amateur company that the French colony there had established. From Molière to Feydeau, his repertory was abundant. Where had he acquired his taste for cynical soliloquies? 'In the secret services,' replied those in the know.

Indeed Pierre Marion was no stranger to SDECE. An engineer from Marseilles, he joined Air France in 1942, and slowly climbed the ranks of the hierarchy. This was the position until 1963, when he was suddenly appointed the company's representative in East Asia and the Pacific. At about that time he was recruited to the Secret Services. His address in Tokyo became a rendezvous for French intelligence. After his appointment to the directorship of SDECE, Colonel Michel Garder paid repeated tribute to the qualities of this former 'honourable correspondent'.[5]

Upon his return to Paris Pierre Marion was appointed Deputy Director-General of Air France, responsible for commercial matters. From this time onwards he was often in the company of Charles Hernu. He had known him during the period of the Fourth Republic. The Minister of Defence was then deputy for the Le Bourget constituency, and Pierre Marion was working in the town for Air France. They had campaigned side by side in the Convention for Republican Institutions, a socialist group founded by François Mitterrand. But Pierre Marion had no great taste for politics. He had often taken them up, but had always abandoned them. In the tumultuous post-Gaullist era he had linked up for a short while with the Centrist group around Jean-Jacques Servan-Schreiber. The adventure ended in fiasco.

Pierre Marion saw his hopes of becoming Director-General of Air France vanishing. He took off for other fields, and in 1977 joined SNIAS. Two years later he was in Washington. The change of government in 1981 opened wide to him the portals of Tourelles HQ. Tall and still athletic in his sixties, the newcomer certainly possessed the necessary physique for the job. This hot-tempered man, with a liking for theatrical gestures, did not lack backbone. And he needed it if he meant to lay claim to the leadership of a body where it was easy to be distracted by factional in-fighting, and the constant buzz of false rumours and of genuine plots.

Above all, however, Pierre Marion lacked political support. He was not President Mitterrand's man; he hardly knew François de Grossouvre, the faithful counsellor at the Elysée. Pierre Marion was not unaware that, at an earlier stage, the head of state had asked Alexandre de Marenches to stay on. For health reasons, he had turned down the offer. In the government Pierre Marion had only one friend, but an influential one: by getting one of his protégés appointed, Charles Hernu had succeeded in keeping SDECE under his own control. The tie of freemasonry that joined them was a salient factor in the case, because a close acquaintance of Charles Hernu, Guy Penne, was also appointed to the Elysée, to take care of African affairs. He too was a freemason, a former member of the Council of the Grand Orient Lodge of France. The three men intended to use their connections on every continent to coordinate the clandestine activities of France.

François Mitterrand, who had finally let himself be won over by Charles Hernu, received the new head of the secret services at the Elysée. Their discussion lasted two hours. The president gave the director of SDECE very detailed instructions: as a matter of priority, to focus intelligence work upon the Eastern bloc, to unmask Soviet 'moles' in France, to dismantle terrorist networks, to improve the 'yield' of industrial intelligence and, finally, to eliminate from SDECE those senior officials who might be tempted to obstruct the new French policy. The task was immense. Without any additional financial or technical resources, Pierre Marion tackled it with great zeal.

The Time of Reform

A change of acronym was the ritual symbol of any reform in depth. Pierre Marion did not break with the tradition. On 4 April 1982 SDECE vanished, giving way to the new General Directorate of External Security (Direction Générale de la Sécurité Extérieure: DGSE). By a decree published in the *Journal officiel* the specific tasks of the French secret services were also spelt out.[6] From then onwards DGSE was no longer allowed to operate on national territory. The text was clear:

The General Directorate of External Security has as its mission, on behalf of the government and in close collaboration with the other bodies involved, the research and exploitation of intelligence concerning the security of France, as well as the detection and prevention outside the national boundaries of espionage activities aimed against French interests, so as to forestall their consequences. In order to carry out its tasks DGSE is especially instructed to maintain the necessary links with the other services or bodies concerned; to carry out, within the limits of its functions, any operation that may be entrusted to it by the government; and to submit intelligence syntheses that become available to it.

This clarification was essentially aimed at a clear-cut definition of DGSE's areas of responsibility in relation to the Directorate for the Safety of the National Territory (Direction de la Sûreté du Territoire), which came under the Minister of the Interior. In de Marenches's time the SDECE Counter-Espionage Branch had very frequently operated in France, so provoking numerous clashes with the police services. The new text spelt out the prerogatives of each. From the moment of his arrival at Tourelles barracks Pierre Marion also undertook more concrete reforms. Relying skilfully on the military, he scarcely heeded the work of the small Socialist group, in which he had never participated. His preoccupation was to restore order and to keep matters under control. To his collaborators he occasionally gave the impression of an excessively short-tempered and authoritarian captain of industry.

First of all he got rid of the closest collaborators of Alexandre de Marenches: René Dalmas, the Polytechnicien, Yves Beccuau, the psycho-technical adviser, and Michel Roussin. General René Crignola, who occupied the post of Director of Intelligence within the Research division, also left SDECE. In all, under various pretexts, almost 50 agents of the 'Firm' were asked to resign for 'failing in their duty'.

This purge was accompanied by considerable changes in structure. Pierre Marion proceeded to carry out a complete reorganization. The major directorates – Research, Counter-Espionage, and Action Branch – were now placed under a General Directorate. This put an end to the excessive independence of the departments, which had gradually turned into fiefdoms.

Around the Director-General three major branches were linked together: the Operations Directorate, in the hands of Colonel Codet and Commandant Ricard, his deputy; the General Directorate, with three subsections (personnel, control and security); and finally a small group, 'Planning, Forecasting and Evaluation', entrusted to sub-prefect Arsène Lux. This last structure was, more particularly, resposible for drawing up syntheses directly usable by the government. For this purpose it had to intensify research into scientific and technological intelligence, which until then had (improperly) been neglected in favour of more strictly political intelligence. Furthermore, Pierre Marion also took on a scientific adviser so as personally to follow up this line of enquiry.

The General Directorate had a supervisory role over the four great functional divisions of SDECE: Research, Action Branch, Counter-Espionage, and Staffing. General Jacques Sylla Fouilland and Colonel Jean-Albert Singland, who respectively held the posts of Director of Research and head of Counter-Espionage, were brought into the General Directorate by Pierre Marion. They directly looked after a small section focused on 'Russian disinformation' that the Director had set up in agreement with the Americans.

The structuring flowed logically from the new directions laid down for DGSE. The Socialist government, perpetuating an old custom of the SFIO, established as its priority infiltration into countries of the Eastern bloc. This was not only to counter them, but also to obtain intelligence of a kind that for years had been grievously lacking. Counter-espionage traditionally obtained such mediocre results that the former heads of the secret services had gradually lost interest in this sector. On the other hand, Pierre Marion reinforced it considerably, since the number of counter-espionage agents grew during his time from 250 to 350. There was a will to 'penetrate' the Eastern bloc, but also a desire to succeed (finally) in 'manipulating' some terrorist networks reportedly based in Budapest or Prague. The restructuring appeared all the more necessary because, under Alexandre de Marenches, a dozen officers operating in the Eastern bloc countries had been abruptly transferred, on suspicion – not always unjustified – of maintaining connections with communist services in that area. At the end of de Marenches's time in office there were no French agents left behind the Iron Curtain. For instance, during the State of Siege in Poland, the French secret service had to send officers on foot to cross the border and investigate the mood of the Polish population. In fact these officers were almost captured.

Other measures followed. The South Africa station under Colonel Hamon was closed down on the orders of Pierre Marion. Here too it was a matter of adapting the organization of DGSE to the new government policy. In order to make it more of an operational unit, Action Branch became the Action Division. It was broken up into three specialized entities: one whose task was air support; a second to train the commandos; a third to undertake sea missions. Training was still carried out at Cercottes under the direction of Colonels Charrier[7] and Saint-Gest, and also at Aspretto, Beuil (Alpes-Maritimes) and the fort of Noisy-le-Sec on the outskirts of Paris. At the head of the division Colonel Grillot, who never failed to voice his opposition to the newly appointed team, was soon replaced. Colonel Jean-Pol Desgrées du Lou assumed temporary command.

Finally, Pierre Marion pleaded the cause of his service at the Elysée in order to procure fresh funds. Up to 1981, none of the SDECE records sections had used information technology. One by one they had settled for hiring computers to help with the management of the 'Firm'. However, the new director launched a three-year 'information technology plan', designed to computerize the principal basic records, including those devoted to 'sources'. Although it was behind the times by several years in this field, DGSE thus prepared to catch up with its American, German and British counterparts.

African Thorns

President Mitterrand had gone to sleep with a *coup d'état* on his hands. When he woke up, the skies were clear once more. It had only been a false rumour. And this made the occupant of the Elysée pose a few questions about the credibility of the French secret services.

At 6.23 p.m. on 28 October 1981, an AFP dispatch announced that a column of Libyan armour had just entered Ndjamena. The president of Chad, Goukouni Oueddei, had apparently disappeared. The news was taken up by Radio-France International, and the French troops stationed on the Cameroon frontier were placed on a state of alert by their colonel. Acyl Ahmat, a pro-Libyan, had allegedly attempted to take control of the Chad capital.

The Elysée asked Pierre Marion to provide further information. From Tourelles barracks, the directorate of DGSE attempted to contact its agents in Ndjamena. It was impossible to reach either of them. Today an officer in the secret services laughingly admits: 'Espionage is not always carried out in earnest. One of our agents was on leave at the time, and the other was out of the capital.' In short, Pierre Marion was unable to offer the slightest scrap of information to the political authorities. Finally, Pierre Ricard, the future ambassador to Chad, who had just spent the day with Goukouni, informed

Paris shortly before midnight that everything was calm in Ndjamena. After an investigation, the head of DGSE, in whom the events had provoked a memorable fit of anger, concluded that the alarmist item of news had come from a confidential publication, *La Lettre d'Afrique*, which was linked to certain Gaullist networks. From here it was only a step to the idea that certain agents had tried to play a dirty trick on the French government.

Pierre Marion easily took that step when a second affair blew up, this time in the Central African Republic. Already there had been some delay in informing the Elysée of the transfer of power in that territory on 1 September 1981. But this time it was more serious. 'Rebel' officers attempted to topple President Kolingba in favour of an opponent, Ange Patassé. Officially Paris gave its support to General Kolingba, and the instructions issued by Pierre Marion were in accord with this. But, there again, as observers were to discover after the event, the French military presence in Bangui had seen fit to take initiatives without informing their government. The Central African Republic's police even went so far as to show their mistrust by searching the house of Colonel Faure, the French military attaché in Bangui. Another DGSE officer, Colonel Mansion, was accused of playing a double game. François de Grossouvre at the Elysée made praiseworthy efforts to establish the good faith of these agents, but he was wasting his time. At Figuera, in Corsica, a French military plane transporting equipment to Central Africa was grounded by an act of sabotage. Who other than DGSE agents would have dared to risk such an operation, under the very nose of Action Branch? The French secret services seemed to be acting just as they pleased.

In the Four Corners of the World

Every time that he left the fort of Noisy-le-Sec, the subterranean training centre of Action Branch, 'Michel' stifled a smile. Just opposite Action Branch HQ was a hostel for immigrants, the 'Sonacotra'. And the senior officials of SDECE regularly checked the registers in that building, which housed a large number of immigrants of Arab origin.

In recent months the surveillance had been reinforced, particularly since the day in 1982 when France had declared war on the Syrian secret services. On 22 April an Opel Kadett had been blown up in front of the buildings of the weekly paper *Al Wattan al Arabi*, in the Rue Marbeuf in Paris. This attack by the Syrian secret services against opponents of President Assad's regime was deplored by the French government. Immediately the 'anti-terrorist war council', which included all the heads of the security services, met at the Ministry of the Interior. Two concrete measures were undertaken: to eliminate, if possible, one of the terrorist leaders, and to reactivate the old French networks, which were still in place in Beirut and Damascus.

Very early in the morning two days later 'Michel' left Noisy, which was less closely watched by agents of opposing powers than the headquarters of Tourelles. His mission was to reach Beirut via Cyprus in order to investigate terrorist ramifications in Lebanon. The same morning a small group of commandos slipped discreetly out of the Action Branch training centre and left for Madrid. On 27 April 1982 Hassan Dayoub, the Syrian cultural attaché in the Spanish capital, who was known to have organized numerous attacks against opponents in Europe, avoided a hail of bullets on his way home. The diplomat-cum-spy narrowly escaped death. Had they missed him, or had it been a warning? 'From now on,' said a French senior official in confidence, 'we shall reply like this to all terrorist attacks.'

A similar offensive policy, approved by President Mitterrand, was carried out in Chad. Whilst in the desert nearly 3,000 French soldiers were confronting detachments of Gadaffi's Islamic Legion and the troops of Goukouni Oueddei, Charles Hernu authorized SDECE to recruit some 40 mercenaries, commanded by René Dulac, a veteran of the Comoros expedition. The objective was to mount guerrilla operations behind the Libyan lines. Liaising with Colonel Monti, attached to the Chad armed forces, these men succeeded in cutting off Gadaffi's columns from their supply zones for some weeks.

Nor was DGSE idle in Africa. After much hesitation, the French government had decided to resume its aid to the anti-Marxist guerrillas in Angola, led by Dr Jonas Savimbi. Yet at the beginning of his term of office, François Mitterrand had decided to cut off supplies to him. The Moroccan and Senegalese secret services had then taken over from France. (Most of the UNITA officers are now trained in the military schools of Morocco.) But after the recent successes of UNITA on the ground, Paris seemed once again to have become more 'realistic', believing that it was now possible to inflict a humiliating defeat on the 'Progressive' Angolan forces, which were strongly supported by the USSR and Cuba. Aid was restored, and DGSE experts were sent to work on the spot.

Farther afield, in Asia, DGSE was once again plunged into the Cambodian maelstrom, still somewhat timidly, but nevertheless significantly. The French secret services once again played the Sihanouk card, with the idea of building up a third force. However, the French support remained insufficient if the former head of state was to take over the leadership of the Cambodian opposition. In fact, he did not have at his disposal forces that were large or well-organized enough to compete against those of the Khmer Rouge, which were supported by China.

For its part, the CIA criticized French actions. According to reports drawn up in 1984 the best option was a permanent conflict between the Vietnamese occupation forces and the Khmer resistance, with neither party having the upper hand. It would be a running sore that would prolong the Chinese–Russian struggle. The dilemma is enlightening. The CIA thought in terms of geo-strategy: William Casey, CIA's director asked himself: 'How can the varieties of communism be checked?' Pierre Lacoste, of DGSE, retorted: 'How can the resistance of the Khmer peoples be supported so as to bring about a return to an independent Cambodia?'

It was the same situation in Afghanistan, where, after Régis Debray or General Jeannou Lacaze had visited Peshawar, on the Pakistan–Afghan border, the DGSE in its turn lent logistic support to certain units of the Afghan Mujahedin resisting the Red Army.

To some of those who voted for François Mitterrand the move would seem paradoxical. But he intended to show the superpowers that his secret services counted on the international chess board.

The Director-General's Downfall

'I had been given the task of reorganizing the secret services in accordance with new objectives. I did so, but it was very plain that immediate results could not be achieved. I still do not know why I was dismissed,' Pierre Marion complained to his friends.[8] He was clearly not satisfied with his new post as chairman of the Paris Airports Authority, which the government had offered him after he left the service. He was an ambitious man. This fanatical worker – up to 14 hours a day – had done his utmost in his attempt to restructure the DGSE.

And at one stroke, in a fit of temper, François Mitterrand had sacked him. The President's Office had thanked him for his brilliant qualities as a reorganizer, but nobody was fooled. Even Charles Hernu was unable to save his friend. There were many reasons for this. Firstly, there were purely personal grounds. The personality of Pierre Marion was much discussed at the Elysée. The President did not care very much for this Polytechnicien who embarked on flights of geo-political analysis in his presence, such as to irritate any prince of the Fifth Republic.

But, above all, Pierre Marion was the victim of his own will to carry out reforms. He kept the secret services on a short rein. And in trying to control them too rigidly and make himself too prominent by introducing extreme centralization, he laid himself open to attack. By concentrating all power in himself, he made it inevitable that he would be blamed for any errors. The thorns of Africa had pierced him.

Furthermore, the Elysée declared itself unhappy with the results achieved by DGSE in the struggle against terrorism. The secret services were ill-prepared and had shown themselves incapable of competing in this field with other police bodies, whether it was the Directorate for the Surveillance of the National Territory (DST) or Renseignements Généraux (RG). At the meetings of the Inter-ministerial Committee for the Fight Against Terrorism, presided over by Secretary of State Joseph Franceschi, the Director of DGSE usually arrived empty-handed. Doubtless too much was expected of a service that was not geared to this kind of mission. It was no longer a matter of attempting to penetrate the organizations of hostile states, but of forecasting the possible operations of groups scattered throughout the country. Secret service agents were wont to say: 'It is difficult to infiltrate terrorist networks that are very tenuous, mobile both in time and space, very scattered, and capable of sudden disappearances. To take only one example, to disentangle Shiite connections in the Middle East requires long and minute preparation, as well as luck, and DGSE has still not mastered this.'

Those at the pinnacle of the state were also surprised by the poor quality of intelligence about the USSR: usually DGSE came up with nothing more than a bunch of commonplaces. This was a glaring fault.[9] But could this long-standing defect in the secret services be imputed to Pierre Marion? It had grown worse under Alexandre de Marenches, and the new director had wished to remedy it. When Charles Hernu went to Mortier HQ to witness the formal transfer of power from Pierre Marion to Admiral Lacoste, the minister made no mistake about apportioning blame. Speaking to senior officials assembled in the courtyard of DGSE, the Minister of Defence took a threatening tone: 'Discipline is as necessary as unity, and it is a condition of unity. Hierarchy must and will be respected. To obey and to be accountable, these are the pillars of your organization's obligations, and these imperatives hold for everybody, whether civilian or military.'

The message seemed to have struck home. After the arrival on the scene of Admiral Lacoste, who immediately recruited as his Director of Intelligence General Roger Emin, the former military attaché in Rome, DGSE settled down again. It was the first time since 1945 that a sailor had been appointed to head the secret services. With the Greenpeace scandal he was to meet the biggest storm of his career.

Mission 'Satanic':
'Sink the Rainbow Warrior'

Even for the crew of an F38 sloop classified as top class, the southern hemisphere winter is harsh round about the Tasman Sea. On that day, 22 June 1985, a gusty north wind sweeping along at 30 knots was whipping up waves 9 feet high. The four men on course for New Zealand in the *Ouvea*, a yacht they had hired in New Caledonia at an exorbitant price (90,000 French francs), were not on a pleasure cruise. Their orders were to keep a rendezvous. Where? It remains a mystery. It was not the kind of mission that is recorded in a ship's log.

On that same day, two other 'tourists', Alain-Jacques and Sophie-Claire Turenge, aged 36 and 34 respectively, who apparently spoke only broken English and passed themselves off as Swiss, landed at Auckland airport. They drove immediately to the Travel Lodge Hotel. On the following day, another Frenchman, Jean-Louis Dorman, arrived in Auckland from Paris, via Los Angeles. He put up at the South Pacific Hotel. From room 819, on the eighth floor, he had a view over the whole of Auckland harbour. He could see precisely the spot where the Greenpeace ship *Rainbow Warrior* was soon to berth.

Let us go back to our seafarers. Once through the reefs and the waves breaking on the harbour bar, the *Ouvea* finally cast anchor in the tiny creek of Parengarenga. It was an isolated spot on the northern headland of North Auckland Island, where only a few Maoris live. On that day they hardly ventured out of their huts on the heathland swept by the storm. The scene was deserted, and somewhat sinister.

There were of course no customs men in sight. The dirty weather had prevented the Customs and Excise launches from venturing into these waters. Moreover, there are regulations prohibiting vessels from approaching New Zealand by way of this extreme northerly and inhospitable coastline. A French yacht had broken up on the rocks at the beginning of 1985.

It was only three days later that the *Ouvea* and its crew, which really consisted of Roland Vergé, a senior sergeant-major at the Frogman Training Centre (CINC) in Aspretto, Corsica, Sergeant-Majors Andries and Barcelo, also from the Centre, and Xavier Maniguet, a doctor, went through customs. They had gone southwards down the coast to Opua. On that day – 25 June – the incurious customs officers noticed nothing unusual on board. Much later they were to tell the New Zealand investigators that the yacht had a sophisticated navigation system, of a kind installed on quite a few craft of this type, which worked through the Satnav satellite. On the other hand they had been a little surprised to see that the ship's radio was supplemented by a quartz transceiver of 8 megahertz, thus allowing very long distance communications – with Paris, for example.

Mission 'Satanic' was set to begin.[1] On 29 June the men from the *Ouvea* hired a red Ford Orion from Avis. The day before, Dormand, the tourist, had rented a camping van from Horizon Holidays. A few days later, the Turenges, in their turn, hired a Toyota camping van. From then on an astonishing game began.

We can now reveal that the crew of the *Ouvea* had been assigned the task of transporting to New Zealand the bombs that were to sink the *Rainbow Warrior*, as well as their Zodiac dinghy, together with the necessary diving equipment. The Turenges, for their part, were to organize the getaway. As for the mysterious Dormand, he was in fact Louis-Pierre Dillais, the head of the Centre at Aspretto, who had come in person to supervise operations. He kept an eye on the slightest detail. In under a fortnight he was to cover a distance of 2,424 kilometres on an island that was less than 300 kilometres in length.

On 5 July the Turenge couple went to Paihia. Alain and Sophie had rented for two days Room 12 in the Beachcomber, a motel opposite the spot where the *Ouvea* had cast anchor a few days earlier. From their windows they could observe the movements of the few boats that ventured out to sea. For the rest of the time they struck the hotel staff as very sociable. They liked to engage in conversation with other guests passing through. A New Zealand policeman was to emphasize later in an explanatory note for his superiors that in this area any other attitude would have appeared suspicious. There people easily struck up an acquaintance. Sophie made only one slight slip, which the lady who owned the hotel was to remember. Since she wanted to do some washing, she asked in perfect English for some explanation as to how the machine worked. This was astonishing on the part of a tourist who pretended to have only a vague idea of the language of Shakespeare. This mistake was to be analysed several weeks later by the Auckland police. But we have not yet come to that point.

From Opua the members of the yacht's crew had gone to Whangarei, where they stayed in the Six Motel. On 6 July a meeting was arranged by telephone between the Turenges and the crew of the *Ouvea*. At 11.30 a.m. a witness was to notice near Hokianga a camping van similar to that of the Turenges parked beside another vehicle. The two teams met up again a few days later near the village of Kaiwaka. By now the Turenges had taken delivery of the Zodiac and the diving equipment. That still left the explosives.

The seamen had doubtless deposited them in a discreet spot in the north of the island. This is the only explanation for their trip among the reefs, where several times they had almost split their hull. The Bay of Islands is a desolate spot, the sort of wilderness smugglers dream of. In the 1970s it sheltered the local drug king nicknamed Mr Asia, who ended his days in prison. Over a thousand creeks are sheltered from prying eyes. On 23 and 24 June the *Ouvea* was moored in Kaourou Bay, far from civilization. It was there that the sailors concealed the explosives, near the little village of Kaitaia. There is one curious detail: the name Kaourou, which the police were later to find written in the logbook of the *Ouvea*, was completely unknown to New Zealanders. They thought it was a secret code used by the French agents. They finally discovered that the name figures on the charts of nineteenth-century whaling ships.

Who later retrieved the explosives? A witness from Kaitaia is certain that on 9 July at 6.30 a.m. he met a couple who were looking for a place to get a cup of coffee. Was it the Turenges? Nobody knows.

Only the essential element was now missing: the two frogmen who had been given the job of blowing up the *Rainbow Warrior*. On 7 July, the team in question landed at 8.15 a.m. on a flight from Tahiti. Sergeant-Major Jean C. and Captain Jean Luc K. were two experienced frogmen who had been rehearsing Operation 'Satanic' for a month in the Bay of Aspretto.[2] On the same day the Greenpeace ship returned to Auckland harbour, warmly welcomed by the supporters in the city. On the following day the last 'tourist' landed in Auckland, flying in from Tokyo. François Verlet had been given the task of inspecting the *Rainbow Warrior* before the final phase of the attack.[3]

On 10 July 1985, at 8 p.m., on board the environmentalist ship there was a noisy celebration for the birthday of Steve Sawyer, the international coordinator of the Greenpeace organization. The environmentalists had invited on board a young Frenchman who had happened to be passing by, François Verlet, a 'computer operator from Singapore'. About 9 p.m. the latter left the ship to catch his plane for Tahiti, which was taking off in two hours' time. A few minutes later the French secret agent was making a detailed report to Dillais in an Auckland parking lot. 'Steve Sawyer,' he said, 'is to leave the ship at 10.30 p.m. to give a lecture at Piha. The men on board the *Rainbow Warrior* will go to bed soon after. It's then that we can strike.'

Operation 'Satanic' entered the operational stage. The frogmen gave the following account of it:

On our mission we were instructed to avoid casualties at all costs. Thus the main bomb was to be placed on the side nearest the quay. As a safety measure, after we had dived in we were linked to each other by a strap one and a half metres long attached to our wrists. Thus in case of accident we could each save the other. And above all it meant that we couldn't lose each other. In night attacks one can never see more than two metres ahead. During the dive secret agents like us never use a torch. We were going to position the two explosive charges one after the other, joined together.

With my hand I felt the hull of the *Rainbow Warrior*. It was covered with slight growths, and small pieces of seaweed and some shells clung to it. The first bomb, the smaller one – mine – was placed on the rudder blade at the stern of the trawler. The senior man in the team always carries the lighter charge, if there are two of them, because he must concentrate on navigation. My mate fixed it against the driving shaft of the rudder. I tightened the straps. Then the control mechanism – O.K., it was fixed. The second charge had to be attached to the stabilizer on the side nearest the quay. From this mini-keel we measured out the ten strokes that took us up to engine-room level. I signalled to my mate that he could place his charge. He undid his straps and fixed the 15-kilogram bomb at the point we had selected. Whilst he was 'holding the baby' I proceeded to fix the straps and clamp them, then the control mechanism . . . I turned to my mate and gave the thumbs up. I set in motion the countdown for firing the main charge. Three hours' delay precisely. It was 8.50 p.m. We went back aft and set the second countdown mechanism to go off 60 seconds after the first, with the same delay. . . . 'Satanic' was well and truly under way; nothing could stop the course of destiny.[+]

Nothing, indeed. Destiny was to be of very ill omen for the French secret agents. Having regained the surface, the two French frogmen hastily dressed again and disappeared. They abandoned their equipment on the spot. This is the rule in the secret services. Another team, known as 'Surface Protection', is given the job of retrieving the equipment and disposing of it. It was there that the first setback occurred. Because of the numerous thefts committed in the Auckland yacht marina, the night watchmen had been ordered to keep their eyes peeled. Consequently, two of them, David Collins and Danny Feeny, on the evening of 10 July, noted down the registration number of a Toyota 4X4 whose movements appeared suspicious to them. It was of course the vehicle hired by the Turenges, who had been given the job of retrieving the equipment. At 9.30 p.m. the watchmen noticed one or two persons – the evidence differs as to the number of shapes made out on the beach – landing from a Zodiac craft and making towards the vehicle, carrying sacks.

Before vanishing in the Toyota 4X4, one of the two figures moored the rubber dinghy to a bollard, using no padlock and taking no other precautions. The watchmen were later to tell the investigators that they had been surprised at this, for the Zodiac was brand-new and ran a risk of being stolen. This was doubtless what the suspects were hoping for, concluded the New Zealand police: if there were no boat, there would be no evidence. All this was to be remembered two hours later when the first charge exploded on the hull of the *Rainbow Warrior*. Only 12 people were still on board, among them the captain, Peter Willox, and Fernando Pereira, the expedition's photographer. Awakened by the explosion of the first bomb, the men hurriedly left the ship. But the photographer then remembered that he had left his photographic gear on board. He had scarcely entered his cabin before the explosion of the second charge tipped the ship on its side. Fernando Pereira was killed on the spot. It was now a case of murder, something that the French secret services had not foreseen.

The New Zealand police then launched a thorough investigation. Superintendent Alan Galbraith, who was in charge of the enquiry, was an intelligent man. What is more, he was persistent. On the day after the attack, 11 July, the watchmen gave him the description of the Toyota they had seen on the quayside at Auckland. The police had not even time to send out a search notice. On the following day, 12 July, the Turenges turned up at the car-hire firm. The clerk tipped off Galbraith's men. This time the Turenges were caught in the net. They were not to escape from it.

Our two so-called tourists showed their Swiss passports, in the names of Sophie Frédérique Claire Turenge, maiden name Payot, born in Geneva in 1949, and Alain Jacques Turenge, born at Lancy in 1951. Immediately Galbraith sent off to Interpol to learn the source of these documents. The reply came two days later. The passports had been sold. The questioning began.

The men from the *Ouvea* were to have better luck. Questioned some days later at Norfolk, in Australia, the three men from Aspretto (Dr Maniguet had taken the extreme step of flying out), denied everything. The pleasure yachtsmen had done nothing on North Island that they needed to hide. They had even left many clues behind them. They had signed – using their false names, naturally – the visitor's book of a pizzeria at Whangarei, where they had dined on 29 June. They had added the cryptic comment: 'Will something else happen to us in New Zealand?' They had spent a lot of money. They had not been able to resist buying jogging trainers of a Canadian make, New Balance. This was a slip-up that was, for a while, to make them suspect: the New Zealand police said that they had detected the imprint of one of these shoes in the Zodiac. The travellers had also made female conquests. One of them even said to the investigators: 'Are you asking me where I was on a certain day at a certain time? Well, I'll let you into a secret: I was out after the ladies.' The police ended up by letting them go. Before vanishing completely – the secret services were to sink the boat and pick up their men[5] – the crew of the *Ouvea* could not resist playing a final practical joke: they gave their position as being close to the Ile des Pins in New Caledonia, which must have been incorrect because it was physically impossible.

The two frogmen who sank the ship remained on North Island for some time. At all costs they had to avoid being spotted. They went skiing, and then climbing. They finally left Auckland on 26 July under the very nose of the New Zealand police. As for Dillais, alias Dormand, he went off with a party of sportsmen to sail down the rapids on the Shotover River. Their leader was later to say that he thought he seemed 'a little tense'. Dillais was to leave Auckland only at the end of July.

In the meantime the New Zealand police were busy. The French secret services had compounded their mistakes. Firstly, there were the false passports of the Turenges, which were unusable. Then Galbraith's men found the oxygen bottles that had been left behind in the harbour. Finally, the British police informed them that Sergeant-Major Andries himself had bought the Zodiac boat in London, and that he did not speak a word of English. The New Zealanders were now convinced that it had been a French operation. In New Zealand public opinion demanded exemplary punishment.

In Paris too the atmosphere became more menacing. As early as 14 July one of the authors of this book, the journalist Roger Faligot, asked in the Sunday newspaper *Le Journal du Dimanche*: 'Was it the French secret services that carried out the attack on Greenpeace?' No one believed this at the time. It was too outlandish. As the days passed, however, the rumour became more persistent. On 28 July Roger Faligot returned to the attack, revealing that several months previously a 'mole' (Christine Cabon) had infiltrated Greenpeace. On 7 August the co-author of this book, Pascal Krop, in *L'Evénement du Jeudi* and another journalist in the weekly magazine *VSD*, prepared to publish fresh revelations about the involvement of the French secret services in the affair.[6] Immediately Prime Minister Laurent Fabius sent off dispatch riders, so anxious was he to read these papers before they were put on sale. At the Elysée Palace a crisis committee met under the chairmanship of François Mitterrand. The President asked his prime minister to throw light on the affair. A long-standing Gaullist, Bernard Tricot, a former secretary-general of the Elysée, was given the task of drawing up a detailed report within a fortnight.

On Monday, 25 August, journalists at the Matignon (the prime minister's Office) jostled one another as Bernard Tricot made his report public. On the whole, he exonerated the French government from all responsibility. 'All that I have heard and seen,' he said in his report, 'makes me certain that, at governmental level, no decision was taken to cause damage to the *Rainbow Warrior*.' The press was enormously disappointed. Bernard Tricot did not answer the questions that were put to him. Several days previously the links between the *Ouvea* and the Turenges had become known through the New Zealand investigators. In Auckland it was asserted that the two groups had met several times. 'Hypotheses, not certainties,' retorted the Tricot report. For the time being the matter rested there.

But the press continued its investigations.[7] It badgered the politicians to such an extent that Prime Minister Laurent Fabius asked Charles Hernu, his Defence Minister, for further details. 'Question marks persist. I have my doubts. I demand the truth.'

The moment of truth finally came on Tuesday, 17 September. Spread over four columns on its front page, the distinguished French newspaper

Le Monde, revealed: '*Rainbow Warrior* sunk by a third team of French military personnel.' According to the newspaper 'the attack may have been carried out by frogmen of the French Army'. On 20 September Charles Hernu, the Defence Minister, and Admiral Lacoste, the head of DGSE, were forced to resign. By sacrificing themselves in this way the two men saved the President politically. In fact there is no longer any doubt that François Mitterrand had personally been informed of the operation.[8]

What in fact really took place? In order fully to understand the development of this whole affair we must go back to the beginning of 1985. The military and civilian personnel, working in France at Villacoublay and in Melanesia at Mururoa, who make up the Directorate of the Centre for Nuclear Experimentation (Direction du Centre des Expérimentations Nucléaires: DIRCEN), were then in a ferment. The Army's Deuxième Bureau at Mururoa had passed on to them a very alarmist report: for the first time Soviet submarines had allegedly been identified during the series of French nuclear tests. Moreover, Charles Hernu was soon to send the submarine *Rubis* to warn off these 'strange passers-by'. What was more serious was that communist groups (two, in fact, the third having failed to live up to its promise) originating in Panama, had allegedly infiltrated the Greenpeace ships. Under the leadership of an American naval man suspected of being linked with the KGB (this emerged in the message from the Deuxième Bureau) the ships might be preparing a large-scale provocative operation. With the assistance of four fast Zodiac craft, civilians, notably members of the Polynesian independence movement would be landed on the atolls of Mururoa and Fangatofa. They would then announce that they had suffered exposure to radiation. This would be the pretext for a vast campaign to sensitize public opinion at the very moment when a festival of the Pacific arts, which was expected to be anti-French in tone, would be taking place in Tahiti.

In order to understand thoroughly what followed it is necessary to assess the mentality of the French military personnel in DIRCEN. Very conscious of their role and their importance, they considered themselves to be the guardians of the French nuclear deterrent force – as it were the vestal virgins of the national flame – and the ultimate guarantors of a genuinely independent defence policy.

They had had several brushes since 1970 with the Greenpeace organization, whose ships they had unceremoniously arrested, after having already suggested to Robert Galley, a former Defence Minister, that they should sink them. Greenpeace constituted in their eyes a kind of abominable synthesis of the forces of evil. Bearded environmentalists, often springing from Leftist organizations, and therefore part of the international subversion movement, could only be, wittingly or unwittingly, KGB agents, whilst those of the movement's leaders who were of 'Anglo-Saxon' origin clearly worked for US or British imperialism, which, with the complicity of the Australian and New Zealand pacifist movement, was seeking to sabotage the French nuclear defence effort.

In the minds of these military men, things were all of a piece: it was the same Soviet–British–American link-up that was attempting to rob France of New Caledonia by financing the FLNKS, the local independence movement, and by encouraging the Polynesian independence groups, and thereby seeking to banish the French from the Pacific. The consequence of this would be that their strike force would become inoperative and useless, because it could not carry out tests.

Among those around Admiral Fagès, the head of this celebrated DIRCEN organization and an intelligent and competent man, there was certainly confidence in Charles Hernu. He was a 'genuine nationalist', they said, who knew how to mollify the Army and who understood the importance of the French nuclear effort. But what could be said of those other socialists, who only a little while before had condemned the nuclear strike force and had shamelessly gone along with the environmentalist movements? Thus they remained watchful and mistrustful.

This was the climate that reigned when, at the beginning of January 1985, Admiral Fagès met Admiral Lacoste, the head of DGSE, and shared his grievances with him. He passed on the intelligence that he had received from the Deuxième Bureau, insisting on the gravity of the situation that the offensive by Greenpeace might spark off. He then accused the French intelligence services of being ineffective and of not taking any initiative worthy of the name in the Pacific area. Lacoste, however, remained cautious: he would only act when ordered to do so. Fagès then drew up a memorandum intended for Charles Hernu. Once more he emphasized the extreme danger that the alleged intentions of Greenpeace represented, and made two separate suggestions, which were, in his view, complementary:

1 The secret services must be asked to intensify the quest for information concerning Greenpeace intentions, the movements of its ships, the nature of the equipment they carry, the composition of their crews, their contacts with the land, etc. This search for intelligence is designed to foresee, but also, if need be, to forestall the operations of Greenpeace.
2 Action must be taken in such a way that the French Pacific forces are legally justified in forbidding the environmentalist ships access to territorial waters.

Admiral Fagès was thus very clear: there should be no question of allowing Greenpeace to intrude into French territorial waters, and even less of permitting a landing on the atolls. On the other hand, he seemed clearly to draw a distinction between this and an intelligence operation entrusted to the secret services but still under the control of his own services, which would serve to dissuade the environmentalists from further action.

After reading this memorandum, which he took very seriously, Charles Hernu gave vent to an angry outburst, the monumental nature of which was emphasized by several who witnessed it. In substance, he asked why DGSE was not doing its job. 'We're nobody at all in the Pacific,' he thundered. He broached the subject during a lunch with General Lacaze, the army Chief of Staff, who pointed out to him that he, the 'Aztec Wizard',[9] had not concerned himself with intelligence for 15 years. Prudently Lacaze referred Hernu back to Admiral Lacoste.

On 4 March Hernu received Admiral Fagès, who repeated his anxieties to him, and also reiterated what he wanted. The minister assured him he had understood, affirmed that he shared his sentiments, and pledged himself as a result to give the necessary orders to Admiral Lacoste. In fact, at the beginning of March he summoned the head of DGSE. He ordered him to intensify the quest for information concerning Greenpeace intentions, and to infiltrate the organization. He was to use every means for discovering what was brewing on board and around the *Vega*, another environmentalist ship, and the *Rainbow Warrior*. Finally, he was to 'ponder' – the word was disclosed to Bernard Tricot by Lacoste himself – on the means, if the case arose, of 'countering' the offensive by the pacifist movement.

It was upon this occasion that Charles Hernu showed Lacoste the memorandum of Admiral Fagès, in which the word 'forestall' had been underlined twice. But by whom? By Hernu himself. At this stage Hernu knew that the operation for 'information' was linked with one of 'forestalling'. He had just set in train an operation that might extend to sabotage.

After this discussion the decision was taken to send several teams of French agents to work on the spot. But these were not from Intelligence Branch but from Action Branch. This in itself was already a clear indication that it would concern a ship. Operation 'Satanic' was born.

Lacoste then went off to the Elysée to report on the state of preparations. There he was received by the head of the President's staff, General Saunier. It was he who released the funds necessary for the operation – 4 million francs. The head of the secret services also had several private conversations with François Mitterrand.

He now had the go-ahead. The Admiral therefore gave General Emin, the deputy head of the secret services, the task of finalizing the operation. On 18 May, at the fort of Noisy-le-Sec, Colonel Lesquer, head of Action Branch, solemnly announced to his officers that Operation 'Satanic' was to be launched. We know what followed.

Was it the plot of a bad novel? Undoubtedly. Sentenced by the New Zealand courts, the Turenges were finally freed and, after an agreement with France, transferred to the Hao atoll. In addition, after arbitration by an international tribunal, Paris had to pay the sum of 50 million francs damages and interest to the Greenpeace environmentalist movement. The French secret services had committed one of the biggest blunders in their history.

Notes

Prologue: Amid the Ruins of the Third Reich

1 Conversation with the authors.
2 The Law of 16 February 1943 instituted compulsory labour service in Germany (Service du Travail Obligatoire en Allemagne: STO).
3 Conversation with the authors.
4 Ibid.
5 Testimony of Voltaire Ponchel, obtained by the authors.
6 Account by Paul Aussaresses.
7 Conversation with the authors.
8 Ibid.
9 Testimony of François Saar Demichel.
10 In reality, there were some 30 partisans.
11 War diary of the Calvary mission.
12 Kokorin fled shortly afterwards, with a group of Italian communist partisans. He was in fact Lieutenant Makarov, alias Carlos Alamo, member of the famous Soviet spy network 'Red Orchestra' (see the CIA Handbook on the 'Rote Kapelle').
13 War diary of the Calvary mission.

Chapter 1 Ali Baba's Cave

1 Finally, at the beginning of 1946 he presided over the setting-up of the Service of External Documentation and Counter-Espionage (Service de Documentation Extérieure et de Contre-Espionnage: SDECE). The secret services were to keep this name until 1982.
2 Charles de Gaulle, *War Memoirs*.
3 The Cagoule was a secret organization of the extreme Right that had hatched a plot to seize power at the time of the Popular Front.
4 Conversation with the authors.
5 Paul Paillole likewise founded the Service de Sécurité Militaire, a counter-espionage service within the army. Today he is the chairman of the Association of former Members of the Special Services for National Defence (Association des Anciens des Services Spéciaux de la Défense Nationale: ASSDN).

6 P. Paillole, *Services spéciaux, 1935–1945*, Paris, 1975.
7 Among these men and women are names of intelligence specialists that occur frequently in the course of this account: Naval Captain Henri Trautmann, Captain Lucien Lochard, an expert on Russia, Colonels Henri de Buttet and Jean Mercier ('Big Mercier'), the White Russian Yevgeny Delimarsky, and Lucienne Quercy, secretary to the heads of the SR since 1924; and counter-espionage specialists Colonel Jean Chrétien, then Roger Lafont, his successor at the head of the CE, as well as his assistants, Captains Jean Allemand, Marcel Mercier ('Little Mercier'), Jean Fontès and Roger Morange.
8 An intelligence station often works on the near side of a frontier: in Strasbourg, for Germany; in Nice, for Italy; in Vienna, for Czechoslovakia; in Hong Kong, for China, in order better to protect the officers under diplomatic cover in the countries to which they are appointed.
9 Intervention in Parliament of the deputy Pierre Le Brun, secretary of the CGT, on 16 March 1945.
10 The FTP were started by the Communist Party in the spring of 1942.
11 In 1945 this budget amounted to 256.8 million francs.
12 Conversation with the authors.
13 Intervention by Pascal Copeau in the National Assembly, 27 December 1944.
14 *Paris-presse*, 20 June 1947.
15 Ibid., 18 June 1947.
16 *Cité-soir*, 3 March 1946.
17 *L'Humanité*, 9 September 1945.
18 *L'Aurore*, 11 September 1945.
19 *Action*, 14 September 1945.
20 *L'Humanité*, 13 September 1945.
21 *Franc-Tireur*, 21 September 1945.
22 *Cité-soir*, 3 March 1946.
23 Conversation with the authors.
24 *Action*, 7 September 1945; *Fraternité*, 17 October 1945.
25 A. Wurmser, *De Gaulle et les siens*, Paris, 1947.
26 Quoted in P. Robrieux, *Histoire intérieure du parti communiste, 1945–1972*, vol. II. Paris, 1980.
27 *France d'Abord*, 22 February 1949. For the history of the French wartime Communist intelligence set-up, see Roger Faligot and Rémi Kauffer, *Service B* (Paris: Fayard, 1985).
28 Wurmser, *De Gaulle*.
29 Cf. A. Brayance, *Anatomie du parti communiste français*, Paris, 1952, p. 274. 'Brayance' was the pseudonym of Alain Griotteray, liaison officer with SDECE and the DST in the Private Office of the minister of Defence, Paul-Henri Teitgen.
30 A. Marty, *L'Affaire Marty*, Paris, 1952, p. 90.
31 *Rapport parlementaire Delahoutre*, July 1950.
32 He was to commit suicide in the Fort of Châtillon.
33 *Rapport Ribière*. It was sent to Félix Gouin, the prime minister, on 20 May 1946. Published for the first time in the Communist daily *Ce Soir*, on 1 and 2 June 1947, it is partly reproduced in *Le Monde*, 3 June 1947.
34 *Rapport Ribière*.

35 Press release by Colonel Passy, 11 September 1946.
36 'Captain Vaudreuil' (François Thierry-Mieg) was one of the heads of the Counter-Espionage section.
37 *Rapport Ribière.*
38 Wurmser, *De Gaulle.*
39 *France-soir*, 12 September 1946.
40 Rassemblement du Peuple Français (RPF): the first truly Gaullist party after the War. In 1949, however, a 'Union Gaulliste pour la IVe République' had been created.
41 Conversation with Colonel Passy, 15 May 1984.

Chapter 2   Tracking down the Nazis

1 Conversation with the authors.
2 The BICE later changed its name to become the Bureau de Documentation (B-doc).
3 Paul Gérar-Dubot died on 20 May 1984, at the age of 96. Cf. the *Bulletin de l'Amicale des anciens membres des services spéciaux de la défense nationale*, no. 122, 1984/II, and the pamphlet produced by P. Gérar-Dubot in September 1951 (Sécurité militaire, DSM/F), *Maintenant, il faut le dire.*
4 For its part, the US counter-espionage branch belatedly launched its CROWCASS programme (Central Registry of War Criminals and Security Suspects) in May 1945. The suspects interned by the Allies in Germany were systematically recorded. At the CROWCASS centre, in the Rue des Mathurins, in Paris, 300 officers sorted out 40,000 files. The Americans were aiming too high: overwhelmed with cardboard files, they gave up the task. In the end they contented themselves with selecting German officers and agents likely to be of assistance to the US secret services.
5 A SDECE agent, Alain Roy, tells in his book *Le Cheval à Bascule* (Paris, 1975) how he succeeded in neutralizing von Merode in Spain by infiltrating his network. Beaugras died in 1963, 'having retired from politics'. As for Bickler, in 1983 he was found by the authors in Italy. Bickler died in March 1984.
6 He died in 1981. Under the pen-name 'Delimars' he had published articles on the Russian services in the review *Le Contrat social* (1966), which was published by the former communist leader, Boris Souvarine.
7 Henri-Gorce Franklin was the head of 'Gallia', the former BCRA intelligence network in the southern zone of France.
8 See especially Patrick Fridenson, in *La France de 1939 à nos jours* (Paris, 1985), and Peter Müller, *Ferdinand Porsche: un génie du XXe siècle* (Paris, 1980).
9 Ferdinand Porsche died on 30 January 1951.
10 Another investigator at Tübingen was the SDECE lieutenant Jean Paucot, the future leading light in the Defence Committee of the socialist party.
11 Conversation with the authors.
12 Conversation with the authors.
13 The Soviet espionage network in Switzerland during the Second World War was directed by a Hungarian, Sandor Rado.

14 Testimony of Colonel Roger Trutat, head of the SR station in The Hague before the War. Colonel Trutat died on 27 March 1988.

15 Admiral Canaris, head of Hitler's military intelligence service, the Abwehr, was accused by the Nazis of having worked for the British and, above all, of having sought a separate peace. Using as a pretext the attempt on Hitler's life in July 1944, they arrested and then executed him shortly before Germany capitulated.

16 Cf. E. H. Cookridge, *The Grey Hand: The Story of General Reinhard Gehlen* (London: Hodder & Stoughton, 1971): 'Heinz was considered to be an excellent spy, particularly by the SDECE.'

17 Bundesamt für Verfassungsschutz – German counter-espionage, the equivalent of the French DST and the British MI5.

18 Under the pen-name of Walter Hagen, Hoettl published *The Secret Front* (Vienna, 1950), a memoir on the Nazi services in which he pays off some old scores. In 1952 the book was published in France as *Le Front secret*, in a series produced with the help of Boris Souvarine.

19 Conversation with the authors.

Chapter 3 SDECE and the Socialist Party

1 André Dewavrin, 'Du BCRA au SDECE', *Le Monde*, 17 February 1966.

2 Cf. below, the Ribière Report on the Passy Affair and the secret funds of the DGER. According to John MacGregor Bruce-Lockhart, the station head in Paris of the Secret Intelligence Service (SIS) and later deputy director of SIS, 'Passy was imprisoned for misappropriation of public funds, but I do not know whether he was guilty or innocent' (testimony given to the authors).

3 Testimony of Louis Mouchon, taken by the authors shortly before his death. (He died on 4 February 1983.)

4 In conversation with the authors.

5 Georges Groussard, *Service secret, 1940–1945*, Paris, 1964.

6 Colonel Passy, *2ᵉ Bureau, Londres*, Paris 1947.

7 Testimony of Claude Bourdet.

8 Testimony of Pierre Fourcaud and Jean-Marie L'Allinec, on 2 March 1950, before the commission of enquiry regarding the affair of the generals, *Rapport parlementaire Delahoutre*, July 1950, pp. 735 and 2434.

9 From the Rue François-Ier, then the Rue de Grenelle, Pierre Fourcaud was to continue running a network of 'super-honourable correspondents', made up mainly of politicians. But his team was henceforth reduced to three people: Jean-Marie L'Allinec, his secretary, Mlle Blanc, and himself.

10 Pierre Nord, *Mes camarades sont morts*, Paris, 1947.

11 *L'Intoxication*, Paris, 1971.

12 *Bulletin de l'ASSDN*, no. 4, pp. 11–12.

13 The best agent of Intelligence branch in China, Lucien-Paul Bridou, was none other than the father of Marie-Madeleine Fourcade, the famous leader of the 'Alliance' Resistance movement linked to the British SIS during the Second World War. M. Bridou was officially the representative of Messageries Maritimes in Shanghai.

14 Unpublished conversation, from the authors' archives.

15 Yves Ciampi, Pierre Accoce, Jean Dewever, *Le Monde parallèle (ou la vérité sur l'espionnage)*, Paris, 1968.

16 Henceforth SDECE was familiarly known as the Piscine ('swimming pool'), because it faced the Tourelles swimming baths.

17 The 11th Shock Troops were established on 1 September 1946. The battalion was commanded first by Edgar Mautaint, and then Robert Rivière. Paul Aussaresses succeeded him in May 1947.

18 Born in 1901, Henri Boris died in 1972. Since then an 'Henri Boris' cup has been awarded to the best aeroplane and helicopter crews for their accuracy in navigation.

19 Captain René Bertrand and Colonel Gustave Bertrand were not related in any way.

20 Gustave Bertrand, *Enigma*, Paris, 1973.

21 He was again to be director of Research Branch in SDECE in 1962.

22 In conversation with the authors.

23 At his request, 'Jules' here preserves one of the pseudonyms that he used in SDECE until 1976.

24 Colonel Passy, *Missions secrètes en France*, Paris, 1951.

25 In conversation with the authors.

26 Afterwards Léon Kastenbaum was to be the archivist of SDECE until the appointment in 1957 of General Grossin as head of the organization.

27 During the War, using the pseudonym 'Claude', he was part of 'Azure', a British intelligence network.

28 Louis Mouchon has himself recounted the missions he directed in London, in the periodical of the former members of Action Branch, *Gens de la lune*, nos. 176–7 (1977).

29 Recalled at the age of 63 to go to the Russian front as engineer in chief of the Todt Organization, Demichel's father died there.

30 The officer Pierre Cambon had had a relationship with a Romanian immigrant woman. Henri Trautmann, the head of Intelligence Branch, then dismissed him from the secret services and reduced him in rank. Did his humiliation cause this brilliant officer to take his own life? The official enquiry concluded that it was an accident.

31 In conversation with the authors.

32 At the beginning of 1947, he 'turned' Sano Stanić, a Yugoslav intelligence officer, who gave away to the French information about many of his country's defence plans.

33 Until 1949 François Saar Demichel was to remain in SDECE as special adviser to Henri Ribière.

34 Cf. Rafael Gomez Para, *La Guerrilla antifranquista, 1945–1949*, Madrid, 1983.

35 Cf. p. 29.

36 Commissioner for Jewish Affairs of the Vichy government.

37 Testimony given to the authors.

38 Ibid.

39 *Résistance*, 14 September 1945.

40 Cf. David Wingate Pike, *Jours de gloire, jours de honte (le parti communiste d'Espagne depuis son arrivée en 1939 jusqu'à son départ en 1950)*, Paris, 1984.

41 His children, accompanied by the directress of the French Institute in Prague,

were soon to rejoin him in Paris. They were reunited in the Paris apartment of François Saar Demichel. Hubert Ripka was soon to leave France for the United States, where he died on 7 January 1958.

Chapter 4   The Cold War

1 From the authors' archives.
2 In 1949 Lieutenant Jellicoe was the British representative in Washington of the 'Special Political Committee' that tried but failed to set up an underground network in Albania.
3 The 'Jedburgh' commandos had been started in 1943. They grouped together elements from the Allies' secret services (OSS, SOE, DGER, SAS) and their purpose was to liaise with the Resistance and to stage guerrilla attacks behind the enemy lines during the Allied landings.
4 He was later to be the press attaché of the Princess of Monaco, and then the Director of the Société des Bains in the Principality.
5 James Burnham, *Pour vaincre l'impérialisme soviétique*, Paris, 1950.
6 General Maurice Guillaudot was to write a virulent pamphlet, *Criminels de paix*, Paris, 1948.
7 Louis Terrenoire, *De Gaulle, 1947–1954. Pourquoi l'échec?* Paris, 1982.
8 Testimony of Paul Aussaresses during a conversation with the authors.
9 Born in 1917, Dominique Ponchardier became famous through his spy novels, published in the 'Série Noire' library. 'The *barbouze* [literally "beard"],' he wrote regarding the French secret services, 'is ferocious and even nasty. But what is less widely known is that he is fairly clean. It cannot be said often enough that the secret agent is not at all the seedy, randy creature that a certain type of literature has made him out. The *barbouze* functions in a simple-minded way. For not a cent, not a stripe, not a decoration. (When a *barbouze* is awarded the Legion of Honour his appointment is not even gazetted in the *Journal officiel*.)' Ponchardier died in April 1986.
10 Testimony of Louis Mouchon in a conversation with the authors.
11 Cf. Dominique Loisel, *J'étais le commandant X*, Paris, 1970. The *Journal officiel* (10 March 1953) announced in an indirect way the promotion of Lieutenant-Colonel Dumont.
12 *Le Monde*, 9 January 1951.
13 Born in 1898, Lamy was to end his career in SDECE as a radio operator in the Federal Republic. He died on 14 April 1972.
14 Testimony given to the authors by Colonel de Lannurien.
15 Posted back to Baden-Baden, in charge of liaison with the CIA, Lannurien was afterwards to set up the first SDECE station in Finland. Colonel de Lannurien died on 1 March 1988.
16 Conversation with the authors.
17 Under the name of Jean-Paul Serbet, Lucien Gouazé published the story of his imprisonment: *Polit-Isolator*, Paris, 1961. M. Gouazé confirmed the version given by the authors in the original French publication of *La Piscine*.
18 As early as 1940, Pierre Faillant de Villemarest formed a Resistance network specializing in Intelligence. Later he was an officer in the *Armée Secrète*, fighting

in the famous Maquis du Vercors. Then he joined SDECE in Austria under Commandant Gavigniet; he took part in the hunt for former Nazis and organized networks against the Soviets. He later joined the French Press Agency (AFP) and, with his wife Danièle Martin, founded the Centre Européen d'Information. He is the author of many books on the intelligence war. His most recent work is the first history of the Red Army intelligence service: *GRU: Le plus secret des services soviétiques* (Paris, Stock: 1988).

19 Cf. Herman Zolling and Heinz Höhne, *Le Réseau Gehlen*, Paris, 1973.

20 Tsukor was to be assassinated at Nice in 1972 by the UDBA, Tito's secret services.

21 The authors possess a dossier containing 40 cards with organization charts drawn up in the 1960s, on which still figure Albanian émigrés and ex-Guomindang Chinese in Paris.

22 In 1949 SDECE refused to take part in the launching of the Committee for Free Albania, at the Hotel Crillon in Paris, despite the request of the CIA to do so. According to a former assistant to Colonel Fourcaud, this committee was considered to be an unrepresentative fabrication.

23 In *On chantait rouge* (Paris, 1977, p. 451) the communist dissenter Charles Tillon accuses Lieutenant-Colonel Mischke of having organized the infiltration of his ministry by the secret services (Mischke was also the author of *Paratroupes*, Paris, 1946).

24 D. M. Sotirović has expounded his theories in *L'Europe aux enchères*, Paris, 1952.

25 The former commander of the ELA 56 'Vaucluse' from March 1953 to October 1956, General Charles Christienne was head of the Historical Services of the air force in 1984.

26 One former member of the Normandie-Niemen squadron opted for the communist camp: a hero of the Franco-Russian squadron, Charles Jurquet de la Salle committed suicide on 8 August 1969, when the DST came to arrest him for belonging to a Romanian espionage network.

27 Conversations with those responsible at the time show a considerable difference as to the numbers of men that were sent – from several dozen to several hundred – and dates vary between 1951 and 1954. These divergences clearly spring from the role played by each person within a severely compartmentalized system, and also from the fact that a distinction must be drawn between operations carried out from beginning to end by SDECE and those realized jointly with the CIA. All agree in pointing out that few came back and in denying the rumour that numerous émigrés died during training, when making very low-level jumps into trees, and were buried secretly in Luzarches cemetery.

28 Conversation with the authors. It must be noted, in addition, that SDECE trained several dozen more Czechs between 1963 and 1967.

Chapter 5   Indo-China

1 It was Colonel Passy's own brother, one of the first to have parachuted into Indo-China, who sent this sarcastic note. (Conversation with Colonel Passy.)

2 Conversation with the authors. Colonel Passy counted on retailing this anecdote in the fourth volume of his memoirs concerning the DGER. It has never been published.

3 In the former Action Branch of the BCRA, the names of tools were used for saboteurs: 'Axe', 'Hoe', 'Pick'. The motor-cycling champion and future minister for the Quality of Life under President Giscard d'Estaing, André Jarrot, was called 'Gouge'.

4 This was a kind of 'intelligence exchange' between allied powers.

5 Recalled by his government, Trevor-Wilson was sent to a junior post in Malaysia.

6 Conversation with the authors.

7 *Rapport sur l'affaire des généraux*, 1949, p. 409.

8 *Rapport parlementaire sur le trafic des piastres*, May 1953.

9 Ibid.

10 Jacques Despuech, *Le Trafic des piastres*, Paris, 1953.

11 At Cao Bang, on the Chinese frontier, on 3 October the French began the evacuation of their positions. This turned into a disaster.

12 Conversation with the authors. The nucleus that was the forerunner of Action Branch thus comprised six men who were to be found on all the battlefields of the secret war: Bichelot, Dunant-Henry, Gauthier, Maloubier, Pellay and Sassi.

13 Conversation with the authors.

14 'A unique fact was that the Viets possessed whole regiments for intelligence-gathering,' emphasized Colonel René Delseny, then responsible for counter-espionage in Indo-China. Conversation with the authors.

15 Conversation with the authors.

16 *La Guerre moderne*, Paris, 1960. Colonel Trinquier acquired great influence among British and Americans experts in counter-insurrection, with the Americans in Vietnam and the British in Ireland. Cf. Roger Faligot, *Guerre spéciale en Europe*, Paris, 1980.

17 Cf. also Antoine Savani, *Visages et images du Sud-Viêt-nam*, Saigon, 1955.

18 Roger Trinquier, 'L'opium des Méos', *Historia*, no. 25 (special issue).

19 Afred McCoy, *La Politique de l'héroïne en Asie du Sud-Est*, Paris, 1980, p. 119. McCoy interviewed numerous members of Vietnamese intelligence, both American and French.

20 US Senate, 88th Congress, *Report on Organized Crime and Illicit Traffic in Narcotics: Hearings before the Permanent Subcommittee on Government Operations . . . Pursuant to Resolution 278*, 30 July 1964, Part 4. Cf. also, A. Jaubert, *D . . . comme Drogue*, Paris, 1974.

21 Conversation with General Belleux. Roger Bellon was a reserve officer in SDECE's Action Branch. Paul Jacquier was to become Director-General of SDECE in 1962.

22 Roger Trinquier, *Maquis d'Indochine*, Paris, 1976.

23 We should point out that meanwhile the GCMA had been renamed 'Groupement Mixte d'Intervention' (GMI).

24 Trinquier, *Maquis d'Indochine*.

25 Yves Roucaute, *Le PCF et l'Armée*, Paris, 1983.

26 Colonel Sassi, however, assured the authors that no member of the GCMA had gone over to the Vietminh.

27 Testimony of General H. Jacquin.

28 Shortly after the incident, Perrez enlisted in the Foreign Legion. Despite 'investigations', he was not found.

29 General Mast did not figure among those officially due to receive the report. But,

as a friendly gesture, Revers, as chief of staff, had handed him a copy (no. 27), which was returned by Mast on 27 July.

30 Having become president of the Chamber of Commerce in La Paz, Bolivia, Roger Peyré was in 1970 to help Dominique Ponchardier, the ambassador, to have Régis Debray set free from the hands of the military dictatorship.

31 *Rapport parlementaire Delahoutre*, July 1950.

32 Against all logic, the DST did not inform SDECE of its first investigations, though SDECE was in charge of counter-espionage at the time.

33 *Rapport . . . Delahoutre*. Only Jean-Marie L'Allinec, counsellor at SDECE and a friend of Fourcaud, was to dispute that such orders had been given by the deputy director.

34 Ibid.

35 A former secret service agent, Jacques Locquin ran a DGER network in the Federal Republic nicknamed 'Der Gast' (The Visitor). After the affair of the generals, he was to be the correspondent of Agence France-Presse in Peking, and then in charge at SDECE of the syntheses on foreign policy, under General Grossin.

36 In his book of memoirs, *Roger Wybot et la bataille pour la DST*, Paris, 1975, written in collaboration with Philippe Bernert, the former chief of the DST gives a very complete account of this affair.

37 *Rapport . . . Delahoutre*.

38 Conversation with the authors. The hypothesis that Raoul Salan was the principal informant of *L'Express* is confirmed by Serge Siritzky and Françoise Roth in *Le Roman de l'Express*, Paris, 1979.

39 Personal archives of the authors.

Chapter 6   The Secret War in the Maghreb

1 Genet, *Manuel d'histoire* (school text), Paris, 1985.

2 Conversation with Colonel Germain.

3 In the jargon of the secret services, to 'neutralize' means to kill.

4 The Counter-Espionage Branch of SDECE, directed by Colonel Maurice Dumont and then Colonel René Delseny, was organized as follows during the Algerian war: *Head* – Colonel Germain; *Egypt* – H. Geniès; *Tunisia* – P. Conty; *Algeria* – Nougaret; *Morocco* – R. C. Duprez; *Tangiers* – Boureau-Mitrecey.

5 In the French *Who's Who* for 1961 the biographical entry for Jacques Chevallier mentions that in 1945 he was 'head of the Liaison Services of French Counter-Espionage in America'. The former mayor of El Biar, the future deputy for Algiers, and in 1955 the Minister of State for National Defence, he was head of the DGER station in Washington. According to Philippe Robrieux (*Histoire intérieure du parti communiste*), Boris Souvarine, the founder of the French Communist party (PCF), figured among his agents.

6 There was a murderous attack by night in the Casbah.

7 On 16 January 1957, a home-made rocket launched against General Salan missed its target, but killed his aide-de-camp, Commandant Rodier. This group of activists, the instigators of the attack, was run by Gaullists.

8 The Servizio Informazioni Forzi Armate Republicane, like the DGSE today, came under the Minister of Defence.

9 During the Algerian war SDECE brought about the arrest of six ships, with a total of 1313 tonnes of arms and explosives, or double the ALN armament in 1962. The ships involved were: *Athos* (Cypriot, October 1956); *Slovanja* (Yugoslav, January 1958; *Granita* (Danish, December 1958; *Lidice* (Czech, April 1959); *Bies-Bosch* (Dutch, December 1959); *Trigito* (Panamanian, September 1961).

10 Geniès was head of Counter-Espionage in Cairo. At the embassy was also to be found the head of Intelligence for the station, the assistant military attaché Henri Picq. Colonel Picq was to return to civilian life in May 1956, when he embarked on an important career with the Crédit Lyonnais, from Singapore to Teheran. He was succeeded by Colonel de Lannurien.

11 A veteran of Indo-China, in 1970 Commandant Blouin became the commander of the reserve company in SDECE.

12 Raymond Tournoux, *Secrets d'Etat*, Paris, 1960.

13 A plane was to be sent to Morocco to evacuate the families.

14 A = Ben Bella; C = Boudiaf.

15 As head of the Action section in Colonel Simoneau's CCI.

16 Testimony of Colonel Vincent Monteil to the authors, confirmed by that of the former head of Israeli counter-espionage, Baruch Nadel (*Européo*, 4 July 1971).

17 Paul Léger, *Aux carrefours de la guerre*, Paris, 1983.

18 'Steamboat' died in 1958, as the result of the treatment he had suffered at the hands of the Gestapo during the Resistance.

19 Testimony of General Jacquin to the authors.

20 Before taking over as director of the DST in 1959 Gabriel Eriau was successively Secretary-General for the Protectorate of the French Republic in Morocco, then of the High Commission, and finally of the embassy in Morocco.

21 The SLNA was formerly called the Committee for Information and Studies (Comité d'Information et Etudes: CIE).

22 Roger Trinquier, *La Guerre*, Paris, 1980.

23 Conversation with the authors.

24 Cf. *Le Monde*, 19 May 1961: 'The Centre for Joint Army Coordination is the object of an enquiry', particularly because of its methods, and also because of its links with the pro-French Algeria activists. 'One of the most important centres of the CCI, the Améziane farm at Constantine, to which numerous Muslims were taken for "interrogation", has been closed down.' (It should be noted that in 1960 Colonel Simoneau had been replaced at the head of the CCI by Colonel Blanchet.)

25 The DOP was not an 'Algerian' invention. Back in Indo-China, as Colonel Belleux explained to us, a DOP had been set up 'in relation to counter-espionage, under the auspices of SDECE and military security. Gendarmes were present to ensure the legality of the interrogations.' So far as we know the DOP in Indo-China did not stir up criticism as did its Algerian counterpart. It is true that it had fewer members and fewer prerogatives, and was made up of real professionals in intelligence work who had won their spurs against Nazism ten years earlier.

26 Cf. the works of Pierre Vidal-Naquet, and particularly *La Torture dans la République*, Paris, 1975.

27 Conversation with the authors, 15 November 1984.
28 Jacques Massu, *La Vraie Bataille d'Alger*, Paris, 1971.
29 Conversation with the authors.
30 The term *bleuite* arose from the psychosis of treason aroused by those who were called, because of their dress, the 'blue boiler suits'.
31 Henri Jacquin, *La Guerre secrète en Algérie*, Paris, 1977.
32 Commandant Prévôt was wounded, and a lieutenant killed. According to Jean-Raymond Tournoux (*L'Histoire secrète*, Paris, 1962), Michel Debré, the prime minister, sent a telegram personally congratulating this unit on the execution of Si Mohammed.
33 Among them, some 'virtuosos' of special operations: Georges Barazer de Lannurien, Hélie Denoix de Saint-Marc, Yves de la Bourdonnaye-Montluc, Léonce Barrière and Raymond Muelle.
34 Captain Rocolle was killed in action at the beginning of 1958.
35 Philippe Bernert, *Roger Wybot et la Bataille pour la DST*, Paris, 1975.
36 Captain Mantéï died in Corsica in 1961, trying to save a mountain climber in difficulty – according to the official version.
37 To take a single instance: if several former members of the 11th Shock Troops are now in the ranks of management at Citroën, it is as a result of a ridiculous episode. One day, at the beginning of the 1950s, the SDECE lieutenant Joseph Vermot, severely wounded in 1940, an officer of the 'Jedburghs', had a conversation with the head of military personnel, who predicted that he would have a 'short career' because of his lack of qualifications. Disheartened, the fighter went to sit Citroën's psychological tests. He was to become one of the senior staff in the car firm (he was even burnt in effigy in 1968), and never forgot his old comrades.

Chapter 7   Grossin's 'Firm'

1 This mobile 'insulated chamber' installed in a room at the French embassy is sound-proof to the ultra-sensitive nail-size microphones the KGB has the habit of fitting in walls. It thus allows the ambassador to give instructions without the risk of being 'bugged'.
2 This Higher Council for Intelligence, presided over by the head of state is, so far as the authors are aware, regulated by no official decree published in the *Journal Officiel*. It differs from the Inter-ministerial Council on Intelligence (Comité Interministériel du Renseignement: CIR), which, under the orders of the prime minister, has the task of coordinating the activities of the various services for documentation and intelligence.
3 A member of the family of Dr Botkin – the personal doctor of the Tsar who was assassinated at Ekaterinburg in 1918 by the Bolsheviks – Constantin Melnik became fascinated by the secret services very early in his life. Frequenting American circles, among them the Rand Corporation, and an ex-member of Marshal Juin's Deuxième Bureau at the Liberation, from 1959 to 1962 he was in charge of security problems in Michel Debré's Office. During the war in Algeria it was his job to ensure liaison between the prime minister's Private Office,

SDECE and the DST. The supporters of French Algeria, enraged, called him 'Melnik the Russian', because they were convinced that he had succeeded in suborning some of their members. In so doing they strengthened the enigmatic image that Melnik liked to cultivate. He was soon to switch to publishing and edit the 'Guerre secrète' series for Fayard.

4 Pierre Fourcaud, the former technical director of SDECE, was at the time running his own separate miniature secret service. He was directly under the Office of the Prime Minister, to which he handed in his reports.

5 The son of General Mangin, this St-Cyr graduate was given the job by de Gaulle of coordinating paramilitary action in Occupied France during the War.

6 Engineer-General of Marine Engineering, under the Fourth Republic Abel Thomas was several times in charge of the Private Office of Bourgès-Maunoury.

7 Testimony of General Grossin, given to the authors.

8 Ibid.

9 Ibid.

10 The slang name given to SDECE by its agents.

11 There is another Grand Hôtel Gambetta, just on the corner of the Avenue Gambetta and the Rue des Tourelles, opposite SDECE.

12 Marie Bell, whose real name was Bellon, had a brother, Raoul Bellon, a counter-espionage agent (SSM/TR) in Marseilles during the War, where he became the friend of Roger Blémant, the astounding DST superintendent turned gangster. Upon his retirement Colonel Dumont took an interest in the theatre, before returning to Lorraine, where he ran a business reproducing the popular French prints of the 18th and 19th centuries known as the 'images d'Epinal'.

13 Conversation with the authors.

14 Ibid.

15 René Backmann and Claude Angeli, *Les Polices de la nouvelle société*, Paris, 1971.

16 Cf. Jean-Marie Pontault, *Le Secret des écoutes téléphoniques*, Paris, 1978.

17 SDECE was then under the prime minister, and its budget was made public each year, since the National Assembly voted the funds for the prime minister's Office (Matignon).

18 Conversation with the authors.

19 Several French officers who were communists were subjected to the lie detector test during the Indo-China war.

20 Testimony of General Paul Aussaresses, given to the authors.

21 Gilbert Cohen-Séat died in 1980. He wrote many articles in the *Revue internationale de filmologie*, and three books, including *Essai sur les principes d'une philosophie du cinéma*, Paris (the book went out of print in 1973).

22 Conversation with the authors.

23 For a while he was attached, with his friend François Bistos, to the Minister of Information, Jacques Soustelle.

24 Tropel, a former member of Action Branch, was to leave SDECE in 1966, to enter the Union Générale des Pétroles, and then Elf, where he was in charge of security (his name was to crop up again in connection with the affair of the 'sniffer' planes).

25 Upon this subject see the book by L. Roy Finville, *SDECE, 'Service 7'*, Paris, 1980.

26 Testimony of Jean Violet, given to the authors.

27 General Eugène Guibaud became head of SDECE in 1966. He succeeded General Paul Jacquier, who himself had replaced General Grossin in 1962.
28 Conversation with the authors.
29 Since 1948 Father Dubois had belonged to several groups for the 'defence of Western values'. Afterwards he was the Chaplain-in-Chief of the expeditionary corps in Indo-China.
30 *Combat*, 23 January 1957.
31 Alfred Grosser, *Affaires étrangères*, Paris, 1984.
32 In 1962 the writer Pierre Nord, alias Colonel Brouillard in the Resistance, published a novel entitled *Pas de scandale à l'ONU* (Paris). In this work a certain Colonel Dubois, the head of the French secret services, puts a stop to a conspiracy mounted by an 'Afro-Asian coalition of totalitarian and "slave-trading" states, who were even cannibals'. Fiction is often inspired by contemporary happenings. On a more serious note, for almost 30 years Pierre Nord remained an 'honourable correspondent' of the secret services, a sort of 'moral authority' within SDECE.
33 The term 'Church of Silence' gradually came to designate the oppressed Catholic Church in communist countries. Cf. François Bernard, *Où en est l'Eglise du silence?*, Paris, 1960, and Alain Guérin, *Les Commandos de la guerre froide*, Paris, 1969.
34 James Burnham, *Pour en finir avec l'impérialisme soviétique*, Paris, 1950.
35 *Ce soir*, 21 April 1948.
36 Certain activities of Father Dubois were to be hotly criticized after his death. Thus Father Bouchet, the Provincial of the Dominican Order in Paris, said: 'I found a document in his archives regarding subversion in Latin America and Marxist infiltrations: so a certain Church was acting against another, the Church of South America. He took an interest in affairs that, to say the least, were strange for a priest.' *Rapport parlementaire sur les avions renifleurs*, 1984.

Chapter 8   Signed: The 'Red Hand'

1 Cf. Hervé Hamon and Patrick Rotman, *Les Porteurs de valise*, Paris, 1979.
2 Testimony of M. Raptis, given to the authors.
3 Between September 1956 and October 1960 22 attacks attributed to the 'Red Hand' took place. Most were outside France and of those in Europe many were in Germany, where, it was alleged, the West German secret services gave tacit support to SDECE-prompted assassinations and 'accidents'. These 22 were just the successful ones, or those that got press coverage. There was a noticeable lull in such operations for a year after September 1957, corresponding to General Grossin's first 12 months as head of SDECE. It was six months after de Gaulle's return to power in May 1958 that Grossin was confirmed in office. During this period too the FLN suffered serious reverses in the battle of Algiers.
4 *Daily Mail*, 27 November 1959. It was this interview, one suspects, that was picked up by the French press. Durieux later denied having given it. But he gave another, this time to *Der Spiegel*, on 21 February 1960.
5 *Paris-presse*, 23 April 1960.
6 His real name was Kurt-Emile Schweizer, and he was born in Monaco in 1931.

He has published a number of novels, and more recently has been the editor of the Eurédif series of erotic novels 'Aphrodite-Classique'.

7 Jacques Latour died in 1976, according to his mother's testimony, given to the authors.

8 Colonel Mercier took an interest in spy books. Gabriel Veraldi (author of *Le Roman d'espionnage*, Paris, 1983, and of *Les Espions de bonne volonté*, Paris, 1966) points out that he was a very close friend of the great spy novelist Pierre Nord, whose source of inspiration was very close to reality. Pierre Nord (who died on 20 December 1985) regretted that he had not seen his friend Mercier since the 1960s (conversation with the authors).

9 In contrast to 'Big Mercier' or 'Von Kluck bis', Colonel Jean M. Mercier, among other posts, head of Research in SDECE 1948–55. (He died in October 1988.)

10 He had been incorporated into SDECE as a P2 agent of the SSM/TR (the 'Camelia' network, from 1 February 1944 to 5 June 1945) as a 'second category' head of mission.

11 As other identities he used the names 'Charpentier', 'Dubois', 'Monnot' and 'Morel'. Colonel A. de Dainville (*L'ORA – la résistance de l'armée durant la guerre 39–45*) describes him as being 'an indefatigable liaison agent'.

12 Conversation with the authors.

13 Reinhard Gehlen, *Mémoires*, Paris, 1972.

14 Conversation with the authors.

15 Tangiers was swarming with 'honourable correspondents' at the time: Jo Renucci was trading in cigarettes; Antoine Lopez ran an agency for Air France at the airport; and Alexandre de Marenches lived in a villa on 'La Montagne'.

16 Centring round Carmen Cocu, Jo Attia's girl, the stratagem was thought up by Despierres, of SDECE, Michel-Pierre Hamelet, a *Figaro* journalist well in with Pierre Boursicot, and Roger Lentz, another notorious figure of the underworld, an SDECE agent under contract, whose name is constantly being mentioned in the Monfort-l'Amaury and Ben Barka affairs.

17 From 1966 to 1971 Colonel Zahm was to be an SDECE station head in the Federal Republic.

18 At the Liberation Bistos was entrusted with counter-espionage against Spain, with Déodat du Puy-Montbrun. After having successfully directed the Spanish section, Bistos became the head of office administration in 1963, and in 1970 he was transferred to become head of the General Services in the directorate relating to the infrastructure and resources of SDECE (the central registry). He died on 17 September 1981.

19 According to a senior member of the Action Branch in SDECE, 'Radio Somera' was broadcasting to Algeria in 1961, but had only a small audience. Nearer home, this offshoot of SOFIRAD, financed by the Quai d'Orsay, has been an object of criticism. In 1982 the French government called for an enquiry into 'Somera'. In fact, listening to recordings from the time of the Lebanese conflict reveals that certain programmes, produced by supporters of the Christian Phalangists, constituted an incitement to murder. The Elysée was to block a ministerial report.

20 Besides Pierre Gondolo, nine telecommunications technicians were implicated: Pierre Bresson, Pierre Lacaze, Emile Ghibaudo, Edmond Montagne, Roger Richard, Georges Winger, Claude Dhainaud, Lucie Atlan and Charles Wirt.

21 *Le Monde*, 12 February 1959.
22 Conversation with the authors.
23 The 'resident' of the Bundesnachrichtendienst (BND) then in Tunis, Richard Christmann, as he has revealed to the authors, helped his 'honourable correspondent', Ali M'rad, to dismantle the Magenta network.
24 'Lieutenant-Colonel Paul Conty (a veteran of Tunisia) died suddenly on 17 November 1964 at Tours.' *Bulletin de l'Amicale des anciens membres des services spéciaux de la défense nationale*, no. 44, 1964/IV.
25 Yves Ciampi, Pierre Acocce and Jean Dewever, *Le Monde parallèle*, Paris, 1968. Note that Yves Ciampi produced short instructional films for SDECE.
26 Thyraud de Vosjoli, *Lamia*, Montreal, 1970.
27 *Le Terrorisme international et la CIA*, Moscow, 1984.
28 *Le Monde*, 19 April 1962. Then running a bar at Villefranche-sur-Mer, Louis Soliveau had formerly taken part in the parachute landings at Arnhem.

Chapter 9   The Colonies are Finished

1 The German arms trafficker Georg Puchert, alias Captain Morris, was killed by Action Branch on 3 March 1959.
2 Conversation with the authors.
3 During one of these meals Jacques Foccart had a violent argument with Pierre Viansson-Ponté, who had described him as a *barbouze* in his book *Les Gaullistes*, Paris, 1963.
4 Contrary to everything that has been written, Jacques Foccart was never sent on to Holland to interrogate German prisoners of war.
5 In 1968 General de Gaulle was to reproach Jacques Foccart for continuing to practise parachute jumping.
6 Conversation with the authors.
7 Centre Bordelais d'Etude d'Afrique Noire, *La Politique africaine du Général de Gaulle*, 1980.
8 Roger Barberot, *A bras le cœur*, Paris, 1972.
9 *La Politique africaine*.
10 *Rapport parlementaire sur le SAC*, vol. 2, 1982.
11 In 1974 Valéry Giscard d'Estaing summarily sacked Jacques Foccart from his post as Secretary-General for African and Madagascan Affairs. Foccart learnt of it a few minutes before it was announced officially by Agence France-Presse.
12 Conversation with the authors.
13 Ibid.
14 Since 1970 Alexandre de Marenches, a friend of Pompidou, had been the head of SDECE.
15 In his book *Affaires africaines*, Paris, 1983, the journalist Pierre Péan has drawn up a list of tragic disappearances for which no satisfactory explanations have been given: Germain M'ba (1971), Robert Bossard and his wife (June 1979), and, in France, Robert Luong Truat (October 1979).
16 Conversation with the authors, 1984.
17 *La Politique africaine*.
18 Conversation with the authors, 1983.

19 Conversation with the authors. Paul Perrier was to resign from the Mauritian secret services when Paul Bérenger married his daughter.
20 Conversation with the authors.
21 Engineer-General Canbeaux, 'Nécessité d'une Eurafrique', *Revue de défense nationale*, December 1957. Colonel Muller, 'La subversion et l'Afrique noire française', *Revue de défense nationale*, May 1958.
22 Conversation with the authors.
23 This detail figures in *Affaires africaines*. It has been confirmed to the authors by Maurice Robert.
24 SDESC was later to become DIRDOC.
25 Maurice Delauney, *De la casquette à la jaquette ou de l'administration coloniale à la diplomatie africaine*, Paris, 1982.
26 *Carnets secrets de la colonisation*, Paris, 1967.
27 If the political authorities had not given their agreement there would have been sanctions imposed at the top of and within the secret services, as in the Ben Barka affair. There were none.
28 Ernest Ouandié, the last great leader of the UPC, was condemned to death in 1971 by Ahidjo.
29 This pseudonym disguises an officer of Action Branch who, at the time the original edition of this book was published, was still alive.
30 Landing in Indo-China in October 1945, the 'Conus' commando, led by Adrien Conus, was made up of some 30 parachutists recruited from the DGER, from the 1st Paratroop Infantry Regiment and former Action Branch men.
31 The French authorities clearly did not wish the young student to recount his memories of that meal. He was expelled from France in February 1961. Having become the permanent delegate of the UPC, Jean-Martin Tchaptchaët was arrested in Ghana during the coup of 1966.
32 Jean-Francis Held, *L'Affaire Moumié*, Paris, 1961.

Chapter 10   Secret Missions on the Dark Continent

1 The Centre Bordelais d'Etude d'Afrique Noire, *La Politique africaine du Général de Gaulle*, 1980.
2 *Revue de défense nationale*, July 1960.
3 This testimony is taken from the trial at Conakry during 1970–1, after the attempted coup on 22 November. The interrogation, which was carried out in very brutal fashion, was published in the *Revue tricontinentale* (February 1972). One must be cautious in using the evidence given under pressure at this trial. Nevertheless, for the period 1958–61, the senior officials of SDECE at the time admit that the complaints against France were well founded.
4 Ibid. The person in question is Captain Boureau-Mitrecey, whom we encountered in Tangiers during the 'Red Hand' affair.
5 The CFA franc is the unit of currency of the French Community of African States (Communauté Française d'Afrique). In 1960 CFA francs were printed by the Institut d'Emission of West Africa. The notes are identical for all French-speaking Africa.
6 The director of *Horoscope* was Jean-Noël Beyler, whose father belonged to the supervisory committee of the Saint-Phalle bank (the SDECE bank).

7 *Horoscope*, Special issue, 1974.
8 Ibid.
9 Ibid.
10 *La Politique africaine.*
11 Ibid.
12 *Les Complots de la CIA*, Paris, 1976. The Church Commission on the CIA was to reveal that in 1975 Joseph Scheider, the scientific specialist of the American agency, had perfected some ten poisons intended to be mixed with the food or toothpaste of Patrice Lumumba. Colonel Mobutu had no need of these additional 'refinements' to eliminate Lumumba.
13 B. Eliacheff, *Mémoires*, Paris, 1972.
14 *La Politique africaine.*
15 *La Libre belgique*, 29 January 1982.
16 Ibid., 30 January 1982.
17 Testimony of Robert Lemoine, given to the authors.
18 Ibid.
19 *Revue de défense nationale*, March 1969.
20 Rolf Steiner, *Carré rouge*, Paris, 1976.
21 In his press conference de Gaulle seemed not to know that Nigeria comprises 250 different tribes, and that the Ibos were not the sole inhabitants of the Eastern region.
22 Several African countries, among them Gabon, Ivory Coast, Tanzania and Zambia, recognized the new state.
23 These figures are put forward by Daniel Bach, a researcher at Ife University (Nigeria). He reckons, moreover, that Biafra may have received 384 million dollars' worth of heavy equipment, as against Nigeria's 6,758 million dollars (*La Politique africaine*).

Chapter 11   The Hunt for Moles

1 Etienne Manac'h was reproached with knowing the writer Han Suyin; Daniel Doustin, the head of the DST, was to ask for the ambassador in China to be relieved of the task of organizing General de Gaulle's visit.
2 Piotr Deriabin has told his story, *Policier de Staline*, in the 'Guerre secrète' series published by Fayard (Paris, 1966) and edited by Constantin Melnik.
3 Anthony Blunt confessed to the investigators of MI5 the role he had played. As a result he was given immunity from prosecution, but he was nevertheless publicly accused in 1979. Andrew Boyle, the author of *A Climate of Treason* and the journalist who had identified Blunt, has confirmed to the authors that James Angleton was the source of his investigations.
4 Among the suspects, David Murphy, the head of CIA's Soviet division, was given a clean bill. But in 1973 Murphy became station head in Paris, and de Marenches, the head of SDECE, discovered to his stupefaction that Angleton had placed him there in order to trap him. When he learnt this Bill Colby, the head of the CIA, decided to dismiss Angleton (W. Colby, *Trente ans dans la CIA*, Paris, 1978).
5 Daniel Doustin was the director of the DST from 1961 to 1964, Marcel Chalet

from 1975 to 1982. Louis Niquet was then the director of Section E2. (Niquet died on 25 April 1988.)

6 To cite another instance, the DST kept under surveillance the famous actress Madeleine Robinson, whose real name was Svoboda, merely because she was of Czech origin.

7 Krotkov testified before the American Congress under the pseudonym 'Karlin' (cf. *Testimony of George Karlin*, Parts I, II and III. Sub-committee to Investigate the Administration of the Internal Security Act and other Internal Security Laws, Committee of Judiciary, Senate/H SSIS, November 1969–March 1970). Moreover, John Barron of *Reader's Digest* interviewed him about the Dejean affair for his book *KGB*, but the story was omitted from the French version of the work.

8 One cannot for a moment imagine that the Russian diplomats stationed in Paris would agree, as do the French in the Eastern bloc countries, to having their staff provided by the host country.

9 A director of Shell and President of the Société Franco-soviétique de Coopération Industrielle (SOFRACOP), Maurice Dejean died in January 1982.

10 Conversation with the authors.

11 The prime minister, Georges Pompidou, who had overall responsibility for SDECE, was, however, personally opposed to it.

12 In 1966 he was to be the deputy of Maurice Dejean in SOFRACOP.

13 Testimony of François Saar Demichel. He gave up his commercial activities in Eastern Europe on the day he became administrator of SOFMA in 1976. This very 'sensitive' post, in a state-run company that exported equipment for land warfare, could be occupied only after a detailed vetting by the French security services.

14 President Pompidou wanted to avoid any 'witch hunt' within SDECE. He asked de Lannurien to restrict his enquiries to Léonard Hounau alone. Indeed the government was not at all certain whether the whole thing was not a CIA set up, aimed at discrediting the French services.

15 Conversation with the authors.

16 '23' signified Colonel Verneuil's Counter-Espionage Branch.

17 In the book by Philippe Thyraud de Vosjoli, which Colonel de Lannurien wanted to have withdrawn (*Lamia*, Montreal, 1970), the former reproduced a letter of congratulation from Mareuil (Colonel Mercier), thanking Lamia on behalf of General Jacquier, who had been delighted by his trip to the United States in October 1962.

18 A. Tully, *CIA – Central Intelligence Agency*, Paris, 1962.

19 Thyraud, *Lamia*.

20 Without being able to verify further, we note that in September 1963 the Cuban press reported that State Security had arrested 'Pierre Owen de Ure, agent of the CIA, a French citizen living in Cuba'. Was he also Thyraud's agent?

21 Numerous senior officials, among them at least one director of SDECE, have indicated to the authors that they would have found it normal for Lamia to be executed. On the other hand, the department for the protection of the Service dismissed this hypothesis as fantasy, recalling that in 1972 Thyraud gave lectures in Belgium without any trouble (cf. the interview carried out by Yvon Toussaint, 'Un ancien lieutenant-colonel du SDECE raconte . . .', *Le Soir*, Brussels, 25 March, 1972).

22 *Lamia* had very poor sales in France, partly because Colonel de Lannurien, who was accused in it, just as was Colonel Hounau, lodged a legal complaint. Later, in 1975, Thyraud published *Le Comité* (Montreal), describing the downfall of Le Roy Finville and his 'Service 7', and pursuing his campaign of denouncing his old 'Firm'.

23 *La Gazette de Lausanne*, 2 May, 1962.

24 Gilles Perrault, *L'Erreur*, Paris, 1971.

25 After the publication of Perrault's book, some eminent people, alerted by Maître Soulez-Larivière, Rousseau's lawyer, had written to the President of the Republic asking him to intervene. Among them were Colonel Rémy, Yvon Morandat, General Billotte and Romain Gary.

26 *Le Nouvel observateur*, 14 June 1971. Alexandre de Marenches had been the director of SDECE since November 1970.

27 On 10 December 1971, the Deuxième Bureau changed its name to the Centre for Exploitation of Military Intelligence (Centre d'Exploitation du Renseignement Militaire: CERM), but was still directed by Colonel Bourgogne.

28 This was the rather unflattering portrait of Beaumont painted by the press. This one was published in *Le Monde* on 27 November 1971, over the signatures of Michel Legris and Kosta Christitch.

29 He died in 1984.

30 Conversation with the authors. Mme Bertrand insisted that it be plainly stated that in her opinion Colonel Beaumont was entirely innocent.

31 There was a sequel to this affair: in 1984 it was discovered once again that a former senior official of Security Branch, a member of the Director's office in the 1960s, and now dead, had been working for the Romanians.

Chapter 12   In the Turbulence

1 A facsimile of the DST work log was reproduced in the account by René Backmann, Franz-Olivier Giesbert and Olivier Todd, 'Ce que cherchent les agents de la CIA en France', *Le Nouvel observateur*, 19 January 1976.

2 P. Bernert, *SDECE, Service 7 (l'extraordinaire histoire du colonel Le Roy-Finville et des clandestins)*, Paris, 1980.

3 Testimony of Marcel Chaussée. In his book Le Roy Finville gives no credence to Chaussée's testimony.

4 Report on the interrogation (No. 253), 16 March 1966.

5 Report on the interrogation, 9 December 1966.

6 Christian David, imprisoned in the USA for drug trafficking, was extradited to France in January 1985 to answer a charge of murdering Commissioner Gallibert in 1966. The head of the anti-gangs brigade had been enquiring into Figon's death.

7 Gilles Perrault revealed this in *Un Homme à part*, Paris, 1984.

8 Cf. Robert Lemoine, *Profession: barbouze*, Paris, 1980.

9 The information was published by Claude Angeli in *Le Nouvel observateur*, on 20 April 1966 and involved him in trouble with the judicial authorities.

10 Cf. Henri Navarre, *Le Temps des vérités*, 1979.

11 Cf. P. Thyraud de Vosjoli, *Le Comité*, Montreal, 1975.

12 Matsui was to be expelled from Karachi in 1966 on grounds of subversion.

13 Norodom Sihanouk, *La CIA contre le Cambodge*, Paris, 1973.

14 In 1981, after having appeared before the commission of enquiry on the RCMP, Trudeau replied to the journalists who were pressing him with questions: 'I have no intention of talking about the affair concerning the French Embassy, nor of making judgements about embassies suspected of sheltering spies. In any case, no French diplomat has ever been declared *persona non grata*, or asked to leave the country.' (*Le Monde*, 30 August 1981).

15 In 1970 the Canadian Solicitor-General sent an RCMP agent to Paris to check whether SDECE maintained connections with the separatist movements in Quebec. At the same time, the RCMP accused a university professor, Jacques Parizeau, of having organized a network linked to the French secret services. Finally, these services were suspected of having handed over $350,000 to René Lévêque's Parti Québecois. In 1981 a commission of enquiry was to give France a clean bill.

16 Regarding the FLQ, in his book, *FLQ, histoire d'un mouvement clandestin* (Quebec, 1982), Louis Fournier noted that 'Rossillon was put in contact with an FLQ militant called Gilles Pruneau, whom he allegedly helped to take refuge in Algeria.'

17 Conversation with the authors.

Chapter 13   De Marenches at SDECE

1 G. Pompidou, *Pour rétablir une vérité*, Paris, 1982.

2 There he made the acquaintance of Vernon Walters, the future second-in-command of the CIA. On the national Defence general staff of Marshal Juin, he met an officer of the Deuxième Bureau, Constantin Melnik, the future coordinator of intelligence matters, after the end of the war in Algeria.

3 Lieutenant-Colonel Jeannou Lacaze succeeded him.

4 Under the *nom de plume* of J. Henry, Jacques-Henri Hervé published, in collaboration with the journalist Jean-Michel Barrault, *Vademecum du parfait agent secret*, Grenoble, 1970.

5 At the time the press spoke of 800 dismissals. One can imagine the orderlies helping the whole barracks to pack their bags.

6 Authors' archives. Memorandum dated 27 December 1970.

7 One must not confuse, as people did at the time – not unintentionally – 'Colonel Paul Fournier' with Roger Fournier of SDECE, Trinquier's assistant at the GCMA, and then the GMTI, in Indo-China.

8 In 1973 the decision taken against Captains Paul Santenac and Antoine Paolini was revoked: *Le Monde*, 20 July 1973.

9 Colonel Levacher was to pursue his career in Kenya. In the French Embassy in Cuba at the time there was a real specialist in wartime intelligence, André Tronc, who had nevertheless taken up a diplomatic career. Under the *nom de plume* of Joseph Marsant he wrote *Les Sept vies de Che Guevara*, Paris, 1976.

10 On 28 August 1969 General Guibaud, the head of SDECE, cancelled Delouette's mission to Cuba. Had he learnt something unfavourable about him?

11 Deposition of 6 June 1972.

12 Deposition of 8 June 1972.

13 In November 1971 a SOFRES survey revealed that for 54 per cent of Frenchmen the prime preoccupation at the time was how poorly SDECE was functioning.

14 Among the cronies of Labay there figures a Corsican drug dealer, Félix Rosso. He was to be murdered by Corsican nationalists in 1982, after having agreed to serve as informant for his brother-in-law, Charles Pellegrini, of the anti-terrorist unit of the Elysée, who was in charge of liaison with DGSE.

15 Georges Groussard, *Service secret, 1940–1945*, Paris, 1964.

16 Letter from General Devigny to the authors, following the French publication of this book, 10 June 1985.

17 Among its leaders was Colonel Christophe Delmer, then the head of the Deuxième Bureau of the air force.

18 This structure was to remain until 1981.

19 Michel Roussin was responsible in the Matignon for liaison with SDECE from 1972 to 1976.

20 Guy Laugère, Colonel Lionnet's deputy, took over from him in 1976.

21 Colonel Deuve gives an account of himself in the book he published under the *nom de plume* of Michel Caply, *Guerilla au Laos*, Paris, 1966. A Norman, a science student, a reserve officer in the colonial infantry, he was mentioned in dispatches in 1940, and then was in Niger, before joining the Action Branch of the DGER in Laos. A 'specialist in jungle intelligence', for a long time he was stationed by the post-war SDECE in the Far East. His appointment corresponded to a revival of interest on the part of the leadership of SDECE in that part of the world.

22 Handwritten letter addressed to G. Juquel, Union Fédérale des Ingénieurs Cadres et Techniciens CGT (Authors' archives).

23 In 1981 the Paris courts judged that the transfer order was legally invalid and ordered the Ministry of Defence to pay 40,000 francs to Georges Blanc's family.

24 The authors have not been able to cross-check this piece of information with former members of SDECE.

25 Article 86 of the Decree of 27 November 1967, which was not published in the *Journal officiel*.

26 Roger Duvernois, born in 1914, died on 19 February 1984. This literature teacher joined the Resistance, in which, under the name of 'Barrès', he became the deputy to 'Goëlette', the head of the FFC network in the Auvergne. At the Liberation he joined the DGER, and then SDECE, where he remained till 1977.

27 Conversation with the authors.

28 Mohamed Hassanein Heykal, *Le Retour de l'Ayatollah*, Paris, 1982.

29 In addition, SDECE benefited from the assessments of the Iraqi intelligence services, with whom A. de Marenches was in contact.

30 Cf. Jacques Isnard, 'Des agents du SDECE contestent l'orientation donnée à leurs activités en Afrique', *Le Monde*, 26 October 1979.

31 Interview given to *Al Watan al Arabi*, 1979.

32 Probably by Israel's Mossad.

33 For its naval operations Action Branch had numerous means of transport at its disposal: small submarines that sometimes became entangled in the nets of Corsican fishermen; 'cigar-shaped' boats (60 knots) bought in California, which cost a small fortune, and (jointly owned with SDECE's Counter-Espionage Branch) an oceanographic survey ship.

Chapter 14 *Coups d'état* in Africa

1 Mme Claude's particular friend, the arms dealer Maurice Chabert, for his part has admitted that he 'was trafficking [in arms] with Africa with the blessing of the French government' (*Mercredis de l'information*, TF1 television programme, September 1983).

2 Among the MRA leaders Pierre Lami (March 1969–April 1970) had previously been one of Moïse Tschombe's advisers in the Congo. He was replaced at the top of the MRA by a former administrator in Niger, Henri Paillard, and then by Pierre Claustre. Officially supposed to be digging wells and building dispensaries, in 1972 MRA possessed 80 networks distributed over the whole territory of Chad.

3 N. Fournier and E. Legrand, *E . . . comme Espionnage*, Paris, 1978.

4 T. Desjardins, *Avec les otages du Tchad*, Paris, 1975.

5 Letter from Gourvennec to Bocquel dated 23 June 1970, and the report of Bocquel's interrogation, 22 December 1977. Bocquel was to receive 12 million francs.

6 Source: Report of September 1976 by the SDCI, the intelligence service of the Portuguese Armed Forces Movement. Moreover, SDECE had the Portuguese community under surveillance. This was the case at Nogent-sur-Seine (Aube), where it set up a network in 1975.

7 Published in the Lisbon newspaper *Expresso*, 24 January 1976.

8 When he was asked what he thought of the FLEC, Jonas Savimbi, head of another movement opposed to the MPLA, Unita, which was supported by the West but whose popularity among the people was genuine, replied: 'You know full well that it is an invention of the French secret services, and of SDECE in particular' (interview granted to the special correspondent of *Le Figaro*. Yves Brecheret, and published 17 February 1984).

9 J. Stockwell, *In Search of Enemies (How the CIA Lost Angola)*, London, 1978.

10 Memorandum of 14 November 1975; authors' archives.

11 Jean Kay was also a mercenary in the Yemen, Lebanon and Africa. On 4 December 1971, he attempted to hijack a Pakistani plane at Orly, demanding that it should transport 20 tonnes of medicines to Bangladesh. At his trial André Malraux presented himself as a witness for the defence. The Anglo-American media accused SDECE of having been behind the incident, as a psychological operation to gain the favour of the Bengalis. A former member of Action Branch confirmed to the authors that SDECE had taken a close interest in the secession of Bangladesh, just as it had in that of Biafra previously.

12 Bob Denard suffered various failures in his operations during the 1970s. In contrast, the *coup d'état* that he orchestrated in the Comoro Islands in 1978 was a perfect success. All, or almost all, has been said about the way that Denard went about overturning the radical Ali Soilih in order to bring to power the conservative Ahmed Abdallah. Overseen by René Journiac, the operation was not unconnected with the French secret services. The SDECE station head in the Comoros had smoothed the path for the intervention. At the time the authors followed closely the setting up of the 'Rassemblement des Comoriens en France' (RCF), whose goal was 'to free the Comoran people from the tyranny of Ali

Soilih'. This was at the instigation of their leader, Abdoul Wahab (5–7 Villa Gagliardini, Paris, 75020, which was also the headquarters of the RCF). The first news-sheet of the movement calling for insurrection had been published on 12 April 1978, three weeks before the coup. All this was going on a hundred yards from SDECE headquarters.

13 *Sunday Times*, 29 May 1977.

14 *Le Monde*, 31 March 1977.

15 *Le Monde*, 18 April 1977. Cf. also 'La solitude de l'UNITA', by Dominique de Roux (*Le Monde*, 20 February 1976) and the interview with Jonas Savimbi by D. de Roux (*Quotidien de Paris*, 11 November 1975).

16 P Péan, '*V*', Paris, 1984.

17 Gordon Winter, *Inside BOSS*, London, 1981.

18 It will be noted that several ministers or advisers to ministers of Valéry Giscard d'Estaing were 'Africanists' – top civil servants who had served in Africa before independence. Those who had been in close contact with the secret services are of particular interest to us. Thus in Raymond Barre's Private Office Philippe Mestre was until 1960 Secretary-General for French Equatorial Africa, responsible to the High Commissioner's office in Brazzaville. In 1981 he was put forward as the new head of SDECE, if the outgoing President were re-elected. There is another example: Daniel Doustin operated in the Ivory Coast, Cameroon and Gabon, before becoming the governor of Chad, and then director of the DST in 1961. A notable case is that of Paul Masson, who as head of the Private Office of Yvon Bourges, the Minister of Defence, maintained the link with SDECE. Up to 1960 he had been stationed in Niger, Upper Volta and Guinea. From 1961 to 1967 he was Director-General for the Office for the Development of Agricultural Production (Bureau de Développement de la Production Agricole: BDPA), where he was replaced by Colonel Roger Barberot (1968–72).

19 In *Afrique–Asie*.

20 Testimony of Alain Leluc, given to the authors. In a *roman à clef*, *Mercénaire* (Paris, 1983), Leluc has recounted the experience in Benin, in which he participated.

21 Moïse Tschombe's own son, then a candidate for SDECE in the Congo.

22 Alain Leluc, whom we have encountered with Bob Denard and his mercenaries in Benin, was part of the Africa service of the ATP (Memo: *Service d'information et de diffusion du premier ministre*, 1980).

23 Testimony of 'Michel', given to the authors.

24 *Paris-match*, 15 August 1980.

25 This was a complete turn-about: in 1970 SDECE, the Italian SID, and the British SIS had put a stop to Operation 'Hilton', a plan to overturn Gadaffi, financed by nostalgic supporters of King Idris.

26 Always well-informed, Michel Lambinet's *Lettre d'Afrique* in its issue of 4 September 1980 (No. 35), was the first to offer a detailed version that agreed with that of SDECE: 'The most serious happening took place at Tobruk on 6 August, when the 9th Brigade revolted. The objective was, of course, the elimination of Colonel Gadaffi. The operation was most likely led by the head of Action Branch in the Libyan secret services, Commandant Driss Chehaibi. The rebels' plan was to take Tobruk and then Benghazi, after having secured the support of the great Bedouin tribes in the south, and finally to march on Tripoli

and seize power. The operation failed because one of the conspirators alerted
Tripoli.'
27 A. Gaigneron de Marolles, *L'Ultimatum – fin d'un monde ou fin du monde?*, Paris,
1984.

Chapter 15   Mitterrand's 'Specials'

1 The frogmen of SDECE came for the most part from the Army. Selection was
extremely strict. Out of 500 candidates a year, only two or three were chosen.
These men, trained in commando operations, parachuting and combat swimming,
also underwent numerous courses: sabotage, photography, 'neutralization' etc.
The Navy possessed its own commando groups based at Lorient: 'Hubert',
'Treppel', 'Jaubert', 'De Montfort' and 'De Penfentenyo'.
2 An NCO was even punished for having protested against these undemocratic
methods. The affair went up as far as Charles Hernu's Private Office, which finally
pigeon-holed the file.
3 The Defence Committee of the Socialist Party was officially set up in 1973.
4 'Reflections on SDECE', report drawn up for François Mitterrand by Louis
Mouchon, 15 September 1977.
5 *Bulletin de l'ASSDN*, no. 111.
6 *Journal officiel*, 4 April 1982. That of 4 January 1946, the date of the setting up of
SDECE, had never before been published.
7 Colonel Charrier was the brother of Jacques Charrier, the former husband of
Brigitte Bardot.
8 Testimony of Pierre Marion, given to the authors.
9 To quote only one example, the following is an extract from a note of the DGSE
on the Soviet armed forces, sent in autumn 1981 to the government authorities:
'For the Russians, modern warfare is relentless. This is because of its political
content: the enemy of the USSR is a class enemy. Moreover, the possible
employment of nuclear weapons and the follow-up to nuclear strikes would
increase the bitterness and violence of the struggle . . .'

Chapter 16   Mission 'Satanic': 'Sink the *Rainbow Warrior*'

1 This was the name chosen by the French secret services for the operation mounted
against Greenpeace.
2 We have chosen to preserve the anonymity of these two men.
3 There was also another frogman on the spot: Captain Gérard R., who was given
the task of steering the Zodiac on the evening of the attack.
4 This account is taken from *Mission Oxygène*, Paris 1987, written by a former
frogman using the pseudonym of Patrick du Morne Vert.
5 In the jargon of the French secret services this is called an 'exfiltration'.
6 Pascal Krop, for *L'Evénement*, and J.-M. Bourget for *VSD*.
7 Several journalists, to start with the authors, identified Alain Mafart under the
alias of Alain Turenge, because his life-story had been told, two months earlier, in
the first French edition of this book.

8 On several occasions Admiral Lacoste was to say later that he had personally spoken to President Mitterand about Operation 'Satanic'. Prime Minister Laurent Fabius, on the other hand, was kept in ignorance.

9 Nickname given to General Lacaze in the French secret services.

Index

Abbas, Ferhat, 127, 170
Abdallah, Ahmed, 318 n12
Achard, Jacques, 194
Achiary, André ('Baudin'), 107–8, 109, 119
ACP, 101
Action Branch, 16, 43, 47–50, 90, 104–14, 118, 128–9, 252, 276–7
Action Division (formerly Action Branch), 283
Addam, Sheikh Kamal, 257
Adenauer, Konrad, 35
'Admiral, The', see Trautmann, Henri
Adoula, Cyrille, 251
Afghanistan, 286
AFL, 62
AFP, 283, 303 n18
Africa, 173–90, 191–209, 262–75, 283–4
Agostini, 186
Ahidjo, Ahmadou, 187
Ahmat, Acyl, 283
Aicardi, Maurice, 149
Aït Ahcene, 163
Aït Ahmed Hochine, 112, 114
Al-Fatah, 261
al-Kubaisi, Basil, 260
Alamo, Carlos, see Makarov
Albania, 75
Algeria, 105, 106, 117–24, 173–4
Allain, Yves, 125, 237
Allegre, Manuel, 265
Allemand, Jean, 298 n7

Allenan, Gaby, 108
Allende, Salvador, 54–5
'Alliance' Resistance movement, 300 n13
ALN, 130
Altengrabow, 4
Amade, Louis 56
'Amado' affair, 99
Amaral, Freitas do, 265
Amirouche, 125, 126
AMT, 174
Amt Blank, 36
'Anatole', see Decorse, François
'Andalusia' network, 56, 166
Anders, 69
Andrès, 112, 113
Andries, 288, 293
Anglès, Henri, 182
Angleton, James Jesus, 211–13, 217, 218, 220, 313 n3
Angola, 265, 267–70
Ankara, 117
Antonini, Ange, 63, 65
'Apparat', 34
Argentina, 29
'Arma' Operation, 162–4
Arms Traffic Section, 164–6
Arnal, Frank, 88
Arnaud, 51
Aronowicz, 70
AS, 12
Ashraf, Princess, 258
Assad, President, 284

Athos, 109–10
Atlan, Lucie, 310 n20
ATP, 272–3
Attia, Jo, 163, 233, 310 n16
Aubaume, Jean-Hilaire, 185
'Aubrac', *see* Squadron 51
Auer, Leopold, 6
Auriol, Jean ('Jeannot'), 140
Auriol, Vincent, 40, 137
Aussaresses, Paul, 4, 47, 56, 64, 82,
    144, 147, 310 n17, Plate 2
Austria, 30–1, 36–7
'Austrian, the', 81
Azam, Henri, 253, 254
Aziz, Nayef Ben Abdul, 274
'Aztec Wizard', *see* Lacaze, Jeannou
'Azure', 301 n27

Bachclard, Claude, 169
Badaire, Michel, 129, 131
BAG, 192, 193, 198–9
Bagheera, 81
Bai Vien, 95
Baker, Josephine, 231
Balkan network, 63
Bamilékés, 186
Bamler, Rudolf, 35
Bangkok, 104
Banhiot, 95
Banon, Isadore, 266
Bao Dai, 80, 97
Baranès, André, 102–3
Barberot, Roger, 178, 228, 249–51,
    319 n18
'Barbès', *see* Fourcaud, Pierre
Barbie, Klaus, 27, 251
Barcelo, 288
Bardet, René-Louis, 180
'Barracuda' Operation, 272–3
Barré, Siad, 257
Barrière, Léonce, 307 n33
Barril, Paul, 274
Barthez, 132
Bas, Pierre, 192
Basque country, 260
Bass, André, 85

Bassaler, Yvonne, 70–1
Bauchet, 248
'Baudin', *see* Achiary, André
Bauer, Freddy, 130
Bauge, 132
Baylot, Jean, 102
Bayonne, Henri, 263–4
BCRA, 2, 3, 12, 14–15, 20, 28
BDPA, 249–50
Beauffre, General, 117
'Beaumont, Colonel', *see* Bertrand,
    René
Beccuau, Yves, 253, 281
Bechtell, William ('Big Bill'), 188–90
Begin, Menachem, 257
BEL, 117, 126–8
Beletz, Colonel, 7
Belgian Congo, 200–3
Bell, Marie, *see* Bellon, Marie
Belleux, Maurice, 2, 16, 49, 81, 83–5,
    88–9, 90, 93, 94, 129
Bellon, Marie (Bell), 140, 308 n12
Bellon, Raoul, 308 n12
Bellon, Roger, 83, 304 n21
Bellounis, Mohammad, 130–1
Belvisi, Armand, 169
Ben Barka, Medhi, 151, 163, 175,
    231–8, 247, 248
Ben Bella, Ahmed, 105–7, 109–14,
    119
Ben Boulaid, Mostefa, 129
Ben Faisal, Prince Turki, 258
Ben Gurion, David, 115
ben Mayel, Ibrahim ben Mohamed,
    109
Ben M'Hidi, Larbi, 123
'Benedictines', 173
Benelli, Cardinal, 156
Benes, President, 57
Benet, Jacques, 1–2, 3–5, 62
Benin (Dahomey), 174, 271
Benoît, *see* Bertolini, Louis
Benoît, Pierre, 13
Berenger, Paul, 183, 312 n19
Bergen-Belsen, 3
Beria, Lavrenti, 68, 72

Bernadotte, Folke, 115
Bernier, Marcel, 141
Bernier, Philippe, 234–5
Bertin, 94
Bertolini, Louis ('Benoît'), 121
Bertrand, Gustave, 49
Bertrand, Marthe, 228
Bertrand, René ('Colonel Beaumont'),
    47, 76, 194, 218, 226–9, 237–8,
    245, 247–52
Béthouard, General, 63
Beugras, Albert, 28, 299 n5
Beyer, Georges, 22
Beyler, Jean-Noël, 312 n6
Biafra, 206–9
Bibes, 27
BICE, 27, 299 n2
Bichelot, René, 91, 180, 304 n12
Bichon, 272
Bickler, Hermann, 29, 299 n5
Bidault, Georges, 39, 80, 98, 100
Bidermann, Dr, 51
'Big Ben' Operation, 214
'Big Bill', *see* Bechtell, William
Bigeard, Marcel, 123–4
Billotte, 228, 250
Bingen, Jacques, 12
Binh Xuyen, 93–4
'Binot', *see* Foccart, Jacques
'Bison Base', 182, 245, 249
Bissell, Jnr, Richard, 220
Bistos, François ('Colonel Franck'), 56,
    151, 166–8, 248, 310 n18
Bitterlin, Lucien, 172
Black, Colonel, 49
Blanc, Georges, 254–5, 317 n23
Blank, Theodor, 36
Blaret, Jacques, 227
Blemant, Roger, 308 n12
'Blitz, The', 258–60
Bloch, Jean-Pierre, 12, 53
Blondeau, 65
Blondel, Maurice, 37
Blouin, François, 111, 306 n11
'Blue Bird', 129
'Blue Plan', 62–4

'Blueitis' Operation, 121, 124–6, 163,
    307 n30
Blum, Leon, 5–8, 81
Blun, Georges, 28
Blunt, Anthony, 212, 313 n3
BND, 35, 74, 142, 161, 193, 212–13
Boccone, Aldo, 237
Bocquel, Claude (Léon Hardy,
    'Leonardi'), 264
Bodenan, Francis, 164, 204–5
Bogomolov, Alexander, 60
Boitel, Jacques, 236–7
Bokassa, Emperor, 184, 272–3
Bollaert, Eugène, 86
Bomboko, 204
Bommelaer, Michel, 51, 145, 252
Bond, Nguza Karl I, 204
Bongo, Bernard-Albert, 181, 183,
    196, 207, 271
'Bonito' Operation, 272
Bono, Nadine, 264
Bono, Outel, 263–4
Bordes, 269
Borel, Jacques, 87
Boris, Henri, 47, 301 n18
Borissov, General, 271
BOSS, 184, 269, 271
Bossard, Robert, 311 n15
Boucheseiche, 233
Bouchet, Father, 309 n36
Boudiaf, Mohammad, 112
Boulle, Pierre, 79, 183
Boumedienne, President, 204, 258
Bounier, 141
Bourdet, Claude, 43, 300 n7
Boureau-Mitrecey, 164, 165, 194,
    312 n4
'Bourgeaud, Colonel', *see* Denard,
    Robert
Bourgès-Maunoury, Maurice, 112,
    114, 115, 137–8, 148
Bourguiba, Habib, 163, 169, 274
Bourret, General, 138
Boursicot, Pierre, 63, 94, 107, 114–
    15, 147, 152, 162–4, 219
Bousquet, Raymond, 241

Boyle, Andrew, 313 n3
Boymond, Maurice, 83
Bozzi, Jean, 210
BR, 17, 83
Braden, Tom, 62
'Braintrust', 163
Branet, 115
Brayance, *see* Griotteray, Alain
Brazil, 29
Bresson, Pierre, 310 n20
Bresson, Robert, 251
Briand, General, 187
Bridou, Lucien-Paul, 300 n13
British secret services, 115–16, 188;
 see also SIS
Brossin de Meré, Aymar de, 69–70
Brossolette, Pierre, 12
'Brouillard, Colonel', *see* Nord,
 Pierre
'Brotherhood' network, *see* 'Phratrie'
 network
Brouillet, Jean-Claude, 208
Brown, Irving, 62
Bruce, David, 26
Bruce-Lockhart, John MacGregor,
 300 n2
'Bruno', *see* Grillot, Georges
BSLE, 120
BSM, 29
BTLC, 85–6
Buchenwald, 3
Budapest, 71
Bulley, Dominique, 63
Bundesamt für Verfassungsschutz,
 157, 300 n17
BUPO, 161
Burin des Roziers, Etienne, 214
Burnham, James, 62, 155
Buttet, Henri de, 30, 298 n7
BVD, 157
Byelorussia, 75

Cabinda, 267–9
Cabon, Christine, 293
Cabral, Amilcar, 265
Caetano, 266

Cagoule group, 12, 41, 297 n3
Caillaud, Robert, 82, 237
Caillot, Eugène ('Gégène'), 49, 60,
 142, 248
Calcutta, 79
Calvary Mission, 5–8
Cambodia, 238–9, 285
Cambon, Pierre, 4, 54, 301 n30
'Camelia' network, 310 n10
Cameroon, 141, 174, 185, 186–8
Camp, Albert, 141
Camus, André, 225, 256
Canaris, Admiral, 35, 300 n15
Candelier, René, 254
Cao Bang, 89, 247, 304 n11
Capitant, René, 245
Cardi, Robert, 161
Cardoso, Agostinho Barbieri, 265–6
Cardot, Pierre, 224–5
'Carlos', *see* Sanchez, Ilich Ramirez
'Carnation Revolution', 265, 267
Caron, 180
Casey, William, 286
Castex, François, 245
Castille, Philippe, 108
Castro, Fidel, 230, 231, 250
'Catena', 159
Cathala, 126
Catherine, Pierre, 150
Catholic Church, 155–6
Catroux, 108
CCI, 106, 119–24, Fig. 6.1
CDS, 265
CE, 13, 16–17
CEA, 136
Central African Republic, 174, 184,
 272, 284
Central Committee of Ukrainian
 Organizations in France, 74
Central Press Agency, 111, 112
CERM, 315 n27
Cetniki, 74, 76
CGC, 62
CGT, 23, 62, 66
Chaban-Delmas, Jacques, 66, 130,
 146

Chabert, Maurice, 318 n1
Chad, 174, 185, 262–4, 285
Chadbourne, Phil, 62
Chaffart, Georges, 186
Chalet, Marcel, 119, 210, 214, 313 n5
Challe, 115, 122
Chamagne, 126
'Chamois' Operation, 121
Chantiers de Jeunesse, 20
Charrier, 283
Chatelain, Maurice, 65
Chaumette, 151
Chaumien, Marcel ('Monsieur Armand'), 57, 76, 151
Chaussade, Pierre, 111
Chaussée, Marcel, 150, 235–7, 315 n3
Chauvière, Mme, 225
Chavanon, Christian, 167
Chehaibe, Driss, 274, 275, 319 n26
Cheka, 72
Chevallier, Jacques, 106, 107–8, 305 n5
Cheysson, Claude, 114
Chiang Kai-shek, 84, 92
Chile, 54
Chin Peng, 84
China, 84–5
Chinese Communist Party, 46
Chinese intelligence, 239
Chrétien, Jean, 45, 298 n7
Christienne, Charles, 77, 303 n25
Christmann, Richard, 311 n23
Chtouki, Larbi, 234–5
Chunowsky, 70
'Church of Silence', 155–6, 309 n33
CIA, 35, 60, 74, 75, 84–5, 103–4, 171, 193, 201, 203–6, 211–14, 218–21, 230–1, 238–9, 251, 268–71, 274, 278, 285–6
Ciampi, Yves, 311 n25
CIC, 37
CINC, 276–7, 288
CIR, 307 n2
CIRVP, 261
Cjad, 283

'Claude, Madame', *see* Grunet, Fabienne
Claustre, Françoise, 263–4
Claustre, Pierre, 263–4, 318 n2
CLD, 1–2, 3–5
Clément, Maurice, 23, 71, 211, 256
Cléry, Bernard, 51
CNEC, 132
CNRS, 31, 198
CNT, 55
'Cobra 77' Operation, 269
Cochin China, 93
Cocu, Carmen, 310 n16
Codet, 282
Cohen-Séat, Gilbert, 148–9, 308 n21
'Cohors' network, 114
Colby, William, 239, 274, 313 n4
Cold War, 33–4, 60–78
'Coligny' headquarters, 51
Collin, Bernard, 255
Collins, David, 291
Colonial Intelligence Service, 85–6
Colonne, 167
Combat, 43
Comintern, 66
Comité d'Etudes Economiques et Sociales, 62
Commin, Pierre, 110
communism, 33–4, 155–6, *see also* Cold War
Communist Party, 278
'Community' plan for French colonies, 174, 182, 191
Comoro Islands, 318 n12
'Compass Rose', *see* 'Rainbow' Operation
computerization, 252
Conakry, 191–6, 265–7
concentration camps, liberation of, 3–4
Congo (Brazzaville), 174, 184, 199–200
Conty, Paul, 106, 168–9, 311 n24
Conus, Adrien, 312 n30
Copeau, Pascal, 298 n13

Corbel, Jean-Claude, 239
'Coriolan', *see* Demichel, François
    Saar
Cornut-Gentille, Bernard, 192
Corsica, 260–1
Coste-Floret, Paul, 85, 97
Coulon, Christian, 198
Council for Documentation, 40
Counter-Espionage, 13, 16–17, 141,
    173, 305 n4
'Courby', 36
Couve de Murville, Maurice, *see*
    Murville, Maurice Couve de
Couvert, Michel, 150, 236
Crignola, René, 121, 140, 254, 281
Croatia, 75
Cross, 240
CROWCASS programme, 299 n4
cryptography, 49
Cuba, 220, 230–1, 250–1, 260
Cyprus, 116
Cyrenaica, 273
Czech secret services, 222, 224–5
Czechoslovakia, 57–8, 69, 75

'D Measures', 107
d'Astier de la Vigerie, Emmanuel, 42,
    102–3
Dabetić, Lazar, 75
Dabezies, Pierre, 91, 95, 202
da Costa, Jean, 269
Dacko, David, 184, 272–3
Dahomey, *see* Benin
Dalat, 88–9
Dallaporta, Christian ('Qui de droit'),
    261
Dalmas, René, 281
Damon, Henri, 53
'Darius' network, 50, 64
Darquier de Pellepoix, 55
Dassault, Marcel, 31, 152
David, Captain, 96
David, Christian, 236, 315 n6
Dayan, Moshe, 115
Dayoub, Hassan, 285
DCT, 18

de Clary, 202
de Gaulle, Charles, 2, 8, 10–12, 15,
    25–6, 39–40, 42, 55, 57, 63–4, 66,
    107, 114, 121, 127, 133–241
de la Bourdonnaye-Montluc, Yves,
    202, 307 n33
de la Clemandière, Elmire de Courte-
    manche, 175
de la Roncière, Michel Bourel, 69
de la Salle, Charles Jurquet, 303
    n26
de la Source, 112
de Marenches, *see* Marenches
de Vosjoli, *see* Thyraud, Philippe
'Debrand', *see* Guétet, Father
Debray, Régis, 230, 286
Debré, Michel, 135–6, 139, 149, 167,
    182–3, 199–200, 208, 218, 307
    n32
Decore, Roger ('Jean Devis'), 64–5
Decorse, Françoise ('Anatole'), 122,
    128, 131
Defferre, Gaston, 180
Degenne, 273
Degueldre, 121
Dejean, Maurice, 215–16, 217, 314
    n9
Delahoutre Report, 100
Delarue, Alfred, 102, 200
Delauney, Maurice, 186, 208
Delgado, 265
Delimarsky, Yevgeny ('Edward'), 30–
    1, 298 n7
Delmas, Robert, 183
Delmer, Christophe, 317 n17
Delocque-Fourcaud, Boris, 47, 77
Delon, Alain, 228, 245, 249
Delore, Roger, *see* Delouette, Roger
Delorme, 127
Delouette, Roger ('Roger Delore'),
    248–51, 278
Delpal, 65
Delseny, René, 141, 142, 161, 165,
    169, 205, 214
Demichel, François Saar ('Coriolan'),
    5–7, 53–4, 57, 217, 314 n13

Denard, Robert ('Colonel Bourgeaud'),
    181, 200, 202, 207, 268–9, 271,
    318 n12
Denis, Jacques, 220
Depreux, Edouard, 63
Deriabin, Piotr, 211, 313 n2
Deruelle, Henri, 166
Derviche ('Kobus'), 130
des Closières, 253
Desgrées du Lou, Jean-Pol, 283
'Desiré', 107
Desjardins, Thierry, 264
Despierres, Gaston, 164, 310 n16
Despuech, Jacques, 88
Deuve, 254, 317 n21
Deuxième Bureau ('2 bis'), 13, 93, 94,
    111, 315 n27
Devigny, André, 251–2
Devis, Jean, *see* Decore, Roger
Devlin, Lawrence Raymond, 201, 204
Dewavrin, André, 40, 46; *see also*
    'Passy, Colonel'
DGD, 87, 90
DGECE, 13–16
DGED, 258
DGER, 10–26, 39, 56, 79
DGSE, 281–3
DGSS, 10, 14, 22
Dhainaud, Claude, 310 n20
Dia, Mamadou, 197
Diak, Mungul, 204–5
Diallo, Sayfoulaye, 198, 266
'Diaspora II' Operation, 115
Diawadou, El Hadj Barry, 198
Dides, Jean, 102
Dien Bien Phu, 79, 80, 100, 247
Dillais, Louis-Pierre ('Jean-Louis
    Dormand'), 276, 288–9, 290,
    292–3
Dinguibai, 263
Diop, Ibrahima, 198
Diouf, Abdou, 198
DIRCEN, 294–5
DIRDOC, 312 n24
Dlimi, Ahmed, 232, 234, 235, 238,
    257, 258

Do Dai, 96, 97, 98
DOM-TOM, 176, 178
Dombrowski, Siegfried, 72
'Domino', *see* Loisel, Dominique
DOP, 119, 123–4, 360 n25
Doriot, Jacques, 29
Dormand, Jean-Louis, *see* Dillais,
    Louis-Pierre
Dormoy, Mark, 41
Doustin, Daniel, 187, 214, 217, 313
    n1, n5, 319 n18
DPU, 120
DRA, 33–5
Druet, Gaston, 70
drug trafficking, 248–9, 278
DST, 18, 33, 56, 72–3, 102–3, 118–
    19, 214–15, 217, 222–5, 230–1,
    260, 281, 286
du Puy-Montburn, Déodat, 56
Dubois, André, 102
Dubois, Captain, 127
Dubois, Hubert, 168
Dubois, René, 161
Dubois, Yves-Marc, 153–4, 156, 309
    n29, n36
Dubos, Jean-François, 278
Duboÿs, Guy, 50, 66, 150
Duchemin, Jacques, 272
Duclos, Jacques, 22, 102, 231
Duclos, Maurice ('Saint-Jacques'),
    12, 23, 29
Ducournau, 111
Dulac, René, 285
Dulles, Allen, 2, 62, 85, 103, 220
Dumas, Robert-Charles, 13
Dumont, Maurice, 27, 68, 114, 144,
    308 n12
Dunant-Henry, 304 n12
Dung, Tran Viet, 230
Dunkirk Intelligence Group, 54
Dupas, Jacques, 81–2
Durand, Paul, 248, 252
Durieux, Christian ('Napoleon'), 158,
    309 n4
Dutch intelligence, 84
Dutet, Captain, 16

Duvalier, François, 251
Duvernois, Roger, 256, 317 n26
Duvivier, 129
Dzerzhinsky, 72

East German secret services, 275
Ed Dib, Fathi, 109
Eden, Anthony, 115
'Edward', *see* Delimarsky, Yevgeny
Egé, 131, 202
Egypt, 110, 114–18, 257, 274
El Fassi, Allal, 163, 246
El Mahi, 235
Elbling, 119
Eliacheff, Boris, 201
ELP, 265
Elsaneaux, 36
Ely, Paul, 101, 121, 122, 136
EMIAT, 90
Emin, Roger, 287, 296
ENI, 170
Enigma machine, 49
EOKA, 116
Eriau, Gabriel, 306 n20
Erouard, 107, 129
Erulin, 272
ETA, 260
Etiau, Fabriel, 118
Evang, Wilhelm, 212
Eyadema, Etienne, 184

Fabius, Laurent, 293, 321 n8
Fagès, 295, 296
FAI, 55, 56
Faligot, Roger, 293, Plate 5
Faulques, Roger, 131, 200, 202, 207
Faure, Edgar, 105, 112, 284
Faure-Beaulieu, Didier, 83, 253, 256
Fauvert, Louis, 24
Fayolle, 246
FBI, 220
Febvre, Louis, 56
Fedyahin, 117, 260
Feeny, Danny, 291
Felfe, Heinz, 213
Fellagha, 117, 128

Fernandès, Raoul, 153
Ferré-Patin, 253
Ferry, Jules, 201
FFI, 55
FHO, 35
Fichard, 165
Fifth Bureau, 120
Figon, Georges-Auguste, 234–6
Fille-Lambie, Henri, *see* Morlanne,
    Jacques
Finland, 140
'Finville', *see* Le Roy, Marcel
'Firm, the', 135–56
Flaud, Jacques, 239
FLB, 241, 260
FLEC, 267–9, 318 n8
FLERD, 271
Flcutiaux, Michel, Plate 7
FLN, 105–32, 141, 157, 164–5, 252
FLNC, 261
FLNKS, 295
Floirat, Sylvain, 87
FLQ, 240–1, 316 n16
FNLA, 269
Foccart, Jacques, 1, 3, 4–5, 83, 135,
    138, 172, 174–9, 182, 187, 191,
    195–7, 203–4, 215, 217, 232, 237,
    241, 270, 311 n3, n11
Foch, Marshal, 246
Fochidé, 185
Folliguet, Professor, 49, 51
Follot, Nicole, 83
Fontès, André, 298 n7
Fontès, Jean, 34
'Force K', 121, 129
Force Ouvrière, 62
Fouchet, Christian, 101–2
Fouilland, Jacques Sylla, 254, 282
Fourcade, Marie-Madeleine, 180,
    300 n13
Fourcaud, Boris, 16
Fourcaud, Pierre ('Barbès', 'The Slav'),
    12, 16, 23, 24, 40, 41–3, 47, 70, 76,
    89–90, 96, 99–100, 138, 144, 167,
    188, 217, 300 n8, 308 n4
Fournet, 70

Fournial, Georges, 220
Fournier, Edith, 83
Fournier, Louis, 316 n16
Fournier, Paul, 208, 249, 250, 316 n7
Fournier, Roger, 316 n7
Fourth International, 157
'France-Sud' group, 199
Franceschi, Joseph, 287
Franchini, Mathieu, 87
Francia, 261
Francis, Ahmed, 110
Francisci, Marcel, 94
'Franck, Colonel', *see* Bistos, François
Franco, Francisco, 55–7
Franco, Lieutenant, 167
'Francophonic' movement, 205–6
Frandon, General, 111, 112
Franque, Luis Ranque, 267, 269
Frederick of Prussia, Prince, 8
Free Czech Movement, 57–8
Free France, 10, 12, 42
freemasonry, 280
Frelimo, 265
Frenay, Henri, 1
French Connection, 248
Frey, Roger, 172, 210, 233
Fried, 60
Frolinat, 262–4
Froment-Maurice, Henri, 111
FTP, 18, 60, 298 n10
Furuya, Yukata, 260

Gabon, 174, 183, 185
Gadaffi, 257, 264, 273–5, 319 n25
Gafsa, 274
Gaillard, Félix, 149
Galbraith, Alan, 292
Galley, Robert, 294
'Gallia' network, 57, 299 n7
Galopin, Pierre, 263–4
GAM 56 ('Vaucluse'), 252, 273
Gambetta, Grand Hotel, 139–43
'Garanin', *see* Sinitzin, Yevgeny Ivanovich
Garaudy, Roger, 155
Garcia, Cristino, 55, 56

Garder, Michel, 37, 280
Gardes, Jean, 111, 120
Gastaldo, 69, 217
Gaullist Republic, 133–241
Gaullists, 41, 62
Gauthier, 304 n12
Gbenye, Christophe, 203
GCMA, 89–92, 93–6, 97, 128, 304 n23
GCR, 121, 143, 254–5
'Gégène', *see* Caillot, Eugène
Gehlen, Reinhard, 35, 36, 142, 161–2
Gehlen Organization, 35–7, 74, 75–6
GEI, 271
General Directorate, 282
generals, treason of the, 85, 96–8
Geneva Conference (1954), 95
Genève, Pierre, *see* Schweizer, Kurt-Emile
Geniès, Henri, 110, 141, 165, 306 n10
Genot, Eugène, 161, 165
Geoffray, Jean, 168
Gérar-Dubot, Paul, 27–8, 34, 299 n3
Germain, Colonel, 28, 44, 45, 76, 105–12, 114, 120–2, 129–31, 160, Plate 3
German intelligence, 35–7, 157
Gevaudan, Honoré, 119, 123
Ghibaudo, Emile, 310 n20
'ghost service', 52–3
Giap, Vo Nguyen, 89, 92, 96
GIC, 142
GIGN, 274
Gillier, Genest, 266, 274
Gingouin, Georges, 162
Girard, 64
Girardot, 99
Giraud, 12, 14
Giscard d'Estaing, Valéry, 255, 257, 270–3, 277
GLI, 129
GMI, 304 n23
Godard, Yves, 82, 123, 126, 128, 131
Goldschild, Gaston, 53

Golytzin, Anatoly Alexandrovich ('Martel'), 210–11, 213–15, 218, 221
Gondolo, Pierre, 168, 310 n20
Gorce-Franklin, Henri, 31, 299 n7
Gorse, Georges, 169, 215
Gottwald, Klement, 57
Gouazé, Lucien ('Little Cleric'), 71–2, 302 n17
Gouin, Félix, 25, 40
Gourlay, Larry, 231
Gourvennec, Camille, 263, 264
Goussault, 120
Gowon, 206
GPRA, 110–11, 127–8
Gracieux, 90
Grall, Edmond, 91, 93, 94, 95
Gramatges, Harold, 230
'Grand Mercier, Le', *see* Mercier, Jean
Grangeaud, 4
Gras, Yves, 272
GRE, 125–6
Greene, Graham, 84, 90
Greenpeace affair, 288–96
Grellier, 113
Gribanov, Oleg, 215–16
Grillot, Georges ('Bruno'), 252, 273, 274, 276–7, 283
Griotteray, Alain (A. Brayance), 298 n29
Grivas, 116
Grosser, Alfred, 154
'Grosses Paluches, Les', *see* Meunier, Raymond
Grossin, General Paul, 72, 109, 118, 135–56, 170–2, 177, 181–2, 189, 192, 200, 213–16, 220, 232, 239
Grossouvre, François de ('Monsieur Leduc'), 65–7, 278–9, 284
Groussard, Georges, 42, 251
GRU, 211
Grué, Bernard, 254
Grunet, Fabienne ('Madame Claude', 'Violette'), 262
Grunitzky, Nicholas, 184

Guéna, Yves, 194
Guérin, André, ('Toto'), 210, 223–4
Guerini, Antoine, 94
Guesde, Jules, 52
Guétet, Father ('Debrand'), 83
Guetz, 33
Guevara, Ernesto (Che), 230
Guibaud, Eugène, 151, 152, 236, 238, 246, 248, 270, 309 n27
Guibaud, Louis, 216
Guillaudot, Maurice, 63
Guillaumat, Pierre, 136
Guillermaz, Jacques, 84
Guinea, 174, 177, 191–6, 198–9
Guinea-Bissau, 265–7
Guivante Saint-Gast, Paul ('Saint-Gast'), 49, 81
Guomindang, 46, 84, 303 n21
Guy, 247
Guyot, Raymond, 23

Habaki, 115
Habré, Hissène, 262–4
Hacène, Mayhouz, 125
Hached, Ferhad, 158
Hadj, Messali, 130
Hagemeister, Ludwig, 35
Haiphong, 87
Hall, Mervin, 84
Hamel, Raymond, 31, 66
Hamelet, Michel-Pierre, 310 n16
Hammarskjöld, Dag, 155, 201
Hamon, 283
'Hand of the Fathma', 158–60
Hardy, Léon ('Leonardi'), *see* Bocquel, Claude
Hassan II, 257, 258, 271
Haulin, 185
Havana, 220–2
Héblé, 119
Hechberg, 205–6
'Hedgehog, The', *see* Rizza, Jo
Heer, General von, 7
Heinz, Friedrich Wilhelm ('Tulip'), 35–6
Held, Jean-Francis, 189

Helms, Richard, 218
Henriot, Philippe, 227
Hentic, Pierre, 91, 129
Hermault, Pierre, 110
Hernu, Charles, 277–80, 285, 286–7, 293–6, Plate 6, Plate 10
Hervé, Jacques, 136, 154, 214, 220, 237, 248, 316 n4
Hessel, Stéphane, 12
Heux, Pierre, 126–7, 130
Higher Council for Intelligence, 135, 307 n2
'Hilton' Operation, 319 n25
Hitler, Adolf, 8, 35
Ho Chi Minh, 79, 80–1, 84, 91, 97, 104
Hoettl, Wilhelm, 37, 300 n 18
'Homo' Operation, 162–4
Hong Kong, 84, 86, 94
'honourable correspondents', 141, 150–1, 173
Horoscope, 196–7
Horthy, Miklos, 8
Horton, Philip Clark, 61
Hounau, Léonard, 16, 49, 57, 76, 216–17, 218, 222, 228, 314 n14
Houphouët-Boigny, Félix, 174, 176, 183, 192, 196, 207
Huks, 90
Humm, 71, 140, 256
Hungary, 69, 140
'Hunter' group, 83
Husson, 239

Idris, King, 319 n25
Igouin, Albert, *see* Jallez, David Chaim
IHEDN, 97
Imams, Peul, 199
Indo-China, 79–104
infiltration of Eastern bloc, 282
information technology, 283
Infrastructure and Resources Directorate, 253–4
Intelligence Branch, 252
Intelligence Directorate, 254

Inter-Army Coordination Centre, 119–24
Iran, 257, 258, 267
Iraqi intelligence, 317 n29
Ireland, 260
Israeli secret services, 115
Istanbul, 140
Istiqlâl, 163
Istomin, Konstantin Yeveyevich, 74
Italian secret service, 109
Italy, 5
Ivory Coast, 174, 183

Jacobson, Michael, 158
'Jacques', *see* Soliveau, Louis
Jacquier, Henri, 232
Jacquier, Paul, 52, 111, 152, 213, 216–18, 221, 232, 234, 235, 237, 248, 270, 304 n21, 309 n27
Jacquin, Henri, ('The Legionnaire'), 96, 116–17, 120, 126–8, 167
Jacquinot, Louis, 195
Jakarta, 84
Jallez, David Chaim (Albert Igouin), 70
Janot, Raymond, 177
Jantzen, Bob, 84
Janvry, Yves Choppin de, 255, 256
Japanese counter-espionage, 149
Japanese Red Army Faction, 260
Jardim, Jorge, 265
Jarrot, André, 304 n3
Jaspar, Marcel-Henri, 201
Javorka, Vandelino, 156
'Jeannot', *see* Auriol, Jean
Jeantet, Benoît, 248
'Jedburgh' commandos, 302 n3
Jellicoe, Earl, 62, 302 n2
John, Otto, 35, 36
Joliot-Curie, 33
Jonglez, 99
Journiac, René, 177, 270–2, 318 n12
Joxe, Louis, 67, 136, 215
Juillet, Pierre, 245
Juin, Alphonse, 2, 106, 247
'Jules', 50, 301 n23

K (Kominform) Service, 74
Kabylia, 128–31
Kadaf-Adam, Saif, 275
Kaiser, Raoul, 37
Kaldor, Pierre, 264
Kampuchea, *see* Cambodia
Kandy (Ceylon), 79
Kannengiesser, René, 151
'Karamel', 249
Karim, Bangouri, 193
'Karlin', *see* Krotkov, Yury Vassilievich
Kastenbaum, Léon, 31, 52–3, 54, 301
    n26
Katanga, 200–3
Kaunda, Kenneth, 207
Kay, Jean 269, 318 n11
Keita, Fodeba, 195
Kemp, Jack, 270
Kempeitai, 93
Kennedy, John Fitzgerald, 213, 218
Keramane, Hafid, 163
Kerekou, Mathieu, 179, 271
Kergaravat, 185
Kessler, Roger, 141
KGB, 72, 211, 214–18, 265, 294
Khider, Mohammed, 112, 114
Khomeini revolution, 258
Khonsari, Parviz, 258
Khrushcev, Nikita, 68, 140
'Kilowatt', 260
'Kléber' network, 30, 166–8, 199
'Kobus', *see* Derviche
Koch, Guillaume-Louis, 175
Koenig, General, 53, 63, 64
Kokorin, 8 297 n12
Kolingba, President, 284
Kominform, 74
Kondek, 224, 225
Kosciusko-Morizet, Jacques, 203
Kountche, Seyni, 180
Kovacs, René, 108
Krassin, Leonid, 42
Kronberg-Sobolevskaya, Lara, 215–16
Krop, Pascal, 293, Plate 6
Krotkov, Yury Vassilievich ('Karlin'),
    215–16, 314 n7

Krotoff, René, 129
Kubitschek, Juscelino, 154

La Bourdonnaye, 126
La Boudonnaye-Montluc, 131
La Guerre Moderne (Trinquier), 92–3
Labadie, Maurice, 86, 87
Labat, Paul, 254
Labay, André, 251
Labbens, Albert, 140, 216
Labrusse, Roger, 103
Lacaze, Jeannou ('Sorcerer', 'Aztec
    Wizard'), 3, 111, 166, 252, 254,
    273, 276, 286, 296, Plate 6
Lacaze, Pierre, 310 n20
Lacheraf, Moustapha, 112
Lacheroy, 120
Lacoste, Pierre, 286, 287, 294–6,
    Plate 8
Lacoste, Robert, 32, 46, 107, 111,
    112, 123
Laer, André van, 6
Lafont, Roger, *see* Verneuil, Colonel
Lageneste, Jacques de, 253, 265
Laguerre, Jacques, 98
Lahana, Captain ('Landrieux'), 16,
    24
Lai Van Sang, 93
Lalanne, Louis, 106, 115, 162–3
L'Allinec, Jean-Marie, 43, 300 n8
Lamazina, Sangoulé, 184
Lambert, Claudine, 113
Lamberton, Jean-Marie, 187
Lambinet, Michel, 268–9
Lambroschini, Joseph, ('Colonel
    Nizier'), 202
Lami, Pierre, 318 n2
Lamia (Thyraud), 220–1, 314–15
    nn17–22
Lampe, Alexis de, 74
Lamy, Léon, 69, 197, 302 n13
'Landrieux', *see* Lahana, Captain
Landsdale, Edward, 90, 94, 103, 239
Langella, 167
Langlade, François de, 79
Laniel, Joseph, 101

Lannurien, Georges Barazer de, 69, 71, 109, 110–11, 184, 217–19, 221–2, 307 n33, Plate 5
Lannurien, Jean de, 249
Lanquetin, 196
Laporte, Michel, 218
Laporte, Pierre, Canadian Minister of Labour, 240
Larminat, General de, 63
Larzul, Robert, 272
Lasimone, 202
Lassabe, Maurice, 119, 130
Latin America, 29, 154, 220
Latour, Jacques, 159, 310 n7
Lattre de Tassigny, Marshal de, 84, 87, 129, 239
Laugère, Guy, 317 n20
L'Aurore, 88
Lavaud, 115
Le Brun, Pierre, 298 n9
Le Guerney, Roger, 175
Le Roy, Marcel ('Finville'), 66, 150–1, 232–7, 248
Le Tac brothers, 172
Le Terron, Philippe, ('Monsieur Philippe'), 207
Le Van Vien, 93
'Leb', *see* Penguilly
Lefaucheux, Pierre, 32
Léger, Paul-Alain, 91, 115–16, 124–6, 163
'Legionnaire, The', *see* Jacquin, Henri
Lehmann, 165
Lejeune, Max, 112
Leluc, Alaine, 319 n20
Lemaigre-Dubreuil, Jacques, 158
Lemarchand, Pierre, 172, 237
Lemoine, Robert, 54, 70, 205–6, 237
Lenoir, Jean-Pierre, 150, 237
Lentz, Roger ('Poupon the Stéphanois'), 236, 310 n16
Léonard, 79
'Leonardi', *see* Bocquel, Claude
Leopold, Marcel, 163, 166
Leopold II, 201
Leroux, 99

Leroy, Jean-Jacques, 169
Lesquer, 296
Lester, Charles, 205, 231
Leusse, Pierre de, 114
Levacher, Jacques, 140, 250, 316 n9
Lévêque, René, 240
L'Helgouach, Louis, 83, 140
Libération-Nord, 16, 41, 51, 114
Libération-Sud, 42
Libya, 273–5
lie detectors, 147
Lignières, Charles de, 269, 274
L'Intoxication (Nord), 44
Lion, Elisabeth, 83
Lionnet, Georges, 16, 51–2, 140, 147, 222, 225, 236, 253, 256
Lithuania, 75
'Little Cleric', *see* Gouaze, Lucien
'Little Father', *see* Verneuil, Colonel
'Little Fathers', death of the, 67–9
'Little Liars', 83–5
'Little Lieutenant', *see* Robert, Maurice
Lloyd, Selwyn, 115
Lochard, Lucien, 30–1, 45, 74, 298 n7
Locquin, Jacques, 54, 100, 305 n35
Loisel, Dominique ('Domino'), 68, 140, 160
Lombard, Paul, 34
Lopez, Antoine, 151, 232–7, 310 n15
Lorillot, General, 112
Lospichel, Dr von, 7
Loustanau-Lacau, 63
Loutrel, Pierre, ('Pierrot le Fou'), 164
Luizet, Charles, 18
Lumumba, Patrice, 201, 203, 313 n12
'Lussac', *see* Penguilly
Lux, Arsène, 282
Lybine, 33
Lygren, Ingeborg, 212

McCoy, Alfred, 94, 304 n19
Machel, Samora, 265
McNab, Harold, 249
Madagascar, 174, 183

'Madame Billy', *see* Roblot, Marie-
  Louise
Mafart, Alain, 277, 288–92, 296, 320
  n7, Plate 11
Mafia, 171
'Magenta' disaster, 168–70
Maghreb, 105–32, 163–4
Maigret, 49
Maillot, Father, 84
Mairey, Jean, 102
Maître, 197
Makarov, Lieutenant (Carlos Alamo),
  297 n12
Malay Races Liberation Army, 84
Malaya, 84
Maleplate, Maxime, 85, 97
Malloum, 262, 263
Maloubier, Bob, 163, 164, 304 n12
Malraux, André, 64, 154, 173, 245,
  318 n11
Manac'h, Etienne, 210, 215, 313 n1
Mangin, Louis, 114, 115, 138
Mangin, Stanislas, 73, 308 n5
Maniguet, Xavier, 289, 292
Mansard, 56
Mansion, 284
Mantéï, Ignace, 131, 307 n36
Mantout, Gilbert, 21, 33
Manuel, André, 16, 24
Mao Tse-tung, 84, 92
Maora, 56
'Mar Verde', 265–7
'Marabouts', 196–9
Marcellin, Raymond, 260
Marcheboeuf, Professor, 32–3
Marchiani, Jean-Charles, 249, 250
'Marching Group', 128
Marcovic affair, 228, 245, 247–51
Marenches, Alexandre de ('Periwinkle',
  'Porthos'), 152, 196, 226–9, 245–
  61, 270–2, 274, 276, 280–2, 287,
  310 n15, Plate 4
Marenches, Anselme de, 246
Marenches, Marguerite, Countess de,
  246
Mareuil, *see* Mercier, Marcel

Mariani, Dominique, 250
Marie, Captain, 194
Marienne, Guy ('Morvan'), 16, 50–1,
  65–6, 147, 150–1, 232
Marion, Pierre, 279–81, 281–3, 283–
  4, 286–7, Plate 6
Marmier, Canon, 156
Marolles, Count Alain Gaigneron de,
  252, 274–5
Marouf, Achkar, 195
'Martel', *see* Golytzin, Anatoly
  Alexandrovich
Martini, Charles, 264
Marty, André, 23
Marty, Bernard, 65
Masaryk, Jan, 57
Maspero, François, 169
Massey, Philippe de, 172
Massignac, 111
Masson, Paul, 319 n18
Massu, 123–4
Mast, 97, 100, 304 n29
Matignon, 182, 183, 186
Matsui, Victor Masao, 239, 315 n12
Mattéï, Captain, 121, 123
Mattéï, Enrico, 170–1
Mauretania, 174
Mauricheau-Beaupré, Jean, ('Mon-
  sieur Jean'), 185, 199–200, 208
Mauritius, 183
Mauro, Mauro di, 171
Mautaint, Edgar, 301 n17
Mauthausen, 3
'Max, Captain', *see* Schlokow, Maxi-
  milian
Mayer, René, 67, 88
Mazza, 273
M'ba, Germain, 311 n15
M'ba, Léon, 181, 183, 185
M'Backe, Falilou, 198
MBHK, 74
Mbumba, Nathaniel, 271
Mecca, 274
Medea, 72
Meffre, 32
Mehiri, Taleb, 168

Meir, Golda, 115
Mella, Tony, 12
Melnik, Constantin, 136, 139, 167, 183, 200, 307 n3, 316 n2
Mendès-France, Pierre, 101–2, 103–4, 106
mental health, 145–7
Menthon, Pierre de, 239
Menzies, Stewart, 219
Meos, 93, 94
Merbah, Kasdi, 258
Merbah, Moulay, 161
Mercier, Jean ('Le Grand Mercier'), 30, 54, 298 n7
Mercier, Marcel ('Le Petit Mercier'), 109, 141, 159, 160–2, 220–1, 253, 298 n7
Merglen, Albert, 131
Merle, 209
Mermet, François, Plate 9
Merode, Rudy von, 29, 299 n5
Merson, Jean, 63
Mertzeisen, Gabriel, 77
Mes camarades sont morts (Nord), 43–4
'Messalists', 130
Messmer, Pierre, 137, 184, 186, 202, 208, 236
Mestre, Philippe, 319 n18
Meunier, Raymond, ('Les Grosses Paluches'), 151
Mexico, 29
Meyer, Albert, 85
MI5, 33–4, 183, 313 n3
'Michel', 284–5
Mihajlović, 36, 74
Miller, Newton, 212
Ministry of Defence, 277–9
'MINOS', 75–8, 151, 227
Mischke, Ferdinand, 57, 76
Mission '48', *see* 'Rainbow' Operation
Mission 'Out', 105–14
Mission 'Satanic', 288–96
Mission 'Valuable', 75–8
Mittel, Charles, 33
Mitterand, François, 2, 65, 102, 276–87, Plate 10

MNA, 130
MNPGD, 1, 2
Mobutu, Joseph, 201, 203–5, 271–2, 313 n12
Moch, Jules, 18, 98, 100, 138
Moghrebi, Mahmoud El, 274
Mohammed V, King, 111, 112
moles, hunt for, 210–29
Mollet, Guy, 108, 110, 112–15, 163
Monahan, Marguerite, *see* Marenches, Marguerite, Countess de
Mons, Jean, 101, 103
'Monsieur Armand', *see* Chaumien, Marcel
'Monsieur Jean', *see* Mauricheau-Beaupré, Jean
'Monsieur Leduc', *see* Groussouvre, François de
'Monsieur Perrier', *see* Paillole, Paul
'Monsieur Philippe', *see* Le Terron, Philippe
Montagne, Edmond, 310 n20
Montarras, Alain, 73, 230
Monti, 285
Morali-Daninos, André, 145–8, 253
Morand, 99
Morange, Roger, 298 n7
Moreau, Alain, 269
Morlanne, Jacques ('Henri Fille-Lambie'), 47, 76, 77–8, 81, 83, 90, 128, 144, 147, 163–4, 176
Moroccan Liberation Army, 109
Morocco, 105, 233–5
'Morris, Captain', *see* Puchert, Georg
'Morvan', *see* Marienne, Guy
MOSSAD, 109, 260
Mouchon, Louis, 53, 54, 65, 66, 138, 150, 278–9, 300 n3, 301 n28
'Moudjahid' Operation, 127–8
Moukhabarat El-Amma, 257
Moulin, Jean, 27
Moumié, Félix ('Big Bill'), 186–90
Mouriot, Charles Albert, 54, 71
Moutet, Marius, 80
Moutin, Henri, 116, 117, 195
Mozambique, 265

MPLA, 265, 267, 270
MRA, 263
M'Rad, Ali, 168, 169
Mroz, Wladislaw, 223
Mubarak, Hosni, 274
Muelle, Raymond, 307 n33
Mujahedin, 286
Mulelé, Pierre, 203
Muller, Léon, 34
Murphy, David, 313 n4
Murville, Maurice Couve de, 135, 201, 245
Musatescu, Mircea, 76
'Muskateer' Operation, 114–18
Mussolini, Benito, 37
MVD, 34
Myjzkiwski, 70

Nadal, 165
Nahmias, Joseph, 115
Naicho, 149
'Napoleon', *see* Durieux, Christian
Narvik operations, 12
Nasser, Gamal Abdel, 110, 114–18
Nassiri, Nematollah, 257, 258
Nat, Daniel, 43
National Council of the Resistance, 12, 41
NATO, 117
Navarre, Henri, 14, 101, 238
Nazis, 27–38
Ndjamena, 283–4
Nehru, 110
Neto, Agostinho, 265, 269, 271
Network A, 107–8
Neumann, 7
New Zealand, 288–90
Ngoc Banh, Trang, 97, 98
Nicholls, General, 3, 4–5
Nicolas, Marcel, 150
Niger, 174
Nikitine, Pierre, 78
Niquet, Louis, 214, 314 n5
Nishri, 115
'Nizier, Colonel', *see* Lambroschini, Joseph

Nkrumah, Kwame, 200
NKVD, 34, 74
Nocq, Captain, 24
Noguères, Henri, 101
Nord, Pierre ('Colonel Brouillard'), 13, 43–4, 309 n32, 310 n7
North Africa, 66
Nossenko, Yury, 213
Nougaret, 107, 119
Nouillan, Inspector de, 87, 88
Noumandian, Keita, 193
Novinat, Gilbert, 53
NTS (the 'Solidarists'), 74
Nyerere, Julius, 207
Nzita, Henrique Tiago, 268

OAS, 121, 145, 158, 171–2
Oddi, Cardinal, 156
Oeldrich, 157
Office Indochinois des Changes, 87, 88
Offroy, Raymond, 206
Ojukwu, 206–9
Okacha, Tharwat, 114
Oliva-Roge, Roger, 64
'Olivier' Operation, 130–1
Olympio, Sylvanus, 184
O'Neill, Stasia, 18
operations, *see under* code-names
Operations Directorate, 282
opium, 92–5, 104
ORAF, 108
ORCG, 21, 33, 55
Orsini, Joseph, 94
ORTF, 237
OSO, 212
OSS, 26, 62, 79, 80, 106, 212
Ouandié, Ernest, 312 n28
Oubangi-Chari, 174
Oueddei, Goukouni, 264, 283, 285
Oufkir, 232, 233, 234
Ouftigouma, Zacharria, 149
Oussedik, Omar, 130
Ouvea, 288–90

'Pablo', *see* Raptis, Michel
Pace, Laurent, 169
PAIG, 266
PAIGC, 265–7
Paillard, Henri, 318 n2
Paillole, Paul ('Monsieur Perrier'), 14, 27, 28, 68, 99, 106, 107, 297 n5
Palestine, 260
Palewski, Gaston, 18
Paolini, Antoine, 316 n8
Papon, 233
Papovici, Mircea, 76
'Paquebot', *see* Pellay, Jean-Marie
Pâques, Georges, 210, 214
'Parent', *see* Rousseau-Portalis, Jean
Parizot, 121
'Passy, Colonel', 2, 5, 10–15, 19–23, 33, 39, 40, 42, 46, 49–50, 54, 56–7, 79–80, 136, 166, 175, 217
Passy affair, 24–6, 300 n2
'Pat', *see* Thébault, Lieutenant
Patassé, Ange, 284
Paucot, Jean, 299 n11
Paul, Marcel, 31, 32, 53
Paye, Lucien, 107
PCF, 22–3, 231
PCR, 119
PDG, 191
Péan, Pierre, 311 n15
Pelabon, André, 18, 73, 101
Pelicier, 192
Pellay, Jean-Marie ('Paquebot'), 116, 304 n12
Pellegrini, Charles, 317 n14
Pelletier, General, 101
Penguilly, Jacques Lebel de, 5–8
Penkovsky, Oleg, 214
Penne, Guy, 280
Pépy, Daniel, 179
Perdon, 127
Pereira, Fernando, 291–2
Peres, Shimon, 115
Périer, Jacques, 193
Périer, Pierre, 86
'Periwinkle', *see* Marenches, Alexandre de

Perón, Juan, 54
Perrault, Gilles, 225–6
Perret, 67
Perrez, Thomas, 96, 304 n28
'Perrier, Monsieur', *see* Paillole, Paul
Perrier, Paul, 183, 312 n19
Perrin, 'Papa', 82
Perronet, Colonel de, 228
Pershing, John, 247
Pétain, Henri Philippe, 42, 72
Peter, Gabriel, 69
Peters, John, 206
'Petit Mercier, Le', *see* Mercier, Marcel
Peugeot brothers, 63
Peyré, Roger, 97–100, 305 n30
Pflimlin, Pierre, 149
PFLP, 260
Pham Van Dong, 80
Philby, Kim, 76, 106, 212
Phnom Penh, 87
'Phratrie' ('Brotherhood') network, 83
'Pick', *see* 'Pioche'
Picq, Henri, 306 n10
PIDE, 193, 265–7
Piech, Dr, 32
Pierre-Brossolette, Claude, 267
'Pierrot le Fou', *see* Loutrel, Pierre
Pierson, Maurice, 249, 250
Pietri, Aimé, 261
Pignon, Léon, 85, 86, 89
Piguet, Gabriel, 8
Pika, General, 58
Pilquet, Robert, 239
Pinay, Antoine, 88, 151–3
Pineau, Christian, 114
'Pioche' ('Pick'), 81
Pius XII, 155
Plan Bolero-Paprika, 56–7
'Plan X', 155
Planchais, Jean, 226
Planet, 126
Planning, Forecasting and Evaluation group, 282
Plantey, Alain, 177
Pleven, René, 56

PLR, 181–6
Pognon, Gratien, 271
Poirot-Delpech, Bernard, 269
Poland, 69–71, 75, 140
Polish secret services, 222–3
Pommes-Barrère, Jacques, 2, 4–5,
47, 76
Pompidou, Claude, 228, 245, 249
Pompidou, Georges, 136, 179, 209,
217, 218, 226, 238, 245–6, 270,
Plate 4
Poncet, Jean-François, 272
Ponchardier, Dominique, 64, 172,
302 n9
Ponchardier, Pierre, 64, 172
Ponchel, Voltaire, 2, 3, 4
Poniatowski, Michel, 149
Popott, Vladimir, 74
Popović, Miloslav, 75
Popular Front, 41
Porsche, Ferdinand, 31–2, 299 n9
'Porthos', *see* Marenches, Alexandre
de
Portugal, 265–7
Poste, 172
Potsdam Agreement, 79
Pouget, Daniel, 151
'Poupon the Stephanois', *see* Lentz,
Roger
Poujat, 74
PPF, 20
Pradel, Albert, 65
Pradère-Niquet, Daniel, 125
Pradier, Claude, 249, 250
Prague, 140
Prévôt, 91, 127, 307 n32
Prieur, Dominique, 288–92, 296,
Plate 10
'Prometheus', headquarters of BCRA,
50
Pruneau, Gilles, 316 n16
PSS, 198
PTT, 18
Puchert, Georg ('Captain Morris'),
163, 164, 173, 311 n1
Puy-Montbrun, Déodat, 91, 310 n18

Quan Bao, 91
Quebec, 239–41
Quebec Liberation Front, 239–41
Quercy, Lucienne, 298 n7
Queuille, Henri, 96, 98, 100
Quiet American, The (Greene), 90

Radio Cairo, 116
Radio Corse Internationale, 261
Radio 'Somera', 116, 167
Radl, Karl, 37
Rado, Sandor, 80, 299 n13
Raffini, Toussaint, 53
'Rainbow' Operation, 65–7
Rainbow Warrior, 288–96, Plate 12,
13
Raïs, the, *see* Nasser, Gamal Abdel
Ramadier, Paul, 8, 60, 63, 98, 100
Ramier, 141
Ramos, Ernesto Lopes, 265
Rançon, 172
'RAP 700', 115–16
Raptis, Michel ('Pablo'), 157
Rateau, Jacques, 64
Rauzy, 113, 119
Ravensbruck, 3
RCF, 318 n12
RCMP, 239–40, 316 nn14, 15
'Red Hand', 157–72, 309 n3
Red Hand, The (Latour), 157–9
'Red Orchestra', 297 n12
Renault, 32, 60
Renaux, Fernand, 69–70
Renucci, Jo, 94, 233, 310 n15
Research Branch, 46, 140, 252, 254
Resseguier, Olivier de, 6
Réunion, 183
Revers, 96–9
Revol, 219
RG, 33, 56, 286
Ribière, Henri, 24, 40–1, 43, 47, 48,
51, 52–3, 54, 56, 57, 63, 66, 70,
99–100, 219
Ricard, Pierre, 282, 283–4
Richard, Paul, 141, 165
Richard, Roger, 310 n20

Richard, Tristan, 173, 193, 195, 233–4, 248, 252–4
Richon, 96
Richter, Captain, 7
Ricord, Auguste, 30
RIN, 241
Ripka, Hubert, 57–8, 302 n41
Rivet, Louis, 14, 44
Rivière, Robert, 301 n17
Rizza, Jo ('The Hedgehog'), 108, 121
Robert, Maurice ('Little Lieutenant'), 173, 176, 179–82, 184–5, 193–4, 196–7, 200, 208, 254, 268, 270
Robertson, T. A., 33
Robineau, André, 69–71
Robinson, Madeleine, 314 n6
Roblot, Marie-Louise ('Madame Billy'), 262
Rocca, Raymond, 212
Rocolle, 130, 307 n34
Rohmer, Georges, 97
Rollet, 99
Romain, 65
Romania, 69, 75, 225, 227
Romanian Iron Guard, 75
Roos, Joseph, 79
Ropagnol, 202
Rose, Mlle, 246
Rossi, Francesco, 171
Rossignol, Pierre, 195
Rossillon, Philippe, 240–1
Rossin, 142
Rosso, Félix, 317 n14
Roucaute, Yves, 95
Rougemont, Jean-Louis du Temple de, 214
Rousseau, Eugène, 225–8
Rousseau affair, 256
Rousseau-Portalis, Jean ('Parent'), 29
Roussel, 182, 250
Roussillat, Colonel, 122, 164, 165, 187
Roussin, Michel, 253, 281, 317 n19
Roux, Dominique de, 269–70
ROVS, 74
Roy, Alain, 56, 299 n5
Royal Yugoslav Army, 74

Royo brothers, 56
Rozenne, 94
RPF, 54, 62, 64–5, 88, 179, 299 n40
RPIMA, 273
RTF, 167
Ruat, Clément, 121, 122
Ruchenko, Nikolay, 74
Rusconi, 180

SA, 43
SAARF, 3–5
Sabri, Ahmed, 124
SAC, 178, 249
Sadat, Anwar al-, 257
Safar, 16
'Safari Club', 257
'Safira', 265–7
Saigon, 84, 87, 90
Saint-Gast, *see* Guivante Saint-Gast, Paul
Saint-Gest, 283
Saint-Hilaire, Guy de, 85
'Saint-Jacques', *see* Duclos, Maurice
Saint-Marc, Hélie Denoix de, 307 n33
Saint-Paul, Tony de, 202
Sakharovsky, 214
Salan, Raoul, 89, 93, 94, 100–1, 108, 120, 305 n38
Salazar, 265, 266
Salmson, Philippe, 82
Sanchez, Ilich Ramirez ('Carlos'), 258–60
Sanitzer, Johann, 35
Santen, Sal, 157
Santenac, Paul, 249, 250, 316 n8
Santeny, Jean, 80
Sapin-Lignères, Victor, 29, 99
SAPO, 212
'Sapphire' network, 214, 216–18, 221
SAS, 62
Sassi, 132, 304 n12
Saudi Arabia, 274
Saudi Arabian secret services, 257–8
Saunier, 296
SAVAK, 257, 258, 267

Savani, Antoine, 93–4
Savary, Alain, 114
Savimbi, Jonas, 269–70, 285, 318 n8
Sawyer, Steve, 290
Scandinavia, 212
Schacht, Dr, 8
Schaeffer, 99
Scheider, Joseph, 313 n12
Schlokow, Maximilian ('Captain Max'), 57
Schlütter, Otto, 163, 164
Schneider, Louis, 119
Schneider, Magda, 31
Schoen, Paul, 119
Schoendorffer, Pierre, 180
Schuschnigg, 7
Schweizer, Kurt-Emile (Pierre Genève), 159, 160, 309 n6
Schwerin, Count Gerhard von, 36
SD, 37
SDECE, 9–58; abolition proposed, 278; against CIA, 203–6; becomes DGSE, 281–3; émigrés from the East in, 73–5; establishment of, 39–40; Intelligence Communication Chain, 259 fig. 13.2; organization of, 48 fig. 3.1; personnel, 142–5; renewal, 251–4; structure (1971), 252–3 fig. 13.1
SDESC, 185–6, 312 n24
Security Branch, 51–2
Selassie, Haile, 200
Senegal, 174, 183, 197–8
Senghor, Léopold Sédar, 176, 181, 183, 197
SEPIC, 70
Serbet, Jean-Paul, *see* Gouazé, Lucien
Sérot, André, 115
Servan-Schreiber, Jean-Jacques, 101, 280
'Servias', *see* Simédéï, Colonel
'Service 7', 149–51, 173, 232–7, 248
'Service 29', *see* Action Branch
Servier, Jean, 129–30
Servin, Marcel, 23
Sétif riots, 108

SFIO, 62, 162, 277
SGPDN, 101–3
Shaba, 271–2
Shamir, Itzhak, 115
'Sharq al-Adna', 116
Shock Troops, 11th, 81–2, 116–17, 128–32, 301 n17
'Shrimp' Operation, 271
Si Abdellatif, 127
Si Lakhdar, 127
Si Mohammed, 127
Si Salah, 127
SID, 319 n25
Sidick, Dr Abba, 264
Sidorin, Pavel, 227
SIFAR, 109, 306 n8
Sihanouk, Prince Norodom, 238–9
'Sili', 191–3
SIM, 55
Simédéï, Colonel ('Servias'), 62
Simon, 224
Simoneau, Léon, 32, 106, 120, 122, 123, 128, 144
Simonet, Henri, 272
Singa, 204
Singapore, 84
Singland, Jean-Albert, 282
Sinitzin, Yevgeny Ivanovich ('Garanin'), 74
Siri, Cardinal, 156
SIS, 35, 74, 75, 84, 106, 212, 219, 251, 271, 275
Sitbon, Guy, 168–9
Skorzeny, Otto, 37–8
'Skorzeny' Operation, 113–14
'Slav, The', *see* Fourcaud, Pierre
Slavinsky, Michel, 74
SLNA, 119, 306 n21
'Smerch' executions, 34
SNEP, 240
SNIAS, 279
Socialist Party, SDECE and the, 39–58
Socialists, 62–3, 277–9
Sofia, 140
Soilih, Ali, 318 n12

Soldos, 30
'Solidarists', 74
Soliveau, Louis ('Jacques'), 172, 311 n28
Somalia, 257
Somer, 84
'Somera', Radio, 116, 167, 310 n19
'Sorcerer, The', *see* Lacaze, Jeannou
Sorontiev, Simeon, 74
'Sosies', 64
Sotirivić, Dragan, 76
Soumialot, Gaston, 203
Soustelle, Jacques, 1, 12, 22, 29, 107–8, 139, 146, 166–8, 220, 250
South Africa, 184; *see also* BOSS
South America, 54–5
Soutif, Henri, 21
Souvarine, Boris, 299 n6, 300 n18, 305 n5
Soviet secret services, 34
Spain, 55–7
Spanish Communist Party, 55
Spinola, General de, 265
Spiteri, Professor, 32
Squadron 51 ('Aubrac'), 252
Squadron ELA 56 ('Vaucluse'), 57
SR, 13, 16–17
SRO, 32, 85
SSD, 35
SSM, 28
Stalin, Joseph Vissarionovich, 67
Stanić, Sano, 301 n32
Starnes, John, 239–40
Stauffenberg, Count von, 8
STB, 217, 222, 224–5
Steiner, Rolf, 207
Stent, 230
STO, 1
Stockwell, John, 268
Stolypine, Vladimir, 74
Strauss, Franz Joseph, 137
subliminal images, 148–9
Sudreau, Pierre, 24, 40
Suez affair, 111, 114–18
SURMAR, 109
Suyin, Han, 313 n1

Swiss secret service, 160–1
Sy, Abdoul Aziz, 198
Sy, Sheik Tidiane, 198
Synthesis, 28–9
Syrian secret services, 284
Szczerbinski, 70
Szen, Joseph, 74
Szkolnikoff, Michel, 29, 55

Tacjonis, 157
Tai Li, 84
Taiwan, 84
Tanase, Alexander, 76
Tangiers, 246, 310 n15
Tanguy-Prigent, 8
Tapper, Reinhold, 35
Taro, René-Charles, 140, 166
Tassigny, Marshal de Lattre de, *see* Lattre de Tassigny
Tchaptchaët, Jean-Martin, 188, 312 n31
Tchioufou, Auguste, 268
Te Wu, 239
Teitgen, Paul-Henri, 123, 298 n29
Teply, Jaroslav, 57
Terrenoire, Louis, 64, 88, 176
terrorism, 158, 260, 280–1, 286–7
Tesseyre, 108, 122
Teyssier, General, 71
Thailand, 84, 91
Thébault, Lieutenant ('Pat'), 91, 114, 128
Thierry, Fernand Amedée, 88
Thierry d'Argenlieu, Admiral, 81
Thierry-Mieg, François ('Captain Vaudreuil'), 16, 100, 299 n36
Third Reich, 1–8
Thomas, Abel, 115, 138, 308 n6
Thompson, John, 183
Thomson, 104
Thorez, 231
'Three Reds', 34
Thyraud, Jacques, 219
Thyraud, Philippe (de Vosjoli), 171, 219–22, 238–9, 314 n17, n21
Tillon, Charles, 227–8

'Tilsitt' Operation, 127
Tito, Josip Broz, 36, 110, 228
Togo, 174, 183
Tokyo, 72, 84
Tombalbaye, François, 185, 262–3
Tonkin, 80
Topaz (Uris), 221
Torre brothers, 88
torture, 123–4, 125
TOTEM agreements, 84, 141–2, 149
'Toto', *see* Guérin, André
Touby Lyfoung, 93, 94
Touré, Mamadou, 195
Touré, Sékou, 177, 189, 191–6, 199, 265–7
Tournet, André, 64
Touzelet, 238
TR, 14, 44, 45
traffic in piastres, 85, 86–8
Trautmann, Henri ('The Admiral'), 46–7, 56, 66, 71, 99, 139–40, 145, 170, 180, 217, 298 n7, 301 n30
Trevor-Wilson, 84, 106, 304 n5
Triboulet, Raymond, 195
'Tricontinental', 232
Tricot, Bernard, 293, 296
Trillat, Jean-Jacques, 32
Trinquier, Roger, 91, 92–5, 120, 123, 125, 131, 202, 304 n16
Trocmé, Jean, 239
Tronc, André, 316 n9
Tropel, Jean, 150, 308 n24
Trotsky, Leon, 157
Truat, Robert Luong, 311 n15
Trudeau, Pierre Elliott, 240, 316 n14
Trujillo, Rafael, 154
Truman, Harry S., 62
Trutat, Roger, 300 n14
Tschombe, Jean, 272
Tschombe, Moïse, 131, 200–4
Tshisekedi, 204
Tsiranana, Philibert, 183
Tsukor, Istvan, 74, 303 n20
'Tulip', *see* Heinz, Friedrich Wilhelm
Tully, Andrew, 220
Tunisia, 105

Turenge, Alain-Jacques, *see* Mafart, Alain
Turenge, Sophie-Claire, *see* Prieur, Dominique
Turpin, René, 103
Ty Wan school of guerilla warfare, 90, 129
Tyrol, South, 5

UCR, 5, 217
UDBA, 225, 228, 303 n20
UDR, 178
UJP, 178
Ukraine, 75
Ulrich, 161
Um Nyobe, Ruben, 186
Union, Gilbert, 65
Union Corse, 94
Unita, 269–70, 285, 318 n8
United Croats of France, 74
United Nations, 153–5
UNR, 178
UPC, 186–8
Upper Volta, 174, 184
UPS, 197
'Uranus' network, 140
Uris, Leon, 221
USA, 2, 117; *see also* CIA
USSR, 34, 67, 117, 210–29, 287
UTA, 151

Vaillant, René, 241
Van Co, Huang, 97
Vandenberghe, 180
Vang Peo, 94
Vassall, John, 212
'Vaucluse', *see* Squadron ELA 56
'Vaudreuil, Captain', *see* Thierry-Mieg, François
Vaugelas, Jean, 30
Vega, 296
Vendeuvre, Countess Vassilissa Salomé Evain Pavée de, 83
Venturi, Dominique, 94
Venturi, Jean, 94
'Verbena' Operation, 271

Vergé, Paul, 182
Vergé, Roland, 288
Vergès, Paul, 183
Vergnes, Victor, 62, 63
Verlet, François, 290
Vermot, Joseph, 307 n37
Verneuil, Colonel ('Little Father'), 23,
    43–6, 55–6, 60, 68, 69–70, 99,
    106, 160, 173, 217, 298 n7
Veuve, 150
VIA, 213
Viansson-Ponte, Pierre, 311 n3
Viaud, Jean, 197
'Vicarage' Operation, 3–5
Vienna, 30, 71, 140
Vietminh, 79, 89–92, 95
Vietnam, 80–1, 103–4
Vietnamese intelligence service, 91
Villa, Pancho, 212
Villemarest, Pierre Faillant de, 74,
    302 n18
Villeneuve, du Crest de, 187
Villot, Cardinal, 156
Vin Xa, 97
Vincent, Captain, 57
Violet, Jean, 83, 151–4, 248
'Violette', *see* Grunet, Fabienne
Vlassov Army, 74
'Von Kluck', *see* Mercier, Marcel
von Rosen, Carl Gustav, 208
Vosjoli, de, *see* Thyraud, Philippe
Vulpian, Count Edme de, 62, 63

Wagner, Joseph, 4
Wahab, Abdoul, 319 n12
Walters, Vernon, 251, 257, 268, 316
    n2

Warin, *see* Wybot, Roger
Wennerström, Stig, 212
Wessel, Gerhard, 36
Wetter, Father, 155
Whiteway, 27
Whitsun Conspiracy, 64–5
Wilaya, 125, 126, 127, 129, 130
Willox, Peter, 291
Winger, Georges, 310 n20
Winter, Gordon, 270
Wirt, Charles, 310 n20
Witchell, Lady Lilian Mary, 247
Wittinghof, 7
Wurmser, André, 22, 23, 25
Wybot, Roger (Warin), 42, 73, 97, 98,
    99–100, 102–3, 118, 131

'X' Operation, 92–5
Xavier de Bourbon-Parme, Prince, 8

Yaméogo, Maurice, 184
Yazid, M'hamed, 110
Yom Kippur war, 258
Youlou, Fulbert, 179, 184, 199–200,
    202
Yugoslav secret services, 225
Yugoslavia, 69, 75, 76
Yveton, 123

Zahm, Jacques, 165–6, 310 n17
Zaïre, 203, 271–2
Zborowski, Helmut von, 31
Zhukhov, Marshal, 4
Zigmant, Paul, 141, 144, 237
Zollinger, Louis, 234
Zora, Tadjer, 124–5

Index by Fiona Barr